Anonymous

The Essex antiquarian

Vol. 11

Anonymous

The Essex antiquarian
Vol. 11

ISBN/EAN: 9783337713577

Printed in Europe, USA, Canada, Australia, Japan

Cover: Foto ©ninafisch / pixelio.de

More available books at **www.hansebooks.com**

Volume XI.   JANUARY, 1907.   Number 1.

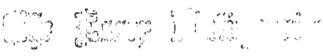

An Illustrated Quarterly Magazine

Devoted to the

Biography, Genealogy, History and Antiquities

of

Essex County, Massachusetts.

SIDNEY PERLEY, *Editor*.
GEORGE FRANCIS DOW, *Business Manager*.

CONTENTS.

ONE DOLLAR PER ANNUM. SINGLE COPIES, TWENTY-FIVE CENTS.
FOREIGN SUBSCRIPTIONS, EXCEPT FROM CANADA AND MEXICO, $1.25.

SALEM, MASS.
The Essex Antiquarian.
1907.

Entered at the Post Office at Salem, Mass., as second-class matter, Oct. 27, 1901.

THE ESSEX ANTIQUARIAN

A QUARTERLY MAGAZINE DEVOTED TO THE BIOGRAPHY, GENEALOGY, HISTORY AND ANTIQUITIES OF ESSEX COUNTY, MASSACHUSETTS

VOLUME XI

1907

SIDNEY PERLEY, EDITOR

ILLUSTRATED

SALEM, MASS.
The Essex Antiquarian
1907

CONTENTS.

ILLUSTRATIONS.

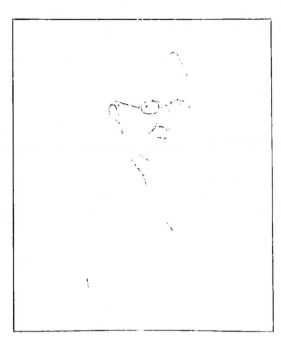

HON. LEONARD WHITE

THE ESSEX ANTIQUARIAN.

VOL. XI.   SALEM, MASS., JANUARY, 1907.   NO. 1.

BRADLEY GENEALOGY.

DANIEL BRADLEY,[1] according to Savage, came in the *Elizabeth* from London in 1635, at the age of twenty. He married Mary Williams in Haverhill May 21, 1662, and was living in Merrimack village in Rowley in 1664. He settled in Haverhill, where he was killed by the Indians, and his crops "fired and spoiled," Aug. 13, 1689. The inventory of his estate amounted to £213, 3s., 10d. His wife survived him, and died, his widow, in Haverhill, Oct. 6, 1714.

Children:—

2—I. DANIEL,[2] b. Feb. 14, 1662-3, in Rowley. *See below* (2).
3—II. JOSEPH,[2] b. Feb. 7, 1664-5, in Rowley. *See below* (3).
4—III. MARTHA,[2] b. in 1667. in Haverhill; m. Ephraim Gild (Giles) Jan. 5, 1686-7; and she was his wife in 1697.
5—IV. MARY,[2] b. March 1, 1669-70, in Haverhill; d. March 14, 1669-70.
6—V. MARY,[2] b. April 16, 1671, in Haverhill; m. Bartholomew Heath Jan. 23, 1690-1.
7—VI. SARAH[2], b. Aug. 19, 1673, in Haverhill; living in 1689.
8—VII. HANNAH,[2] b. May 28, 1677, in Haverhill; m. Joseph Heath in 1697.
9—VIII. ISAAC,[2] b. Feb. 25, 1680, in Haverhill. *See below* (9).
10—IX. ABRAHAM,[2] b. March 14, 1683-4, in Haverhill. *See below* (10).

2

DANIEL BRADLEY,[2] born in Rowley Feb. 14, 1662-3. He lived in Haverhill. He married Miss Hannah Dow of Haverhill Jan. 5, 1686-7; and they were both massacred by the Indians at Haverhill March 15, 1696-7. His estate was insolvent.

Children, born in Haverhill:—

11—I. RUTH,[3] b. May 15, 1688; m. Thomas Johnson Nov. 13, 1706; and was killed by the Indians Aug. 29, 1708.
12—II. DANIEL,[3] b. Oct. 28, 1690.
13—III. MARY,[3] b. May 6, 1693; killed by the Indians March 15, 1696-7.
14—IV. HANNAH,[3] b. June 6, 1696; killed by the Indians March 15, 1696-7.

3

JOSEPH BRADLEY,[2] born in Rowley Feb. 7, 1664-5. He lived in Haverhill, and was a yeoman. He married Miss Hannah Heath of Haverhill April 14, 1691; and died Oct. 3, 1727. She died in Haverhill Nov. 2, 1761.

Children, born in Haverhill:—

15—I. MEHITABLE,[3] b. Nov. 25, 1691; d. Jan. 23, 1691-2.
16—II. JOSEPH,[3] b. March 9, 1692-3; d. March 15, 1696-7, being killed by the Indians.
17—III. MARTHA,[2] b. Sept. 3, 1695; killed by the Indians March 15, 1696-7.
18—IV. MARTHA,[3] b. Nov. 7, 1699; m. James Mitchell of Haverhill, innholder, Dec. 10, 1719; and they were living in 1734.
19—V. SARAH,[3] b. Jan. 26, 1701-2; killed.
20—VI. JOSEPH,[2] b. Feb. 13, 1706-7. *See below* (20).
21—VII. DANIEL,[3] b. March 18, 1708. *See below* (21).
22—VIII. NEHEMIAH,[3] b. Dec. 25, 1711. *See below* (22).
23—IX. WILLIAM,[3] b. July 6, 1717. *See below* (23).

9

ISAAC BRADLEY,[2] born in Haverhill Feb. 25, 1680. He was a husbandman, and lived in Haverhill. He married Elizabeth Clement May 6, 1706; and conveyed his house, barn and land to his son Isaac in 1740. She was his wife in 1738.

Children, born in Haverhill:—

24—I. LYDIA,[3] b. May 31, 1707; m. John Heath, jr., Sept. 3, 1728.
25—II. JOHN,[3] b. April 10, 1709.

26—III. MEHITABEL,[3] b. Dec. 10, 1711; m. Jeremiah Dresser Dec. 3, 1735.
27—IV. RUTH,[3] b. May 26, 1713.
28—V. ABIGAIL,[3] b. May 20, 1714.
29—VI. ELIZABETH,[3] b. Jan. 17, 1716-7; m. Robert Calf of Chester, N. H., Oct. 12, 1738.
30—VII. ISAAC.[3] b. Jan. 10, 1718-9. *See below (30).*
31—VIII. NATHANIEL,[3] b. Feb. 10, 1720-1; d. Oct. 4, 1737, aged sixteen.
32—IX. MOSES[3] (twin), b. Jan. 18, 1723-4; d. March 29, 1724.
33—X. MERIAM[3] (twin), b. Jan. 18, 1723-4; d. April 3, 1724.

10

ABRAHAM BRADLEY,[2] born in Haverhill March 14, 1683-4. He was a husbandman, and lived in Haverhill. He married Elizabeth Philbrick Oct. 18, 1705; and she was his wife in 1730. He was living in Haverhill in 1739.

Children, born in Haverhill:—

34—I. MEHITABLE,[3] b. July 13, 1706; d. Aug. 13, 1706.
35—II. ABIGAIL,[3] b. July 15, 1707; m. Benjamin Richards Dec. 29, 1726.
36—III. JEREMIAH,[3] b. Sept. 28, 1709.
37—IV. TIMOTHY,[3] b. June 16, 1711.
38—V. JONATHAN,[3] b. July 11, 1713.

20

DEA. JOSEPH BRADLEY,[3] born in Haverhill Feb. 13, 1706-7. He was a husbandman, and lived in Haverhill. He married, first, Hannah Marsh July 31, 1733; and she died Jan. 24, 1747-8. He married, second, Sarah French of Newbury Sept. 20, 1748; and died Oct. 1, 1749. In his will he devised his homestead to his son Joseph. The inventory of his estate amounted to about £1,270. His wife Sarah survived him, and married John Marble June 11, 1751. She died April 26, 1809.

Children, born in Haverhill:—

39—I. JOSEPH,[4] b. May 23, 1736. *See below (39).*
40—II. AMOS,[4] b. April 18, 1739. *See below (40).*
41—III. MARTHA,[4] b. March 26, 1744; d. Nov. 7, 1761.
42—IV. JAMES,[4] b. March 13, 1746-7; yeoman; lived in Haverhill, 1768.
43—V. ENOCH,[4] b. June 22, 1749. *See below (43).*

21

CAPT. DANIEL BRADLEY,[3] born in Haverhill March 18, 1708. He was a cordwainer and yeoman, and lived in Haverhill. He was called a gentleman after 1758. He married Elizabeth Ayer Feb. 26, 1729-30; and she was his wife in 1780. He died in 1784; his will, dated Aug. 21, 1780, being proved Sept. 7, 1784. The inventory of his estate amounted to £837, 2s., 6d. He gave his homestead to his son Peter. He had a grist mill.

Children, born in Haverhill:—

44—I. SARAH,[4] b. Sept. 4, 1730; m., first, Benjamin Poor of Haverhill June 1, 1749; he d. in the spring of 1762; she m., second, Abraham Sweet before 1780; and d. July 1, 1815.
45—II. SAMUEL,[4] b. Aug. 4, 1731; trader; lived in Haverhill; m. Sarah Wingate of Amesbury (pub. Nov. 15, 1769); d. before June 3, 1776, when administration was granted upon his estate; she survived him. Probably no children.
46—III. DANIEL,[4] b. Nov. 15, 1732. *See below (46).*
47—IV. RUTH,[4] b. Jan. 6, 1733-4; d. Sept. 10, 1736.
48—V. ELIZABETH,[4] b. Aug. 2, 1735; d. July 6, 1736.
49—VI. MOSES,[4] b. May 12, 1737; lived in Boston; m. Hannah Dakin in Boston (pub. Feb. 14, 1764); living in 1780.
50—VII. NATHANIEL,[4] b. June 1, 1738. *See below (50).*
51—VIII. RUTH,[4] b. June 19, 1739; m. Dr. James Pecker Nov. 29, 1762; and she d. Sept. 1, 1806.
52—IX. DAVID,[4] b. Sept. 20, 1740; yeoman; lived in Haverhill; m. Abigail Marsh June 13, 1781; he d. in Haverhill May 2, 1811; she d. there April 12, 1826; probably no children.
53—X. HANNAH,[4] b. July 12, 1742; m. Samuel Noyes before 1780.
54—XI. ELIZABETH,[4] b. Nov. 19, 1743; unmarried in 1780.
55—XII. PETER,[4] b. Oct. 23, 1745. *See below (55).*
56—XIII. MARY,[4] b. Feb. 1, 1746-7; unmarried in 1780.
57—XIV. LYDIA[4] (twin), b. June 17, 1748; d. Jan. 16, 1748-9.
58—XV. MARTHA[4] (twin), b. June 17, 1748; d. June 17, 1748.

22

NEHEMIAH BRADLEY,[3] born in Haverhill Dec. 25, 1711. He was a husbandman, and lived in Haverhill. He married Lydia Emerson Sept. 1, 1736; and died in 1775; his will, dated March 14, 1775, being proved May 30, 1775. His estate was appraised at £798, 0s., 8d. He devised his homestead to his sons Ithamar and Isaiah. His wife survived him.

Children, born in Haverhill:—

59—I.   NEHEMIAH,[4] b. July 31, 1737; d. Dec. 5, 1737.
60—II. HANNAH,[4] b. Nov. 19, 1738; m. John Emerson May 19, 1763; and was living in 1775.
61—III. NEHEMIAH,[4] b. Oct. 18, 1741; d. Oct. 13, 1747.
62—IV. SIMON,[4] b. Feb. 19, 1743-4; d. Sept. 13, 1747.
63—V.   ELIZABETH,[4] b. April 4, 1746.
64—VI. JONATHAN,[4] b. Oct. 17, 1748. See below (64).
65—VII. ITHAMAR,[4] b. Feb. 15, 1751. See below (65).
66—VIII. NEHEMIAH,[4] b. March 2, 1753; d. May 6, 1753.
67—IX. WILLIAM,[4] b. Sept. 28, 1754; d. Nov. 21, 1754.
68—X.   LYDIA,[4] b. Nov. 21, 1755; living in 1775; perhaps m. Samuel Webster Nov. 26, 177-.
69—XI. MIRIAM,[4] b. April 21, 1758; d. Aug. 29, 1758.
70—XII. WARD,[4] b. Dec. 4, 1759; probably d. before 1775.
71—XIII. ISAIAH[4] (twin), b. May 7, 1762; yeoman; lived in Haverhill, 1786.
72—XIV. JEREMIAH[4] (twin), b. May 7, 1762; husbandman; lived in Haverhill; m. Anna How of Methuen Nov. 6, 1783; d. in 1799; and she was his widow in 1800.
73—XV. CALEB,[4] b. March 11, 1765; living in 1775.

23

WILLIAM BRADLEY,[3] born in Haverhill July 6, 1717. He was a yeoman, and lived in Haverhill. He married Mehitable Emerson Sept. 23, 1741; and died Feb. 28, 1780. The inventory of his estate amounted to £1,684, 11s., 4d., but his debts were about £5,000. She survived him, dying in July, 1811.

Children, born in Haverhill:—

74—I.   MERRILL,[4] b. July 1, 1742; probably d. before 1780.

75—II. JOSEPH[4] (twin), b. Feb. 14, 1744-5. See below (75).
76—III. JONATHAN[4] (twin), b. Feb. 14, 1744-5. See below (76).
77—IV. MEHITABLE,[4] b. Oct. 23, 1747; d. July 22, 1796.
78—V.   SARAH,[4] b. Feb. 24, 1749-50; d. Aug. 4, 1820.
79—VI. WILLIAM,[4] b. May 18, 1752; d. young.
80—VII. HANNAH,[4] b. May 27, 1754; living in 1780.
81—VIII. WILLIAM,[4] b. April 22, 1756; yeoman; lived in Haverhill; probably m. Sally Swarey May 12, 1790.
82—IX. SUSANNAH,[4] b. Sept. 17, 1758; d. Nov. 16, 1785.
83—X.   ABIGAIL,[4] b. Aug. 22, 1760; d. Oct. 23, 1784.
84—XI. ANNE (NANE),[4] b. May 23, 1763; d. March 26, 1798.
85—XII. MOSES,[4] b. Nov. 6, 1765; living in 1780.

30

ISAAC BRADLEY,[3] born in Haverhill Jan. 10, 1718-9. He was a yeoman, and lived in Haverhill. He married, first, Lydia Kimball Nov. 10, 1741; and she died May 23, 1762. He married, second, Rachel, widow of Samuel Ayer of Haverhill Nov. 23, 1762; and died in January, 1802. She survived him, and died in February, 1805.

Children, born in Haverhill:—

86—I.   ELIZABETH,[4] b. Dec. 13, 1742.
87—II. MARY,[4] b. Dec. 13, 1744.
88—III. BENJAMIN,[4] b. Feb. 18, 1746-7. See below (88).
89—IV. ISAAC,[4] b. May 2, 1749; of Dracut, blacksmith, 1783, 1795; wife Abigail, 1795.
90—V.   LYDIA,[4] b. May 17, 1751.
91—VI. JOSEPH,[4] b. May 12, 1753.
92—VII. JOHN,[4] b. Feb. 4, 1756; lived in Haverhill, 1784.
93—VIII. JESSE[4] (twin), b. Aug. 29, 1758.
94—IX. ABIGAIL[4] (twin), b. Aug. 29, 1758; d. Sept. 13, 1760.
95—X.   ABIGAIL,[4] b. May 15, 1761.
96—XI. RUTH,[4] b. Aug. 25, 1763; d. Aug. 27, 1764.
97—XII. RUTH,[4] b. Nov. 27, 1764.

39

JOSEPH BRADLEY,[1] born in Haverhill May 23, 1736. He lived in Haverhill; and married Sarah Hardy of Bradford Feb. 5, 1753. He died July 31, 1754, aged eighteen. His estate was appraised at £349, 2s., 3d. She survived him, and

married, secondly, William Atwood March 29, 1757.

Child, born in Haverhill :—

98—I. JOSEPH,[5] b. Nov. 26, 1753; living in 1757.

40

AMOS BRADLEY,[4] born in Haverhill April 18, 1739. He lived in Haverhill; and married Elizabeth Page Feb. 20, 1759.

Child, born in Haverhill :—

99—I. AMOS,[5] b. May 30, 1759.

43

ENOCH BRADLEY,[4] born in Haverhill June 22, 1749. He was a cordwinder and yeoman, and lived in Haverhill. He was called "gentleman" after 1811. He married Mary Low of Ipswich Oct. 10, 1770; and died May 2, 1834, aged eighty-four. She was his wife in 1812.

Children, born in Haverhill :—

100—I. MARY,[5] b. April 16 (15?), 1771; m. Ezekiel Barnard of Amesbury March 1, 1795; and was living in 1812.
101—II. ABIGAIL,[5] b. May 31, 1772; m. —— Corlis before 1812.
102—III. SARAH,[5] b. Feb. 1, 1774; m. James Ayer, 3d, Dec. 14, 1794.
103—IV. ENOCH,[5] b. April 29, 1778; lived in Haverhill, yeoman, 1834.
104—V. CALEB LOW,[5] b. Feb. 22, 1780; d. Aug. 2, 1821.
105—VI. PATTY,[5] b. Dec. 25, 1781; m. Jesse Page of Warren Oct. 20, 1801; and was living in 1812.
106—VII. JOSEPH,[5] b. Jan. 27, 1784; d. Jan. 14, 1786.
107—VIII. JOSEPH,[6] b. June 4, 1786; living in 1812.
108—IX. BRICKETT,[5] b. April 10, 1789; yeoman, of Haverhill, 1834.

46

DANIEL BRADLEY,[4] born in Haverhill Nov. 15, 1732. He was a cordwainer, and lived in Haverhill. He married Susanna Mitchel Jan. 10, 1754; and was living in Haverhill in 1796.

Children, born in Haverhill :—

109—I. SARAH,[5] b. Jan. 4, 1755.
110—II. JOSEPH,[5] b. March 22, 1756.
111—III. LYDIA,[5] b. Oct. 16, 1757.
112—IV. SAMUEL,[5] b. Jan. 11, 1760; yeoman; lived in Haverhill; United States pensioner; never married; and d. Jan. 1, 1839, aged seventy-eight.

113—V. DANIEL,[5] b. May 20, 1761. See below (113).
114—VI. JONATHAN,[6] b. Sept 18, 1763; probably lived in Andover; and m. Sally Ayer of Haverhill April 14, 1791.
115—VII. DUDLEY,[5] b. June 24, 1765; yeoman; lived in Haverhill, 1798 and 1799.
116—VIII. SIMEON,[5] b. Sept. 7, 1767; lived in Middletown, Conn., and New York; m. Lucretia Russell of Middletown, Conn.
117—IX. SUSANNA,[5] b. Sept. 20, 1770.

50

NATHANIEL BRADLEY,[4] born in Haverhill June 1, 1738. He lived in Haverhill, where he was an yeoman, and in 1776 and 1779 an innholder. He married Elizabeth Ordway of Amesbury (published March 22, 1760). She died March 13, 1799; and he died April 3, 1804. He was called "gentleman" the last twenty years of his life.

Children, born in Haverhill :—

118—I. STEPHEN,[4] b. Dec. 30, 1760. See below (118).
119—II. SARAH,[5] b. Jan. 25, 1762; probably d. before 1802; unmarried, of Haverhill, 1799.
120—III. ELIZABETH,[5] b. Nov. 4, 1763; unmarried in 1802; lived in Haverhill.
121—IV. ABIAH,[5] b. April 23, 1765; m. Moses Emery, jr., Feb. 26, 1789.
122—V. MARY,[5] b. Aug. 12, 1766; m. John Russell before 1795.
123—VI. HANNAH,[5] b. March 11, 1768; m. Simeon Atwood of Bradford Nov. 14, 1790; and was living in 1802.

55

PETER BRADLEY,[4] born in Haverhill Oct. 23, 1745. He was a yeoman and trader, and lived in Haverhill. He married Mehitable Kimball; and she died Sept. 4, 1774. He died Jan. 31, 1817.

Children, born in Haverhill :—

124—I. FRANCIS,[5] b. March 23, 1770. See below (124).
125—II. MEHITABLE,[5] b. April 9, 1774; probably m. Moses Wingate May 30, 1793; and d. Nov. 5, 1807.

64

JONATHAN BRADLEY,[4] born in Haverhill Oct. 17, 1748. He lived in Haverhill; and married Hannah Haseltine, jr.

Children, born in Haverhill :—

126—I. WARD,[5] b. Feb. 16, 1772.
127—II. LYDIA,[5] b. July 11, 1774.

65

ITHAMAR BRADLEY,[4] born in Haverhill Feb. 15, 1751; was a yeoman, and lived in Haverhill until 1782, when he settled in Hollis, N. H. He married Mehitable Stevens of Methuen Oct. 1, 1778.

Children :—

128—I. NEHEMIAH,[5] b. May 17, 1779, in Haverhill.
129—II. EZEKIEL,[5] b. April 27, 1781.
130—III. MEHITABLE,[5] Sept. 8, 1784, in Hollis.
131—IV. ITHAMAR,[5] b. June 22, 1790, in Hollis.

75

JOSEPH BRADLEY,[4] born in Haverhill Feb. 14, 1744-5. He was a cordwainer and yeoman, and lived in Haverhill until 1800, when he removed to Andover. He married Mary Osgood of Andover March 28, 1781. He died in Andover March 21, 1802, aged fifty-six; and she died there, his widow, Aug. 9, 1840, aged eighty-six.

Children, born in Haverhill :—

132—I. JOSEPH,[5] b. March 10, 1782; d. April 1, 1782.
133—II. POLLY OSGOOD,[5] b. June 11, 1783; d. June 11, 1783.
134—III. JOSEPH,[5] b. Aug. 13, 1784; lived in North Andover; m. Charlotte Barker of Andover; d. April 6, 1842. He had children.
135—IV. POLLY OSGOOD,[5] b. Nov. 13, 1786; m. John Poor of West Andover; she became insane, and hung herself with a skein of yarn in "Moose Country" (North Lawrence) Feb. 20, 1829.
136—V. JOHN,[5] b. Feb. 10, 1789; m. Fanny Swan of Methuen; d. Nov. 27, 1830.
137—VI. THOMAS OSGOOD,[5] b. April 10, 1792; d. Oct. 18, 1798.
138—VII. WILLIAM,[5] b. Aug. 20, 1795; m. Harriette Shattuck; he d. Aug. 19, 1838, in West Andover; and she married, secondly, —— Putnam.
139—VIII. THOMAS OSGOOD,[5] b. Aug. 12, 1798; m. Lucy Sutton; d. in South America.
140—IX. GEORGE,[5] b. Dec. 4, 1800; m., first, Louisa Adams of Adams; and, second, Susan Shattuck; d. Jan. 8, 1842, in South Andover, suddenly.

68

JONATHAN BRADLEY,[4] born in Haverhill Feb. 14, 1744-5. He was a yeoman, and lived in Haverhill until about 1780, when he removed to Andover. He married, first, Sarah Osgood of Andover in 1773; and she died in Andover Sept. 14, 1790, aged forty. He married, second, Sally Ayer of Haverhill April 14, 1791. He died Feb. 22, 1818, aged seventy-three; and she died, his widow, Oct. 10, 1820, aged sixty-five.

Children :—

141—I. THOMAS OSGOOD,[5] b. Sept. 28, 1774, in Haverhill.
142—II. SARAH,[5] b. Aug. 10, 1776, in Haverhill.
143—III. WILLIAM,[5] b. Jan. 7, 1782, in Andover; d July 12, 1784.
144—IV. BETSEY,[5] b. June 10, 1784, in Andover.
145—V. JONATHAN,[5] b. Oct. 19, 1786, in Andover.
146—VI. WILLIAM,[5] b. Jan. 16, 1789, in Andover.
147—VII. CHARLES,[5] b. Dec. 17, 1792, in Andover.
148—VIII. HARRISON,[5] b. Dec. 4, 1793, in Andover.
149—IX. JAMES,[5] b. July 1, 1795, in Andover.
150—X. GEORGE,[5] b. Nov. 28, 1796, in Andover; d. Jan. 22, 1797.
151—XI. ANNA,[5] b. Nov. 1, 1798, in Andover.

88

BENJAMIN BRADLEY,[4] born in Haverhill Feb. 18, 1746-7. He was a cordwainer and yeoman, and lived in Plaistow, N. H., until 1784, when he returned to Haverhill, where he afterward lived. He married Sarah Noyes of Plaistow April 20, 1769; and she died in Haverhill April 20, 1817. He died in Haverhill Sept. 2, 1823, aged seventy-six.

Children :—

152—I. LYDIA,[5] unmarried in 1821.
153—II. SALLY,[5] m. Moses Dow of Plaistow Feb. 23, 1800; and was living in 1821.
154—III. BETSEY,[5] m. —— Webster before 1821.
155—IV. ISAAC,[5] d. Sept. 29, 1809.
156—V. JOSEPH,[5] cooper, lived in Plaistow in 1823.
157—VI. BENJAMIN,[5] cooper, lived in Plaistow in 1823.
158—VII. ANNA,[5] b. June 6, 1785, in Haverhill; m. Levi Heard before 1821.
159—VIII. RUTH,[5] b. June 20, 1787, in Haverhill; m. —— Barker before 1821.
160—IX. MARY,[5] b. April 14, 1790, in Haverhill; unmarried in 1821.

161—x.   JUDITH,[5] b. July 17, 1792, in Haver-
         hill; perhaps m. David Stevens be-
         fore 1821.

113

DANIEL BRADLEY,[5] born in Haverhill
May 20, 1761. He was a yeoman, and
lived in Haverhill. He married Sarah
Woodbury Dec. 20, 1795.
   Children, born in Haverhill :—
162—I.   HARRIET,[6] b. March 8 1796.
163—II.   EDWARD WOODBURY,[6] March 8, 1799.
164—III. SARAH JANE,[6] b. Aug. 8, 1800.
165—IV.   LEVERET,[6] b. Sept. 17, 1809.

118

STEPHEN BRADLEY,[5] born in Haverhill
Dec. 30, 1760. He married Abiah Stone
Nov. 23, 1784 ; and lived in Haverhill.
He died Aug. 12, 1792, at the age of
thirty-one.
   Children, born in Haverhill :—
166—I.   ABIGAIL,[6] b. Dec. 23, 1785; living in
          1802.
167—II.   ABIAH EMERY,[6] b. Oct. 30, 1787;
          living in 1802.
168—III. SARAH,[6] b. Aug. 15, 1792, posthu-
          mous.

124

FRANCIS BRADLEY,[5] born in Haverhill
March 23, 1770. He lived in Haverhill;
and married Polly Mooers Nov. 3, 1796.
He died Jan. 5, 1819.
   Children, born in Haverhill :—
169—I.   MARY HAZEN,[6] b. May 1, 1797.
170—II.   HARRIET,[6] b. May 17, 1799.
171—III. MEHITABEL,[6] b. May 22, 1803.
172—IV.   ABIGAIL,[6] b. Oct. 6, 1805.
173—V.   FRANCIS EDWIN,[6] b. Nov. 29, 1811;
          d. Sept. 16, 1819.

WILL OF WILLIAM WILD.

The will of William Wild of Ipswich
was proved in the court at Ipswich Sept.
30, 1662. The following is a copy of the
original on file in the probate office at
Salem.

I william wild of Ipswich in the county
of Effex in New England being at present
Sicke and weake of body but through
Gods mercye Inioyeing my vnderstanding
and memory doe make & ordaine this
my last will and Testament first I giue
my soule into the hands of Jefus christ
my Redeemer my Body to be defently
buried And for my outward estate which
the Lord hath beene pleafed to giue I
difpofe of as followeth After my debts &
funerall expences are difcharged I doe
giue and bequeath vnto [my] beloued
wife Elizabeth wild my dwelling houfe and
all my land for the tearme of her naturall
Life, and after her deceafe I giue all my
fayd houfe and Land I doe giue vnto
John wild the sonn of John wild of Topffield my Kinfman Item I doe giue and
bequeath vnto my Kinfman John wild
Senior of Topffield tenn pounds wch he
the sayd John wild hath in his hands of
myne & doe order the bond I haue of
him for it to be rendered vp vnto him after my deceafe Item I doe giue vnto
Robert Amis the sum of five pounds to
to be payd by my executrix within one
yeare after my death Alfoe I giue vnto
marke warner the Summ of five pound
Alfoe I giue vnto Hanah Lampfon the
summ of ten pounds to be payd by my
executrix as my Overffeers shall apoy[t]
and the rest of my estate I leave vnto my
beloued wife Elizabeth wild whom I make
sole executrix of this my last will and testament And I doe defire my loueing
freinds Theophilus willfon william white
& Robert Lord senior to be my overfeers
to fee that this my last will be pformed
acording to the true intent & meaneing
therof And it is my will and mind that
If my Kinfman John wild Junior depart
this life before he come [to] age or before
the fayd houfe & Land comes into his
poffefion that then it be devided among
the children of John wild senior vnlefs the
Sayd John leaue heires then to be vnto
them In wittnes that this is my last will
& testament I haue heervnto fett my hand
the Sixt day of may in the yeare one
thoufand Six hundred sixty two 1662

      William wild did
subfcrib this & declare   William Wild
it to be his last will
in the prefence of vs
      Theophilus wilfon
      William White
      Robert Lord

HAMILTON INSCRIPTIONS.

ANCIENT BURIAL-PLACE.

This burial ground, originally dedicated to that use in 1706, was conveyed by John Dane to the Hamlet parish. It then measured one-half of an acre in area. Mr. Dane died the next year, and his gravestone is the oldest one in the yard. The following are all of the stones now standing there, bearing dates prior to 1800.

SACRED to the memory of Mifs Betfey Adams the Amiable Daugt of Mr. Samuel & Mrs. Jemima Adams who Departed this Life April 8th 1796, in the 17th year of her age.

Away from fin from forrow & from woe Unto my God & Saviour let me go.

Adieu my friends dry up your tears I muft lie here till Chrift appears My ftate is fix'd my glafs is run My days are paft my life is done.

HERE LYES Yᵉ BODY OF Mʳ IOHN ANNABLE WHO DIED IANUARY Yᵉ 25 1717—16 AGED 68 YEARS

Here lies Interr'd the Remains of Mifs LUCY APPLETON; Daughter of Mʳ OLIVER & Mʳˢ SARAH APPLETON of Ipswich, who departed this Life under the operation of the fmall Pox June 12th 1778. In the 31st Year of her Age.

I am the refurrection and the life; he that believeth in me though he were dead fhall he live JOHN XI: 25th. The hour is coming in which all that are in the grave fhall hear his voice and come forth. JOHN V. 28th & 29th. How fhort, How precarious, How uncertain is life: How quick the tranfition from Time to Eternity: A breath, a gafp, a groan or two, And we are seen no more. Yet on this brittle thread (Alarming thought) Hangs vaft Eternity.

MARY BALCH Dauᵗ of Mʳ FREEBORN & Mʳˢ MARY BALCH Died Sepᵗ 2ᵈ 1758 Aged 3 Years 3 Months & 8 Days.

Here Lyes Yᵉ Body of Sarah Yᵉ Wife of Jacob Brown who died Yᵉ 9 1729 In Yᵉ 51 year of her Age.*

MEMENTO MORI   FUGIT HORA

HERE LIES Yᵉ BODY OF JOHN DANE SENʳ WHO DEPARTED THIS LIFE DECEMBᴿ Yᵉ 23 1707 IN Yᵉ 65 YEAR OF HIS AGE

HERE LIES Yᵉ BODY OF Mr. WILLIAM DAUISON WHO DIED JANUARY Yᵉ 17th 172930 AGED 66 YEARS

Here lies Buried the Body of PAUL DODGE who Departed this Life Janʳʸ yᵉ 3ᵈ 1773 in yᵉ 64th Year of his Agᵉ

*The month was not inserted.

In memory of 4
children of Col.
ROBERT & MRS.
MARY DODGE.

ROBERT died Feb. 3,
1774. Æt. 5 months.

POLLY died April 19,
1779. Æt. 7 months

POLLY 2 died July 8,
1790. Æt 19 months

PEARLY died May 29,
1799. Æt. 14 years

A breath, a gasp a groan or two
And we are seen no more,
Yet on this brittle thread alorming
Hangs vast eternity   (thought

———

Here Lies the Body of
Mr THOMAS DODGE
who Died August the 23
1 7 5
In   the   47th   *
of his

———

Here Lyes Buried
the Body of Mr
DANIEL   GILBERTT
Who Decd Nouembr
the 2nd 1723, in the
44th Year of His Age

———

Here Lyes Buried
the Body of Deacon
JOHN GILBERTT,
Who Deceafed March
the 17th 1723 in the
67th Year of His Age

Bleffed are ye Dead, yt Die in ye Lord.

——— .

Here Lyeth ye Body of Mr John
Hubbard Who Died January ye
1750 Aged 74

Ye MEMORY OF Ye JUST IS BLEFFED.

*Broken.

ELIZABETH,
the Wife of
Dr. Nathan Lakeman,
died May 17th 1796 ;
Æt 29.

The rifing morning can't affure
That we fhall end the day ;
For Death ftands ready at the door,
To feize our lives away.

———

In Memory of
Mrs HANNAH LUMMUS
the virtuous confort of
Mr JOHN LUMMUS ;
fhe furvived & mourned
him till Decr 13th 1787,
and fell afleep, in the 64th
year of her age ; beloved and
lamented.

" *Away from fin from pain & ev'ry woe*
Now to my God & Savior let me go."

Her pray'r is heard ; the gentle fpirit flies;
The poor bewail her as fhe mounts the fkies;
Each friend bemoans her love with aching breaft,
And ev'ry child fhall rife & call her bleft.

———

In
Memory of
Mr JOHN LUMMUS who
died May 18th A D 1785
in the 63d year of his Age
He was an affectionate hufband
a kind father ; the poor man's friend ;
Retired in his turn of mind but fo-
ciable, liberal, & a lover of hofpitality ;
An attentive & public fpirited member of fociety ; punctual to every
duty of his ftation, faithful to his
engagements, upright in his dealings, and
eminently of a meek & quiet fpirit.

Bleffed are the peace-makers.

———

HERE LYES Ye BODY
OF MARY Ye WIFE OF
SAMUEL   LUMMUS
WHO DIED NOVEMbr
Ye 29th 1744 IN Ye
58th YEAR OF HER
AGE

Here Lyeth the Body of
Mr Samuel Lummus Who
Was Born June y^e 7th
1639 & Died y^o 24th Feb^y
1 7 2 0   A g e d   8 0
years.

———

Here   lyes   Buried
y^o   Body   of   M^r
SAMUEL   LUMMUS
Who   Departed   this
Life *December* ye 9th
1754 in ye 74th Year
o f   H i s   A g e.

———

Here lies
Interr'd the Remains
of Mrs ELIZABETH PARSONS,
the Amiable Confort of M^r
OBADIAH PARSONS, and
youngeft Daughter of the Rev.
Mr SAMUEL & M^{rs} MA^rTHA
WIGGLESWORTH, who Departed
this Life Jany 17th 1771 in the
23^d Year of her Age.

———

IN Memory of
DEA. JOHN PATCH,
who died Aug. 8, 1789;
Æt. 90.
RACHEL his wife died
March 4, 1806,
Æt. 80.
How still & peacefull is thy grave
Where life's vain tumults past,
The appointed house by Heaven's decree
Receives all at last.

———

IN Memory of
Mrs. SARAH PATCH,
who died Novr 28th
1798, aged 48 years
She was the wife of
Mr. SAMUEL PATCH,
who died in
Pointpeter.

———

In memory of
Mr. JOSEPH POLAND
who died Octr 14, 1798
In the 95 Year of his age.
Hear what ye Voice from heav'n proclaims
For all the pious dead,
Sweet is the favour of their names
And soft their sleeping bed
Far from this World of toil & strife
They're present with ye LORD;
The labours of their mortal life
End in a large reward.

———

HERE   LIES   Y^e   BODY
OF   M R   R O B E R T
QUARLES   WHO   DIED
SEPTEMBER Y^e 7th 1730
I N   Y^o   5 5th   Y E A R
O F   H I S   A G E

———

HERE   LIES   THE
BODY OF MR WILLIAM
QUARLES   WHO   DIED
Y^e 9 OF JUNE 1726
I N   Y^e   5 6   Y E A R
O F   H I S   AGE

———

In Memory of
MRS. MARY ROBERTS,
wife of
Mr. Thomas Roberts,
who died
April 17, 1795;
Aged 36.

———

Here Lyes Y^e Body
of Abraham Telten
Who died March the
28 1728 and the
90 year of
Age.

In Memory of
Mr JOSEPH TILTON;
who departed this Life
Janry 24th 1779. Aged 69 Years.
He was an affectionate Husband—a kind
Parent—a sincere Friend— an exemplary
Christian.   At death he resigned his spirit
with great serenity, having a Confident
Hope of an interest in ye Redeemer.
Mark ye perfect man, & behold ye upright
for the end of that man is Peace.
He's gone, he's past ye gloomy shades of Night,
Safe landed in the eternal realms of light.
Happy exchange to part with all below
For worlds of bliss, where joys unceasing flow.

———

In Memory of
MR. CHARLES TUTTLE
who died Decr 1st
1 7 8 8
in the 80th year
of his age.

My children look as you pass by,
As you are now, so once was I,
As I am now soon you will be;
Prepare for death & follow me.

———

IN Memory of 3 children of
Mr. Charles & Mrs. Lucy Tuttle.
Daniel Tuttle"died Decr 16th 1798
in the 9th year of his age.

Anna	Hepzibah
Tuttle died Jan.	Tuttle died Jan.
29r 1799, in the	30th 1799, in the
16th year of	11th year of
her age	her age.

A breath,'a gasp, a groan or two, ⎫
And we are seen no more,   ⎬ *Alarming*
Yet on this brittle thread   ⎭ *thought.*
Hangs vast Eternity.

———

Here Lies the
Body of Mrs Hannah
Whipple the Wife
of Capt John
Whipple Who Died
Jany the 24
17   * ye 66 Year
of her Age.

*Broken.

CAP JOHN
WHIPPLE
1722*

Here lies Buried
the Body of
Capt JOHN WHIPPLE;
who departed this Life
Febry the 9th 1781
Aged 91 Years
The memory of the Just is blessed
Be thou faithful unto death
And I will give thee a crown of life.

———

ERECTED In memory
of John Whipple 5th
second son of Mr. Willm
& Mrs. Katharine Whipple
who died Jany 10th 1797,
in the 18th year of his age.
Early in life I'm call'd to die,
To sing his praise who reigns on high
                            ds
But as for you, my weeping frien
My God will make you all amends
Your care & kindness shewn to me
Shall all by him rewarded be,

Here Lyes Buried ye Body of
Mrs MARTHA WHIPPLE
The Wife of MATTHEW
WHIPPLE Esqr who died
September 12th 1728
In ye 60th year of his Age.
Blessed are the dead
that die in the Lord.

Here is interred
the Body of
Capt MARTHY
W H I P E L
Who DeParted
this   Life
Ienuery   The
8 th   1 7 7 3
Aged 70 years.
come Mortal man
& cast An eye
come read thy dOOm
PrePare To Die

*Footstone (?).

Here Lyes ye Body of
Matthew Whipple Esqr
Who died y^o 28th of
Janu^{ry} 1738/9 in y^e
* of his
Age

ERECTED
In Memory of
Mr WILLIAM WHIPPLE,
who departed this Life
June 29th
1784
In the 57th year of his age

HERE LYES Y^e BODY OF
Mrs MARY WIGGLESWORTH
WIFE TO Y^e REU^D M^r
SAMUEL WIGGLESWORTH
AGED 28 YEARS
DEC^D JUNE Y^e 6th
1 7 2 3

In memory of
MRS. SARAH WOODBURY,
1st wife of
Mr. Barnett Woodbury,
who died
Jan. 11, 1782;
Æt. 45.

WILL OF JOHN BRABROOKE.

The renuncupative will of John Bra-
brooke of Newbury was proved in the
court at Ipswich Sept. 30, 1662. The
following is a copy of the original instrument on file in the probate office at Salem.
It was sworn to by Henry Short and
Richard Knight.

This 27th of June 1662 I John bra-
brooke of newberie being fick in body
butt of good memorie do here make my
laft will and teftament as foloweth firft
I Comit my foule to god to Inioy him
fecondly for my outward Eftat I giue
vnto my mother on Cow and all my wering
Clothes that Cow I mene which is in my

*Unintelligible.

vnkl fhorts hands 3dly I giue vnto my
mother and my brother famuell and my
brother Jofey and my fifter Elizabeth and
my fifter farah and my fifter Rebeca and
my fifter Rachell all that Eftate which is
mine in England to be Equaliy devided
between them

4^{thly} I giue vnto my brother Thomas
and my brother Jofey my mare and Coult
to be devided between them Likwis I
giue vnto my brother Jofey on yew lamb
Likwis I giue vnto my frend Cormack fiue
fhillings Likwis I giue vnto my mother
mor fifteen fhillings

Laftly I giue vnto my brother Thomas
all my Intreft in the houfe and Land at
watter toune after my mother defese allfo
I giue vnto my fifter Elizabeth on Cow
which is at famuell Moodys

Likwis I defier my vnkell fhort as my
frend to fe this my will to be performed

Wittnes Richard Knight
James Jackman

NOTES.

Joseph Boovy of Lynn, aged twenty-
seven, 1658.—*Court records.*

William Bosson of Roxbury, tailor, appointed administrator of the estate of his
brother John Bosson of Marblehead, mariner, Oct. 6, 1714.—*Probate records.*

Jonathan Davis Bosen married Martha
Young, both of Salem, June 18, 1783.—
Salem town records.

Joshua Basson of Beverly, joiner, formerly of ye Island of Jersey, in Hantshire,
England, son of Elizabeth Fall alias Basson, 1702.*—*Registry of deeds.*

William Borroughs, son of George, of
Ipswich, baptized Oct. 21, 1722.—*Manchester church records.*

Mrs. Ann Boshon married John Coles
Oct. 31, 1769, at Hampton Falls, N. H.
—*Manchester town records.*

Lydia Boston married Joseph Henfield,
both of Salem, Sept. 14, 1710.

*See *The Antiquarian*, volume VIII., page
132.

Sarah Boston of Lynn married Benjamin Nurse of Salem (published Sept. 4, 1714) in 1718.

Boston (negro servant of Rev. John Barnard of Marblehead) published to Rose (negro woman servant of Warwick Palfray of Salem) March 22, 1760.

—Salem town records.

SALEM IN 1700. NO. 26.

BY SIDNEY PERLEY.

The map on page 14 represents that part of Salem which is bounded by Walnut, Essex and Liberty streets and the South river. It is based on actual surveys and title deeds, and is drawn on a scale of two hundred feet to an inch. It shows the location of all the houses that were standing there in 1700.

The braces marked "a" show where Charter street runs; and the braces marked "b" where Derby street runs.

Essex street was one of the original highways of the town. It was called the street or common highway in 1658; ye highway, 1678; the main street, 1705; and Essex street in 1799.

Walnut street was called a highway in 1694; a lane leading to ye South river, 1705; Elder Brown's lane, 1725; Brown's lane, 1734; and Walnut street, 1795.

Elm street was an ancient way to the cove; and was called the street or common highway in 1658: a way in 1669; a lane or street, 1674; the lane or highway that goes down to South river, 1685; ye street or town highway, 1687; highway by Peter Osgood's tanhouse, 1695; the highway or lane that goeth toward Maj. John Higginson's wharf and warehouse, 1696; the lane which leads downe from Col. John Higginson's house to ye South river, 1699; the lane which leads down from the main street to ye South river, 1699; a lane leading down to Peter Osgood's, 1705; the lane that leads from the maine street downe to the South river nigh Capt. Osgood's, 1710: ye lane that goes down to Capt. Osgood's, 1711; Osgood's lane, 1737; Lowther's lane,

1755; Lowder's lane, 1759; Loder's lane, 1785; Loader's lane, 1785; Lother's lane, 1785; Lodder's lane, 1792; and Elm street, 1796.

Liberty street is also an ancient way. It was called Ye lane next to John Pitman's in 1670; ye lane or highway that leads down to the river, 1672; the lane or highway that goes down to the South river, 1678; the lane that goes down to ye burying place, 1683; the burying place lane, 1690; highway that leads down to ye water's side, 1697; Liberty lane, 1789; and Liberty street, 1800.

The western half of that part of Charter street shown on the map as a lane, was a strip of land conveyed by Hilliard Veren, jr., of Salem, merchant, to William Browne, jr., of Salem, merchant, Nov. 8, 1679,[*] for a way into the grantee's land. When the lot of land, to which this lane led, was conveyed by Richard Moore, sr., of Salem, mariner, to William Browne, jr., of Salem Sept. 27, 1671,[†] the grantor reserved a right of way over the lot from his house to what is now Essex street. To free his land from this incumbrance, Mr. Browne bought of Mr. Veren the strip of land of eighteen feet in width above-mentioned and with a strip off the southern end of his own lot made a way for Captain Moore out to what is now Liberty street. This part of the street was called in the year it was laid out, 1679, the lane or highway that goes to Captain More's; the lane that goes to Capt. Richard More's orchard, 1683; Captain More's lane, 1687; and ye lane that leads down to Captain Osgood's, 1709. The lane was extended to what is now Walnut street soon after the Long (or, Union) wharf was built, about 1730. It was called the lane leading from the burying point lane to the long wharf in 1747; the highway, 1772; the street, 1773; highway leading to the long wharf, 1779; a lane leading to the long wharf called Union wharf, 1783; and the street

[*]Essex Registry of Deeds, book 5, leaf 104.
[†]Essex Registry of Deeds, book 3, leaf 128.

leading from Liberty street to the long wharf there so called, 1789. In 1795, that part of the street lying between Walnut and Elm streets was called Neptune street, and from Elm to Liberty street, Vine street. In 1853, both sections were called Charter street.

The present Derby street, the location of which is shown on the map by the braces marked "b" was made by filling the river shortly before 1784. It was called the highway near the South river in 1784; Water street, 1795; and Derby street, 1871.

The river was so called in 1654; the sea, 1687; the South river, 1687; the river or salt water, 1705; and the harbor or South river, 1722.

The cove was so called in 1688; and called the dock in 1789. It was probably not filled up and the street extended over it until about 1840(?).

In the sketches that follow, after 1700, titles and deeds referred to pertain to the houses and land adjoining and not always to the whole lot, the design being, after that date, to give the history of the houses then standing principally.

William Curtis House. This was the homestead of Daniel Rumball, the blacksmith, in 1659. Upon condition that his son-in-law, William Curtice, and wife Alice, daughter of Mr. Rumball, support him for life and also pay his burial expenses, he conveyed his estate to Mr. and Mrs. Curtice March 18, 1681-2-* Mr. Curtice was also a blacksmith, and lived here. In consideration of love, Mr. and Mrs. Curtice conveyed the house, barn and land to their daughter Elizabeth and her husband, John Lowther of Salem, Feb. 17, 1704-5.† Mr. Lowder died in 1717, leaving his wife Elizabeth, and children, Jared (or, Garrett) Lowther, Nicholas Lowder, James Lowder, Abigail Lowder, Martha Lowder, Daniel Lowder, and Elizabeth, wife of John Callum of Salem, mariner. Jared lived in Salem,

being a shipwright; Daniel lived in Salem, being a barber; and Nicholas lived in Salem, being a cordwainer. Daniel bought out the heirs of his father; Nicholas, Oct. 22, 1717;* Jared, Dec. 1, 1718;† and Elizabeth, Nov. 10, 1720.‡ Daniel Lowder died in 1722, having devised the estate to his mother, widow Elizabeth Lowder. She conveyed the house and land around it to her son-in-law Benjamin Allen of Salem, joiner, Dec. 13, 1737.§ Mr. Allen died before Jan. 20, 1768, when his heirs made partition of the estate.|| In this division, the house is called "ye old house," and with the land around it was assigned to Abigail, wife of Joseph Gilford of Salem, mariner, and Martha, wife of John Teague of Salem, hatter. Feb. 20, 1768, Mrs. Gilford and Mrs. Teague, with their husbands, made a division of the estate, the house and land around it being assigned to Mrs. Gilford.¶ Mrs. Gilford died in 1797, having devised the house and land around it to her son Joseph Gilford of Salem, laborer, and her daughter Sarah Gilford of Salem, singlewoman. In the inventory of Mrs. Gilford's estate, the house is called "an old dwelling house." It was gone in 1799, when Joseph and Sarah sold the land to Benjamin West, who built the brick block upon the lot.

John Higginson Lot. This was a part of the lot of Samuel Archer April 27, 1665, when he conveyed it, being then a part of a larger lot, to James Browne of Salem, merchant.** Mr. Browne was murdered in Maryland Nov. 12, 1675. By an agreement between the widow and the children of the deceased, dated Sept. 15, 1694, this land was assigned to his daughter Elizabeth Browne.†† For two pounds, Miss Browne conveyed it to Col. John Higginson, jr., of Salem, mer-

---

*Essex Registry of Deeds, book 6, leaf 68a.
†Essex Registry of Deeds, book 18, leaf 17.

*Essex Registry of Deeds, book 33, leaf 249.
†Essex Registry of Deeds, book 33, leaf 250.
‡Essex Registry of Deeds, book 37, leaf 163.
§Essex Registry of Deeds, book 74, leaf 76.
||Essex Registry of Deeds, book 121, leaf 241.
¶Essex Registry of Deeds, book 117, leaf 250.
**Essex Registry of Deeds, book 2, leaf 111.
††Essex Registry of Deeds, book 10, leaf 69.

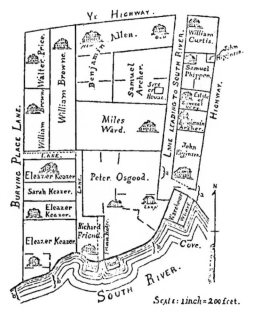

PART OF SALEM IN 1700. NO. 26.

Ye Highway.

Burying Place Lane.

William Browne. Walter Price.

William Browne.

Benjamin Allen.

Samuel Archer.

Site of House.

Miles Ward.

Lane leading to South River.

William Curtis.

John Higginson.

Samuel Phippen.

Estate of Samuel Very.

Benjamin Archer.

Highway.

John Higginson.

Lane.

Eleazer Keazer.

Sarah Keazer.

Eleazer Keazer.

Eleazer Keazer.

Peter Osgood.

Richard Friend.

N

Watchhouse.

Wharf.

Cove.

South River.

Scale: 1inch=200feet.

chant, Oct. 6, 1699.[*] Colonel Higginson owned it for many years after 1700.

Samuel Phippen House. This lot belonged to Samuel Archer of Salem April 27, 1665, when he conveyed that part of it lying east of the dashes to James Browne of Salem, merchant.[†]   Mr. Browne was murdered in Maryland Nov. 12, 1675. By an agreement between his widow and children this lot, then called the great garden, was released to his daughter Elizabeth Browne Sept. 15, 1694.[‡] Miss Browne conveyed the land to Samuel Phippen (or, Phippeny), sr., of Salem, blockmaker, Oct. 6, 1699.[§]

That part of the lot lying westerly of the dashes remained the property of Samuel Archer until his death in December, 1667, when it was valued at five pounds. The estate was insolvent, and William Browne, sr., of Salem, esquire and merchant, the principal creditor, took the place. Samuel Archer's widow, then Susannah, wife of Richard Hutchinson, released her dower interest in the lot to Mr. Browne July 5, 1669.[||] He erected a house upon the lot, and, for eighty pounds, conveyed the house and this part of the lot to Mr. Phippen, who owned the remainder of this lot, March 30, 1681.[¶] Sept. 27, 1687, Samuel Archer (or, Archard) of Salem, house-carpenter, eldest son of the deceased Samuel Archer, released the land to Mr. Browne.[**] Samuel Phippen died Feb. 1, 1717-8, at the age of sixty-eight, intestate. The house and an old shop and the land were then appraised at eighty pounds. The real estate was divided among his children May 21, 1733, when it was valued at one hundred and twelve pounds and ten shillings. The house and the land around it were assigned to his son Nathaniel Phippen of Salem, cooper. Nathaniel Phippen died

in 1756, possessed of the house and land around it, which was described in the inventory of his estate as "One Old house & Land in y[e] Lane former Sam[l] Phippens dec[d]," and valued at sixty-five pounds, six shillings and eight pence. In his will he devised his real estate to his children, David, Israel, Thomas, Margaret and Anstes. In the division of the real estate, Nov. 15, 1759, this old house and the land around it were assigned to son Thomas Phippen, who then lived in the house.[*] The executor of the will of David Phippen of Salem, gentleman, deceased, brought suit against Thomas Phippen; and, May 13, 1785, this lot with the old house thereon, was set off to the estate in satisfaction of the judgment.[†] July 9, 1785, the executor of David Phippen's will, for sixty-four pounds, ten shillings and six pence, conveyed the lot and buildings thereon to John Fisk of Salem, merchant;[‡] and the house was gone before 1792, when Mr. Fisk sold the lot.

Estate of Samuel Very House. This lot belonged to John Archer as early as 1665. He lived in Salem, and was a cooper. He gave this lot of land by deed to his daughter Abigail and her husband Samuel Very May 9, 1685.[§] Mr. Very built a house upon the lot in which he lived. He died in 1697, possessed of the estate. Probably after the death of his widow Abigail, the remainder of his real estate was divided, and the house and land were assigned to his eldest son Samuel Very Oct. 29, 1716. In 1697, the house and land were valued at forty pounds. Samuel Very, jr., lived in Salem, being a mariner. For eighty pounds, he conveyed the house and land to David Montgomery of Salem, mariner, July 20, 1734.[||] Mr. Montgomery died in 1737. The house, barn and land around them were then valued at one hundred and

---

*Essex Registry of Deeds, book 13, leaf 178.
†Essex Registry of Deeds, book 2, leaf 111.
‡Essex Registry of Deeds, book 10, leaf 69.
§Essex Registry of Deeds, book 13, leaf 229.
ˮEssex Registry of Deeds, book 7, leaf 27.
ˑEssex Registry of Deeds, book 7, leaf 146.
**Essex Registry of Deeds, book 3, leaf 75.

*Essex Registry of Deeds, book 111, leaf 1.
†Essex Registry of Deeds, book 144, leaf 187.
‡Essex Registry of Deeds, book 144, leaf 47.
§Essex Registry of Deeds, book 43, leaf 224.
||Essex Registry of Deeds, book 62, leaf 209.

twenty-five pounds. His widow and administratrix, Sarah Montgomery, for sixty-five pounds, conveyed the house and land around it to David Phippen of Salem, joiner, Jan. 27, 1740.* Deacon Phippen apparently removed the house soon afterward.

Benjamin Archer House. This lot belonged to John Archer quite early. He was a cooper, and died in 1693, intestate. The estate passed to his son Benjamin Archer, who was also a cooper. Benjamin Archer probably built a house on the land about 1694. He died about 1705, and the house and lot descended to his children, namely: John Archer, Benjamin Archer, Sarah, wife of John Swasey, and Josiah Archer. John Archer of Salem, cordwainer and fisherman, released his interest in the house and lot to his brother Benjamin Archer of Salem, mariner, Dec. 18, 1722.† Josiah and Sarah probably did the same. The house was gone a few years later.

John Higginson House. John Archer owned this house and lot quite early. He lived in the house, and died in 1693. That part of the estate lying northerly of the dashes became the property of John Higginson of Salem, merchant, about 1696.

On the triangular part of the lot lying below the dashes Mr. Higginson built a brewhouse before Nov. 26, 1695, when the administrator of the estate of John Archer, for thirty shillings, conveyed the land to Mr. Higginson.‡

Mr. Higginson died March 23, 1719, and, for sixty pounds, his surviving executor conveyed the house and entire lot to Jonathan Archer of Salem, carman, Feb. 1, 1721-2.§ Mr. Archer probably immediately removed the house.

The wharf site and small piece of land back of it was conveyed by John Archer, sr., of Salem, cooper, for eight pounds, to

*Essex Registry of Deeds, book 81, leaf 104.
†Essex Registry of Deeds, book 40, leaf 209.
‡Essex Registry of Deeds, book 11, leaf 47.
§Essex Registry of Deeds, book 39, leaf 239.

John Higginson Dec. 12, 1684.* For four pounds, Mr. Higginson conveyed one-half of it to Lt. Thomas Gardner of Salem Feb. 14, 1686-7.† Messrs. Higginson and Gardner built a wharf and warehouse thereon, and, June 6, 1637, divided the warehouse, Higginson to have the northern end, and Gardner the southern. Fifty feet of the wharf before the warehouse was to continue in common between them.‡ They, also, laid out a highway as marked on the map, twenty feet wide, Nov. 10, 1691.‡ Mr. Higginson died in 1719, and his surviving executor conveyed his half of the warehouse, wharf and land to Peter Osgood of Salem, tanner, Feb. 27, 1721-2.§ Thomas Gardner conveyed his interest to Captain Osgood at about the same time.

Benjamin Allen Houses. That part of this lot lying north of the dashes early belonged to William Allen of Manchester, carpenter, and he conveyed it, with the house thereon, to John Bridgman of Salem 9:4 mo: 1652.‖ Mr. Bridgman died in 1655, leaving a will: "that his whole estate shal bee deliuered into mr curwins hand and when hee hath satisfied him selfe to giu the rest to his daughter." George Corwin of Salem, merchant, for eighteen pounds, conveyed the house and that part of the lot to Thomas Barnes of Salem, blacksmith, 25:11:1658.¶ The title passed from Thomas Barnes to Capt. Benjamin Allen in or before 1695. Mr. Barnes' blacksmith shop was conveyed with the land. Captain Allen died in 1703, possessed of the old dwelling house, in which Mr. Habakkuk Gardner then lived, and the smith's shop and land. Captain Allen died intestate, and his daughter, Rachel Allen of Salem, conveyed the house and that end of the lot to her brother-in-law Capt. John Richards of

*Essex Registry of Deeds, book 7, leaf 137.
†Essex Registry of Deeds, book 7, leaf 138.
‡Essex Registry of Deeds, book 7, leaf 139.
§Essex Registry of Deeds, book 43, leaf 173.
‖Essex Registry of Deeds, book 1, leaf 18.
¶Essex Registry of Deeds, book 1, leaf 48.

Salem, mariner, Oct. 28, 1709.* Captain Richards conveyed the house and that end of the lot to John Phippen of Salem July 23, 1711.† Mr. Phippen removed the old house a few years later.

Captain Allen probably erected the house on the western end of this part of the lot soon after 1695. He died possessed of it in 1703; and the house and land, with the barn and woodhouse, came into the possession of Capt. John Richards, probably the inheritance of his wife Mary, daughter of Captain Allen. Captain Richards removed to Boston, where he was a mariner, and, with his wife Mary, for three hundred and seventy pounds, conveyed the house and land around it to Joseph Grafton of Salem, mariner, Nov. 30, 1727.‡ Captain Grafton died in the winter of 1766-7, having in his will devised this estate to his three daughters, Susanna, Mary and Anna, all unmarried. For four hundred and sixty pounds, they conveyed the house and land around it to Joseph Peabody of Salem Sept. 30, 1790.§ Mr. Peabody became a merchant, and for fifty-four hundred dollars, conveyed the house, "wherein I now live," and the barn and land under and adjoining them to Dr. Moses Little of Salem March 7, 1799.‖ Doctor Little probably removed the old house immediately after his purchase.

That part of the lot lying between the dashes was in the possession of Samuel Archer, sr.. before 1658. He died in 1667, and it descended to his son Samuel Archer. Samuel Archer of Salem, carpenter, conveyed it to Capt. Benjamin Allen Aug. 9, 1695 ;¶ and he died possessed of it in 1703.

That part of the lot lying south of the dashes was also early in the possession of Samuel Archer (or, Archard) who died in 1667. William Browne, sr., of Salem,

merchant, was the largest creditor of the deceased, and he apparently took the land for his debt. Susannah, the widow of Mr. Archer, married, secondly, Richard Hutchinson, and she conveyed her dower interest in the premises to Mr. Browne July 5, 1669.* Mr. Browne conveyed the land to Joseph Phippen of Salem, fisherman, Dec. 28, 1674.† Mr. Phippen conveyed it to his brothers, David Phippen and Samuel Phippen, both of Salem, Jan. 15, 1694-5.‡ David Phippen and Samuel Phippen conveyed it to Capt. Benjamin Allen Aug. 5, 1695 ;§ and Captain Allen died possessed of it in 1703.

Samuel Archer Lot. Samuel Archer, sr., of Salem, owned this lot in 1658 ; and he died possessed of the lot and the house thereon in 1667. That part of the lot lying north of the dashes descended to his son Samuel Archer, who owned it until after 1700.

That part of the lot lying south of the dashes and the house were taken by William Browne, sr., of Salem, merchant, in satisfaction apparently of his claim against the estate of Samuel Archer, sr., being the largest creditor ; and Susannah, widow of Mr. Archer, and then wife of Richard Hutchinson, conveyed her dower interest in this part of his estate to Mr. Browne July 5, 1669.* Mr. Browne conveyed the house and land around it to Joseph Phippen of Salem, fisherman, Dec. 28, 1674 ;† and Mr. Phippen conveyed the estate to his brothers David Phippen and Samuel Phippen, both of Salem, Jan. 15, 1694-5.‡ David Phippen and Samuel Phippen, for fifty pounds, conveyed the house and this part of the lot to Capt. Benjamin Allen of Salem Aug. 5, 1695.§ Captain Allen removed the house the same year.

Miles Ward House. This lot belonged to Joshua Ward as early as 1669. He died in 1680, leaving this lot of land, with a house thereon, the estate being valued

*Essex Registry of Deeds, book 21, leaf 133.
†Essex Registry of Deeds, book 22, leaf 278.
‡Essex Registry of Deeds, book 50, leaf 5.
§Essex Registry of Deeds, book 153, leaf 91.
‖Essex Registry of Deeds, book 163, leaf 262.
¶Essex Registry of Deeds, book 11, leaf 12.

*Essex Registry of Deeds, book 3, leaf 75.
†Essex Registry of Deeds, book 4, leaf 128.
‡Essex Registry of Deeds, book 10, leaf 113.
§Essex Registry of Deeds, book 11, leaf 14.

at one hundred pounds. It descended to his son Miles (or Michael) Ward, who was a chairmaker. The latter conveyed the house, barn and land, "where I now dwell," to his son Ebenezer Ward of Salem, joiner, March 7, 1755.[*] The father died in 1764, having continued to live in the house, and Ebenezer probably removed the house soon afterwards.

Peter Osgood House. That part of this lot lying within the dashes at the northwesterly corner was the property of William Chichester in 1654; and Henry Bartholomew of Salem conveyed it to Richard More of Salem July 11, 1664.[†] Mr. More was a mariner, and conveyed the land to William Browne, esq., and Mr. Benjamin Browne, both of Salem, May 14, 1688;[‡] and they conveyed it to Peter Osgood of Salem, tanner, May 1, 1696.[§] The remainder of the lot was the homestead of Capt. Richard More in 1664, and there his house stood. He mortgaged a little strip of land next to the "primm" hedge, extending from his house to the South river, including his outkitchen and leanto, to Philip Cromwell of Salem, slaughterer, Dec. 17, 1687;[||] and Captain More conveyed the fee in the same property to Mr. Cromwell May 10, 1690.[¶] The bound of the northeast corner of the lot conveyed was a plum tree; and a right of way was granted through Captain More's orchard to the lane leading down to Richard Friend's house. Mr. Cromwell died, and his executor conveyed the lot to William Browne and Benjamin Browne, the owners of the land adjoining, April 20, 1696.[**] Captain More conveyed the western or old part of his dwelling house and the land within the dashes, except the strip mortgaged to Mr. Cromwell, to William Browne, esq., and Mr. Benjamin Browne, both of Salem, May 14,

1688;[*] and the two Brownes conveyed the same estate to Mr. Osgood May 1, 1696.[†]

The wharf at the southern corner of the lot was built by Richard More, sr., before Oct. 29, 1687, when he conveyed the wharf and flats it was built on, for nine pounds, to John Higginson, jr., of Salem, merchant.[‡] The deed also conveyed the way for cart and on foot that already existed from Captain More's gate to the wharf. Mr. Higginson died in 1719, and his surviving executor conveyed the property to Mr. Osgood Feb. 26, 1721-2.[§]

Captain More conveyed the easterly part of the house, called by the name of new room or ye long room, barn and land to the eastward lying between the dashes to his son Richard More, jr., July 10, 1688.[||] Probably the land conveyed by this deed included the larger portion of the lot lying northerly of the dashes. Richard More, jr., who was, also, a mariner and lived here, conveyed this part of the house and the barn and lot to Mr. Osgood May 1, 1690.[¶]

That part of the lot lying at the northeasterly corner of the premises was early owned by Capt. Richard More, and he apparently conveyed the southern part of it to his son Richard More, jr., before 1688. Both father and son join in a deed of this part of the lot to Mr. Osgood July 5, 1688.[**]

Thus Captain More obtained possession of the entire lot and buildings. He owned the estate for many years after 1700, and the house was probably removed soon after that date.

Richard Friend House. William Chichester owned this lot in 1654; and Henry Bartholomew of Salem conveyed it to Richard More, sr., of Salem July

[*]Essex Registry of Deeds, book 101, leaf 127.
[†]Essex Registry of Deeds, book 2, leaf 82.
[‡]Essex Registry of Deeds, book 8, leaf 85.
[§]Essex Registry of Deeds, book 12, leaf 82.
[||]Essex Registry of Deeds, book 8, leaf 15.
[¶]Essex Registry of Deeds, book 8, leaf 151.
[**]Essex Registry of Deeds, book 11, leaf 184.

[*]Essex Registry of Deeds, book 8, leaf 85.
[†]Essex Registry of Deeds, book 12, leaf 82.
[‡]Essex Registry of Deeds, book 8, leaf 9.
[§]Essex Registry of Deeds, book 43, leaf 173.
[||]Essex Registry of Deeds, book 8, leaf 95.
[¶]Essex Registry of Deeds, book 9, leaf 18.
[**]Essex Registry of Deeds, book 8, leaf 94.

11, 1664.* Mr. More's son-in-law Samuel Dutch of Salem, husband of his daughter Susannah, built a house upon the lot before June 4, 1684, when Mr. More conveyed the land to Mr. Dutch and his issue by said Susannah,† including a right of way to the lane, as marked on the map. Mr. Dutch was a mariner, and died in 1694, possessed of the house and lot, which descended to his children. The land was then valued at twenty pounds, and the house at ten pounds.

Richard Friend owned the house and lot in 1705, and lived there. He died in 1706, when the house and land were appraised at thirty-one pounds. His widow and administratrix, Martha Friend of Andover, for thirty-four pounds, conveyed the house and land to Capt. Peter Osgood of Salem, tanner, Nov. 15, 1707.‡ The house was removed probably soon afterward by Captain Osgood.

That part of the lot lying easterly of the dashes, Mr. Dutch conveyed to John Conant of Marblehead, house-carpenter, Nov. 23, 1692,§ but the title was soon again in Mr. Dutch.

Eleazer Keazer House. This lot belonged to Major William Hathorne of Salem in 1654. He conveyed the lot, except the two little lots shown by the dashes on the map, to George Keazer of Lynn, tanner, 28 : 18 : 1654.‖ There was at that time a cellar on the lot, within the six dashes, "over the which a warehouse is to be erected." The little lots lying within the dashes Major Hathorne conveyed to his son Eleazer Hathorne of Salem, merchant, Dec. 28, 1664.¶ There was then "an old seller" upon the lot, lying within the six dashes, and George Keazer built a house upon it before Oct. 7, 1670, when Eleazer Hathorne conveyed the lot to him.** For eight pounds and

ten shillings, Mr. Hathorne undertook to convey the smaller of the two lots to his wife Abigail, who was daughter of Capt. George Corwin of Salem, March 20, 1671 ;* and he conveyed it to Mr. Keazer Nov. 12, 1672.† Thus Mr. Keazer became the owner of the entire lot. He lived in this house, and died in 1690, having devised the estate to his eldest son Eleazer Keazer. The house was probably gone soon after 1700, when Eleazer Keazer owned the land.

Eleazer Keazer House. This lot belonged to Maj. William Hathorne, and he conveyed it to George Keazer of Lynn 28 : 8 : 1654.‡ Mr. Keazer removed to Salem, where he was a tanner; and died possessed of the land in 1690, having in his will devised it, with a barn thereon, to his son John Keazer of Haverhill. John Keazer was massacred at Haverhill by the Indians March 15, 1696-7. In the division of his real estate this lot was assigned to his son Eleazer Keazer. Apparently, Eleazer had conveyed the lot to his uncle Eleazer of Salem about 1699, when the latter probably had built a house thereon. How long the house stood is unknown.

Sarah Keazer Lot. This lot belonged to Maj. William Hathorne who conveyed it to George Keazer of Lynn 28 : 8 : 1654.‡ Mr. Keazer removed to Salem, where he was a tanner; and died possessed of the land in 1690, having devised it, with the barn thereon, to his son John Keazer. John Keazer removed to Haverhill, where he and his son George were massacred by the Indians March 15, 1696-7. In the division of his real estate, this lot was assigned to his daughter Sarah Keazer, who continued to own it until 1705.

Eleazer Keazer House. This lot early belonged to William Hathorne, who conveyed it to George Keazer of Lynn 28 : 8 : 1654.‡ Mr. Keazer removed to Salem,

*Essex Registry of Deeds, book 2, leaf 82.
†Essex Registry of Deeds, book 6, leaf 123.
‡Essex Registry of Deeds, book 20, leaf 75.
§Essex Registry of Deeds, book 10, leaf 122.
‖Essex Registry of Deeds, book 2, leaf 57.
¶Essex Registry of Deeds, book 2, leaf 93.
**Essex Registry of Deeds, book 3, leaf 101.

*Essex Registry of Deeds, book 3, leaf 140.
†Essex Registry of Deeds, book 3, leaf 164.
‡Essex Registry of Deeds, book 2, leaf 57.

where he was a tanner; and March 16, 1677-8, deeded this lot to his daughter Mary and her husband Thomas Mould and the heirs of her body.[*] Mr. Mould built a house upon the land, and in some way the title to the land was again in Mr. Keazer before his death, in 1690. In the division of Mr. Keazer's estate, the lot was assigned to Capt. Eleazer Keazer of Salem, tanner, who died possessed of it in 1721. The house, however, continued to belong to Mr. Mould until his decease, before Feb. 13, 1699, when administration was granted upon his estate. The house was then appraised at fifteen pounds and ten shillings. There was also a small barn, "butting on the burying place lane," which was valued at four pounds and ten shillings. The house was bought apparently of the estate of Mr. Mould by Eleazer Keazer, who, for sixty-five pounds, conveyed the house and land around it to Capt. Eleazer Moses of Salem, mariner, Oct. 15, 1709.[†] Captain Moses died in 1718, and the house and lot came into the possession of his son Eleazer. The house probably was removed a few years later.

William Browne House. This lot belonged to Peter Palfrey of Salem, planter, very early. He removed to Reading, and conveyed the land to John Porter of Salem, yeoman, Dec. 10, 1653.[‡] Mr. Porter's son, Joseph Porter, married Anna, daughter of Maj. William Hathorne of Salem, Jan. 27, 1664-5. Twenty-five days previously the parents conveyed the marriage portions of their children. Mr. Porter conveyed this lot and other land to his son.[§] Joseph Porter lived in Salem, and conveyed the land to Hilliard Veren, jr., of Salem, merchant, Sept. 17, 1678.[‖] Mr. Veren, for fifteen pounds, conveyed the lot to his father, Hilliard Veren, sr., of Salem, Nov. 29, 1679.[¶] For twenty-six pounds and five shillings, Mr. Veren

conveyed the land to Robert Hodge of Salem, mariner, May 15, 1680.[*] Mr. Hodge erected a house upon the lot, and, for one hundred and sixty pounds, he conveyed the house and land to William Browne, esq., of Salem Jan. 3, 1682-3.[†] The estate belonged to Mr. Browne in 1710, and the house was standing some years thereafter.

Walter Price House. This lot belonged to Peter Palfrey of Salem, planter, very early. He removed to Reading, and conveyed the land to John Porter of Salem, yeoman, Dec. 10, 1653.[‡] Mr. Porter's son, Joseph Porter, married Anna, daughter of Maj. William Hathorne of Salem, Jan. 27, 1664-5. Twenty-five days previously the parents conveyed the marriage portions of their children to them. Mr. Porter conveyed this lot to his son.[§] Joseph Porter lived in Salem, and conveyed the land to Hilliard Veren, jr., of Salem Sept. 17, 1678.[‖] Mr. Veren built a house upon the lot, and died possessed of the estate in 1680. The house then had in it a parlor, hall, shop, leanto and garret chambers. The estate was then valued at two hundred and forty pounds. In his will, he devised the estate to his wife Hannah.[¶] They were apparently childless. She died in the autumn of 1683, having devised the estate to her brother John Price of Salem. Captain Price died in 1691, and the estate was then appraised at two hundred and fifty pounds. It descended to his only child, Walter Price of Salem, esquire and merchant. He died in March, 1731, possessed of the estate. For one hundred and fifty pounds, Mr. Price's widow and executrix conveyed the house in which she then lived, and the lot of land

*Essex Registry of Deeds, book 6, leaf 62.
†Essex Registry of Deeds, book 21, leaf 129.
‡Essex Registry of Deeds, book 1, leaf 21.
§Essex Registry of Deeds, book 3, leaf 139.
‖Essex Registry of Deeds, book 5, leaf 8.
¶Essex Registry of Deeds, book 5, leaf 55.

*Essex Registry of Deeds, book 6, leaf 104.
†Essex Registry of Deeds, book 6, leaf 74.
‡Essex Registry of Deeds, book 1, leaf 21.
§Essex Registry of Deeds, book 3, leaf 139.
‖Essex Registry of Deeds, book 5, leaf 8.
* As there was some question about the legality of the will, his father, his heir, released the house and lot to his daughter-in-law, Hannah Veren, July 23, 1680. Essex Registry of Deeds, book 6, leaf 108.

to Dr. Joseph Bartlett of Salem April 30, 1748.* Doctor Bartlett died in the autumn of 1751, possessed of the house and lot. In his will, he devised two undivided thirds of his real estate to his son Walter and the other third to his wife Sarah. The house, barn and land were then appraised at two hundred pounds. The son, Walter Price Bartlett of Salem, auctioneer, came into the possession of the entire estate at the death of his mother, and he removed the old house between 1793 and 1801.

William Browne House.† This land, with a house thereon, belonged to John Horne of Salem 13 : 7 : 1655, when, for twenty-four pounds, he conveyed the same to Richard Moore of Salem.‡ The house was gone Sept. 27, 1671, when Richard Moore, sr., of Salem, mariner, for thirty pounds, conveyed the lot to William Browne, jr., of Salem, with a right of way from the grantor's house to the street.§ Captain Browne erected a house upon the lot. He became an esquire and merchant, and, for one hundred and ninety-five pounds, conveyed the house, orchard and land, reserving the barn or stable at the southern end of the lot, to James Putnam of Salem Village June 16, 1710.‖ Mr. Putnam was a bricklayer, and by deed conveyed the northern half of the messuage to his son Bartholmew Putnam of Salem, mariner, May 17, 1716.¶ The house was gone about that time.

WILL OF ABRAHAM MORRILL.

The will of Abraham Morrill of Salisbury was proved in the court held at Hampton Oct. 14, 1662. The following is a copy of the original instrument on file in the probate office at Salem, Mass.

I being weake in body, yet hauing the perfect ufe of my memory doe make this as my laft will & teftament ;

*Essex Registry of Deeds, book 9, leaf 5.
†This is the Browne estate on Essex street.
‖Essex Registry of Deeds, book 2, leaf 82.
§Essex Registry of Deeds, book 3, leaf 128.
'Essex Registry of Deeds, book 22, leaf 269.
*Essex Registry of Deeds, book 63, leaf 148.

Im: my will is that whatt euer debts I owe to any man be firft payd out of my eftate, And the reffidue of my eftate I doe difpofe of as followeth,

I giue unto my Deare & louing wife the one halfe of my whole eftate whether in Houfing lands cattle debts due to me from any or moueables or what euer els is mine ; & this to be hers to difpofe of as fhe fhall fee caufe either in her life *time or** at her death,

2ly I giue to my eldeft fonne Ifaack Morrill a double portion *of** the othar halfe of my eftate to be payd to him at the *age* of one & twenty yeares or day of marriage ;

3ly The reft of the fayd halfe of my eftate I giue unto my *other** five children Abraham Jacob sarah Mofes & Lidda Morrill to be equally deuided betweene them, & to be enioyed by them as they come to the age of one & twenty yeares ; or at the day of marriage ;

4ly My will is if any of my forefayd fix children die before the come of age to inioy there portion that then there portion be deuided betweene the feruiuing children equally.

5ly My will is my whole eftate be kept, & improued together & noe deuiffion made untill my eldeft fonne Ifaack come to age to reciue his portion ; & afterwards as much as may be with any conueniency ;

6ly My will is that my deare & louing wife & my eldeft fonne Ifaack Morrill fhall be the executors of this my will

7ly My requeft is that my louing friend Mr Thomas Bradburry & my louing brother Job Clement be the ouerfeers of this my laft will & teftament.

June the 18th
62

        Abraham Œ & Morrill
        his   marke

witneffe John ftebines
          Tobias Daues
          Rhoda Remington
          Mary wife

*Worn off; words supplied from the record.

IPSWICH COURT RECORDS AND FILES.

Continued from volume X, page 179.

Court, March 27, 1655.

Judges: Mr. Symon Brodstreet, Mr. Samuell Symonds, Maj. Daniell Denison and Mr. Will: Hubard.

Trial jury: Mr. Jo: Apleton, Tho: Borman, Tho: Bishop, Robort Day, Joseph Reding, Hugh Smith, Sam: Brocklbanck, Ezek Northen, Ben: Swett, John Bishop, Robt Coker and Will: Evans.

Richard Coye v. Mr William Hubbard, sr. Review. [Copy of verdict, which was upon the bargain made with Mr. Whittingham, ten years' service, 27 : 1 : 1655.

Haniell Bosworth testified that while we were in London and all the way we came to New England I never heard any other time mentioned that Richard Coy came over with Mr. Whittingham but ten years. Sworn in Ipswich court 27 : 1 : 1655.

John Anable testified that he heard Mr. Whittingham say that Richard Coy was to be with him ten years, and that he heard his (Richard's) sister Mary Coy say that her brother Richard Coy was to serve Mr. Whittingham ten years, and it was so spoken of generally amongst us that were servants.

Robert Smith testified that it was so reported all the way we came to New England. Sworn in Ipswich court 27 : 1 : 1655.

Samuel Kent and Benjamin Muzy deposed that Richard Coy served Mr. Hubberd after seven years one and one-half years. Sworn in court March 28, 1655.

Samuel Kent deposed that a month before the trial Richard Coy and Mr. Hubberd were talking together about Richard's time. Mr. Hubberd said he was going to Boston and would talk with Richard's sister there. Richard was sent away meanly clad, his best suit being a slight stuff, and the breeches having no lining in them, and one old suit more. Sworn in Ipswich court 27 : 1 : 1655.

Benjamin Mussy, aged about twenty years, testified that he was living at Mr. Hubard's when Richard Coy and Mr. Hubard talked about Richard's time. Sworn 27 : 1 : 1655.

Mr. Whittingham brought over Richard Coy and his brother Mathew Coy in 1638 with divers other servants who first came from Boston in Lincolnshire to London where Mr. Whittingham kept them upon his own charges from May 1st till June 24th, so that his bringing up to London and charges of his staying there could not be less than forty shillings, his passage to New England five pounds, for a boy of thirteen years of age. His brother is two years older, served eight years to Mr. Haugh.

Mathew Coy, aged thirty-three years or thereabouts, deposed that at their coming to New England, his mother sent Richard Coy with his sister Mary to Mr. Whittingham, then at Boston, in England, and told them she was willing that her son Richard Coy should serve but seven years with Mr. Whittingham or else Richard should return home. Sworn March 20, 1655, before Ri: Bellingham, governor.

—Files.]

An Mighill, executrix to her late husband Thomas Mighill, v. Mr. ffrances Norton. Trespass. Mr. Jewett undertakes to answer it.

ffrances Johnson and partners v. Mr. Richard ffoxwell. Debt.

Capt. Robert Bridges, attorney to Mrs. Mary Washbourn, widow, administratrix to the estate left by Mr. William Woodcoke, v. Mr. Edward Ting, Elder William Colbourne, Elder James Penn and Mr. Thomas Joanes, overseers to the will of Capt. William Ting. Debt. Jury does not consider things mentioned in Mr. Ting's books concerning provisions left in the ship Expedition. Appeal to court of assistants, Mr. Edward Ting and Mr. Edward Rawson, sureties. The original petition preferred to the general court by Capt. Bridges.

[Writ : Capt. Robert Bridges, attorney of Mrs. Mary Washbourne, widow, administratrix to the estate left by Mr. William Woodcock, sometime of London, deceased, v. Mr. Edward Tinge, Elder Willm Colbourne, Elder James Penn and Mr. Thomas Jones, overseers to ye will of Capt. Willm Tinge, deceased, as they are guardians to act in place of the executrix; dated at Boston 10: 1mo: 1655; signed by the court, Jonath: Negus. Served by Ri: Wayte, marshall, by attachment of the dwelling house, land, warehouse and orchard, now the house of Mr. Edward Tinge that he now dwells in of Boston.

Mrs. Mary Bridges testified that she talked with Mr. William Tinge, deceased, about the debt he owed to the estate of her deceased father. She said : My grandmother, Mrs. Mary Washbourne wrote to me to speak to him. He asked me how many children she had living. I said, six : that he would pay the money to my uncle Herriott Washbourne, he being my grandmother's eldest son. Signed. Sworn to 26 : 1 : 1655, before Rob. Bridges.

Declaration of Robert Bridges, attorney for the plaintiff : That in or about 1638, said Wilbur Woodcooke made an adventure in partnership with Capt. Willm Tinge in ye ship Expedition to ye Barbados ; I hired £400 of my mother-in-law, Mrs. Mary Washbourne, now about seventy years of age, she having a maternal affection toward his parentless children (to whom she is a grandmother) ; that Captain Tinge with his family removed from ould England hither ; and after being here several years (having buried his wife) he took a voyage for England in one of those ships that were cast away upon ye Spanish coast (Captain Hawkins' being one), but ye Lord sparing Captain Tinge from ye eminent danger; he arrived in England, after some time he returned hither again. He has written to my sister and my wife. Elders of the church in Boston, Mr. Jones of Dorchester.

The following is a copy of a letter which is on file as evidence : —

"Loueinge ffriend,

"I doe vnderftand by my fonne Bridges, yᵗ yᵉ Lord hath beene pleafed, to take away my deare freind yoʳ Broth', Capta. Tinge, there was fome acco. betweene him & my fonne Woodcocke, wᶜʰ if yᵉ Lord had fpared him Life, I make noe queftion, but hee would have cleered, And nowe feeinge it is foe, yᵗ hee hath lefte foe faithfull a freind, as yoʳ felfe, oufeer of his eftate, for to fee his Juft debts fattisfied. I make noe doubt, but yoʷ will take fuch order, whereby I may receeve yᵗ wᶜʰ is due to my fonne Woodcock, from yoʳ bro. Capta. Tinge, I beeinge adminiftratrix, for yᵉ good of his Children, there is many of them, to bee fet forth into yᵉ world, one yᵗ is newely a freeman, & anothʳ wᶜʰ is a foldier in Ireland, & a Daughter wᶜʰ is married in Ireland, befids & they haue bin at cheirge bringinge vpp & puttinge to prentice, wᶜʰ hath coft mee more, then I haue receed for them, therefore I fhould defire yoʷ to pay vnto my fonne Bridges, yᵗ money, wᶜʰ is behind, wᵗʰ yᵉ pfitts beelonginge to yᵉ eftate of my fonne Woodcock, I haue giuen him power by Lre of Atturney for to receeve yᵉ fame, & to giue a Releafe, & an acquittance, I haue alfoe fent yoʷ a certificate vnder yᵉ hands of two Notary publque, whoe I caufed purpofedly to Serch yᵉ regifter of the progatiue office, whoe hath certified vnder theire hands, yᵉ truth of yᵉ Admiftracon, I haue receed of yoʳ bro. in his life time 50ˡˡ by bill of Exeᶜ & 20ˡˡ yᵉ Capta pd mee himfelfe when hee was in London, & 20ˡˡ my fonne Bridges Receed of him by my oueer, wᶜʰ comes to in all, 90ˡˡ wᶜʰ is all I receed of him, It is agreate while fince it fhould haue bin pd, therfore, I defire yoʷ to pay it forthwᵗʰ to my fonne Bridges, & to pay him Confideracon for yᵉ forbearance of yᵗ fame as is meete, Then wᵗʰ my Louinge Comendac⁵ to yoʳ felfe, & to yoʳ Bro. Tings Children, wᵗʰ my prayers to Allmighty god for them, I reft,

"Yoʳ Loueinge ffriend vnknowne,
    "mary Wafhbourne.
"Northall ffebr yᵉ 18ᵗʰ 1653.

"ffor m{r} Edw : Tinge thefe p{r}fent att his howfe in Newe England

" This is a true Coppy of y{e} Originall examined

"By Wm. Davis 5 : 5 : 1654."

Account in above case. The general court ordered that the administrator be summoned into court, etc.

—Files.]

Thomas Rolinson v. Mr. John Appleton. Trespass. Withdrawn.

Robert Starkeweather v. Thomas Kemball.

John Gifford v. Capt. Robert Keaine. False imprisonment; keeping him in prison after execution was satisfied. Withdrawn.

Mr. John Appleton v. Mr. Henry Dunster. Withdrawn.

Daniell Salmon, assignee and attorney of Joseph Bouey, v. Mr. John Beaks and company and Mr. John Gifford, agent. Nonsuit.

ffrances Ingalls v. Mr. Jo: Beaks and company and Mr. Jo: Gifford, agent, etc. Debt. Nonsuited.

Daniel King " the like."

Jo : ffrances " the like."

Mr. Jo: Gifford, agent to Mr. Jo: Becks and copy, etc. Account, about the works.

[Plea against the illegality of Mr. Gefford's attachments in suing me, at Ipswich court Sept. 25, 1655.

At general court at Boston May 23, 1655, in said case, plaintiffs nonsuited.

—Files.]

Edward Woland v. Capt. Jo: Manings. " Wheras there was a pfell of land Sould by Tho : Hale by vertue of a letter of Attorney from Jofeph Carter y{e} court orders y{e} letter of Attornye to be recorded."

Richard Browne's bond to pay his wife's son John Bager £34 at eighteen years of age, besides the half of the land left by the latter's father, March 27, 1655.

William Marchent released from ordinary training.

Richard Wattells freed from trainings during his lameness.

John Warner freed from ordinary trainings, paying four shillings a year to the use of the company.

—— —— of Rowley freed from ordinary trainings, paying three shillings a year to the use of the company.

Arthur Sanden presented by Marblehead to keep an ordinary there, license granted.

Mr. Nathaniell Rogers acknowledged satisfaction of Mr. Samuell Winslow for a judgment.

" Johnathan Platts indevoring to draw awaye the afections of m{r} Rogers his mayd is Judged to haue broke the Law and is fined 5{l}."

Abigail Averill, dying intestate, administration on her estate was granted to her son William Averill. Eldest son to have a double portion, and the rest of the children a single portion.

Daniell Poore of Andover and John Scales, Sam : Mighill and Richard Lighton of Rowley made free.

William Goodhue sworn constable for Ipswich.

John Emery, sr., sworn constable for Newbury.

William Tittcum and Harchales Woodman sworn commissioners for Newbury.

John Knight sworn clerk of ye market for Newbury.

William Law sworn clerk of ye market for Rowley.

Anthony Potter and Tho: Rowlinson fined.

Maxemilion Jewett and ffrances Parrett, ye deacons of Rowley, appointed administrators of the estate of Henry Smith ; and to dispose of the children for the present.

Mr. Will: Hubbert and Mr. Rich Dummer sworn " asosiats."

John How fined or to be whipped for several misdemeanors. James How, the father, agrees to pay the fine.

Benjamin Scott fined and admonished for theft.

Mr. Henry Sewall fined for striking Will Asye and " Justleing " Mr. Jewett; execution respitted.

Willm Smith discharged of his presentment.

James White and Jacob Davis, for stealing apples on the Sabbath day, fined or to sit in the stocks.

John Smith of Rowley admonished and bound to good behavior for breach of the peace. Witnesses : Mark Quilter and Mary Browne.

Case of widow Elitrop referred to the general court ; ordered with consent of the overseers that Hugh Smith, John Pickard and John Trumble pay her twenty shillings, etc., the produce of the two younger children's portions.

William Holdred's wife's presentment for unseemly carriages with John Chator, etc., referred to Mr. Symonds and Maj. Daniell Denison. Proved to be lasciviousness, he being sick and she his only nurse, and her own husband present in the house. She is troubled with fits. No censure on her.

[Inventory of estate of widow Alice Ward of Ipswich taken 23 : 11 : 1654. Amount, £37, 14s., 11d.; personal, £21, 14s., 11d.; real, £16. House and one acre of land about it. Appraisers: Robert Lord and John Warner.

Joanah, wife of Thomas Smith, Elizabeth, wife of Jacob Perkins, and Jane, wife of ffrances Jordon, testified that widow Alice Ward, upon her death bed, committed her daughter-in-law Sarah Ward to John Baker and his wife Elizabeth, to bring up the child in the fear of God. Sworn in Ipswich court 27 : 1 : 1655.

Will of Nathaniel Merrill of Newbury proved 27 : 1 : 1655, by John Merrill and Anthony Somerby. This will was printed in full in *The Antiquarian*, volume VI, page 38.

Inventory of estate of Nathaniel Merrill of Newbury who deceased March 16, 1654-5 ; taken March 23, 1654-5, by Daniel Thurston (his D mark), Richard Knight and Archelaus Woodman. Amount, £84, 6s. ; real, £20 ; personal, £64, 6s. No buildings. Owes £5 rent to Mr. Cutting ; and is also indebted £2 to others.
— *Files*.]

Court, 25 : 7 : 1655.
Judges: Mr. Sam : Symonds, Mr. Rich: Dumer and Mr. Hubard.

Grand jury : Lt. Sam : Apleton, William Addam, sr., John Prockter, Isaack Commings, Philip ffowlar, Tho : Browne, Geog : Little, John Hutchings, James Barker, Rich : Swan, Will : Hobson, Will : Ballard and Lt. Will Howord.

Jury for trials : Math : Boyes, Reg : ffoster, Sam : Younglove, Will : Lampson, John Wiate, Aron Pengry, Will Stickney, Will : Boynton, John Palmer, Arch : Woodman, Rich : Browne and Edw : Towne.

Tho : Loe fined for not appearing to serve on the jury.

Mr. John Gifford v. Capt. Robert Kayne and Mr. Josias Winslow. For detaining five cows and two calves and the breed of them almost two years.

Robert Lord, attorney to Mr. Joseph Jewatt, acknowledged judgment to Mr. Rich : Dummer.

Mr. John Gifford v. Capt. Robert Kayne and Mr. Josias Winslow. For false imprisonment. Gun tendered to Mr. Knight.

Willm Wyld v. Robt. Swan. For carpenter work of a house and diet. Withdrawn.

[At the general court at Boston May 3, 1655, in the case between Robert Lord, marshall, and Mr. Webb, upon the question whether the personal estate of Mr. Webb, an owner or undertaker of the Iron works, is liable upon the execution against said owners. Decision : It is not.

At a general court at Boston May 7, 1651, rule about executors in suits at law.
— *Files*.]

Christopher Collings v. John Mansfield. Appeal from Captain Bridges to court of assistants.

[Grounds of Christopher Collins' (autograph) appeal as above, for molesting John Mansfeeld in going through my ground in a way which he said was a common highway laid out by the town.

John Mansfeild's (autograph) answer to the grounds of Christopher Collings' appeal from the court held before worshipful Captain Bridges to this court at Ip-

^swich. Refers to testimony of Richard Chadwell and Joseph Armitage.

Copy of summons to Christopher Collins to appear before ye worshipful Captain Bridges to answer to Jn° Mansfield, for resisting him upon the highway, and molesting him. Dated at Lynn 30 : 5 : 1655 ; by the court, Edw : Burcham. Copy by Rob : Bridges.

Record of above action. Found for plaintiff, and Christopher Collins appealed.

Deposition of Andrew Mansfeild, brother of plaintiff, and of Isaac Ramsdeale who testified similarly. Both sworn by Robt Bridges 4 : 6 mo : 1655. Rich : Chadwell testified that all ye lots from ye house that was his to ye Rocks northward were to be three acres apiece and that there was to be a highway on ye west side of ye little run to ye Rocks from ye country highway. Dated 12 : 11 mo : 1649. Sworn 12 : 12 : 1649, before Robt Bridges. Copy attested by John ffuller.

Copy of a vote of town meeting 28 : 5 : 1644 : Ordered that Nich^a Potter and Edw. Baker shall again stake out ye highway, which heretofore was laid out by Lt. Tomlins, Mr. Howell, Mr. Sadler and Nich^a Potter two rods broad, beginning at Corporal Baker's and so running by Mr. Souther and James Bowtall's house up to ye Rocks. Copied by John ffuller, clerk.

Joseph Armitage testified that several years since he sued John Mansfeild concerning a highway from ye Rocks to ye country highway on ye west side of a little run by Goodman Gillo Dow, and that ye highway was to be two rods wide on that side ye river, and made use of it, and now ye way lieth through John Mansfield's lot, near Collins which the latter bought of Jno Gillo, and so went right through John Gillo's pasture to ye fresh marsh. Sworn 30 : 5 : 1665, before Rob : Bridges. Copy.
—*Files.*]

Joseph Armitage v. Mr. Thomas Purchase. Horses and mares plaintiff bought of defendant. Withdrawn.

Rich : Jacob v. John Burnam. For detaining 3000 pipe staves.

Mr. William Payne v. Mr. Jonathan Wade. For money laid out in England for him.

Mr. Willm Payne v. Samuell Bennett. Bond.

Mr. Rich : Dummer v. John Mighill. For a horse bought of him. Withdrawn.

William Curtice v. John Shaw. Slander. For saying he was a thief and base rogue. Withdrawn.

ffrancis Smith, being attached by John Hathorne, action not entered. Costs allowed.

Will and inventory of the estate of Humphry Brodstreet proved.

Thomas Moore and Hockaliah Bridges, one for running away from his master and the other from his father, fined.

Charles Hushlantan to be whipt twelve stripes for fornication.

Bridgett Brodstreet bound to discharge legacies given in her husband's will. She signed with a mark.

Court being informed that there is no ferry over the Merrimack river at Haverhill, Robert Haseltine is ordered to keep a ferry there. Fees : Strangers, four pence cash, six pence on book ; town's people, two pence cash, four pence on book. He is to keep entertainment for horse and man for one year unless the general court otherwise orders.

John Remington and Elizabeth Osgood of Andover fined twenty shillings each for frequenting each other's company, and bound to good behavior and he not to frequent her company unseasonably.

Jafery Sknelling, on his presentment, to pay fine or be whipped.

Joseph Armitage imprisoned for divers affronts to the court. Released upon his petition and bound for good behavior.

Difference about the line between Newbury and Rowley to be presented to the general court, unless they agree between themselves.

Town of Rowley, presented for defect in highway, being now amended, discharged of the presentment.

Robert Amis to sit half an hour in the stock for fore-swearing himself.

William Knowlton died intestate ; and administration on his estate was granted to his brother Thomas Knowlton, to whom is committed ye care of ye widow and children.

Ten actions presented from Salem court to be tried here. Returned to Salem court.

Mordicha Larkcum complained of by his master, Mr. Rich : Jacob, for neglecting his service. To pay his master twenty-five shillings.

Mathew Stanlye discharged of his presentment.

Ipswich presented for defect in highway. No witness. Discharged.

Andrew Creeke presented. Bound to good behavior, and not to frequent the house of Will Symons nor the company of his daughter.

Isaack Davis fined three pounds or be whipped, for running away from his master. He was absent from his master thirty-two or forty-two days in the summer time. His father undertook to pay the fine.

Thomas Bishopp sworn clerk of the troop of horse.

[Vital records of Rowley for 1655, certified by John Trumble of Rowley:—

Samuell Balie, son of James and Lidiah, born 10 : 6 mo.

Andrew Hidin, son of Andrew and Sarah, born 7 mo.

Rebecka Law, daughter of William and Mary, born 1 : 4 mo.

Thomas Dickanson, son of Thomas and Jenet, born 26 : 8 mo.

John Tod, son of John and Susannah, born 12 mo.

Samuell Brown, son of Charls and Mary, born 5 : 11 mo.

John Jonson married Hannah Crosbie Dec. 6.

Jonathan Plats married Elisabeth Johnson Dec. 6.

Sarah, wife of Nickolas Jackson, buried Aug. 12.

Samuel, son of Benjamin and Margaret Scot, buried March 10.

Andrew, son of Andrew and Sarah Hidin, buried 11 mo.

Sarah Pearson, daughter of John and Dorcas, buried 10 : 8 mo.

John Tod, son of John and Susanna, buried " the twelft month finis."

Mary Wood, daughter of Thomas and Ann, born 15 : 1 mo.

Sarah Pearson, daughter of John and Dorcas, born 3 : 3 mo.

Mary Burbanke, daughter of John and Jemimah, born 15 : 3 mo.

John Hassen, son of Edward and Hannah, born 22 : 10 mo.

ffrancis Brokelbanke, son of Samuell and Hannah, born 26 : 7 mo.

Humphrey Hobson, son of William and Ann, born 2 : 4 mo.

Samuel Scot, son of Benjamin and Margaret, born March 7.

Hannah Burkbie, daughter of Thomas and Martha, born 1 mo.

Hannah Harriman, daughter of Lenart and Margaret, born 22 : 3 mo.

Vital records of Newbury from March 25, 1654, to March 25, 1655, certified by Anthony Somerby, clerk :—

Mary, daughter of Benjamin Swet, born May 2, 1654.

Benjamin, son of Richard Dole, born June 14, 1654.

Thomas, son of Thomas Smith, born July 7, 1654.

Edmund, son of Richard Browne, born July 17, 1654.

Isaac, son of John Baily, born July 22, 1654.

Thomas, son of Aquilla Chase, born July 21, 1654.

Joseph, son of Joseph Plumer, born Sept. 11, 1654.

Elizabeth, daughter of Capt. Will Gerrish, born Sept. 20, 1654.

Nathaniell, son of Richard Pettingall, born Sept 21, 1654.

Mary, daughter of Edward Woodman, born Oct. 10, 1654.

John, son of Lancelot Granger, born Jan. 15, 1654.

Elizabeth, daughter of Will Titcomb, born Dec. 12, 1654.

Mary, daughter of Roger Wheeler, born Feb. 12, 1654.

William Richardson married Elizabeth Wisman Aug. 23, 1654.

Nicholas Wallington married Sara Travers Aug. 30, 1654.

Richard Fitts married Sara Ordway Oct. 8, 1654.

Robert Morse married Anne Lewis Oct. 30, 1654.

Daniell Peirce married Anne Milward Dec. 26, 1654.

William Bolton married Jane Bartlet Jan. 16, 1654.

Francis Tharly married An Morse Feb. 5, 1654.

Mary, wife of Thomas Browne, died June 2, 1654.

Richard Kent, sr., died June 15, 1654.

Will Mitchill died July 16, 1654.

Sara, wife of Daniell Peirce, died July 17, 1654.

Daniell Greenleafe died Dec. 5, 1654.

Hannah, wife of Samuell Moore, died Dec. 8, 1654.

Dorcas, wife of John Tillotson, died Jan. 2, 1654.

Inventory of the estate of Henry Fay of Newbury, weaver, who deceased June 30, 1655, taken by Thomas Hale, Thomas Browne and Abraham Toppan. Amount, about £58; personal, about £20; real, £38, 15s. House, barn and land. Owed to Mr. Woodman, Steven Greenleafe, Robert Coker, Thomas Smith; Will: Bolton, Will Richardson, Goodman Hutchins, Robert Long, John Bishop, John Bartlett, Antho: Somerby, Steven Swett, Daniell Peirce, John Bishop, Mr. Dumer, Peter Godfry, Nicholas Noyes, Mr. Jewet, Steven Kent, John Davis, Rich'd Fits and James Ordway.

Robert Long testifies that Henry Fay said, two days before he died, when he thought he was going to die, that he would leave the estate in his hands, etc. Sworn in Ipswich court 25 : 7 : 1655.

Thomas Noyes of Sudbury, yeoman, appoints, under seal, his friends, Mr. Nicholas Noyes of Newbury, gent., and Robert Long of Newbury, wearer, his attorneys to let his house and lands in Newbury, sometime the house and land of

Henry Fay etc. Dated Sept. 20, 1656. Witnesses: Rich: Lowle and Joseph Mors.

"Witnesse by theise p'sents that Henry fay of Newbary in the County of Essex weaver did in his life time, giue and bequeath vnto his brothers children his whole estate his debts being discharged, and that he did desire his freinds Robert Long and James Jackman that they would looke to it for said he I will leaue it in your hands vntill they come, this he said oftentimes

"witnes

" Richard fitts
Robert Long
James Jackman
Joane Jackman

" The Court Inclynes to ap'hend by the testimonys this to be the will of Henry fay yet suspend the full determination of it till Ipswich court next but leave the estate in there hands & give them power in the meane tyme to pay inst debts & to receiue what is due to the estate

" p me   Robert Lord cleric

"The Deposition of Richard fits of Newbery the said Deponent Testifieth that Henery fay Said to him that if hee Died a Singll man then his brothers Children shal haue his estatt   this he said often

"the mark R of Richard fits

"Taken vpon oth befor me william Titcom commissioner for newbery September 24 1655."

—Files.]

To be continued.

NOTES.

S A L E M, July 11.

The Reverend NATHANIEL WHITTAKER, D. D. late Pastor of a Church at Chelsea, in Connecticut, came to Town last Saturday, with his Family, he having accepted an Invitation of settling in the Ministry over the Church and Congregation, of which the late Reverend Mr. HUNTINGTON was Pastor.

John Prince advertised for sale best Isle of May salt.

—Salem Gazette, July 4-11, 1769.

Mary Bost married John Fern Sept. 1, 1747, in Lynn.

Lydia, daughter of Gideon Boston, born Dec. 27, 1689, in Lynn.

—Court records.

Hannaniah Bosworth of Ipswich, deceased, 1727.*—Registry of deeds.*

Children of widow Prudence Boston: Prudence and Sarah, baptized April 30, 1727.

William Boston married Betty Harris, negroes, Oct. 29, 1778.

Widow Boston died May 10, 1745.

Hannah Bosworth published to John Fitts Aug. 20, 1726.

John, son of John and Hannah Bosworth, baptized May 23, 1736.

—Ipswich town records.

WILL OF GEORGE FARR.

The will of George Farr of Lynn was proved in the court at Salem 26 : 9 : 1662. The following is a copy of the original instrument on file in the office of the clerk of courts at Salem, volume VIII, leaf 92.

The will of goodman far

my will is that my fonne John fhould haue the lot of ground that lieth between the ground of Captan martialls and the ground of goodman winters allfo I giue tow acers of falt march which is in Roumly march to my fonne John to him and his ares for euer

Alfo it is my will that my fons lazerous and Bengamin fhould haue my hous and all the land About it and the lot that lyeth near the land of Captan ||martiall|| and john lueces to them and to thare ares for euer and if onny of them die before he be at age then thare porfhon fhall goe to my fones that doth life ether iohn lazerous or Bengamin

Alfo it is my will that my wife fhall haue hare thirds of all my eftat fo long as fhe doth reman a widdow but in Cas fhee fhould marry then hare thirdes fhould ceafe and thee fhall haue that which fhee and hare fones fhall Agree for

and after har defeafe hare thirdes fhall goe to my three fones namely iohn lazerous and Bengemin

Alfo it is my will that my fone iofeph fhall haue fifty fhillings when he Comes to age

Alfo it is my will that my fones dauter[s] namly mary marthr : Elifebeth and farah fhall haue fitti fhilins apefe and mary and martha fhould haue it paed to them tow yeare after my defeafe and that Elizebeth and farah fhall haue thares paed to them fouer yeare after my defeaf

Alfo it ||is|| my will that ||my|| mare and Cattel and my houfould goods fhall be for the cufe of my famely

It is my will m^r laton and ffrancis Burrill and allin Brad iuner fhall be the ouerfeers of my wif and Children

Henery Sillfbey   his
ffrancis Burrill   George G far
                                mark

dated the firft of July 1662

THE OLD OX-TEAM.

BY AUGUSTUS WIGHT BOMBERGER.

Full fifty years have passed, and yet
Amid the city's noise and fret,
With wistful feelings of regret
    I do remember still
The quiet farm I used to love,
Its sunlit fields so sweet to rove,
And, best of all, the days I drove
    Its old ox-team to mill.

Ah, those were happy days, I ween:
And fresh and beautiful and green,
And all the long, long space between
    Seems nothing now and fades away,
And, lo, a barefoot boy and gay,
And lord of all my eyes survey,
    I mount that lumbering cart !

Yes, slow and sleepily we went,
And yet, how careless and content !
Oh, would those hours were still unspent,
    And this loud, restless mart,
Which grows so wearisome and sad,
Were dream itself—and I the lad
I used to be, supremely glad,
    Within that old ox-cart !

OLD NORFOLK COUNTY RECORDS.

Continued from volume X, page 113.

Sam^ll Dudley of Exeter, gent, with consent of my now wife Elizabeth, for £148, conveyed to Andrew Wiggins of Swampscott, in Norfolk county, one-half of a saw-mill now standing upon Humphrey Wilson's creek, with 80 acres of pine swamp granted to Mr. Sam^ll Dudley by Exiter in 1650, bounded by Sam^ll Levitt, Humphrey Wilson, Lt. Hall, ye great plain, Abraham and Nath^ll Drake and town common, and 30 acres of upland, bounded by Hampton highway, ye commons of Exiter, Jno ffoulsham, sr., and land of Ric: Morgan now in the occupation of Sam^ll Levitt, June 8, 1661. Wit: Seaborn Cotton and Edw: Smithe. Ack. in court at Hampton 8 : 8 : 1672.

Andrew Wiggins of Swamscott in ye river of Pascataway conveyed to Jno ffoulsham, jr., of Exiter, in ye river aforesaid, one-half of 80 acres of swamp land that was granted to Mr. Sam^ll Dudley Feb. 19, 1650, in Exiter, the whole bounded by Sam^ll Levitt, Humphrey Wilson, Lt. Hall, ye great plain, Abraham and Nath^ll Drake and ye town's common, in 1672. Wit: Jonathan Thing, jr., and Sam^ll Levitt. Ack. in court at Hampton 8 : 8 : 1672.

Andrew Wiggins of Swamscott in ye river of Pascataway conveyed to Sam^ll Levitt of Exiter in said river one-half of the 80 acres described in above deed, June 1, 1672. Wit: John ffolsham and Jonathan Thing, jr. Ack. in court at Hampton 8 : 8 : 1672.

Nath^ll Batchelder of Hampton, for £8, conveyed to Jno Marston of Hampton 3 acres of salt marsh as it was laid out in Hampton "this side ye ffalls river," bounded by Taylers river, marshes of Jno Cliffords, Tho: Sleeper and Tho: Chase, July 3, 1671. Wit: Henry Dow and Jno Moulton. Ack. in court at Hampton Oct. 8, 1672.

Morris Hobbs (his ∞ mark), sr., of Hampton, planter, conveyed to Ralfe Hall of Exiter, planter, 10 acres of land in Hampton, in ye grassi swamp, between land of Christopher Palmer and Nathl Batchelder, on both sides of a brook running into Exiter river, Sept. 9, 1672. Wit: Mary Smith and Edw: Smithe. Ack. in court at Hampton 8 : 8 : 1672.

Henry Roby of Hampton, planter, for 2000 feet of pine boards, conveyed to Lt. Ralph Hall of Exiter 3 acres of marsh in and granted by Exiter lying below ye now dwelling house of grantee, being on the southermost branch of Wheelwright's creek, June 6, 1672. Wit: Edw: Smith and Mary Smith. Ack. in court at Hampton 8 : 8 : 1672.

Moses Cox of Hampton, for £14, conveyed to Jno Marston of Hampton 9 acres of upland and swamp in ye mill field in Hampton, bounded by Wm. ffuller, Morris Hobbs, a common way, Jno Brown and grantee, Oct. 11, 1673. Wit: Henry Dowe and Joseph Moulton. Ack. in court at Hampton 8 : 8 : 1672.

Moses Cox of Hampton, for £8, conveyed to Jno Marston of Hampton 2 acres of salt marsh in Hampton, bounded by grantor, Godfrey Dearborn, creek, Nath^ll Batchelder and grantee, Feb. 16, 1671. Wit: Mary ffifcild and Henry Dowe. Ack. in court at Hampton 8 : 8 : 1672.

Inventory of estate of Timothy Worcester of Salisbury, deceased, taken by John Ilsley and Willi: Buswell. Amount, £90, 17s.: real, £78; personal, £12, 17s. Due to one of Salem, to Mr. Checkly, Wil: Townes, Joseph ffrench, Jno Severans, and Steven Flanders. Attested by oath of Susana Worcester in Hampton court 8 : 8 : 1672.

Inventory of estate of Richard Wells of Salisbury, late deceased, taken Sept. 3, 1672, by Tho: Bradbury and Wm Buswell. Amount, £311, 1s., 2d.; real, £172; personal, £139, 1s., 2d. House, barn, etc. Sworn to by Elizabeth Wells, administratrix of the estate, in Hampton court, 8 : 8 : 1672.

Inventory of estate of Widow Satchwell, deceased May 3, 1672, appraised May 23, 1672, by William White and

Henry Palmer. Amount, £203; real, £171; personal, £32. Debts due from the estate, £40. Sworn to by Hananiell Bosworth and Jn° Griffyn, administrators.

William Holdred (his X mark) (also, Holdridg) of Exiter, sr., and wife Isabell Holdridg (her W mark), for £40, to Zakerie Davis of Nubery, about 40 acres in Haverhill near Holts rocks, "The spring called Coffyns ordinary being y° bounds on y° weft," bounded also by James Davis, ye uppermost corner of Amesbury and Salisbury bounds away to ye water side between Henry Tuxberies land, Merrimack river, and another way, July 11, 1672. Wit: Anthony Somerby, Rebecca Somerby and Augustin Steadman. Ack. by both July 16, 1672, before Samuel Symonds.

John Bayly (his [mark) of Nuberie to Mr. Edward Goodwyn of Salisbury, shipwright, 4 acres of upland in Salisbury " in y¹ divifion of land wch belongs to y¹ place called y° newtowne upon y° weft fide of y° Pawwaus River," bounded by Merrimack river, a little run, a highway and grautor, and "to run feventeen rodd from y° River in breadth," June 11, 1665. Wit: Richard Currier and Wm: Sargent. Ack. Feb. 7, 1670, before Robert Pike, commissioner.

Edward Goodwin promises that if he ever sells the above described lot John Bayly shall have the refusal of it, June 11, 1669.

Edward Goodwin conveys above described lot to his son Richard Goodwin Nov. 15, 1672. Wit: Wm. Wickham and Nicolas Heskins. Ack. at Portsmouth Dec. 16, 1672, before Elias Stileman, commissioner.

Jn° Severn of Salisbury mortgaged to Mr. Jn° Joyliffe his dwelling house, barns, stables, land, etc., in Salisbury; also, 6 acres of meadow at *Rose's* island; also, 8 acres of meadow at ye higledee piglede, adjoining Capt. Thomas Bradbury's; also, 6 acres of meadow adjoining his orchard; also, 15 acres of upland on ye north side of Capt. Bradbury's ferry; also, 5 acres on ye west side of William Bradbury's

comonly called ye swamp, by deed acknowledged Dec. 25, 1672. Certified by Isaac Addington, recorder, to the recorder of Norfolk county.

John Ilsley of Salisbury, for £25, to James Chase of Hampton, planter, my two divisions of upland in Salisbury I bought of Jn° Easman and Abraham flitt, in a place comonly called by ye name of Hall's farm, on its northeasterly side, bounded by Edward ffrench and Mr. Stanian; ye lot bought of Easman containing 16¾ acres, and ye lot bought of flitt contains 9 acres and 13 rods, they being numbered 7 and 8 in the town book, Jan. 28, 1672. Wit: Cutting Noyes and Moses Pike. Ack. by grantor, his wife Sarah releasing dower, Jan. 28, 1672, before Robert Pike, commissioner.

Samuell Winsley, sr., of Salisbury, planter, to my son Samuell Winsley (by the hands of Mr. Josua Scotto at Boston), the household goods that were mine when I married M^s Ann Boad my now wife, and a pcell of diaper napkins, Dec. 22, 1660. Wit: Isaac Cullimore, Margery Cullimore (her M mark) and Robert Howard, not: pub.

Nathanil Smith of Haverhill conveyed to John Decker of Haverhill a parcel of upland and meadow in Haverhill near the bridge over ye Sawmill river, bounded by a little brook yt runs into ye sawmill river, way and said river, Nov. 18, 1672. Signed also by Elizabeth Smith (her O mark). Wit: John Hassalton and Mathew fforriman. Ack. Nov. 25, 1672, before Simon Bradstreet, asst.

Abraham Drake of Hampton, for £3 (£2 to Capt. Pendleton and £1 to Isaac Cosens), conveyed to Phillip Lewis of Greenland 5 acres of salt marsh beyond the falls river, bounded by ye marsh that was Thomas Levet's and Giles ffuller's marsh, 2 : 1 mo : 1659-60. Wit: Martha Car and Giles ffuller. Ack. 8 : 8 : 1662, before Tho : Wiggin.

Giles ffuller of Hampton, for £3, conveyed to Phillip Lewis of Greenland 5 acres of salt marsh beyond ye fals river, bounded by marsh yt was sometimes

Abraham Drake's and marsh sometimes of Anthony Tayler's, 2 : 1 mo : 1659-60. Wit : William Godfrey (his W mark) and Abraham Drake. Ack. 8 : 8 : 1662, before Tho : Wiggin.

John Marian (his mark M) of Hampton, yeoman, for love, conveyed to my daughter Elizabeth, ye wife of Henry Dearborne, and their two eldest male children one dwelling house, barn and house lot of five acres in Hampton, bounded by Tho : Levitt, Phillip Toule, common way, Gillse's swamp ; also, 2 small lots of swamp land (4 or 5 acres more or less) in Wigwam field in Hampton below ye hill against my house lot, bounded by Tho : Levitt, Phillip Towle ; also, one-half of my 12 acres of planting land above Gillse's swamp (to be divided between said Henry and Isaac Godfrey ye husband of my daughter Hannah) ; also, half of my fresh meadow and ye upland belonging to it (10 acres in all), bounded by Ed Colcord, Robert Page, Sam¹¹ Dalton and Will : Swaine ; also, one-half of 11 acres of marsh lying near birch island, bounded by Mr. Christopher Hussey, Tho : Levett ; also, 2 shares of cow's common, Jan. 1, 1671. Wit : Sam¹¹ Dalton, jr., and Hannah Dalton. Ack. 2 : 11 mo : 1671, before Sam¹¹ Dalton, commissioner.

HAMPTON MARRIAGES.

Nath¹¹ Eyer married Tamosin Turlear May 10, 1670.

Jn° Collins married Elizabeth Gutterson Nov. 17, 1670.

Sam¹¹ H[a]seltine married Deborah Cooper Dec. 28, 1670.

Isaac Godfrey married Hannah Marian 15 : 5 : 1670.

Jn° Clifford, jr., married Sarah Godfrey 18 : 6 : 1670.

Benjamin ffifeild married Mary Colcord 28 : 10 : 1670.

Jn° Clifford, sr., married Bridgett Huggins, sr., 6 : 2 mo : 1671.

Jn° Samborn, sr., married Margerite Moulton 2 : 6 mo : 1671.

Jn° Marian, sr., married Margerie Godfrey 14 : 7 : 1671.

Joseph Chase married Rachel Partridge 31 : 10 : 1671.

SALISBURY BIRTHS.

Susanah, daughter of Phillip and Mary Brown, born 8 : ⁷ mo : 1670-1.

Joseph, son of Jedediah and Mary Andross, born March 10, 1669-70.

Sam¹¹, son of Sam¹¹ and Abigail ffrench, born March 24, 1670-1.

Joseph, son of John and Mary Osgood, born April 12, 1671.

Ruth, daughter of Henry and Abigaill Wheelar, born July 15, 1671.

Abraham, son of Isaac and Phebe Morrill, born Aug. 22, 1671.

Ephraim, son of Tho : and Mary Hoyt, born Oct. 16, 1671.

Jerimie, son of Cornelius and Sarah Conner, born Nov. 6, 1671.

William, son of Henry and Jane True, born June —, 1670.

Joseph, son of Mr. John and Sarah Stockman, born 20 : 12 : 1671.

Elizabeth, daughter of Mr. Willi : and Elizabeth Hooke, born 22 : 12 : 1671.

AMESBURY DEATHS.

Tho : son of Tho and Rachell Sargent, died March 18, 1669-70.

William, son of Willia and Elizabeth Brown, died Nov. 11, 1669.

Henry Brown of Salisbury, shoemaker, for love, conveyed to my son Nath¹¹ Brown of Salisbury, husbandman, and his wife Hannah, my division of the 500 acres of land granted by Salisbury to its inhabitants, to wit : 10 acres, bounded by Jn° Stevens, sr., Mr. Tho : Bradbury, and a drift way leading to gunner's point ; also. my first higledee pigledee lot of salt marsh lying between ye lots of Jn° Eaton and Robert Downer, formerly ye lot of Wm. Partridg, March 25, 1672. Wit : Tho : Bradbury and Mary Weed (her m mark). Ack. March 14, 1672-3, before Robert Pike, commissioner.

Joseph Davis of Haverhill, planter, for £40, conveyed to Peter Brackett of Boston 27 acres of upland in Haverhill in ye cow comon adjoining ye fishing river,

bounded by a swamp to ye fishing river, ye fishing river upon ye north to a horne beach tree and ye deep swamp; also, 10 acres of meadow in Haverhill at Hog hill meadow to be laid out of the meadows belonging to me when the grantee shall require the same, July 20, 1667. Wit: Sam¹¹ Jacklen, Tho: White and Nath¹¹ Williams. Ack. 20 : 5 : 1667, before Ric : Bellingham.

Laid out by Henry Palmer and Bartholimew Heath (signed by mark) in the behalf of Mr. Brackett of Boston abovementioned 10 acres of meadow, bounded by Tho. Dow, etc., the line running over a rocky island, Aug. 11, 1667.

AMSBERY BIRTHS.

Jn°, son of Henry and Mary Blasdall, born May 27, 1668.

Mary, daughter of Phillip and Mary Challis, bore Aug. 27, 1668.

Hannah, daughter of John and Marah Pressie, born Sept. (written over "May" ?) 29, 1668.

Mary, daughter of John & Mary Ash, born May 20, 1668.

William, son of Thomas and Hannah ffowler, born June 8, 1668.

Mary, daughter of Sam¹¹ and Mary Bickford, born Nov. 18, 1668.

Edward, son of Edward and Susannah Goodwin, born June 22, 1669.

John, son of William and Sarah Hackett, born April 15, 1669.

John, son of James and Elizabeth ffreeze, born Oct. 1, 1669.

William, son of William and Mary Sargent, born April 19, 1669.

Jn°, son of John and Mary Ash, born Feb. 3, 1669.

John, son of John and Hannah Pressie, born Feb. 15, 1669.

Thomas, son of Thomas and Rachell Sargent, born Feb. 24, 1669.

Abigail, daughter of Jn° and Mary Kimball, born June 12, 1669.

George, son of Ezekiel and Hannah Wathen, born 15 : 10 : 1669.

Sara, daughter of James and Sarah Georg, born Oct. 24, 1669.

William, son of John and Marra Pressie, born June 2, 1671.

AMSBERY MARRIAGES.

Tho: Sargent married Rachel Barnes March 2, 1668.

William Sargent married Mary Colby Sept. 23, 1668.

Tho: Currier married Mary Osgood Dec. 9, 1668.

John Jimson married Hester Martyn March 15, 1669 70.

Sam¹¹ ffelloes (his X mark) of Salisbury, weaver, for love, conveyed to my children Nath¹¹ Brown of Salisbury, husbandman, and his wife my daughter Hanna, my 10-acre lot of upland on which his house stands in Salisbury, bounded by Rodger Easman, a highway, highway leading to ye mill, and Georg Carr, sr.; also, my sweepage lot of salt marsh at ye beach in Salisbury, between the lots of Maj. Robert Pike and Willia Osgood, March 20, 1672. Wit : Tho : Bradbury and Mary Weed (her m mark). Ack. March 14, 1672, before Robert Pike, commissioner.

Susana Goodwin (her S mark), wife of Edward Goodwin of Amesbury, shipwright, as his attorney, for £60, conveyed to Caleb Moody, of Newbury, maltster, all chattels of said Edward, Dec. 25, 1672. Wit : Walter Tayler and mark W of Wm Laman. Ack. March 14, 1672-3, before Robert Pike, commissioner.

EXITER BIRTHS.

Jn°, son of Jr.° Currier, born June 11, 1670.

Elizabeth, daughter of Hen : Magoon, born 29 : 7 : 1670.

Jn°, son of Allex : Gordin, born 26 : 8 : 1670.

Margerite, daughter of Jn° Bene, born 27 : 8 : 1670.

Israel, son of Jonathan Smith, born March —, 1670-1.

James, son of Christian Dolhoff, born 25 : 10 : 1670.

Jn°, son of Jonathan Robinson, born 7 : 7 : 1671.

Thomas, son of Tho : Raulins, born 14 : 5 : 1671.

HAMPTON BIRTHS.

John, son of Nicolas and Sara Norris, born 10 : 5 mo : 1667.

Robert, son of Thomas and Mary Page, born 17 : 5 : 1667.

Abigall, daughter of Edward and Hannah Goue, born 23 : 5 : 1667.

Ebenezer, son of Tho : and Sarah Webster, born 1 : 6 mo : 1667.

Susanah, daughter of Jn° and Rebecka Hussie, born 7 : 7 : 1667.

William, son of Wm. and Rebecka Marston, born 7 : 8 mo : 1667.

Symon, son of John and Jemima Knowles, born 22 : 9 : 1667.

Theodata, daughter of Jn° and Hulda Smith, born 16 : 10 : 1667.

Abigail, daughter of Nath¹¹ and Deborah Batcheller, born 28 : 10 : 1667.

Mary, daughter of Joseph and Mary Dowe, born 15 : 11 : 1667.

Isaac, son of Abraham and Mary Cole, born 15 : 12 : 1667.

James, son of Sam : and Mary ffogg, born 18 : 2 : 1668.

Caleb, son of Sam : and Mehetable Dalton, born 29 : 2 : 1668.

Mary, daughter of Henry and Jane True, born 30 : 3 : 1668.

Peniell, daughter of Edw : and Hannah Goue, born 10 : 5 mo : 1668.

Mehetable, daughter of James and Ane Philbrick, born 19 : 5 : 1668.

Mary, daughter of Jn° and Martha Cass, born 1 : 6 mo : 1668.

Lidia, daughter of Hezron and Martha Levitt, born 5 : 6 mo : 1668.

Mehetable, daughter of Jn° and Mary Godfrey, born 15 : 6 : 1668.

Mary, daughter of Jn° and Hannah Souter, born 25 : 6 : 1668.

Debora, child of Mary Read, born 4 : 7 mo : 1668.

Dorethia, daughter of Jasper and Deborah Blake, born 17 : 7 : 1668.

Luther, daughter of Tho : and Joanna Sleeper, born 14 : 9 : 1668.

William, son of Sam¹¹ and Hannah Tilton, born 11 : 9 mo : 1668.

Jonathan, son of Gershom and Mary Elkins, born 24 : 11 : 1668.

Benjamin, son of John and Mary Samborne, born 20 : 10 : 1668.

Tho : son of Tho : and Sarah Nud, born 15 : 12 : 1668.

Elizabeth, daughter of Nath¹¹ and Grace Boulter, born 27 : 12 : 1668.

Abiah, daughter of Mr. Seaborn and Dorethi Cotton, born 5 : 2 mo : 1669.

Joseph and Benjamin, sons of Phillip and Isabell Towle, born 4 : 3 mo : 1669.

Ann, daughter of Jn° and Rebeckher Hussey, born May 4, 1669.

John, son of John and Lidea Moulton, born 3 : 3 : 1669.

Sarah, daughter of Benjamin and Ester Shaw, born 22 : 4 : 1669.

John, son of John and Hulda Smith, born 21 : 6 : 1669.

Nath¹¹, son of Nath¹¹ and Elizabeth Weare, born 29 : 6 : 1669.

Mary, daughter of Benjamin and Argentine Cram, born 6 : 6 : 1669.

Maria, daughter of Jn°, jr., and Martha Redman, born 12 : 9 mo : 1669.

Sam¹¹, son of Joseph and Elizabeth Merrie, born 16 : 9 : 1669.

Sarah, daughter of Jn° and Sarah Hobbs, born 30 : 10 : 1669.

Jane, daughter of Nath¹¹ and Debora Batcheller, born 8 : 11 mo : 1669.

Sam¹¹, son of Henry and Elizabeth Dearborn, born 27 : 11 : 1669.

Isaac, son of Tho : and Sarah Webster, born 12 : 2 mo : 1670.

Abigail, daughter of Edward and Hannah Goue, born 17 : 2 : 1670.

Meriah, daughter of Mr. Seaborn and Dorethie Cotton, born 22 : 2 : 1670.

John, son of Benjamin and Ester Swett, born 17 : 3 : 1670.

Abiah, daughter of Sam¹¹ and Mehetabel Dalton, born 3 : 4 mo : 1670.

William, son of Tho : and Hannah Philbrick, born 27 : 4 : 1670.

Sam¹¹, son of Tho : and Sarah Nud, born 13 : 7 : 1670.

Jacob, son of John and Mary Stanian, born 11 : 11 : 1670.

Christopher, son of Tho : and Mary Page, born 20 : 7 : 1670.

John, son of Sam[ll] and Hannah Tilton, born 23 : 8 : 1670.

Abigail, daughter of Daniel and Mehetabel Tilton, born 28 : 8 : 1670.

John, son of Hezron and Martha Levitt, born 26 : 9 : 1670.

Moses, son of Gershom and Mary Elkins, born 4 : 10 mo : 1670.

Rebecka, daughter of John and Hannah Souter, born 5 (?) : 10 mo : 1670.

Hannah, daughter of John and Mary Godfre, born 12 : 10 mo : 1670.

James, son of Joseph and Mary Dow, born 17 : 7 : 1670.

Caleb, son of Joseph and Elizabeth Shaw, born 31 : 11 : 1670.

Tho : son of ffrancis and Hannah Jennis, born 23 : 12 : 1670.

Sam[ll], son of ffrancis and Meriba Page, born 3 : 1 mo : 1671.

Hannah, daughter of Sam[ll] and Mary ffogg, born 6 : 2 mo : 1671.

Deborah, daughter of Jn° and Huldah Smith, born 11 : 2 mo : 1671.

Joseph, son of Benjamin and Argentine Cram, born 12 : 1 mo : 1671.

Hannah, daughter of Isaac and Hannah Godfrey, born 24 : 2 : 1671.

Abraham, son of Abraham and Mary Cole, born 12 : 3 mo : 1671.

Philemon, son of Jasper and Deborah Blake, born 23 : 3 : 1671.

Ebenezer, son of Edward and Hannah Goue, born 23 : 3 : 1671.

Lidia, daughter of Jn° and Lidia Moulton, born 13 : 5 : 1671.

Mercy, daughter of Abraham, jr., and Elizabeth Perkins, born 3 : 5 mo : 1671.

Edmond, son of Peter and Ruth Janson, born 8 : 5 mo : 1671.

Ebenezer, son of Jn° and Martha Cass, born 17 : 5 : 1671.

Abigail, daughter of Ben : and Ester Shaw, born 22 : 6 : 1671.

James, son of James and Mary Prescott, born 1 : 7 mo : 1671.

Steven, son of Willi : and Mary Samborn, born 4 : 7 mo : 1671.

Bathshuah, daughter of Jn° and Rebecka Hussey, born 21 : 7 : 1671.

Ju.°, son of Benjamin and Mary ffifcild, born 21 : 9 : 1671.

Isaac, son of Jacob and Mary Pirkins, born 18 : 10 : 1671.

John, son of Jn° and Sarah Clifford, born 7 : 12 mo : 1671.

Jabez, son of Henry and Hannah Dowe, born 8 : 12 mo : 1671.

Robert Ring of Salisbury, planter, conveyed to Wm. Osgood of Salisbury, millwright, about 15 or 20 acres of upland in Salisbury, on ye north side of yt land I now live upon, bounded by a brook near ye mills, and ye head of ye 10-acre lots, Jan. 9, 1672. Wit : Tho : Mudgett and Isaac Morrill. Ack. 21 : 11 : 1672, before Robert Pike, commissioner.

To be continued.

NOTES.

Haniel Bosworth of Ipswich, 1653-1694 ; came from London to New England ; wife Abigail, daughter of Thomas Scott, sr.; Elizabeth Bosworth was his executrix, 1697 ; his widow was Abigail Bosworth in 1694 ; and she was "in old age" in 1698. His daughter Mary was born in Ipswich April 6, 1665 ; died Aug. 9, 1666.—*Records.*

Hannah Botman married Peter Bridge Feb. 18, 1752, in Beverly.

John, son of Richard and Mary Botson, died July 9, 1687, in Gloucester.

James Bott of Salem married Dolly Newhall of Lynn March 15, 1768.

James Bott married Ruth Hathorne, both of Salem, Feb. 11, 1787.

Frances Bott married Abner Goodhue, both of Salem, July 10, 1796.

Hannah Bott married John Ferguson, both of Salem, Sept. 2, 1798.

John Bott married Lydia Henfield, both of Salem, Oct. 21, 1798.

Sally Bott published to Hugh Irwin, both of Salem, May 26, 1798.

—*Salem town records.*

James Bott of Salem, sadler, 1774-1796; wife Dolly, 1781-1785.

James Bott of Salem, chaise-maker, 1781.

James Bott of Salem, gentleman, wife Ruth, 1793.

—*Registry of deeds.*

Elizabeth Bosworth married Nicholas Pearl Oct. 25, 1686, in Ipswich.

Samuel Bosworth of Andover, 1662.

—*Court records.*

ROWLEY IN ENGLAND.

BY OSCAR FAY ADAMS.

Population: 512 (1891). Acreage: 6,428. About seven miles from Hull. Parish church, St. Peter; register from 1565; living, a rectory. Chapels: Chapel-of-ease; Wesleyan chapel. Parish council composed of eleven members. The manor belongs to the Harrison-Broadley family.

According to Cotton Mather's "Magnalia" the Massachusetts Rowley was so named by its first minister, the Reverend Ezekiel Rogers, a native of Wethersfield, in Essex, "who called the town Rowley and continued in it about the same number of years that he had spent in that Rowley whence he came on the other side of the Atlantick ocean."

"That Rowley," whence the Reverend Ezekiel departed in 1638 to his new charge over seas, is a very extensive parish in the East Riding of Yorkshire about one hundred and seventy miles from London. Within its borders are the various hamlets of Bentley, Hunsley, Ribblingham, Risby, Rowley and Little Weighton. The hamlet of Rowley is some five miles north of Brough station on the Hull and Selby division of the North Eastern system, but a much nearer station is that at Little Weighton (locally weé-tn), on the Hull and Barnsley railway. Approaching from the direction of Brough the highway, after passing through the village of Elloughton, presently ascends the chalk wolds whence opens an extended prospect across the Humber into Lincolnshire. A stretch of upland next crossed the road descends one slope only to ascend a second on which is the hamlet of Ribblingham with its four houses, and a mile beyond these is the hamlet of Rowley. A footpath that leaves the main road to cross a wide pasture, that is almost like a wooded park in places, furnishes the most direct access to the object of the journey, and soon brings one before a large rectory in the midst of lawns and gardens, and immediately adjoining these on the west is seen the diminutive church of Saint Peter.

And church and rectory set midmost of the spacious glebe are all there is of Rowley hamlet. By day and in the summer sunshine it is indeed a pleasant spot, this fair green pasture encircled by ancestral trees and with cattle picturesquely distributed, one might almost say posed, about the expanse, but at night and in winter, it can hardly fail of being somewhat lonely.

The church, which will seat only one hundred and fifty persons, consists of a nave of three bays, chancel, low western pinnacled tower and south porch. It is of brick faced with cement and is in great part in the transitional Norman style. The tower, which has but one bell, opens from the nave through a low arch in character scarcely more than a doorway, and from the south side of the chancel a low wide arch, with rosettes in the soffit, affords entrance into the mortuary chapel of the Elleker family that now serves as a robing room.

In the hamlet of Bentley is the small Chapel-of-ease, and in Little Weighton, which contains some thirty houses and is the largest of all the hamlets, is a Wesleyan chapel, but in the whole wide parish no other churches will be discovered.

From Rowley church, a pleasant path extends across the glebe to the high road leading to Little Weighton, half a mile further, and here the train for Hull may be taken. Little Weighton cannot be honestly characterized as an attractive village but as a place of residence it is distinctly preferable to the ugly village of Walkington, three miles to the northeast, with its parish church situated in the midst of an unkempt, neglected churchyard.

There is little in the way of scenery to be noted in Rowley parish but the traveler will find the seven-mile walk to Beverley a pleasant one, and he will be likely to note that in the East Riding, as in Massachusetts, Essex, Beverley and Rowley are in neighborly proximity. Save once in the state of Iowa the name of Rowley finds echo only in New England.

HON. LEONARD WHITE.

Hon. Leonard White of Haverhill, whose portait appears as the frontispiece of this number of *The Antiquarian*, was born in Haverhill May 3, 1767, being son of Hon. John and Sarah (Le Barron) White. The father graduated at Harvard college in 1751; was a merchant, and a member of the provincial congress in 1775.

Leonard White was also educated at Harvard, graduating in 1787. He was the patron of Josiah Quincy while in college. With Mr. White, John Quincy Adams was a student of Rev. John Shaw of Haverhill, and together, in the same class, they pursued their college course. Rev. Peter Eaton, afterward pastor of the Second church in Boxford for about half a century, was also in the same class.

Mr. White lived in Haverhill, and married, first, Mary, daughter of Hon. Tristram Dalton of Newburyport Aug. 21, 1794. Her father was a member of the first senate of the United States, and during the years Mr. Dalton was in Washington, Miss Dalton was on very friendly terms with the president's family, visiting Mrs. Washington for weeks at a time.

Mr. White served on the school committee; was town clerk and treasurer of Haverhill, 1804-1810, 1815, 1818, 1821-1831, 1838 and 1839; and represented the town in the legislature in 1809. From 1811 to 1813 he was a member of congress.

The Merrimack Bank in Haverhill was established soon afterward, and he was chosen its first cashier, holding the office for a quarter of a century, until the in-firmities of age compelled its relinquishment.

Though having all the advantages of good birth, education and the highest society, he was neither brilliant nor ambitious. He was a gentleman of the old school, modest, unassuming, and of a kindly and cheerful disposition. He was eminently faithful, punctual and honest in the discharge of every duty that came to him.

He was a religious man, and a member of the Baptist church, believing most firmly and happily and living in the benign light of gospel truth.

Mrs. White died June 18, 1839, at the age of sixty-eight, after they had lived together for about forty-five years. Three years and three days later, he married secondly, Mrs. Hannah Cummings.

For about two years before his death he had repeated attacks of paralysis, and he died, Oct. 10, 1849, at the age of eighty-two, as quietly and as undisturbed as an infant going to sleep. He was the survivor of his class in college.

Mr. White's children were, Mary Ann, who married David How, jr., a merchant of Haverhill, and afterwards of New York; Leonard D.; Sarah D.; Katherine; George; Frederick, who lived in New York; Robert Hooper, who lived in New York; Katherine; Edward, who lived first in New York city and subsequently at Dalton, Ga.; and John L., who lived in New York. Several of the children died young.

NOTES.

Dorcas Bosworth married Edward Clarke; and died Feb. 13, 1681.

Susanna Bosworth married Theophilus Shatswill before 1650.

Abigail Bosworth of Ipswich married Israel Ela Nov. 11, 1680; and died Dec. 14, 1717.

—Haverhill town records.

Mary, daughter of Samuel and Ruth Bots, born Aug. 12, 1747.—*Wenham town records.*

Will of Daniell Bosworth of Ipswich proved Sept. 25, 1683; mentions wife, and daughters Abigail and Elizabeth. His wife survived him.—*Probate records.*

SOLDIERS AND SAILORS OF THE REVOLUTION.

Continued from volume X, page 185.

JOHN BOND of Cape Ann (also given Gloucester); Capt. Gideon Foster's co., Col. John Mansfield's reg.; receipt for advance pay dated Cambridge, July 4, 1775; *also*, priv., muster roll dated Aug. 1, 1775; enl. June 14, 1775; service, 1 mo., 19 days; *also*, Capt. John Baker's co., Col. Mansfield's reg.; co. return [probably Oct., 1775]; *also*, Capt. Baker's co., Col. Israel Hutchinson's (19th) reg.; order for bounty coat dated Winter Hill, Oct. 27, 1775; *also*, order for bounty coat dated Camp at Winter Hill, Dec. 25, 1775; *also*, Capt. Samuel Page's co., Col. Ebenezer Francis' reg.; pay abstract; 49 days subsistence allowed from date of enlistment, Feb. 5, 1777, to time of arrival at Bennington; *also*, Capt. Page's co., Col. Benjamin Tupper's reg.; Continental Army pay accounts for service from Feb. 20, 1777, to Dec. 31, 1779; residence, Gloucester; credited to town of Gloucester; *also*, Maj. William Lithgow's co., Col. Tupper's (15th) reg.; muster roll for March, 1779, dated West Point; enlistment, 3 years; *also*, Continental Army pay accounts for service from Jan. 1, 1780, to Jan. 23, 1780; reported discharged.

JOSEPH BOND of Gloucester; priv., Capt. John Burnam's co., Col. Michael Jackson's reg.; Continental Army pay accounts for service from Feb. 18, 1777, to Dec. 31, 1779; reported transferred to corps of invalids June, 1779; *also*, Capt. Moses McFarland's co. of invalids, Col. Lewis Nichola's reg., muster rolls made up to Sept. 9, 1779, and Oct. 2, 1779; reported stationed at Boston; *also*, muster roll for Oct., 1779; reported stationed at Boston; *also*, Continental

Army pay accounts for service from Jan. 1, 1780, to Dec. 31, 1780; enlistment, during war; reported stationed at Boston.

ROLLINSON BOND of Gloucester; descriptive list of men enl. from Essex co. in 1779 to serve in the Continental Army; Capt. Warner's co.; age, 55 years; stature, 5 ft., 10 in.; complexion, light; residence, Gloucester; enlistment, 9 mos.; delivered to Col. Collins (also given Lt. Lilley); *also*, return of men mustered by John Cushing, muster-master for Essex co., to join Continental Army for 9 mos., dated Boxford, Dec. 8, 1779.

SAMUEL BOND of Gloucester; priv., Capt. Daniel Warner's (1st) co.; pay rolls for service from date of enlistment, July 19, 1775, to Dec. 31, 1775, 5 mos., 26 days; co. raised in and stationed at Gloucester for defence of sea coast; *also*, Capt. Samuel Page's co., Col. Ebenezer Francis' reg.; pay abstract; 49 days subsistence allowed from date of enlistment, Feb. 5, 1777, to time of arrival at Bennington; March 12, 1777, reported as date of marching; *also*, serg., Capt. Page's co., Col. Benjamin Tupper's reg.; Continental Army pay accounts for service from Feb. 5, 1777, to Dec. 31, 1779; *also*, Maj. William Lithgow's co., Col. Tupper's (15th) reg.; muster roll for March, 1779, dated West Point; enlistment, 3 years; reported on command with Col. Hay; *also*, Continental Army pay accounts for service from Jan. 1, 1780, to Feb. 5, 1780.

SAMUEL BOND of Ipswich; priv., Capt. Richard Dodge's co., Col. Loammi Baldwin's (26th) reg.; pay abstracts for Jan.-June, 1776; *also*, list of men who agreed to serve for 6 weeks from Dec. 31, 1776, dated Trenton; *also*, order for wages, etc., for 1776, dated Uppermerry, Dec. 26, 1777; *also*, return of men enl. into Continental Army from 3d Essex co. reg., dated Ipswich, Feb. 17, 1778; residence, Ipswich; enl. for Ipswich; joined Capt. Child's co., Col. Wesson's reg.; enlistment, 3 years; reported mustered to serve in Capt. Pettingill's co., Col. Wesson's reg., by Nathaniel Barber, muster-

master; *also*, Capt. Samuel Carr's co., Col. James Wesson's reg.; Continental Army pay accounts for service from Jan. 1, 1777, to Dec. 31, 1779; also, Lt.-col.'s co., Col. Wesson's (9th) reg.; Continental Army pay accounts for service from Jan. 1, 1780, to Dec. 31, 1780; *also*, descriptive list of enl. men dated Hutts, West Point, Jan. 28, 1781; age, 29 years; stature, 5 ft., 3 in.; complexion, light; hair, light; occupation, mariner; residence, Ipswich; enl. Jan. 2, 1777, by Capt. Carr; joined Capt. Edes' co., Col. Henry Jackson's reg.; enlistment, during war.

THOMAS BOND of Danvers; priv., Capt. Samuel Epes' co., Col. Pickering's reg., which marched on the alarm of April 19, 1775; service, 2 days; *also*, Capt. Gideon Foster's co., Col. John Mansfield's reg.; receipt for wages dated Cambridge, June 26, 1775; *also*, receipt for advance pay dated Cambridge, July 4, 1775; *also*, muster roll dated April 1, 1775; enl. May 8, 1775; service, 3 mos.; *also*, Capt. John Baker's co., Col. Mansfield's reg.; co. return [probably Oct., 1775]; *also*, Capt. Baker's co., Col. Israel Hutchinson's (19th) reg.; order for bounty coat dated Camp at Winter Hill, Oct. 27, 1775, and Dec. 25, 1775; *also*, return of men enl. into Continental Army from Capt. Caleb Low's (2d) co., dated Feb. 14, 1778; residence, Danvers; enl. for Danvers; enlistment, 3 years.

EDMOND BOODON of Marblehead; Capt. Francis Symonds' co., Col. John Glover's reg.; order for bounty coat dated Camp at Cambridge, Dec. 25, 1775.

JONATHAN BOOLES of Beverly; lad, brigantine "Saratoga" (privateer), com. by Capt. Ebenezer Giles; list of crew certified to by the owners, John and Andrew Cabot; endorsed "1780."

BENJAMIN BOOTMAN of Beverly; priv., Capt. John Low's co., Col. Hutchinson's reg.; muster roll dated Aug. 1, 1775; enl. May 12, 1775; service, 2 mos., 25 days.

DANIEL BOOTMAN of Danvers; priv., Capt. Jeremiah Page's co., which marched on the alarm of April 19, 1775; service, 2 days.

DAVID BOOTMAN of Danvers; priv., Capt. Jeremiah Page's co., which marched on the alarm of April 19, 1775; service, 2 days.

ISRAEL BOOTMAN of Salem; priv., Capt. Nathan Brown's co., Col. Mansfield's reg.; muster roll dated Aug. 1, 1775; enl. May 25, 1775; service, 9 weeks, 5 days; *also*, co. return dated Oct. 6, 1775; *also*, Capt. Brown's co., Col. Israel Hutchinson's (19th) reg.; order for bounty coat dated Camp at Winter Hill, Oct. 27, 1775.

JOHN BOOTMAN. Return of men mustered by John Cushing, muster master for Essex co., to join the Continental Army for 9 mos., dated Boxford, Dec. 8, 1779; enlisted for Newburyport.

JONATHAN BOOTMAN. List of men mustered in Essex co. by Michael Farley, muster mariner, dated Sept. 16, 1775; Lt. Joseph Lane's co.; raised for defence of sea coast in Essex co.; stationed at Gloucester; *also*, corp., Capt. Joseph Whipple's co.; enl. July 19, 1775; roll made up to Dec. 31, 1775; service, 5 mos., 25 days; co. raised for defence of sea coast in Essex co.; stationed at Manchester and Gloucester.

AARON BORDMAN of Lynn; priv., Capt. David Parker's (1st Lynn) co. of minutemen, which marched to Concord; service, 2 days. Roll sworn to Dec. 20, 1775.

ABEL BORDMAN of Ipswich; priv., Capt. Daniel Low's co. of volunteers, 3d Essex co. reg.; engaged Sept. 30, 1777; marched Oct. 2, 1777; dis. Nov. 7, 1777, at Cambridge; service, 1 mo., 10 days, at the Northward and guarding Gen. Burgoyne's troops to Prospect hill, under command of Maj. Charles Smith; *also*, Capt. Simeon Brown's co., Col. Nathaniel Wade's reg.; enl. July 20, 1778; dis. at East Greenwich, R. I.; service, 5 mos., 17 days; co. raised in Essex and York counties; enlistment to expire Jan. 1, 1779; *also*, Capt. Benjamin Gould's co., Col. Wade's (Essex co.) reg.; enl. July

6, 1780; dis. Oct. 10, 1780; service, 3 mos., 17 days; enlistment, 3 mos.; co. raised to reinforce Continental Army.

AMOS BORDMAN of Lynn; priv., Capt. David Parker's (1st Lynn) co. of minute-men, which marched to Concord; service, 2 days; roll sworn to Dec. 20, 1775; *also*, Capt. John Bacheller's co., Col. Ebenezer Bridge's reg.; order for advance pay dated Cambridge, June 6, 1775; *also*, muster roll dated Aug. 1, 1775; enl. April 29, 1775; service, 3 mos., 9 days; *also*, co. return dated Cambridge, Sept. 25, 1775.

DANIEL BORDMAN of Topsfield; priv., Capt. Stephen Perkins' co., which marched on the alarm of April 19, 1775; service, 1 day.

IVENEY BORDMAN of Lynn; priv., Capt. David Parker's (1st Lynn) co. of minute-men, which marched to Concord; service, 2 days. Roll sworn to Dec. 20, 1775.

JOHN BORDMAN of Lynn; priv., Capt. David Parker's (1st Lynn) co. of minute-men, which marched to Concord; service, 2 days. Roll sworn to Dec. 20, 1775.

JOHN BORDMAN of Ipswich; sergt., Capt. Richard Dodge's (3d) co., Col. Baldwin's (late Gerrish's) 38th reg.; muster roll dated Aug. 1, 1775; enl. June 11, 1775; service, 7 weeks, 9 days; *also*, Capt. Dodge's co., Lt.-col. Loammi Baldwin's reg.; muster roll for Sept. and Oct., 1775; appointed June 11, 1775; reported entered service April 19, 1775.

JOHN HOW BORDMAN of Ipswich; Capt. Abraham Dodge's co., Col. Moses Little's reg.; order for bounty coat dated Dec. 21, 1775; *also*, corp., Capt. Dodge's co.; muster roll for April, 1776; enl. Jan. 1, 1776.

NAT. BORDMAN of Salisbury; priv., Capt. Henry Morrill's co., Col. Caleb Cushing's reg., which marched April 20, 1775, in response to the alarm of April 19, 1775; service, 7 days.

SAMUEL BORDMAN of Lynn; priv.; Capt. David Parker's (1st Lynn) co. of minute men, which marched to Concord; service, 2 days. Roll sworn to Dec. 20, 1775.

THOMAS BORDMAN of Ipswich; serg., Capt. Nathaniel Wade's co. of minute-men, which marched on the alarm of April 19, 1775, to Mystic; service, 21 days; co. ordered to Salem April 20, 1775, to Ipswich April 21, 1775, from thence to headquarters at Cambridge; remained in service until May 10, 1775.

WILLIAM BORDMAN of Lynn; priv., Capt. David Parker's (1st Lynn) co. of minute-men, which marched to Concord; service, 2 days. Roll sworn to Dec. 20, 1775.

JAMES BORMAN of Salem; mariner, ship "Salem Packet," com. by Capt. Joseph Cook; descriptive list of officers and crew sworn to May 13, 1780; age, 34 years; stature, 5 ft., 3 in.; complexion, light; residence, Salem.

JAMES BORMAN of Salem; descriptive list of officers and crew of the ship "Salem Packet," com. by Capt. Joseph Cook, sworn to Nov. 25, 1780; age, 17 years; stature, 5 ft., 2 in.; complexion, light; residence, Salem.

JOHN BORMAN of Ipswich; seaman, brigantine "Defence," com. by Capt. John Edmonds; descriptive list of officers and crew dated Aug. 21, 1781; stature, 5 ft., 10 in.; complexion, light; residence, Ipswich.

JOHN BORREH of Salem; seaman, ship "Pilgrim," com. by Capt. Joseph Robinson; descriptive list of officers and crew dated Aug. 2, 1780; age, 24 years; stature, 5 ft., 9 in.; complexion, dark; residence, Salem.

ANTHONY BOSTON of Newburyport (also given Boscawen); descriptive list of men enl. from Essex co. for 9 mos. from the time of their arrival at Fishkill, June 18, 1778; age, 34 years; stature, 5 ft., 8 in.; complexion, black; hair, black; eyes, black; residence, Newburyport; *also*, priv., Capt. Amasa Soper's co., Col. Thomas Marshall's reg.; muster roll dated West Point, Feb. 1, 1779; enl. June 15, 1778; enlisted, 9 mos.; reported sick at Fishkill.

EDWARD BOSTON of Ipswich; seaman, ship "Pilgrim," com. by Capt. Joseph

Robinson; descriptive list of officers and crew dated Aug. 2, 1780; age, 17 years; stature, 5 ft., 4 in.; complexion, dark; residence, Ipswich.

TONEY BOSTON of Newburyport (also given Salem); list of men enl. from Essex co. for 9 mos. from the time of their arrival at Fishkill, June 18, 1778; also, list of men returned as received of Jonathan Warner, commissioner, by Col. P. Putnam, July 20, 1778.

WILLIAM BOTMAN of Newbury; list of men enl. into Continental Army from Essex co. [year not given]; residence, Newbury; enl. for Newbury; also, priv., Capt. Carr's co., Col. Wesson's reg.; Continental Army pay accounts for service from May 17, 1777 [service not given]; reported deserted.

ISRAEL BOURRAL of Lynn; Capt. Ezra Newhall's co., Col. John Mansfield's reg.; order for advance pay dated Cambridge, June 8, 1775; also, priv.; muster roll dated Aug. 1, 1775; enl. May 6, 1775; service, 3 mos., 2 days.

JOHN BOVEL of Marblehead; seaman, ship "Rhodes," com. by Capt. Nehemiah Buffington; descriptive list of officers and crew dated Aug. 14, 1780; age, 22 years; stature, 5 ft., 5 in.; complexion, light; residence, Marblehead.

STEPHEN BOW of Marblehead; Capt. Ebenezer Winship's co., Col. John Nixon's (5th) reg.; receipt for advance pay dated Cambridge, June 22, 1775; also, priv.; muster roll dated Aug. 1, 1775; enl. May 3, 1775; service, 3 mos., 6 days; also, co. return dated Sept. 30, 1775; also, order for bounty coat dated Dec. 22, 1775; also, Capt. Winship's (4th) co., Col. Nixon's (4th) reg.; return of men in service Sept. and Oct., 1776, dated North Castle; also, order for wages for Oct., 1776, dated Camp Peekskill.

BEN BOWDEN of Marblehead; return of men enl. into Continental Army from Col. Jonathan Glover's (5th Essex co.) reg.; dated Nov. 7, 1777; residence, Marblehead; enl. for Marblehead; enlistment, 3 years.

BENJAMIN BOWDEN of Lynn; certificate stating that he took the oath of the army July 24, 1775, in Middlesex co.; also, priv., Capt. Lindsey's co., com. by Lt. Daniel Gallusha, Col. Benjamin Ruggles Woodbridge's reg.; muster roll dated Aug. 1, 1775; enl. July 28, 1775; service, 3 days; also, Capt. Eleazer Lindsey's co., Col. Samuel Gerrish's reg.; order for advance pay dated Malden, Aug. 3, 1775; also, Capt. Daniel Gallusha's co., Col. Woodbridge's reg.; order for bounty coat dated Malden, Dec. 22, 1775.

To be continued.

NOTES.

William Botham married Martha Bray Dec. 7, 1715; lived in Gloucester; lost on a fishing voyage near the Isle Sables Aug. —, 1716, aged twenty-five; his wife Martha survived him, and died in Gloucester, his widow, in 1757, her will, dated April 7, 1757, being proved June 27, 1757. Their only child was Anna (or Ann), born in Gloucester April 10, 1717, posthumous; married Isaac Day Nov. 5, 1749; and she was his wife in 1757.—*Records.*

Charles, son of Michael and Mary Boucher, born in Salem Sept. 13, 1693. (Belonged in Lynn.)

Thomas Boucnton married Sara Sothwick 30 : 10: 1670. Children: Thomas, born March 1, 1671; Benjamin, born July 24, 1675; Abigail, born July 25, 1695.
—*Salem town records.*

Joseph Boude of Marblehead, 1669.

Nathaniel Boulton of Ipswich, 1657.
—*Court records.*

Children of Moses and Phebe Boudy: Lydia, born Jan. 10, 1742; Ruth, born Dec. 29, 1746.—*Amesbury town records.*

William Bound married Mary Haverlad July 12, 1669, in Lynn.

Ruth Bound married John Goodale Nov. 11, 1724.

John Bound married Eunice Fuller Dec. 15, 1725.

Mary Bound married Ebenezer Hutchinson Dec. 13, 1726.

Jack Bourn published to Lucy Thomas, both negroes and of Salem, June 19, 1797.
—*Salem town records.*

Abial Bound married Leonard Madeson Jan. 20, 1712-3.—*Marblehead town records.*

Aaron Bourn of Marblehead, physician, married Hannah Ridd..n of Lynn March 1, 1719-20, in Marblehead. They lived in Marblehead, 1720-1723, and in Bristol, 1728-1741. He was called a physician, 1723, 1740 and 1741; "barber chirurgeon," 1724; and surgeon, 1728.

—— Bourn had children: 1. Mary, married Samuel Jordan, esq., of New Biddeford, Me., and was his wife in 1770; 2. Melatiah, lived in Boston, 1756, 1770-1772; esquire, 1770-1775; merchant, 1756; wife Mary, 1756; and had sons Melatiah and Sylvanus; 3. William, lived in Marblehead; colonel, honorable and esquire; married, first, Sarah Legallais May 30, 1756; she died in 1764, aged thirty-three; he married, second, Deborah (Tasker), widow of James Freeman (published May 7, 1768); he died in 1770; at the age of forty-seven; his will, dated Aug. 9, 1770, being proved Nov. 5, 1770; his estate was valued at £4,886, 2s., 7d.; his wife Deborah survived him, and died, his widow, in Marblehead, May 30, 1810, aged seventy-seven. Children, born in Marblehead: Sarah, born May 26, 1757; Lucretia, born July 13, 1758; married Capt. Joshua Orne of Marblehead, gentleman, Aug. 14, 1783; Charlotte, born April 14, 1760; married Dr. John Barnard Swett of Newburyport May 4, 1780; Frances, born March 31, 1761; married Oliver Peabody, esq., of Exeter, N. H. (published Feb. 9, 1782).

—*Records.*

John, son of John and Mary Bourne, born 11 : 8 mo: 1651.—*Gloucester town records.*

Infant of John Bourn died Jan. 20, 1759.—*Wenham church records.*

Joanna Bourne, grandchild of Mary Bourne of Salem, 1644.

Susanna Bourn married Andrew Newhall Dec. 21, 1752, in Lynn.
—*Court records.*

Paid coronor for taking up the body of Joseph Borne out of Salem harbor and burying it, Aug. 1, 1727.—*Sessions court records at Salem, page 40.*

Mary Bours married William Bours Dec. 10, 1760.

Rev. Peter Bours died Feb. 24, 1762, aged thirty-six.
—*Marblehead records.*

Hannah Boutel married Rev. Samuel Bacheller about 1735.—*Haverhill town records.*

Margaret Bofee married Zebedee Day Feb. 19, 1743.

Thomas Boffee married Margaret Denning Nov. 9, 1736.
—*Gloucester town records.*

Mrs. Mary Bovill married Benjamin Eborns of Lynn June 2, 1786.

John Bovill married Mrs. Mary Milford March 28, 1780.
—*Marblehead town records.*

Samuel Boreman of Ipswich, 1639; probably removed to Wethersfield, Conn., with his son Isaac, born Feb. 3. 1642; had there, Mary, born Feb. 14, 1644, and other children.

Samuel Boswell of Bradford about 1663; of Rowley, 1671; had Samuel (who perhaps lived in Boston).

Hananiel Bosworth of Ipswich, 1648; removed, I suppose, to Haverhill, where Hannah Bosworth is found in 1674.

Robert Botham of Ipswich, 1652.

Stephen Boulter of Newbury, 1668.

William Bound of Salem, freeman May 17, 1637, by wife Ann, had baptized there James, Aug. 25, 1636; Andrew, Aug. 12, 1638; and Philip, Dec. 7, 1640; married, second wife, July 12, 1669, Mary Haverlad. (Felt.)

John Bourne of Salem, 1637; removed to Gloucester, 1649, had there, by wife Mary, Bethia, born Oct. 11, 1651; removed next year.

Richard Bourne of Lynn, 1637: removed to Sandwich, was the first instructor of the Indians at Mashpee, beginning

in 1658; ordained, in 1670, by Eliot and Cotton; married, July —, 1677, Ruth, widow of Jonathan Winslow, daughter of William Sargent; children, by a former wife: Job; Elisha, born 1641; and Sheariashub, 1643. He died in 1682. See Gookin's Hist. Coll.; Hubbard, 659, 60; and Davis' Ed. of Morton's Mem., 408.

James Boutell of Salem and Lynn, 1635; freeman March 14, 1639; died in 1651, in his will of Aug. 22, proved Nov. 26, of that year, names wife Alice, sons James and John and daughter Sarah.
—*Savage.*

Rev. Peter Bours of Marblehead; will dated Feb. 21, 1762; proved April 26, 1762; gave to his wife Abigail all his estate and appointed her executrix.—*Probate records.*

John Botton married Esther Gardner Sep'. 24, 1782.

Samuel Bovee married Mrs. Mary Lee Oct. 19, 1794.
—*Gloucester town records.*

Eliezer Bow married Sarah Waters May 31, 1754; children, baptized in St. Michael's church: Amos, Oct. 3, 1756; and Stephen, Sept. 4, 1757.

Stephen Bow married Abigail Boden Sept. 30, 1783; children, baptized in Second church: Sarah, Feb. 29, 1784; Nabby Harris, June 4, 1786; Stephen, April 20, 1788; and Polly, Sept. 12, 1790.
—*Marblehead records.*

Robert Bow married Lydia Carter of Salem Aug. 16, 1721.

Sarah Bow married Edward Smith Nov. 22, 1761.
—*Records of St. Michael's church, Marblehead.*

Will of widow Mary Bow of Marblehead, dated Feb. 20, 1749, proved July 11, 1753; bequeathed all her estate to her daughter Patience Poor.—*Probate records.*

Moses Boudy of Haverhill, blacksmith, 1731-2.

Moses Bowday of Amesbury, blacksmith, 1742.

Joseph Bowd of Marblehead, "liquor stiller," 1666.

Joseph Bowed of Marblehead, yeoman, 1667.
—*Registry of deeds.*

Joseph Bowed (also Boude, Boud, and Bowde) of Marblehead, 1669, 1670.

Joseph Bowed of Salem, 1669.
— *Court records.*

John Ingersoll, mariner, was appointed administrator of the estate of Henry Bowdell of Gloucester Nov. 17, 1760.—*Probate records.*

Children of Benjamin and Mary Bowden: Benjamin, baptized Oct. 28, 1759; Lydia, baptized Nov. 21, 1773.

Ebenezer Bowden married Rebecca Holman Feb. 3, 1763; children: Ebenezer, baptized Sept. 4, 1763; Rebecca, baptized April 13, 1766; Samuel, baptized May 29, 1768.

Francis Bowden married Elizabeth Boden Feb. 28, 1768; children: James, baptized May 15, 1768; Francis, baptized Jan. 21, 1770; Rebecca, baptized Sept. 15, 1771; Elizabeth, baptized Oct. 3, 1773; Mary, baptized Dec. 10, 1775; John, baptized June 14, 1778; Deborah, baptized April 6, 1783; Hannah, baptized July 30, 1786.

Francis Bowden married Sarah Brown Sept. 10, 1772; children: Francis, baptized Aug. 30, 1772; Mary, baptized Feb. 2, 1777.

John Boden married Rebecca Vickrey Feb. 12, 1754; and had daughter Rebecca baptized Sept. 1, 1754.

Francis Bowden married Mary Horton June 10, 1792; children: Mary Dennis, baptized Sept. 23, 1792; Francis, baptized April 13, 1794; Francis, baptized May 11, 1795; Elizabeth, baptized Sept. 3, 1797; Benoice Johnson, baptized Sept. 1, 1799.

John Bowden married Rebecca Trefry April 8, 1780; children: Sally, baptized Oct. 5, 1783; John, baptized April 30, 1786.

Children of John and Mary Boden: Lydia, baptized Jan. 23, 1757; Eleaner, baptized April 3, 1757; John, baptized Sept. 30, 1759; Meriam, baptized Aug. 2, 1761.

Samuel Bowden married Mary Collyer Dec. 10, 1792; children : Ruthy Besome, baptized Aug. 3, 1794; Samuel, baptized and " died before baptism," Nov. 11, 1798 (his mother is called " Polly.")

Samuel Bowden, 4th, married Elizabeth Holden April 15, 1798; children: Elizabeth, baptized July 14, 1799; Samuel, baptized June 7, 1801 ; Nathaniel, baptized Feb. 24, 1805 ; Sally, baptized May 26, 1806 ; Mary Holden, baptized Sept. 18, 1808 ; Mary Holden, baptized Aug. 14, 1811, aged five months.

Rebecca, daughter of John and Patience Boden, baptized Dec. 19, 1736.

John Trefry son of John and Hannah Bowden, baptized March 13, 1797.

Sally, daughter of Quin and Sarah Bowden, baptized Jan. 13, 1782.

Mrs. Abigail Boden married Benjamin Robinson May 17, 1778.

Deborah Boden married Ebenezer Le Grow Dec.15 (10—church records), 1767.

Elizabeth Boden married John Jarvis Dec. 7, 1788.

Mrs. Elizabeth Boden married Philip Follet Dec. 7, 1788.

Hannah Boden married Samuel Hitchins Dec. 6, 1716.

Hannah Boden married Isaac Wadden Dec. 14, 1752.

Hannah Boden married Phillip Corral Oct. 1, 1765.

Hannah Boden married John Copp Aug. 11, 1768.

Hitchins Boden married Hannah Chubb Sept. 17, 1761.

Lydia Boden married Thomas Renew Jan. 10, 1760.

Mary Boden married Peter Daley, at Salem, Aug. 26, 1753.

Mary Boden married Amos Grandy Dec. 20, 1759.

Mary Boden published to Samuel White Nov. 12, 1774.

Polly Boden married John Peach June 6, 1782.

Rebecca Boden married John Gilbert Aug. 18, 1772.

Ruth Boden married Ebenezer Brown of Lynn Feb. 21, 1782.

Sarah Boden married Ambrose Grant Aug. 19, 1746.

Sarah Boden married Elias Le Grow Dec. 15, 1765.

Sarah Boden married William Davis Feb. 8, 1770.

Sarah Boden married Jacob Vickery Jan. 12, 1786.

Susanna Boden married Amos Collins of Gloucester Jan. 7, 1733-4.

Sympson Boden married Charity Tucker 10 mo : 27 : 1720.

Tabitha Boden married Benjamin Dodd 10 mo : 13 : 1722.

Mary Bodin married Richard Horton Feb. 24, 1712-3.

Tabitha Bodin married John Rhodes, 3d, Oct. 31, 1700.

Benjamin Bowden married Mary Vinson Sept. 4, 1773.

Edward Boden married Sarah Hales Aug. 6, 1741 ; children : Sarah, baptized Sept. 19, 1742; Edward, baptized Oct. 21, 1744; Thomas, baptized Aug. 23, 1747.

Benjamin Bowden, jr., published to Sarah Quiner Jan. 17, 1777.

Elizabeth Bowden married Ambross James Jan. 17, 1740.

Elizabeth Boden married Samuel Gouldsmith Feb. 25, 1768.

Elizabeth Bowden married Samuel Mescrvy Dec. 8, 1768.

Elizabeth Bowden married William Proctor Dec. 14, 1769.

Hannah Bowden married Thomas Williston Dec. 31, 1767.

Hannah Bowden published to Samuel Russell May 15, 1790.

Joseph Bowden married Ruth Cloutman Jan. 20, 1799.

Lydia Bowden married John Lemain April 22, 1773.

Mary Bowden married Moses Stacey Aug. 5, 1756.

Mary Bowden married Benjamin Russell Nov. 10, 1757.

Mary Bowden married Joseph Grant April 14, 1772.

Rebecca Bowden married Thomas Nicholson May 8, 1790.

Sarah Bowden married Charles Wheeler Dec. 25, 1787.

Mrs. Sarah Bowden married Edward Fettyplace, esq., Aug. 26, 1794.

Susannah Bodin buried Jan. 19, 1730-1. Widow Sarah Bowden died Oct. 2, 1789.

Children of Susanna Bodin : Tabitha, baptized July 31, 1698 ; Samuel, baptized Oct. 31, 1703.

—Marblehead records.

Michael Bowden, aged thirty years, lived on Marblehead Plains in 1681.— *Court Files*, volume XXXVI, leaf 59.

Administration was granted on the estate of Benjamin Boden of Marblehead, fisherman, Dec. 30, 1763, to his son John Boden of Marblehead, fisherman.

A guardian was appointed for Rebecca, aged ten, and Sarah, aged eight, children of John Boden of Marblehead, fisherman, in April, 1792. Their mother was a niece of Samuel Orne of Marblehead.

Administration was granted on the estate of Michael Bowden of Marblehead, housewright, July 10, 1783. His estate was valued at £120. He had two hundred acres of land at Windham, Me.

Will of Robert Boden of Salem, merchant, dated April 7, 1750, proved April 23, 1750. He gave his property to strangers, and apparently had no family. His estate was appraised at £184, 1s., 7d., all personal. It was insolvent.

—Probate records.

Peter Bowden (signed *Baudouin*), protestant, merchant, of the city of Wexford, Ireland, now living in Salem, Mass., sold ship, lately of Dublin, 1684-1686.

Benjamin Bowden, jr., cordwainer, and wife Hannah, Sarah Boden, Mary Boden, Isaac Wodden, fisherman, and wife Hannah, and others, all of Marblehead, sell property in New Town in Marblehead, formerly estate of Benjamin Bowden, deceased, 1768.

Amos Grandy of Marblehead, mariner, and wife Mary, daughter of Benjamin Bouden of Marblehead, deceased, 1770.

Estate of Benjamin Boden of Marblehead, shoreman (1785), sold land to Benjamin Boden of Marblehead, mariner, 1786.

Benjamin Boden of Marblehead, mariner, 1771.

John Bowden of Marblehead, fisherman, and wife Mary, our late sister Ruth Curtis of Marblehead, singlewoman, sell estate of our grandparents Robert and Mary Girdler, 1793.

Widow Sarah Bowden of Marblehead, 1792.

Samuel Bowden of Marblehead, shoreman, and wife Sarah, to James Bowden of Marblehead, fisherman, 1793, 1795.

Joseph Bowden of Marblehead, housewright, 1795, 1796.

—Registry of deeds.

Edward Bowden, rigger, sailmaker and mariner, lived in Beverly, 1781-1790; married Esther Harriden (published Nov. 25, 1781); she was daughter of John and Esther Harmon of Beverly, and had minor children, William Langdell, jr., and Love Langdell, in 1790; children of Edward and Esther Bowden, born in Beverly : Andrew, born April 16, 1788; Sarah, born Jan. 17, 1790.

Simpson Boden, shoreman, lived in Marblehead, 1773-1780; will dated May 19, 1777, proved July 3, 1780; married Elizabeth Power June 3, 1773; and had son-in-law John Poor of Marblehead, mariner, 1777.

—Records.

Thomas Bowden, born about 1770 ; lived in Beverly ; married, first, Lucy Woodbury March 8, 1795 ; married, second, Mehitable ———, who died, his widow, Jan. 3, 1835, aged sixty-seven ; he was lost at sea July 27, 1827, aged fifty-seven ; in her will, she called Charles Elliott, deceased, her "son ;" children born in Beverly : 1. Thomas, born Dec. 18, 1795 ; 2. James, born Dec. 13, 1798 ; 3. Warren Woodberry, born Aug. 22, 1801 ; 4. Lucy B., born Oct. 5, 1804 ; married, first, Thomas Standley, and, second, Shadrack Fisk of Beverly, cordwainer ; and they were living there in 1835 ; 5. John Simmons, born July 30, 1806 ; married Elizabeth Woodbury ; 6. William, born March 14, 1809 ; 7. Porter D., born March 30, 1810 ; married, first,

Christian Utsen; and, second, Eliza (Pulsipher) Woodbury.

Benjamin Boden, mariner, lived in Marblehead, 1768-1774; married Miss Martha Vickary of Marblehead May 22, 1764; children, baptized in Marblehead: 1. Martha, baptized Oct. 9, 1768; died young; 2. Martha, baptized April 22, 1770; married Samuel Glover of Marblehead, merchant, Feb. 9, 1786; and died ("Patty") Dec. 1, 1786, aged seventeen years and eight months; 3. Benjamin, baptized March 22, 1772; died young; 4. Benjamin, baptized April 17, 1774.

Michael Bowden, planter, lived in Topsfield, 1669, 1670, and in Marblehead, 1688, 1694, 1695; married Sarah Nurse of Salem Dec. 15, 1669; she was his wife in 1695; daughter Susanna, born in Topsfield June 10, 1670; living in 1688, when she claimed to be with child by John Oak of Lynn (conception latter part of August, 1687—court files, volume XLVII., leaf 134).

John Boden, fisherman, lived in Marblehead; married Mary Giffard Aug. 18, 1748, in Marblehead; administration was granted on his estate July 7, 1766; she survived him, but probably died next year; children, baptized in Marblehead: Sarah, baptized July 19, 1752; living in 1766, fourteen years old ; Mary, baptized Aug. 25, 1754; aged under fourteen years in 1766

—Records.

Mary Bowden of Marblehead appointed administratrix of the estate of her husband Francis Bowden, jr., of Marblehead, fisherman, March 31, 1746.—*Probate records.*

Joseph Bowden of Marblehead published to Lydia Collins of Lynn Nov. 29, 1717.—*Lynn town records.*

Jonathan Bodin married Susanna Nicholson Oct. 21, 1697, in Marblehead; was a fisherman; lived in Marblehead, 1719-1721; and she was his wife in 1720.—*Marblehead town records and Registry of deeds.*

Edward Bowden, sojourner, published to Mary Wheeler June 11, 1771.

Samuel Boden married Catey Huffains (recorded Dec. 9, 1791.)

—Gloucester town records.

Michael Bowden of Marblehead married Sarah Davis of Lynn (published Nov. 20, 1697); she was his wife in 1741; bought house and land near the burying place in Lynn in 1707; innholder, 1729-1741, waterman, 1722-3; will dated Sept. 26, 1741, proved Oct. 12, 1741; estate appraised at £555, 16s.; children: 1. John, of Exeter, N. H., wife Huldah, joiner, 1755; 2. Sarah, married John Riddan of Marblehead (Redding—*publishment*) (published in Lynn Aug. 30, 1723) ; 3. Mary, married John (Joseph—*publishment*) Richards in Lynn May 5, 1726; and she was his widow in 1755; 4. Lydia, married Samuel Kelley of Southborough, Mass. (and afterwards of Marblehead), March 30, 1731; 5. Susannah, married Moses Newhall of Lynn, gentleman, before 1755; 6. Benjamin, lived in Lynn, 1749-1772; innholder, 1756-1757; joiner, 1761, husbandman, 1763, housewright, 1770; married Abigail Hawkins of Salem Sept. 28, 1749; child: Frances, stillborn Aug. 6, 1750, in Lynn.—*Records.*

Mary Bowden (also, Bowen) married Peter Crosby, both of Salem, April 27, 1788.

William Boden married Experience Downing, both of Salem, July 18, 1774.

William Boden, jr., married Eunice Barnes, both of Salem, Oct. 12, 1795 (published Sept. 12, 1794).

Charles Bourdon married Mary Davidson, both of Salem, March 13, 1785.

Elizabeth Bowden married James Watts 26 : 5 : 1661.

Grace Bowden married Robert Hamilton, both of Salem, Aug. 14, 1791.

Ann Bowden of Boston published to Joseph Mackintire, jr., of Salem Jan. 2, 1773.

Grace Bowden published to John Dawson, both of Salem, Nov. 14, 1789.

—Salem town records.

Benjamin Boden of Marblehead married Barbary Hood April 22, 1718.— *Lynn town records.*

Samuel Bowden of Gloucester, 1651, 1652.

Mary Bowden of Salem, 1661.

Sarah Bowden of Amesbury married Benjamin Tole of Hampton Nov. 7, 1693, Amesbury.

—*County court records.*

Michael , Bowdoin of Lynn, 1690.—*Savage.*

Sarah Bowditch married Oliver Sawyer before 1752.

Elizabeth Bowditch married Isaac Snow before 1749, perhaps at Bridgewater. She died Nov. 4, 1783.

—*Haverhill town records.*

Judith Bowditch married Timothy Wellman, both of Salem, April 5, 1791.

Widow Anna Bowditch married William Richardson Russell, both of Salem, Nov. 9, 1793.

Deborah Bowditch married Thomas Moriarty, both of Danvers (both of Salem —*publishment*), Oct. 31, 1782.

Samuel Bowel published to Sarah Smith, both of Salem, June 14, 1794.

—*Salem town records.*

Deborah Bowditch married Bartho[m] H. Burger (or, Burges) Oct. 31, 1782.—*Danvers town records.*

Moses Bowdy of Kittery married Miss Phebe Weed of Amesbury June 2, 1730; and lived in Haverhill until the state line was settled, being called of Salisbury and Amesbury District, N. H., in 1746; blacksmith; children, born in Haverhill : Sarah, born April 22, 1731 ; Phebe, born Aug. 19, 1733; John, born Nov. 25, 1735; died Dec. 16, 1735; Hannah, born July 31, 1737; Moses, born Nov. 6, 1739.

Thomas Bowen lived in Marblehead, 1645-1674; born about 1621, 1624 or 1628; fisherman, 1660, planter, 1674; wife Elizabeth, 1646-1674.

William Bowen lived in Marblehead, 1760-1806; laborer; married Martha Homan Feb. 21, 1770; he died May 7, 1806; and she died, his widow, Oct. 24, 1806; children, born in Marblehead : 1. Sarah, baptized Nov. 21, 1773; 2. Margaret Homan, baptized Dec. 18, 1774; 3. William, baptized Sept. 22, 1776;

married Hannah Bogee Jan. 22, 1804; she died "suddenly " July 29, 1819; and he died, "of a Paralitic Shock," May 16, 1830; 4. Hannah, baptized Aug. 23, 1778; died at the poor house, rec. Dec. 11, 1811; 5. Molly, baptized March 31, 1782; 6. Nabby Homan, baptized Feb. 22, 1784; 7. Susy Dixey, baptized April 9, 1786.

—*Records.*

Edward Bowen married Mrs. Lydia Main March 27, 1768.

Elizabeth Bowen married John Walker Nov. 4, 1706.

John Bowen married Hannah Dixey, Dec. 2, 1680.

John Bowen married Eleanor Darling May 9, 1745.

Mrs. Martha Bowen married Capt. John Conway April 13, 1795.

Nathan Bowen, esq., published to Mary Abraham Dec. 15, 1798.

Sarah Bowen married Benjamin Melzard Nov. 26, 1797.

—*Marblehead records.*

Thomas Bowen of Salem, 1648, was of New London, 1657-60, removed to Rehoboth, died in 1663 ; his widow Elizabeth was, in 1669, wife of Samuel Fuller of Plymouth ; had son Richard Bowen and brother Obadiah Bowen.—*Savage.*

Thomas Bowen of Ipswich and his daughter Ruth in 1670.—*Court files.*

Administration upon the estate of Thomas Bowen of Marblehead, yeoman, was granted March 28, 1705. His eldest daughter had married John Roades of Marblehead, shoreman.

John Bowen of Marblehead, blacksmith, 1769.

Administration upon the estate of John Bowen of Marblehead granted Jan. 21, 1750-1.

—*Probate records.*

Andrew Bowen married Elizabeth Haskell July 8, 1756.

Andrew Bowen married Abigail Allen Nov. 7, 1758; children : Andrew, baptized Sept. 16, 1759; and Elizabeth, born March 5, 1761.

—*Beverly records.*

Eleanor Bowen married John Carnes Jan. 15, 1750.

Mary M. Bowen (born March 7, 1786) married Charles Brown (born in 1787) Oct. 19, 1809.

Henry Bowers of Salem published to Rebecca Taber of Dartmouth April 28, 1738.
—*Salem town records.*

William Bowin, son of Ebenezer Johnson's wife, Sarah Bowin Johnson, ———.
—*Andover town records.*

Martha Bowers married Daniel Gowing Nov. 11, 1764.—*Lynn town records.*

Hannah Bowers of Middleton married Rev. Daniel Fuller of Gloucester Aug. 14 (20—*Gloucester records*), 1770.—*Middleton town records.*

William Bowers married Mrs. Sarah Fairfield March 17, 1765.

Sarah and William, children of widow Sarah Bowers, baptized Oct. 20, 1771.

Infant of William Bowers died Dec. 22, 1765.
—*Wenham records.*

Dr. Denison Bowers married Fanny Perly May 19, 1791.—*Boxford town records.*

QUERIES.

Queries are inserted for one cent a word.
Answers are solicited.

466. Ancestry of Ruth Dole who married Philip Butler, Newbury, 1782, desired.   A. H. L.
Elkins, N. H.

467. Wanted, parentage of Jane Perkins who married Joseph Brookings, Newbury, 1773.   A. H. L.

ANSWERS.

331. In this query, John Patch is stated to have come from England with two brothers and settled Ipswich. He was born in 1721 and died in 1799. There must be a mistake in these statements, as the Patch family was in Ipswich in the preceding century.—*Ed.*

465. Elizabeth Waite, daughter of Aaron and Elizabeth Waite of Ipswich, was left fatherless when a child, under fourteen years of age. Her father was son of Capt. Samuel and Ruth Waite. Captain Waite was a weaver, and lived in Ipswich. His wife Ruth was living in 1750. His will, dated Jan. 26, 1750, was proved June 11, 1756. He had two sons, Samuel and Aaron, and a daughter. Ruth Lakeman, all living in 1750. Aaron died before Dec. 15, 1761, leaving widow Elizabeth and children, Elizabeth, Elias and Aaron.—*Ed.*

NEW PUBLICATIONS.

TRANSACTIONS OF THE KANSAS STATE HISTORICAL SOCIETY, 1905-1906. Topeka, Kansas, 1906. This is volume nine of these reports, and one of the most if not the most valuable and interesting of the series. It is cloth bound, and contains 654 octavo pages of fine type, and many illustrations. The contributed articles are principally devoted to Missions among the Indians in Kansas, river navigation, soldiers of Kansas, politics, the railroad convention of 1860, the drought of 1860, the birthplaces of Kansans, reminiscences, etc. The society is doing most excellent work in preserving the detailed history of the state.

WILLIAM YATES AND HIS DESCENDANTS. *By Edgar Yates.* Old Orchard, Me., 1906. This is a pamphlet of fifty octavo pages. It contains the history and genealogy of William Yates (1772-1868) of Greenwood, Me., and his wife, who was Martha Morgan, together with the line of her descent from Robert Morgan of Beverly. There is given a coat of arms of the English Yates family, portraits of William Yates and his wife, and a half-tone engraving of their old home, and several other portraits, autographs, etc. The book has much valuable and interesting matter. The compiler's address is 28 Sherman st., Everett, Mass.

LIST OF GENEALOGIES

PUBLISHED IN

The Essex Antiquarian.

·r, fourteen numbers	. .	$1.20
·s, three numbers	. .	.30
·, one number	. .	.10
·s, one number	. .	.10
·s, thirteen numbers	. .	1.10
·, one number	. .	.10
·MAN, one number	. .	.10
·NDER, one number	. .	.10
·s, thirteen numbers	. .	1.10
·r, three numbers	. .	.30
·OSE, one number	. .	.16
·, three numbers	. .	.30
·RSON, one number	. .	.10
·EWS, eight numbers	. .	.70
·BLE, two numbers	. .	.20
·s, one number	. .	.10
·TON, two numbers	. .	.20
·HER, one number	. .	.15
·OLD, one number	. .	.25
·, one number	. .	.20
·PY, one number	. .	.25
·ON, one number	. .	.25
·EE, one number	. .	.25
·NS, two numbers	. .	.35
·NSON, two numbers	. .	.35
·LL, one number	. .	.25
·OD, three numbers	. .	.60
·N, one number	. .	.25
·NS, two numbers	. .	.35
·ILL, two numbers	. .	.35
·, four numbers	. .	.50
·DGE, one number	. .	.10
·N, one number	. .	.10
·N, three numbers	. .	.60
·OCK, one number	. .	.10
·R, two numbers	. .	.35
·EY, two numbers	. .	.35
·Y, three numbers	. .	.60
·, two numbers	. .	.50
·, one number	. .	.25
one number	. .	.25
·O, two numbers	. .	.50
·CER, two numbers	. .	.50
·S, one number	. .	.25
·ER, four numbers	. .	1.00

BARNARD, two numbers	.	.50
BARNES, one number	.	.25
BARNEY, one number	.	.25
BAER, one number	.	.25
BARRETT, one number	.	.25
BARTHOLMEW, one number	.	.25
BARTLETT, two numbers	.	.50
BARTOLL, one number	.	.25
BARTON, two numbers	.	.50
BASSETT, two numbers	.	.50
BATCHELDER, two numbers	.	.50
BATES, one number	.	.25
BATTEL, one number	.	.25
BEADLE, one number	.	.25
BEAL, two numbers	.	.50
BEAN, two numbers	.	.50
BEAR, one number	.	.25
BECK, one number	.	.25
BECKET, two numbers	.	.50
BECKFORD, one number	.	.25
BELCHER, one number	.	.25
BELKNAP, one number	.	.25
BELL, one number	.	.25
BENNETT, two numbers	.	.50
BERRY, two numbers	.	.50
BESSOM, one number	.	.25
BEST, one number	.	.25
BILES, one number	.	.25
BIRD, one number	.	.25
BISHOP, two numbers	.	.50
BISSON, one number	.	.25
BIXBY, one number	.	.25
BLACK, two numbers	.	.50
BLACKLER, one number	.	.25
BLAKE, one number	.	.25
BLANCHARD, one number	.	.25
BLANEY, one number	.	.25
BLASDELL, one number	.	.25
BLASHFIELD, one number	.	.25
BLUNT, one number	.	.25
BLY, two numbers	.	.50
BOARDMAN, two numbers	.	.50
BODWELL, one number	.	.25
BOLLES, two numbers	.	.50
BOLTON, one number	.	.25
BOND, two numbers	.	.50
BOOTH, one number	.	.25

ADDRESS

The Essex Antiquarian, Salem, Mass.

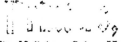

of Essex County, Massachu...

aton includes the complete ...
all volumes in the order of ...
County, in alphabetical ord...
gravestone inscriptions prior...
as abstracts of the Q....

r Annum. Single copies,

Price of Back Numbers:--

... --	
$5.00	No. 1, Vol. I. ...
	" 2, " I, ...
2.00	" 3, " I, ...
ound,	"" 7, " V. ...
	Subsqa...

SEX ANTIQUARIAN, S....

---

nshire Genealo...

agazine devoted to Genealogy. It...

I NEW HAMPSHIRE GE...

---

cript of the genealogical record...
TION: $1.00 per year in advance...

---

r and Publisher,

---

he New England

nd Genealogical

v. April, July and October, ...

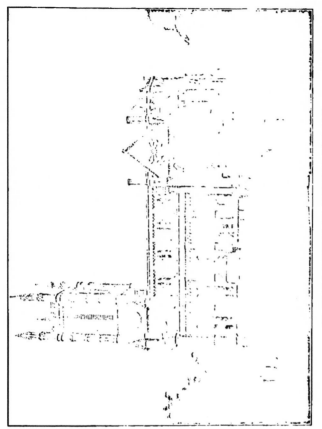

ST. MARY'S CHURCH IN ANDOVER, ENGLAND

THE ESSEX ANTIQUARIAN.

VOL. XI.   SALEM, MASS., APRIL, 1907.   No. 2.

ANDOVER IN ENGLAND.

BY OSCAR FAY ADAMS.

Population : 6,000 (1900). 67 miles from London (Waterloo terminus of South Western railway). Parish church : St. Mary the Virgin, register from 1580: living, a vicarage. Other churches and chapels: 2 Congregational; Primitive Methodist; Wesleyan; Baptist. Schools: Grammar; National; British. 2 banks. Market day: Friday. Cattle market on Monday; wool fair, end of June; Sheep fair, Nov. 17. 2 weekly papers. Corporation: mayor, 4 aldermen, 12 councillors. Gives title of viscount to earl of Suffolk and Berkshire.

Andover is not a place with any very decided claims to be accounted picturesque ; it is in effect nothing more than a busy little market town, the centre of an agricultural district. Still there are points of view whence Andover, at the ford of the Ann or Ande (hence Andover), is well worth looking at, and as the train leaves Andover junction on the London and South Western railway and goes swinging around the long curve on the Southampton line to Andover Town station, the traveller can easily behold one of them. The church tower in the higher part of the picture, with long lines of houses falling away from it to north and south, the river Anton flowing sluggishly between the railway and the town—such a scene, in the judgment of at least one observer, merits the tribute of something more than a passing glance.

It is a very ancient borough indeed that stretches along the wooded valley of the Anton, and spreads itself over the hillsides, the principal town in the northern part of Hampshire, and a place of some little commercial importance. It is situated on the ancient Roman road from Salisbury to Gilchester, some eighteen miles west from Basingstoke and

about as far eastward from Salisbury, and in Saxon days was a royal residence, and the scene of more than one meeting of the Witenagemot. Olaf Tryggvason was entertained at Andover in 988 by Ethelred who induced his Norwegian guest to be baptized and confirmed by Alphege, the archbishop of Canterbury, and in token of his change of heart Olaf vowed never to visit England as an enemy. In the nineteen doleful years of King Stephen, Andover suffered much, and was burned in 1141. In the eighteenth century the place was frequently heard of in electioneering struggles, its inhabitants sharing with those of its neighbour Stockbridge, the dubious reputation of being not beyond the influence of a bribe where votes were concerned.

" Sir Francis Blake Delaval," writes a Quarterly Reviewer, " of the fine old Norman Delavals, the rake and humorist of about a century ago, was one time canvassing Andover. There was a voter there, as far as every appearance went, insensible to every temptation. Money, wine, place, flattery, had no attractions for the stoic. Sir Francis puzzled himself in endeavouring to discover the man's weak point. At last he found it out. The man had never seen a fire-eater and doubted if there existed a class endowed with that remarkable power. Off went Delaval to London and he returned with Angelo in a postchaise. Angelo exerted all his genius. Fire poured from his mouth and nostrils—fire which melted that iron nature and sent it off cheerfully to poll for Delaval."

Three fairly broad and compactly built streets constitute the larger portion of Andover. One of these, in which is the spacious inn of The White Hart, extends eastward from the railway station across the Anton to the long as well as broad market place, an area lined on three of its sides with shops, inns, a bank or two, and lesser establishments. At its upper, or northern end, stands the town hall, erected in 1825, in the classical style then popular; a large stone structure with an open arcaded lower story, and above this a hall seating three hundred people, a council chamber and other rooms. The front of the building displays the town clock. Among the arches of the ground story a corn market is held on Friday, and on Mondays a cattle market is in progress at the Masons Arms in Winchester street. At the left of the town hall a street diverges to the eastward, while at the right the High street proceeds leisurely up the hill toward the parish church. In this thoroughfare are to be seen more shops and a rather imposing Baptist chapel of stone and white brick. At the crest of the hill the street appears to pause and then wanders slowly down the northern slope toward the junction station a half-mile distant. Just where it lingers, as it were, the church may be seen within its spacious churchyard that is reached by a flight of steps from the roadway.

It is a modern stone building in the First Pointed style, with tall western tower, nave, aisles, transepts and apsidal east end. The interior displays an elaborate scheme of color decoration, is lavishly adorned with carvings and very distinctly conveys the impression that it must have cost a lot of money. And so it did, for Dr. William Stanley Goddard, a former headmaster of Winchester college, and long the vicar of Andover, spent in 1848 the sum of thirty thousand pounds in building this church of Saint Mary. It is commodious and apparently comfortable, but it is by no means an admirable specimen of Victorian Gothic, although

the three-sided apse is rather an effective exterior feature, as the illustration of the southern side of the church (see frontispiece), serves to show. The writer, recalling engravings of the church destroyed to make room for the present one, is hardly disposed to commend without reserve the church building zeal of the Rev. William Goddard.

Two curious old tombs taken from the ancient church are preserved in the modern one, the first displaying kneeling effigies of a man and a woman on opposite sides, the second dated 1611, showing a seated male effigy on the left, and on the right seven other figures kneeling. The late and much enriched Norman doorway from the old church, placed between two houses in the High street, now forms an entrance to the churchyard. The tower of Saint Mary's, containing a clock and peal of eight bells, rises high above the trees about it and may be seen for many miles. A priory attached to the abbey of Saint Florence at Samur, to which the Andover establishment once belonged ere alien priories were done away with in the reign of Henry the Fifth, was built here by the Conqueror, and a bit of ivy-clad wall in the churchyard still indicates its position.

Crossing the churchyard by one of its broad, shaded paths one comes to East street in which are several dignified residences, and the Congregational church, built in 1700, but with an organization reaching back to 1662. It was enlarged in 1879, and will seat about six hundred persons. The street extends for some considerable distance to the northeast of the parish church, losing caste rapidly as it proceeds, for the thatched cottages that thickly line its course are plainly the homes of the poor. Some of the poorest, indeed, are sheltered in Marlborough street, where, in 1686, John Pullen, esq., founded an almshouse for six poor men. Another similar shelter for four poor women is situated in the Common Acre. Four would appear to be a favorite num-

ber with Andover benefactors, since the town has two more almshouses intended for four women each.

Perhaps a more practical charity is the Cottage Hospital in the Junction Road. It was built in 1876 and receives forty or more patients yearly, some of whom come no doubt from the Waterloo foundry at the foot of Bury hill. In New street is the endowed Grammar school founded so long ago as 1569, and attended by one hundred boys. Like many another small English town, and, alas! very unlike many a small New England town, Andover possesses public swimming baths, for in Old England the public bath precedes the public library.

Inns and public houses are pretty generally distributed throughout the town. Beside the more pretentious hostelries of the White Hart, and the Star and Garter, the thirsty man might wander on to The Chequers, The Catherine Wheel, The New Inn, or The Waterloo. Or, if none of these proved to his mind he might enter The Globe or The Wellington, patronize the King's Head or be received into the embrace of The Foresters' or the Masons' Arms. Yet, as such things go, however, the number of public houses in Andover, in spite of its several breweries, is rather less than is sometimes found in places of the same size, though more than one would expect to perceive flourishing in the shade of Phillips Academy or the Theological Seminary in the town over seas on the banks of the Shawshine

To the archæologist the vicinity of Andover is very interesting, for all about are

"Grey downs with Danish barrows,"

not to mention the Roman camp on Bury hill two miles southwest, and the large camp still nearer, at Folksbury. From the former locality a fine view of the town may be had, and under the hill is Abbot's Ann, with its brick church built in 1716, by the founder of the Chatham family, Governor Pitt. Another nearby spot offering extended prospects is the recreation ground called The Lady's Mile

Within the limits of the municipal borough are the hamlets of Hatherden, Wildhern, Smannell or Swanhill, Little London, Woodhouse, East Anton and Charlton. There is a Baptist chapel at Smannell, and a Primitive Methodist one at Charlton. Andover was incorporated under King John and sent two members to parliament under Edward first and Edward second and from the twenty-seventh year of Elizabeth's reign until 1867. It then sent but one until 1885, when its representation was merged in that of the county.

It was for this Hampshire borough that the Massachusetts Andover was named, the English locality having been the home of some of the principal personages in the new settlement. The town of Andover, New Hampshire, bore the name of New Breton till 1779, and was then renamed as a compliment, in all probability, to the Massachusetts town. The three other New England Andovers, in Maine, Vermont and Connecticut, very possibly trace their names to the same source. Beyond New England the name occurs in the states of Illinois, Kansas, Missouri, New Jersey, New York and Ohio.

NOTES.

Jacob Bowers published to Miss Elizabeth Stanwood, both of Newburyport, Feb. 8, 1785.

Isaac Bowers published to Mrs. Anne McClarrin, both of Newburyport, Feb. 14, 1784.

—Newburyport town records.

John Bowers of Newburyport, mariner, and wife Lydia, 1780, 1781 ; "our brother" Hezekiah Collins of Newburyport, deceased, 1781.—*Registry of deeds.*

Sarah Bowers, of the Hamlet, married Andrew Cole of Wenham May 12, 1793.

William Bowers married Eunice Low Dec. 31, 1798.

—Ipswich town records.

John Bowers married Lydia Bush June 20, 1779, Newburyport.—*Court records,*

BRADSTREET GENEALOGY.

Gov. SIMON BRADSTREET[1],* baptized at Horbling parish, Lincolnshire, England, March 18, 1603-4. He went to Emmanuel college a year, and at the age of sixteen was tutor or governor of young Lord Rich, son of the earl of Warwick. On the death of his father, Simon entered the service of the earl of Lincoln as assistant of steward Thomas Dudley, at Sempringham, where he staid eight years. In 1628, he married Thomas Dudley's daughter Ann. Later he was steward for the dowager countess of Warwick. Concluding to remove to America, he joined the Winthrop company, and was chosen an assistant before they left England. He was secretary of the Massachusetts Bay colony from his arrival in America, in 1630, to 1643; assistant, 1630-1678; deputy governor, 1678, 1679; governor, 1679-1686, 1689-1692. He lived in Salem, 1630, 1631; Cambridge, 1631-1638; Ipswich, 1639-1643; Andover, 1644-1673; Boston, 1674-1690; and Salem, 1695-1697. His wife Ann died in Andover Sept. 16, 1672, aged sixty. She was the first American poetess. He married, second, Ann (Downing), widow of Capt. Joseph Gardner of Salem, in 1676; the antenuptial agreement being dated May 7, 1676. Governor Bradstreet died in Salem March 27, 1697, at the age of ninety-four, being called "the nestor of New England." His second wife survived him, being known as "Madam Bradstreet," and died in Salem April 19, 1713, aged seventy-nine. See sketch of Governor Bradstreet in *The Antiquarian*, volume II, page 159.

*It is stated on good authority that Governor Bradstreet was a son of Rev. Simon Bradstreet, vicar of Horbling, Lincolnshire, England. The children of the father were baptized at Horbling, probably by himself, as follows: Samuel, Sept. 19, 1602; Simon, March 18, 1604; Mercy, March 9, 1606; John, Feb. 8, 1607. Rev. Simon Bradstreet, the father, was a fellow of Emmanuel college, bred as a puritan, and joined the Non-conformist party. He died there Feb. 9, 1621, and his wife Margaret made her will in 1631, probably dying soon afterward.

Children :—

2—I.   SAMUEL[2], b. in 163-. *See below* (2).
3—II. DOROTHY[2], b. in 163-; m. Rev. Seaborn Cotton June 14, 1651, in Andover; and d. Feb. 26, 1671-2.
4—III. SARAH[2], m., first, Richard Hubbard of Ipswich in 1653; he d. in 1681; she m., second, Maj. Samuel Ward of Marblehead, who d. in the Canada Expedition in 1690.
5—IV. SIMON[2], b. Sept. 28, 1640, Monday. *See below* (5).
6—V. HANNAH[2] (Ann), b. in 164-; m. Andrew Wiggin of Exeter, N. H., June 3, 1659, in Andover.
7—VI. DUDLEY[2], b. in 1648. *See below* (7).
8—VII. JOHN[2], b. July 22, 1652, in Andover. *See below* (8).
9—VIII. MERCY[2], b. in 165-; m. Maj. Nathaniel Wade of Ipswich Oct. 31, 1672; and settled in Medford.

2

DR. SAMUEL BRADSTREET[2], born in 163-. He graduated from Harvard college in 1653; and was a fellow of the college. He became a physician; was a representative to the general court in 1670; and lived in Lynn a short time, subsequently removing to Jamaica. He married, first, Mercy Tyng in 1662; and she died Sept. 6, 1669. He married, second, Martha ——, in Jamaica, and died Aug. —, 1682.

Children :—

10—I.   ELIZABETH[3], b. Jan. 29, 1663-4; d. Aug. —, 1665.
11—II. ANNE[3], b. Nov. 17, 1665; d. June 20, 1669.
12—III. MERCY[3], b. Nov. 20, 1667, in Boston; m. Dr. James Oliver of Cambridge; and d. at Cambridge March 20, 1710.
13—IV. SIMON[3], b. Oct. 15, 1669; d. Nov. 16, 1669.
14—V. ANNE[3], b. Sept. 3, 1670, in Boston; living in Salem, singlewoman, in 1697.
15—VI. JOHN[3], b. about 1676; lived in Boston, clothier, 1697; and probably settled in Jamaica in 1700.
16—VII. SIMON[3], b. about 1680; graduated at Harvard college in 1700; lived in Boston, gentleman, in 1702.

5

REV. SIMON BRADSTREET[2], born Sept. 28, 1640, Monday. He graduated at Harvard college in 1660; and was ordained minister at New London, Conn., Oct 5, 1670. He married Lucy Wood-

bridge in 1668; and died in the autumn of 1683. She survived him, and married, secondly, Daniel Epps, dying in Medford in 1710.

Children :—

17—I. SIMON³, bapt. 24 : 8 : 1669; d. young.
18—II. SIMON³, b. March 7, 1670-1. *See below* (*18*).
19—III. ANNE³, b. Dec. 31, 1672, in New London; d. Oct. 2, 1681.
20—IV. JOHN³, b. Nov. 3, 1676; living in 1697.
21—V. LUCY³, b Oct. 24, 1680; m. Hon. Jonathan Remington of Cambridge Sept. 5, 1711; and d. there April 18, 1743.

7

COL. DUDLEY BRADSTREET², born in 1648. He was an esquire, colonel in the militia, selectman, town clerk, representative, magistrate and school teacher; and lived in Andover. He married Ann (White), widow of Theodore Price, Nov. 12, 1673; and died in Andover Nov. 13, 1702. She survived him, and was "Madam Anne Bradstreet" in 1707.

Children, born in Andover :—

22—I. DUDLEY³, b. April 27, 1678. *See below* (*22*).
23—II. MARGARET³, b. Feb. 19, 1680; m. Job Tyler of Boxford about 1700; and d. before 1740.
24—III. ANNA³, b. March 5, 1681; d. Nov. 12, 1681.
25—IV. ANNE³, m. Nathaniel Perley of Boxford.

8

JOHN BRADSTREET², born in Andover July 22, 1652. He lived in Topsfield; and was called a "gentleman" the latter part of his life. He married Sarah Perkins of Topsfield June 11, 1677; and died Jan. 11, 1717-8, aged sixty-five. She survived him, and died in Topsfield, his widow, April 7, 1745.

Children, born in Topsfield :—

26—I. SARAH³, m. Samuel Porter of Wenham May 20, 1707; and was living in 1740.
27—II. ANN³, b. Sept. 9, 1679; living in 1710; probably d. before 1740.
28—III. SIMON³, b. April 14, 1682. *See below* (*28*).
29—IV. MERCY³, bapt. June 2, 1689; m. John Hazen of New London, Conn.; and was living there in 1718.

30—V. DOROTHY³, bapt. Oct. 25, 1691; m. Samuel Clark of York Dec. 1, 1721; and was living in 1740.
31—VI. JOHN³, b. Jan. 30, 1693-4. *See below* (*31*).
32—VII. MARGARET³, b. Nov. 27, 1695; living in 1710; and probably d. before 1740.
33—VIII. SAMUEL³, b. Aug. 4, 1699. *See below* (*33*).

18

REV. SIMON BRADSTREET³, born March 7, 1670-1. He graduated at Harvard college in 1693; preached at Medford (formerly Mistick) in 1697, and settled in Charlestown the same year. He was a good Greek scholar. He was settled over the church in Charlestown Oct. 26, 1698; and married Mary Long, at Charlestown, May 7, 1700. She died at Charlestown May 21, 1725; and he died Dec. 31, 1741.

Children, born in Charlestown :—

34—I. SIMON⁴, bapt. Oct. 4, 1702; d. young.
35—II. MARY⁴, b. Sept. 9, 1703; m. Rev. Hull Abbot of Charlestown July 27, 1731; and d. May 10, 1763.
36—III. SIMON⁴, b. June 23, 1709. *See below* (*36*).
37—IV. SAMUEL⁴, b. Oct. 2, 1711; lived in Charlestown; m. Sarah (Foster?) March 22, 1738-9; he d. in 1755; and she d. Feb. —, 1802, aged eighty-four.
38—V. JOHN⁴, bapt. Feb. 14, 1713-4; d. Sept. 14, 1714.

22

REV. DUDLEY BRADSTREET³, born in Andover April 27, 1678. He graduated at Harvard college in 1698; and taught school in Andover in 1704. He lived in Andover and Groton, and was a husbandman and Congregational clergyman, being ordained at Groton June 16, 1706. He married Mary Wainwright of Haverhill May 4, 1704. He was dismissed in 1712, and went to England, where he was ordained by the bishop of London into the Episcopal church April 8, 1714. He died in England, suddenly, of small pox, May —, 1714, being buried on the sixteenth of that month. He expected to preach at Marblehead. His family were with him in England; and were destitute. His wife returned to Groton, and married, sec-

ondly, John Parker, subsequently removing to Hollis, N. H.

Children :—

39—I. SIMON⁴, b. March 1, 1705-6, in Andover.

40—II. DUDLEY⁴, b. March 12, 1707-8, in Groton; lived in Groton; was a lieutenant in the expedition to Louisbourg, and at Fort Dummer, near Brattleboro, Vt., in 1747; he d. about 1750, having m. Abigail Lakin April 20, 1727.

41—III. SAMUEL⁴, b. April —, 1711, in Andover.

28

SIMON BRADSTREET³, born in Topsfield April 14, 1682. He was a yeoman, and lived in Topsfield. He married Elizabeth Capen of Topsfield Oct. 12, 1711; and died Aug. 1, 1738, in Topsfield, aged fifty-six. She survived him, and died, his widow, in Topsfield, March 22, 1781.

Children, born in Topsfield :—

42—I. ELIZABETH⁴, b. Aug. 28, 1712; m. Joseph Peabody Nov. 2, 1729; and was living in 1743.

43—II. SIMON⁴, b. April 21, 1714. See below (43).

44—III. DUDLEY⁴, b. May 27, 1716; yeoman; lived in Topsfield; d. Aug. 23, 1743; bequeathed to the church in Topsfield £7, 10s., to be laid out in plate for the use of the church.

45—IV. JOHN⁴, b. March 2, 1717-8. See below (45).

46—V. MARGARET⁴, b. April 24, 1720; m. Thomas Andrews, jr., of Boxford Nov. 27, 1739; and was living in 1743.

47—VI. PRISCILLA⁴, b. Sept. 27, 1722; probably d. before 1735.

48—VII. LUCY⁴, b. Nov. 25, 1724; m. Robert Andrews, jr., of Boxford March 19, 1746-7.

49—VIII. JOSEPH⁴, b. May 13, 1727. See below (49).

50—IX. MERCY⁴, b. Nov. 27, 1728; living in 1743.

51—X. MARY⁴, b. May 10, 1731; m. Elisha Wildes Feb. 27, 1754.

31

JOHN BRADSTREET³, born in Topsfield Jan. 30, 1693-4. He was a yeoman, and lived in Topsfield, then in Windham, and returned to Topsfield in or before 1729. He married Rebecca Andrew of Boxford Feb. 20, 1721-2; and died between 1733 and 1740 (?). She was his wife in 1733. Children, born in Topsfield :—

52—I. ANDREW⁴, b. in 1722; lived in Topsfield, weaver, and bought house and land in Boxford, 1745-6; private in company of Capt. Benjamin Hooper, stationed at Falmouth in 1776.

53—II. SARAH⁴, b. March 8, 1729-30.

54—III. BOENARGES⁴, b. July 1, 1733. This is probably "Benaiah Bradstreet" of Danvers, hatter, on whose estate administration was granted to Andrew Bradstreet of Biddeford, Me., Dec. 28, 1758.

33

SAMUEL BRADSTREET³, born in Topsfield Aug. 4, 1699. He was a yeoman, and lived in Topsfield. He married, first, Sarah Clark April 3, 1722; and she died, in Topsfield, June 19, 1736. He married, second, Elizabeth Chapman March 30, 1738; and died Dec. 1, 1762. The inventory of his estate amounted to about £1,755. His wife Elizabeth survived him, and married, secondly, Dea. Mark How of Ipswich April 26, 1763.

Children, born in Topsfield :—

55—I. ANNA⁴, b. Oct. 23, 1721; m. Benjamin Bixby March 20, 1745-6.

56—II. SARAH⁴, b. Feb. 4, 1726-7; m. —— Stuart before 1760.*

57—III. SAMUEL⁴, bapt. March 30, 1729. See below (57).

58—IV. ELIJAH⁴, b. Aug. 8, 1731. See below (58).

59—V. EUNICE⁴, b. April 15, 1733; m. Samuel Cummings Aug. 25, 1756.

60—VI. ASA⁴, b. April 20, 1736; d. April 14, 1759.

36

REV. SIMON BRADSTREET⁴, born June 23, 1709, at Charlestown. He graduated at Harvard college in 1728; and was ordained over the church at Marblehead Jan. 4, 1738. He married widow Mary Hills Nov. 16, 1738; and she died, his wife, Oct. 18, 1768, aged fifty-one. He died at Marblehead Oct. 5, 1771.

Children, born in Marblehead :—

61—I. MARY⁵, bapt. March 15, 1741.

62—II. ANN⁵, bapt. June 24, 1744; m. Richard Harris Oct. 9, 1764.

63—III. REBECCA⁵, bapt. Feb. 25, 1749.

64—IV. ——⁵, d. —— 22, 1762.

65—V. SIMON⁵, bapt. March 17, 1754.

*James Stuart married Sarah Bradstreet, July 30, 1755.--Brattle Square church.--Boston town records.

66—VI. SARAH[5], bapt. May 4, 1756; m. Gabriel Johonnot of Marblehead, merchant, before 1785.

43

SIMON BRADSTREET[4], born in Topsfield April 21, 1714. He was a yeoman, and lived in Topsfield. He married Anna Flint of Salem Dec. 16, 1740; and died in Topsfield Sept. 18, 1747, at the age of thirty-three. She survived him, and married, secondly, John Baker Feb. 2, 1748-9. She was his wife in 1763.
Children, born in Topsfield :—
67—I. HENRY[5], b. Nov. 30, 1741. See below (67).
68—II. ANNE[5], bapt. April 7, 1745; m. Amos Porter of Chelsea, cordwainer, Jan. 24, 1764, in Danvers.

45

JOHN BRADSTREET[4], born in Topsfield March 2, 1717-8. He was a yeoman, and lived in Topsfield. He married Elizabeth Fisk of Wenham Dec. 23, 1742; and she died in Topsfield Nov. 13, 1801, aged eighty-three. He died in Topsfield Nov. 22, 1807, aged eighty-nine.
Children, born in Topsfield :—
69—I. ELIZABETH[5], b. March 11, 1743-4; m. John Gould, jr., Feb. 9, 1769.
70—II. PRISCILLA[5], b. Jan. 8, 1745; m. Ens. John Killam of Boxford June 12, 1764.
71—III. MOLLY[5], b. Dec. 22, 1748.
72—IV. MARY[5], bapt. June 10, 1750; probably m. John Dodge of Beverly Jan. 31, 1780.
73—V. MEHITABLE[5], b. June 2, 1751; d. Jan. 29, 1776, in Topsfield.
74—VI. HULDAH[5], bapt. Feb. 25, 1753; d. March 7, 1753.
75—VII. HULDAH[5], b. April 15, 1754; d. Sept. 23, 1777, unmarried.
76—VIII. SARAH[5], bapt. Feb. 1, 1756; m. Daniel Gould, jr., of Boxford (pub. May 31, 1778); and d. Dec. 3, 1831.
77—IX. LUCY[5], b. March 27, 1758; d. Jan. 29, 1776, in Topsfield.
78—X. EUNICE[5], b. Aug. 16, 1760; m. Benjamin Emerson March 25, 1783.
79—XI. DUDLEY[5], b. Oct. 8, 1765. See below (79).

49

DR. JOSEPH BRADSTREET[4], born in Topsfield May 13, 1727. He was a physician in Topsfield, having studied physic in Salem Village in 1748-9. He married,

first, Abigail Fuller of Middleton Feb. 8, 1770; and she was separated from him by act of the legislature Oct. 17, 1771, it being decreed that he pay to her twenty-five pounds yearly. He married, second, widow Hannah Ross of Ipswich (published Nov. 16, 1783) ; and died in Topsfield Oct. 5, 1790, at the age of sixty-three.
Child, born in Topsfield :—
80—I. JOSEPH[5], b. March 26, 1771.

57

SAMUEL BRADSTREET[4], baptized in Topsfield March 30, 1729. He was a yeoman, and lived in Topsfield. He married Ruth Lampson of Ipswich (published Oct. 3, 1762) ; and died in Topsfield July 6 (7—gravestone), 1777, aged forty-eight. She died July 25, 1777, in Topsfield, aged forty-four. The inventory of his estate amounted to £4,150, 6s., 1½d.
Children, born in Topsfield :—
81—I. SAMUEL[5], b. Jan. 2, 1764. See below (81).
82—II. RUTH[5], b. March 8, 1766; m. Billy Emerson May 8, 1791.
83—III. ELIJAH[5], b. July 4, 1767. See below (83).
84—IV. ASA[5], b. May 29, 1769. See below (84).
85—V. JOHN[5], b. Dec. 9, 1771. See below (85).
86—VI. MOSES[5], b. Aug. 26, 1773. See below (86).

58

ELIJAH BRADSTREET[4], born in Topsfield Aug. 8, 1731. He was a yeoman, and lived in Topsfield. He married widow Martha Perkins March 9, 1758; and died, in Topsfield, Jan. 14, 1760. She married, secondly, Dea. Anthony Potter of Ipswich Oct. 20, 1762.
Child, born in Topsfield :—
87—I. ELIZABETH[5], bapt. June 24, 1759; and she d., unmarried, at her mother's house in Ipswich, Oct. 23, 1773.

67

HENRY BRADSTREET[5], born in Topsfield Nov. 30, 1741. He was a cordwainer and yeoman, and lived in Topsfield until about 1793, when he removed to Boxford. He married Abigail Porter June 15, 1769 ; and died in Boxford Sept. 2, 1818, aged seventy-six. She survived him, and died,

in Boxford, his widow, June 6, 1820, aged seventy-six.

Children, born in Topsfield :—

88—I. HENRY[6], b. July 12, 1770; d. in Topsfield March 23, 1774, aged three.
89—II. NATHANIEL[6], bapt. Oct. 6, 1771.
90—III. DANIEL[6], bapt. Feb. 14, 1773.
91—IV. BILLE[6], bapt. in 1775.

79

CAPT. DUDLEY BRADSTREET[5], born in Topsfield Oct. 8, 1765. He was a husbandman, and lived in Topsfield. He married Polly Porter of Danvers Sept. 29, 1789; and she died, his wife, May 9, 1815, aged forty-four years, one month and sixteen days. He died April 23, 1833, aged sixty-seven.

Children, born in Topsfield :—

92—I. PORTER[6], b. Dec. 1, 1789; farmer; lived in Topsfield; m. Mehitable Bradstreet (111) April 2, 1812; d. of dropsy June 25, 1849, aged fifty-nine.
93—II. JOHN[6], b. Aug. 8, 1792.
94—III. DUDLEY[6], b. Aug. 16, 1796; d., of consumption, Sept. 25, 1832, aged thirty-six.
95—IV. POLLY[6], b. Aug. 10, 1798.
96—V. JOSEPH[6], b. Nov. 10, 1800.
97—VI. ELIZABETH (Eliza)[6], b. Jan. 11, 1803.
98—VII. ALBERT GRAY[6], b. May 19, 1805.
99—VIII. THOMAS JEFFERSON[6], b. April 6, 1807.
100—IX. JONATHAN[6], b. Oct. 1, 1808.
101—X. SARAH[6], b. March 7, 1812.
102—XI. LYDIA[6], b. Nov. 30, 1813.

81

SAMUEL BRADSTREET[5], born in Topsfield Jan. 2, 1764. He was a yeoman, and lived in Topsfield. He married Matta Foster April 14, 1785; and she was his wife in 1800. His death, which occurred Nov. 26, 1816, at the age of fifty-two, was occasioned by a fall from his carriage.

Children, born in Topsfield :—

103—I. ABIGAIL[6], b. Dec. 31, 1786; m. Dudley Wildes, jr., Feb. 13, 1812.
104—II. SAMUEL[6], b. Aug. 26, 1789; probably m. Mehitable Gould, 2d, of Boxford, Oct. 25, 1810.
105—III. RUTH[6], b. Nov. 4, 1791; d., unmarried, of consumption, April 9, 1817, aged twenty-five.
106—IV. NATHANIEL[6], b. Sept. 20, 1795; d. Nov. 3, 1820, aged twenty-five.
107—V. MOSES[6], b. July 26, 1800; d. at his house in Boxford Aug. 10, 1828, twenty-eight.

83

ELIJAH BRADSTREET[5], born in Topsfield July 4, 1767. He was a blacksmith, and lived in Andover. He married Phebe Ingalls June 3, 1790.

Child, born in Andover :—

108—I. ELIZABETH INGALLS[6], b. May 28, 1791.

84

ASA BRADSTREET[5], born in Topsfield May 29, 1769. He was a cordwainer, and lived in Topsfield. He married Nabby Balch Nov. 30, 1790; and was "killed by ye wheels of a loaded waggon, which passed over his head," Oct. —, 1793, in Topsfield. His age was twenty-four years. She survived him, and married, secondly, Daniel Perkins, jr., Nov. 19, 1795. She was living in 1802. Mr. Bradstreet's estate was valued at £544, 5s., 9d.

Children, born in Topsfield :—

109—I. WILLIAM[6], b. June 26, 1792; lived in Topsfield; and m. Eunice Perkins (pub. March 20, 1814).
110—II. ASA[6], b. Sept. 8, 1793.

85

CAPT. JOHN BRADSTREET[5], born in Topsfield Dec. 9, 1771. He was a cordwainer, and lived in Topsfield. He married, first, Miss Mehitable Balch Jan. 9, 1793; and she died Oct. 4, 1815, aged thirty-seven years and eight and one-half months. He married, second, Priscilla Howe of Ipswich (published Jan. 21, 1821); and died in Topsfield April 4, 1825, aged fifty-three. His wife Priscilla survived him, and married, secondly, Samuel Conant. sr., of Wenham Oct. 16, 1834.

Children, born in Topsfield :—

111—I. MEHITABLE[6], b. March 29, 1793; m. Porter Bradstreet (92) April 2, 1812.
112—II. CORNELIUS BALCH[6], b. Oct. 30, 1796; lived in Topsfield; and m. Eunice Bradstreet (124) Oct. 17, 1820.
113—III. RUTH[6], b. Feb. 16, 1799; m. Solomon Wildes of Boston Jan. 29, 1826.
114—IV. CYNTHIA[6], b. Nov. 3, 1802; m. Samuel Tole Oct. 29, 1826.
115—V. JOSIAH[6], b. Sept. 25, 1804.
116—VI. ——[6], d. Aug. 19, 1808.
117—VII. JOHN[6], b. Nov. 11, 1811; d., of consumption, in Topsfield, Sept. 10, 1847, aged thirty-five.

ᵢₛ–VIII. —— (son)ᵘ (twin), b. July 21, 1815; d. Aug. 5, 1815.
ᵢ₉–IX. —— (son)ᵉ (twin), b. July 21, 1815; d. Aug. 11, 1815.
ₐᵢ–X. ELIZABETH DAYᵈ, b. July 30, 1823; d. Feb. 22, 1835, aged eleven.

86

MOSES BRADSTREET⁵, born in Topsfield Aug. 26, 1773. He was a yeoman, and lived in Topsfield. He married Lydia Peabody May 7, 1795; and died Oct. 29, 1801, aged twenty-eight. She survived him, and married, secondly, John Wright Nov. 2, 1803.

Children, born in Topsfield :—

21–I. LYDIA⁶, bapt. Oct. 12, 1800; m. Nehemiah Perkins (pub. Feb. 23, 1817).
22–II. CYNTHIA⁶, bapt. Oct. 12, 1800; d. Oct. 14, 1801.
23–III. PHEBE⁶, bapt. Oct. 12, 1800; m. Solomon Wildes of Topsfield Oct. 4, 1818.
24–IV. EUNICE⁶, bapt. Oct. --, 1801; m. Cornelius B. Bradstreet (112) Oct. 17, 1820.

DESCENDANTS OF HUMPHREY BRADSTREET.

HUMPHREY BRADSTREET¹, born about 1594, came to Ipswich from Ipswich in England, in the ship Elizabeth, in 1634. His wife Elizabeth, born about 1604, and four children, came with him. He was a yeoman, and lived in Ipswich, on the Rowley line. He died in 1655, having been a representative in 1635. His will, dated July 21, 1655, was proved 25 : 7 : 1655. In it he bequeathed one pound to the poor of Ipswich and one pound to the poor of Rowley. He requested to be buried in Rowley. She survived him, and died, his widow, Nov. —, 1665, in Ipswich.

Children :—

1–I. HANNAH², b. about 1625; m., first, Daniel Rolfe of Ipswich before 1650; and, second, Nicholas Holt of Andover June 12, 1658; and d. June 20, 1665.
3–II. JOHN², b. about 1631; of Rowley, husbandman, 1652; of Marblehead, planter, in 1657, and seaman in 1658; his father gave him a farm at Muddy river; inventory of his estate taken June 14, 1660, when he d. probably.

4–III. MARTHA², b. about 1632; m. William Beale of Marblehead before 1655; and d. April 6, 1675.
5–IV. MARY², b. about 1633; m. John Kimball of Ipswich between 1655 and 1665.
6–V. SARAH², b. in 1638; m. Nicholas Wallis of Ipswich April 13, 1657; and was living in 1665.
7–VI. MOSES², b. about 1644. *See below* (7).
8–VII. REBECCA², m. George Bonfield of Marblehead before 1665.

7

CAPT. MOSES BRADSTREET², was a husbandman, and lived in Ipswich until about 1668, when his residence changed to Rowley. His farm was on the line between Ipswich and Rowley, and perhaps an actual removal did not occur. He married Elizabeth Harris March 11, 1661, and she was his wife in 1667. He had a wife in 1690 who had children by a former husband. He died Aug. 17, 1690. In his will he devised his farm, which had been his father's, to his sons John and Moses. The inventory of his estate amounted to £1,284, 7s., 9d.

Children :—

9–I. JOHN³. *See below* (9).
10–II. MOSES³, b. Oct. 17, 1665, in Ipswich. *See below* (10).
11–III. ELIZABETH³, b. March 22, 1667, in Ipswich; m. Samuel Pickard June 22, 1685; and probably d. before 1691.
12–IV. HUMPHREY³, b. Jan. 6, 1669-70, in Ipswich. *See below* (12).
13–V. BRIDGET³, minor in 1690.
14–VI. ——³ (dau.), minor in 1690.
15–VII. NATHANIEL³. *See below* (15).
16–VIII. JONATHAN³, b. about 1690. *See below* (16).

9

JOHN BRADSTREET³ was a mariner, and lived in Ipswich. He married Hannah Dummer Jan. 29, 1690-1; and died in the island of Barbadoes July 21, 1699. The inventory of his estate amounted to about £500. He owned an interest in the sloop Unity. She survived him, and married, secondly, Nathaniel Elithrop of Boston Dec. 3, 1700. She was the latter's wife in 1711.

Children :—

17–I. MOSES⁴, b. Nov. 11, 1691, in Rowley; m. Martha Beal July 28, 1713, in Marblehead.

18—II. ELIZABETH[4], b. about 1694; m. John Slaughter before 1711; and he was living in Boston in 1715.

19—III. HANNAH[4], b. about 1697; of Boston in 1718.

10

MOSES BRADSTREET[3], born in Ipswich Oct. 17, 1665. He was a yeoman, and lived in Rowley until about 1700, when he settled in Ipswich. He married, first, Hannah Pickard of Rowley July 19, 1686; and she died Jan. 3, 1737. He married, second, widow Dorothy Northend of Rowley Oct. 27, 1737, and died in Ipswich Dec. 20, 1737, aged seventy-three. She was his widow in 1742. His estate was valued at £6,392, 13s., 6d.

Children, born in Rowley:—

20—I. SAMUEL[4], b. May 4, 1687 (his mother is called "Sarah" in the record of his birth).

21—II. ELIZABETH[4], b. April 19, 1689; m. Abraham Parker of Bradford (pub. 5: 3: 1711); and was living in 1743.

22—III. HANNAH[4], b. April 11, 1694; m. Jacob Wood of Boxford (pub. Dec. 6, 1713); and he d. before 1740.

23—IV. BRIDGET[4], b. March 17, 1695-6; d. July 22, 1718, aged twenty-two.

24—V. MOSES[4]. See below (24).

25—VI. NATHANIEL[4], b. about 1705. See below (25).

12

DR. HUMPHREY BRADSTREET[3], born in Ipswich Jan. 6, 1669-70. He was a physician, and lived in Newbury. He married Sarah Pierce of Newbury in or before 1692; and died in Newbury May 11, 1717, at the age of forty-seven. The inventory of his estate amounted to £2,754. He had real estate in Amesbury, Rowley, Newbury and Salisbury, and in Wells alias Cockshall. She survived him, and married, secondly, Capt. Edward Sargent of Newbury June 9, 1719; and she was the latter's wife in 1728.

Children, born in Newbury:—

26—I. DOROTHY[4], b. Dec. 19, 1692; m. Nathaniel Sargent in Newbury Oct. 16, 1710; and was living in 1779.

27—II. JOSHUA[4], b. Feb. 23, 1694-5, in Rowley; drowned May 16, 1710, in Newbury, aged fifteen.

28—III. SARAH[4], b. Jan. 14, 1696-7, in Rowley; m. John Tufts Nov. 9, 1714; living in 1779.

29—IV. HUMPHREY[4], born about 1698; was educated as a physician, and d. in Newbury Dec. 19, 1717, aged nineteen.

30—V. DANIEL[4], b. Feb. 15, 1700-1; was physician; wife Mary; lived in Newbury; d. April 24, 1723, aged twenty-two; his estate was appraised £286, 15s.; his wife Mary survived him.

31—VI. ANNA[4], minor in 1717; m. Benjamin Mondy Nov. 7, 1728; and was living in 1779.

32—VII. BENJAMIN[4]. See below (32).

33—VIII. MOSES[4], b. Feb. 7, 1707. See below (33).

34—IX. BETTY[4], b. May 16, 1713; m. Rev. William Johnson, jr., of Newbury Aug. 30, 1731; and was living 1779.

15

NATHANIEL BRADSTREET[3], lived in Rowley. He married Priscilla Carrell Oct. 16, 1687, in Rowley; and "dyed in ye Canada Voyage 1690." She was his widow in 1691; and probably married Samuel Todd April 26, 1694, in Rowley.

Child, born in Rowley:—

35—I. PRISCILLA[4], b. Sept. 22, 1689; m. Nehemiah Jewett June 14, 1707, in Rowley.

16

CAPT. JONATHAN BRADSTREET[3], born about 1690. He was a yeoman, and lived in Rowley until 1740, when he settled in Lunenburg, where he was an officer of the town and influential citizen. He married Sarah Wheeler of Rowley Nov. 7, 1710; and she was living in 1739. He died in Lunenburg May 22, 1757.

Children, born in Rowley:—

36—I. SAMUEL[4], b. Aug. 9, 1711. See below (36).

37—II. MARY[4], b. May 5, 1714; m. David Chaplin of Rowley Jan. 10, 1737-8.

38—III. JONATHAN[4], b. Feb. 11, 1719-20; lived in Lunenburg; and m. Olive Whitlock of Leominster July 2, 1741.

39—IV. SARAH[4], b. Jan. 11, 1726-7; m. James Colburn of Lunenburg Aug. 12, 1742.

24

MOSES BRADSTREET[4], lived in Ipswich. He married Mary Coburne of Dracut (published March 14, 1723); and died before June 10, 1727, when administration was granted upon his estate. She survived him.

Children :—

40—I. MOSES[5], b. about 1723; living in 1737.
41—II. MARY[5], b. about 1725; m. Samuel Colburn of Dracut before 1747.
42—III. ABIGAIL[5], living in 1740, minor.

25

LT. NATHANIEL BRADSTREET[4], born about 1705. He was a yeoman, and lived in Ipswich. He married, first, Miss Hannah Northend of Rowley April 19, 1727; and she died in Ipswich April 13, 1739. He married, second, Hannah Hammond Aug. 15, 1739; and died in Ipswich Dec. 2, 1752, at the age of forty-seven. He had negroes; and his estate was valued at £2,510, 3s., 4d. His wife Hannah survived him, and died, his widow, in 1792, her will, dated Oct. 26, 1787, being proved May 7, 1792.

Children :—

43—I. MOSES[5], b. Jan. 29, 1727-8, in Ipswich; and was living in 1752.
44—II. ELIZABETH[5], m. Samuel Plummer of Newbury April 14, 1764; and d. before 1787.
45—III. HANNAH[5], b. Nov. 12, 1731, in Ipswich; living in 1752.
46—IV. MARY[5], m. Nathan Person of Ipswich, yeoman, before 1787.
47—V. NATHANIEL[5], b. July 17, 1740, in Ipswich. See below (47).
48—VI. JOHN[5], minor in 1752; of Ipswich, yeoman, 1768-1779; of New Castle, Me., yeoman, 1782; and was living in 1787.
49—VII. SARAH[5], m. Samuel Coburn, jr., of Dracut Dec. 13, 1781.

32

REV. BENJAMIN BRADSTREET[4]. He was a clergyman, and lived in Newbury until 1728, when he settled in Gloucester. He married Sarah Greenleaf Nov. 9, 1726, in Newbury; and died in 1763, his will, dated Sept. 8, 1760, being proved April 4, 1763. His estate, which was insolvent, was appraised at £197, 11s., 8d. She survived him, and was his widow in 1770, living in Gloucester. She probably died Jan. 15, 1779, at the age of seventy.

Children :—

50—I. HUMPHREY[5]. See below (50).
51—II. SARAH[5], b. March 2, 1730, in Gloucester; and was living in 1760.
52—III. THOMASINE[5], b. May 22, 1732, in Gloucester; m. George Denison Feb. 2, 1749.

53—IV. MARTHA[5], living in 1760.
54—V. ELIZABETH[5], m. James Day July 1, 1762.
55—VI. MARY[5], pub. to Timothy Harraden Dec. 8, 1761.

33

MOSES BRADSTREET[4], born in Newbury Feb. 7, 1707. He was a joiner, and lived in Newbury, in that part which was incorporated as Newburyport in 1764. He married Mary Sayward of Gloucester Feb. 16, 1730-1, in Gloucester; and died in Newburyport March 9, 1785, at the age of seventy-seven. She was his wife in 1779.

Children :—

56—I. MARY[5], b. Jan. 15, 1731, in Newbury.
57—II. SARAH[5], b. Jan. 20, 1732, in Newbury.
58—III. BETTY[5], unmarried, of Newburyport, spinster, 1788.

36

SAMUEL BRADSTREET[4], born in Rowley Aug. 9, 1711. He married Dorcas Spofford of Rowley Nov. 9, 1736; and lived in the west parish of Rowley (now the town of Georgetown) until 1739, when they settled in Lunenburg, where he died in 1761.

Children :—

59—I. JOHN[5], b. Sept. 12, 1737, in Rowley; d. at Lunenburg Aug. 30, 1756, aged eighteen.
60—II. SARAH[5], b. July 24, 1740, in Lunenburg.
61—III. DORCAS[5], b. April 7, 1743, in Lunenburg; m. Ezekiel Fowler of Fitchburg Oct. 25, 1768.
62—IV. ABIGAIL[5], b. May 19, 1745, in Lunenburg; d. Dec. 9, 1754, aged nine.
63—V. OLIVE[5], b. May 19, 1748, in Lunenburg.
64—VI. PHEBE[5], b. Sept. 10, 1750, in Lunenburg.
65—VII. MARY[5], b. Aug. 1, 1752, in Lunenburg.
66—VIII. RELIEF[5], b. June 2, 1754, in Lunenburg; m. George Henry.
67—IX. SAMUEL[5], b. June 17, 1757, in Lunenburg.
68—X. ABIGAIL[5], b. Jan. 2, 1759, in Lunenburg.
69—XI. VASHTI[5], b. July 2, 1761, in Lunenburg, posthumous; m. Joel Manning of Townsend.

47

NATHANIEL BRADSTREET[5], born in Ipswich July 17, 1740. He was a yeoman, and lived in Ipswich. He married Elizabeth ——, before 1763; and they were living in Ipswich in 1772.

Children, born in Ipswich : —

70—I.   ELIZABETH[6], b. Sept. 9, 1763.
71—II. DAVID[6], b. Sept. 18, 1765.
72—III. DANIEL[6], b. March 9, 1768.
73—IV. NATHAN[6], b. May 7, 1770.
74—V.   PHOEBE[6], b. Dec. 31, 1772.

50

HUMPHREY BRADSTREET[5], lived in Gloucester in 1758, and in Marblehead in 1759. He married Ann Reed May 4, 1758, in Marblehead.

Child, born in Marblehead :—

75—I.   ANN[6], bapt. Feb. 18, 1759.

WILL OF REV. WILLIAM WORCESTER.

The will of Rev. William Worcester of Salisbury was proved before Samuel Symonds and Daniel Denison Dec. 2, 1662. in the Norfolk county court. The following copy was made from the original on file in the probate office at Salem.

I willi: Worcester being ‖ Sick & ‖ weake of body but of found & pfect memorie doe make & ordeine this my laft will & Teftam[t] as followeth:

Imp my will is that my beloved wyfe: fhall haue that bonde of fiftie pound w[ch] is due vnto me from Thomas clark of Bofton Iron munger: fhe fecureing my daughter in Law Rebecka Bilie of w[t] remaynes due to hir out of y[t] bonde

Alfo my will is that my wyfe fhall haue the vfe & benefit of my dwelling houfe oarchyard & houfe lott duering the time of hir widohood ; & three cowes comonage : duering y[e] fd term

Alfo that my wyfe fhall haue w[t] moneys foever as due in England : for rent : for w[t] lands & houfeing belongs vnto her: or may otherwayes be given vnto her, or any other wayes due

Itt : I doe give & bequeath vnto my Sonn Samuell worcefter my laft higledee pigledee lott of Salt marfh lyng toward Merimack Rivers mouth : & alfo a filve wine bole that hath y[o] letters of his name ingraven vppon it & a thoufand of p board towards the finifhing of his houfe as alfo all my wareing Apparrell ; my minde is y[t] my grandchilde willia : worcefter * * Samuels childe fhall haue y[t] Sylver wine boule * * named

Itt : I doe give & bequeath to my daughter Sufana f * * my pide mare Colt : :

Itt : I doe give vnto my grand childe Rebecka ftacy five pound in houfhold ftuff : fuch as her grandmother fhal thinke meet

It : I doe give & bequeathe to my Sonne william worcefter all my vpland w[th]in y[e] bounds of the new towne of Salifbury : w[th] all rights & privilidges thereunto belonging as alfo my firft Higgle pigledee lott of Salt Marfh : & all my lott of Sweepage at the beache : by my land at y[e] newtown: my meaning is : my twenty acre lott butting vpon merimack River & the fevnty acres granted vnto mee by the towne of Salifbury lyng next : to the land of Cap[t] Pike : n efterly:

Itt : I doe give & bequeath vnto my Sone Timothie worcefter & to my Sonn Mofes wofter all the remaynder of my lands both vpland Marfh & meadow lyng & being w[th]in the bounds of the old towne of Salifbury w[th] all rights, Conomages & privilidges thervnto belonging (Except before Exepted) to bee equally divided between them : pfently after my deceafe Alfo I doe give vnto my faid Sonns Timothe & Mofes: my dwelling houfe, orchyard & houfe Lott : after their mothers death or day of mariage w[ch] firft happens : to bee equally divided between them & to haue the barne pfently after my deceafe wth free egrefs & regrefs vnto y[e] fd barne : to cary hay or corne or y[e] like : Always pvided that the marfh Lott w[ch] was formerly my wyfes by hir former hufband m[r] John Hall : remayne to the

*Turn off.

. : of my Said wyfe hir heires & affignes
. :r ever.

It: I doe giue & bequeath vnto my
.ne william : my pide mare : & a cowe
. .t is cald fhort & fiue povnd in houf-
.ld goods : : all other guifts by any to
.y faid fonne being Comp'hended in y'
.ueffd eftate giuen ‖ by me ‖ vnto him

It: I doe giue & bequeath vnto my
.ne Timothy my old horfe : & a cowe
.ld : Cherry & fiue pound in houfhold
.ods.

It: I doe giue & bequeath vnto my
.nne Mofes my young mare between
.o & three yeare old & alfo the young
.fer & fiue pound in houfehold goods:

It: I doe giue vnto my grandchild
willia worcefter: my Cow cald the Bar-
l.r

It: I do giue vnto my Daughter ftacy :
.' cowe which is cald the young cowe : &
.o my two yearling fteers

It: I doe giue vnto my grand Childe
Rebecka ftacy : my two yeare old fteeref

It: my will is that all the Cattle : before
.amed in this my will : be wintered w'h
.e hay pvide for them if y° owners pleafe

I doe giue vnto my Daughter Rebecka :
Bylie : my braff Chafendifh ; & alfo I giue
.nto her a booke of m' Anthony Burgafes
.ncerning the tryalls of grace, as a fmall
.ken of my Specyall loue vnto hir

It: I doe giue vnto my fervant mayde
Hannah Hendrick : tenn fhillings

It: I doe appoint my loueing freinds
Capt Robert Pike my brother Edward
.rench : Richard wells & m' Tho : Brad-
.ry to bee overfeers of this my will &
.eftam' & for the care & paynes theirin
I doe bequeath vnto each of them twenty
fhillings to bee payd vnto them : out of
my library in fome good ‖ Englifh ‖
.utho'', as they fhall like off

Laftly my will is that my dearly &
welbeeloued wyfe : Rebecka worcefter to
.ee my fole Executrix vnto this my laft
will & teftament

It: my will is that after my wyfe hath
.ken hir owne books out of my library &
.' others fhal think meet for hir vfe ; &

y° • ond x syd in books to
my overfeers as afore   • •
books fhalbe fold   • •
s willia : Timathie   • •
portion :

It : my will is that all   • •
difcharged & pay'd the   • •
remayne & bee to y'   • •
utrix afore named

In wittnefs wherof   • •
hervnto fett my hand
wittnefs

Tho : Bradbury   • •
Robert Pyke
Edward ffrench
Richard Wells
wheras it is be   • •
remainder of   • •
giuen to my Sonns   • •
to each an equall p   • •
that my books fhalbe   • •
yte : to difpofe of a   • •
I haue giuen to my   • •
this 18th day of Octobr   • •

wittnefs to this laft addicon of the will
Tho : Bradbury
John Severance

NOTES.

Eliza, daughter of Samuel and Abigail
Bowers, born July 7, 1797.—*Newburyport
town records.*

Philip Bowers of Billerica married Chloe
Frye June 23, 1796 ; and had son, John
Frye, born Dec. 21, 1796.—*Andover
town records.*

Joseph Bowree of Marblehead married
Hannah Dwinel of Topsfield, at Topsfield,
Jan. 24, 1728-9.

Hannah Bowrey married Isaac Curtis
Oct. 5, 1733.

Hannah, daughter of Hannah Bowery,
baptized Sept. 5, 1731.

Child of Joseph Bowery died April 12,
1730.

—*Topsfield records.*

•Torn off.

BRAGG GENEALOGY.

EDWARD BRAGG[1], born in England about 1616, lived in Ipswich, Mass., as early as 1642, where he was a servant of Mr. Symonds. He became a real estate owner, and a yeoman. He married, first, Elizabeth Whittridge in 164–; and she died May 28, 1691. He married, second, widow Sarah Reddington Oct. 28, 1691; and died, in old age, in 1707. In his will, dated April 26, 1705, and proved Aug. 16, 1708, he gave three pounds to be laid out in a piece of plate for the church, of which he was a member. Robert Kinsman had taken care of him and his wife for several years before his decease. His wife Sarah survived him.

Children, born in Ipswich :—

2—I.   THOMAS[2], born about 1649; lived in Ipswich; m. Phebe Reddington Aug. 24, 1675; and d. Sept. 2, 1675. She married, secondly, Samuel Fiske 6 : 9 mo: 1679, in Wenham.

3—II.   MARY[2], b. about 1650; m. Joseph Eveleth of Ipswich Jan. 1, 1667-8, in Gloucester; she d. Jan. 22, 1713-4; and he was living in Ipswich in 1735.

4—III. TIMOTHY[2], b. about 1652. See below (4).

5—IV.   DEBORAH[2], b. Dec. 22, 1658; m. William Searl of Rowley before 1690; and d. between 1699 and 1705.

4

TIMOTHY BRAGG[2], born in Ipswich about 1652. He was a yeoman, and lived in Ipswich. He married Lydia Gott Feb. 24, 1685; and died before Jan. 6, 1706-7, when administration was granted upon his estate. She survived him; and married, secondly, Jacob Bennett Aug. 27, 1709.

Children, born in Ipswich :—

6—I.   LYDIA[3], b. Nov. 28, 1686.

7—II.   JOHN[3], b. in 1688; eldest son; yeoman; lived in Ipswich in 1710, and in Scarborough, York county, in 1724; m. Mary Bennett May 28, 1711, in Ipswich.

8—III. TIMOTHY[3], b. June 5, 1690. See below (8).

9—IV.   EDWARD[3], b. July 10, 1692. See below (9).

10—V.   NATHANIEL[3], b. Aug. 8, 1694; d. June —, 1699.

11—VI. THOMAS[3], b. Sept. 1, 1696; d. June —, 1699.

12—VII. EBENEZER[3], b. Nov. 13, 1699; carpenter; lived in Marlborough until 17— and removed to Shrewsbury; m. Zeruiah Brigham March 16, 1725, Marlborough; she d. in Shrewsbury July 1, 1736, aged thirty-eight; he second, Sarah ———; and d. Shrewsbury Sept. 4, 1766, aged six.

13—VIII. NATHANIEL[3], b. Dec. 12, 1701. See below (13).

14—IX. ELIZABETH[3], b. Jan. 17, 1704; m. Josiah Kimball of Wenham July 1723; and was living there in 1725.

15—X.   ARIEL[3], b. about 1706; d. in 1723; married. She was lost in a burning house in Shrewsbury.*

8

TIMOTHY BRAGG[3], born in Ipswich June 5, 1690. He was a yeoman, and lived Ipswich. He married Martha Killam Wenham Dec. 23, 1714; and she died his wife, in Ipswich, Dec. 27, 1754.

Children, born in Ipswich :—

16—I.   TIMOTHY[4], bapt. 23: —: 1718. See below (16).

17—II. JOHN[4], a minor in 1723.

9

EDWARD BRAGG[3], born in Ipswich July 10, 1692. He was a carpenter and yeoman, and lived in Wenham as early 1715, and removed from there to Andover about 1720. From Andover removed to Reading about 1728. He married Mary Bridges May 21, 1715, Beverly; and she was his wife in 1729. He died before 1736.

Children :

18—I.   EDWARD[4], b. March 11, 1716, in Wenham. See below (18).

19—II. SARAH[4], b. June 1, 1718, in Wenham.

20—III. THOMAS[4], b. March 2, 1720-1, in Andover. See below (20).

21—IV. LYDIA[4], b. Oct. 9, 1723, in Andover.

22—V.   JOSIAH[4], b. Aug. 23, 1726, in Andover living in 1741.

23—VI. RUTH[4], b. Feb. 10, 1729, in Reading.

24—VII. JOHN[4], b. Sept. 10, 1731, in Reading; cordwainer; lived in Andover; m. Anne Parker of Andover May 8, 1758; living in Andover in 1784.

13

NATHANIEL BRAGG[3], born in Ipswich Dec. 12, 1701. He was a housewright and lived in Wenham until about 17—

*Charles L. Clarke, New York City.

..en he removed to Topsfield. He mar-
-l, first, Mary Trow May 7, 1722; and
e died Dec. 17, 1750, aged about forty-
-.at. He married, second, Mrs. Debo-
.:. Patch of Beverly Dec. 5, 1751; and
..e died June 25, 1756. He married,
..d, Mrs. Ruth Meachem of Beverly
...il 27, 1757; and she died in Wenham
:b. 4, 1784. He died in Topsfield May
.., 1790, aged eighty-eight.
Children, born in Wenham:—

:5-I. MARY⁴, b. Nov. 6, 1722; d. Nov. 10, 1722.
:8-II. MARY⁴, b. Oct. 24, 1723; m. Israel Herrick Feb. 21, 1744-5.
:7-III. BENJAMIN⁴, b. Nov. 22, 1726; d. in Wenham May 8, 1759.
:8-IV. SARAH⁴, b. May 20, 1728; m. Ephraim Towne of Topsfield March 30, 1749; and d., his widow, in Topsfield, Aug. 9, 1800, aged seventy-two.
:9-V. LYDIA⁴, b. Sept. 12, 1730; probably m. James Meachem, jr., of Beverly Sept. 3, 1751.
:0-VI. MOLLY⁴, b. Aug. 31, 1752; m. Jonathan Fiske of Wenham Nov. 26, 1772.
:1-VII. MERCY⁴, b. Feb. 25, 1754; m. Ebenezer Larrabee of Danvers May 27, 1773; and d. Dec. 11, 1775, aged twenty-one.
:2-VIII. NATHANIEL⁴, b. Dec. 4, 1755.

16

TIMOTHY BRAGG⁴, baptized in Ipswich
:3:--: 1718. He was a yeoman, and
.ved in Ipswich. He married Elizabeth
.ow Jan. 24, 1740; and she died June
:3, 1791. He died in Ipswich Dec. 25,
:79S.

Children, born in Ipswich:—

:3-I. ELIZABETH⁵, bapt. March 14, 1742; m. John Harris Dec. 12, 1765; and d. before 1793.
:4-II. SAMUEL⁵, bapt. Dec. 16, 1744; yeoman; lived in Ipswich as late as 1779, and in Dover, N. H., in 1795; m. Mary, widow of James Kinsman of Ipswich Aug. 17, 1765; and she was his wife in 1795.
:5-III. MARTHA⁵, bapt. Aug. 16, 1747.
:9-IV. MARY⁵, bapt. July 16, 1749; m. Capt. Joseph Steel Jan. 18, 1789; and was his wife in 1793.
:7-V. JOSEPH⁵, bapt. Feb. 17, 1750.
:8-VI. MARGARET⁵, of Ipswich, singlewoman, 1799.
:9-VII. NATHANIEL⁵, bapt. Sept. 1, 1754.

18

EDWARD BRAGG⁴, born in Wenham
March 11, 1716. He lived in Andover;
and married Anne —— before 1744.
They lived in Andover in 1751.
Children:—

40-I. ANNE⁵, b. April 24, 1743-4, in Andover.
41-II. SARAH⁵, b. Feb. 2, 1745, in Reading.
42-III. EDWARD⁵, b. June 22, 1748, in Andover; d. young.
43-IV. EDWARD⁵, b. June 8, 1751, in Andover.

20

THOMAS BRAGG⁴, born in Andover
March 2, 1720-1. He was a cordwainer
and yeoman; and was called "gentleman" in the latter part of his life. He
was an innholder in 1762 and 1763; and
deputy sheriff from 1770 until his death.
He married Miss Deborah Ingalls March
5, 1746; and died before Nov. 3, 1788,
when administration was granted upon
his estate. Although his estate was appraised at £1,228, 3s., 10d., it was insolvent, and his creditors received about
twenty-seven per cent of their claims. He
had land in Andover, Methuen and Sud-
bury-Canada, and a saw-mill in Goffstown,
N. H. His wife survived him.
Children, born in Andover:—

44-I. DORCAS⁵, b. Feb. 4, 1746-7; d. Dec. 12, 1748.
45-II. RUTH⁵, b. June 26, 1748; m. Jonathan Abbot, 5th, of Andover Nov. 10, 1768; he d. in Andover, Me.. Jan. 25, 1823; and she d. there Jan. 26, 1833.
46-III. DORCAS⁵, b. April 27, 1751; m. Samuel Farnum of Andover Feb. 22, 1775.
47-IV. INGALLS⁵, b. June 24, 1753. See below (47).
48-V. SUSANNA⁵, b. Aug. 19, 1755; m. Jonathan Stevens of Andover Dec. 15, 1773; he d. in Andover in 1834; and she d. there in 1840.
49-VI. SARAH⁵, b. Oct. 1, 1757; d. Nov. 26, 1758, aged one year.
50-VII. SARAH⁵, b. June 14, 1759; m. Enoch Adams of Newbury Aug. 6, 1778; and lived in Andover, where he was an innholder. They removed to Andover, Me., where she d. July 9, 1801.
51-VIII. LYDIA⁵, b. June 19, 1763; m. Isaac Poor of Andover April 28, 1791.
52-IX. HANNAH⁵, b. June 14, 1767; m.-Elijah Carter of Reading Nov. 29, 1792.

47

INGALLS BRAGGS, born in Andover June 24, 1753. He was a currier and yeoman, and lived in Andover. He married, first, Mary Frye May 9, 1776; and they were living in Andover in 1791. They removed to Andover, Me., where she died June 13, 1796. He married, second, Dorothy (Shattuck), widow of Jacob Russell, in Bethel, Me., Nov. 2, 1803; and died in Andover, Me., Jan. 1, 1808. His wife Dorothy survived him, and married, third, Daniel Gage of Bethel, who died Feb. 22, 1848, aged eighty-seven. She died in Bethel Jan. 24, 1852, aged eighty-eight.

Children :

53—I. INGALLS[6], b. July 15, 1777, in Andover, Mass.; lived in Andover, Me.; m. Betsey Gardner, in Gloucester, Feb. 13, 1809; and d. in Andover Dec. 11, 1840.

54—II. MOLLY[6], b. April 29, 1779, in Andover, Mass.; m. Lt. Stephen Holt of Andover June 1, 1806; and d. in Albany, Me., Aug. 17, 1823.

55—III. ELIZABETH[6], b. March 16, 1781, in Andover, Mass.; d. in Andover, Me., unmarried, April 8, 1856, aged seventy-five.

56—IV. DOLLY[6], b. Feb. 4, 1783, in Andover, Mass.; m. Moses Merrill of Newbury May 6, 1810; and d. in Andover, Me., June 16, 1848.

57—V. THOMAS[6], b. April 7, 1785, in Andover, Mass.; lived in Andover, Me.; farmer; m. Sophia Farrington; and d. in Upton, Me., Feb. 2, 1840.

58—VI. JAMES FRYE[6], b. Dec. 4, 1787, in Andover, Mass.; m. Sarah Graham March 21, 1811, in Rumford, Me.; and d. in Errol, N. H., May 30, 1876.

59—VII. —— (dau.)[6] (twin), b. Jan. 27, 1790; lived one hour.

60—VIII. —— (dau.)[6] (twin), b. Jan. 27, 1790; lived one hour.

61—IX. PAMELA[6], b. Aug. 31, 1791, in Andover; m. Stephen Lovejoy Nov. 8, 1812; and d. in Andover, Me., Jan. 28, 1878.

62—X. SUKEY[6], b. July 21, 1794; d. in Andover, Me., Jan. 19, 1795.

63—XI. SUKEY[6], b. Jan. 19, 1796, in Andover, Me.; d. June 23, 1797.

64—XII. WILLIAM[6], b. Oct. 4, 1804, in Andover, Me.; m., first, Sarah Manning of New Gloucester, Me.; she d. at Bridgton, Me., Aug. 9, 1831; m., second, Eliza Manning; and d. in Boston, Mass.

65—XIII. WASHINGTON INGALLS[6], b. Feb. 22, 1808, in Andover, Me.; graduate Medical school of Bowdoin college; physician; m. Katherine P. Wood (pub. March 17, 1842); and d. in Hartford, Me., Dec. 23, 1843.

WILL OF MRS. MARY SMITH.

The will of Mrs. Mary Smith of Marblehead was proved before William Hathorne 25 : 2 : 1663, and received in the court at Ipswich May 5, 1663. The following copy is transcribed from the original on file in the office of the probate court at Salem.

Marblehed the 28th daye of march 1663.

The last will and Testament of Mary Smith wife vnto the late, Jeames Smith of mabelhed aforsed That is to saye, I bequeth my Soule to God, & my body, to [be] buried at marbelhed at the vsuall place of buring

Nextly I giue my great Braffe kittell vnto my daughter Cathoron Eborne. And for all my peuter, I giue, to boath my Dafters Catharon, And Marye, to be equally shared between them. Allso I giue all my linning vnto my too daughters aforesaied, to be equally shared between them. And my too great Chares I giue the one to my dafter Catheron and the other, to my Dafter Mary Rouland aboued And my tabell, & stooles, I giue to my dafter mary Rouland, and allso the great Chest, Allso my spitt, dripping pan, the smothen Iron, and gridiron. And for my grand childeren, I giue & Conferr vnto Samuell Rouland, and Joseph Rouland all the legafes that my husband Jeames Smith, left for them, And three pounds which is yet behind vnpaid* vnto my grand *child mary Eborne ; And these three Legasies* I doo heerby order and apoynt my tennant Samuell Cutler to* paye, *That is to say tenn* pounds to Samuell aforesaied and five pounds to Joseph & three pounds to mary Eborne, as

* These italicized words are supplied from a copy made at the time, being torn off the original will. The copy referred to is on file in the office of the clerk of courts at Salem, volume IX, leaf 11.

aboue. Morouer I giue to my dafter Mary Roulands fiue children, fiue Cows to each of them one, And for my dafter Catherons Children, I giue to Mary and Rebeca Eboron, each of them a Cow, And the Reft of my Cattell, being three fteers, a heffer & a Calfe of a yeer ould I giue vnto my dafter Cathorons fouer younger Children nanly mofes Hanna & Ieames & Sara; to be equally deuided amongft them, only my will is that Ieames fhall haue the thre yeer ould fteere. My fether bed too bolfters I giue vnto my grandchild Samuell Eborne, and allfo my lron-pott. And to marye Eboron, I giue my littell Joynt Chare, and my Box to Rebeca Eboron, And as for all debts that is dew to me, my on debts, that fhall appeere dew to my Creditors being payed, the Reft I giue & bequeth to my too dafters Catheron Ebron, and Mary Rouland aboufaied.

Allfo, I giue vnto my son Ieames Smith my ffethe bed in the Parler, with all things that doo belong vnto itt, with the bedfteede, My mare, and my Hors I giue vnto my Sonn Ieames to be Improued for his Children, the mare being now in fould, the Coalt when it falls I giue to my to grandchildren Samuell & Jofep Rouland My great Cobber I giue to my dafter Eboren, af allfo my Round tabell, & an Iron fkillet, My Pott I giue to my grandchild Mary Rouland my great Iron kittell I giue to my grandchild Mary Eboron, my braffe fkillett to my dafter Rouland my green Rugg I giue to Samuell Eborn wth the bed aforefaied. my Red Rugg I giue to my dafter Eborne, And my to pare of blankets I giue to my to dafters, to each one pare. And the Reft of the my ftuffe I giue betwen my to dafters aforefaied, to be equally deuided among them.

At the finning heerof, the word Rouland ftrooke out, & the word Eborne put in the margent in the 29 line in the other fide is
*
wittnes our hands the *

*Torn off.

of march aforefayed :
Willm Pitt
Jofeph Rowland
mary aborn

The marke of
Mary 3 Smith

PASSENGERS FOR NEW ENGLAND.

"Wee vnderwritten being now bound from London to New England doe attest that on this day ye Date hereof wee together with Nicholas Hayward Notary Publique of this Citty were prefent and did See mr John Chamberlain & Robert Willfey and Thomaf in Jenney Make Oath in due form vpon ye holy Evangelists to ye Tenour of ye aforegoing depofitions by them Signed before the Right Honourable Sr John Peake Knight Lord Mayor of ye City of London and this wee will Seuernly affirm upon Our Oathes when it shall pleafe God wee ariue in New England if thereunto Required witnefs Our hands in London ye 31 of May 1687.
John Balston
John Herring
Sarah Brickenate
Samuel Hayward "
—*Essex Registry of Deeds, book 11, leaf 28.*

PETITION OF STEPHEN BLANEY.

Boston, March 4, 1778.
Massachusetts Bay.
To the Honble the Council & the Honble the House of Representatives of said State.
Humbly Sheweth Stephen Blaney; That on the 25 April 1775, he Removed with his family from Marblehead to Yarmouth in Nova Scotia (first obtaining Liberty from the Selectman of said Town for that purpose) at which place he has Resided till the present Time, always making it his constant Study to afford every Assistance in his power to any of his Countrymen who have from time to time made their Escape from Enemy, as may be made to appear by many witnesses now in this Town, Particularly Capts Olney & Grimes—Your Petitioner,

being now Desirous to Return to his Native Country, prays Your Honours would Grant him Permission to remove his family & effects from Nova Scotia to Marblehead, & grant him a Safe Passport for that purpose, & he as in Duty Bound will ever pray

Stephen Blaney.

—*Massachusetts Archives, Volume* 184, *page* 17.

The petition was granted March 7, 1778; but Mr. Blaney probably did not return to Massachusetts as he was living in Yarmouth four years later. See Annals of Yarmouth, N. S.

SALEM IN 1700. NO. 27.

BY SIDNEY PERLEY.

The map on page 69 comprises that part of Salem which is now included within Liberty, Essex and Central streets, and the South river. It is based on actual surveys and title deeds, and is drawn on a scale of two hundred feet to an inch.

Liberty street was laid out over land of Maj. William Hathorne as far down as the present Charter street before May 7, 1661.* The way was extended to the river, as provided May 7, 1661, in the deed of Samuel Pickman to John Pickman: " Highway to be left on east side, same width as that said Maj. William Hathorne hath now left out between his fence and farmer John Porter.* This way was laid out as a new way to the cemetery at the time the land between the burial place and the water on the south and west sides was granted and laid out to several parties March 6, 1661. In 1669, the town made this lane a public way; and 20:10:1669, Mr. Eleaz Hauthorne was granted land "for the land wh now maketh the highway from his house to the buringe place." 26:6:1669, the town granted to Samuel Pickman land for "the priuiledge of the highway next to his land." This way was called the town

*Essex Registry of Deeds, book 8, leaf 2, and book 9, leaf 131.

lane in 1671; lane or highway, 1679; lane going to burying point, 1689; burying place lane, 1750; burying point lane, 1757; and Liberty street in 1795.

Essex street was an original highway. It was called ye street that comes from the neck direct to the meeting house in Salem in 1655; the street that goes straight to ye meeting house, 1667; ye main street, 1683; the main street of Salem, 1723; and Essex street in 1824.

That part of Central street which lies between Essex and Charter streets was an original highway to the water; and was called ye street in 1667; highway, 1689; ye highway which leads down to Colonel Browne's wharf, 1722; Ingalls' lane leading from the main street to ye South river, 1760; Ingalls' lane, 1763; a street leading from the Sun tavern so called which is in the main street to the South river, 1785; Market street, 1795; and Central street in 1835. That part of the street lying between Charter street and the point of land was one of the original ways reserved along the water front in the original lay out of the settlement, and was the way to Burying point in the earliest days. When the grants of the lots lying to the south of the lot of Hannah Sanders were made in 1661 a way ten feet wide was expressly reserved. This part was called a highway in 1698; a street or way leading to the wharves of William Gray, Ashby, and others, 1714; a way, 1760; a way leading to the South river, 1787; the street leading from the Sun tavern to the South river, 1792; Fish street, 1794; Derby street, 1873; and Central street in 1880.

Derby street was the way reserved along the water in the first settlement of the town; and when the grants of the lots there were made in 1661 a way ten feet wide was reserved expressly. This was called a highway in 1761; a town way or highway, 1763; Water street, 1810; and Derby street about 1856.

Charter street runs where the dotted lines are shown on the map between the braces marked "a". This was laid out

just before April 4, 1767, when it was called a new town way. It was called a highway in 1784; the street leading by the burying point so called, 1787; and Charter street in 1794.

The South river was so called in 1636; Salem river, 1686; ye river, 1687; ye salt water, 1695; and that part near the western end of Charter street was called ye cove in 1749.

In the sketches that follow after 1700, titles and deeds referred to pertain to the houses and land under and adjoining and not always to the whole lot, the design being, after that date, to give the history of the houses then standing principally.

Ye Burying Point. That part of the burial ground lying south and west of the dashes, being the largest section of the burying ground as marked on the map, was the original burying point, and before the grants of the land adjoining on the south and west to the water were made in 1661, it extended to the river on those sides. On this part, at a town meeting held 14: 6: 1637, John Horne was alowed a pece of grownd for a winde mill vpon or nere the buriall place." 25: 1: 1639, it was voted that Mr. Horne "desist from his inclosure in y⁰ buryall place: and yᵗ y⁰ town shall pay for a quarter of an acre when he hath bought y⁰ same, except the Towne when they shall haue changed the buryall place shall alow him a portion of the same."* This was called the windmill field in 1652. 23: 10: 1661, the selectmen were ordered by the town to "grant liberty for shops to be buikled below ye bank at the buring pt."*

In connection with the grants laid out by the selectmen 6: 1 mo: 1661, it was ordered by the selectmen "that all the bigger lotts that are for ware houfes fhall leaue a sufficyent way of ten foote broode betweene their houfes and the banke and the lefser lotts that are for fhopps fhall leaue a sufficyent way of ten foote brode before theyer houfes or fhopps and thofe 3 shopps laide out togeather are foe to

*Town Records.

wharfe as that they leaue sufficyent rome before wharfes for grauinge of vessells thofe that haue grounde laide out for ware houese haue libertie to wharfe foe lowe as they pleafe and it is further ordered that it fhall be in the libertie of any pfon inhabitant or ftranger to lande at any of thofe wharfes and alfo to more or faffen his foote fciffe or other vefsell at any wharfe provided it is not in the libertie of any pfon to lande any goods whatever at any wharfe vnlefs the owner of the goods Doe firft agree with the owner of the wharf."*

That section of the burial place lying west and north of the dashes, as shown on the map, was undoubtedly purchased of Henry Bartholmew as it was voted by the town 9: 1 mo: 1668-9.

For twenty pounds, Edward Grove conveyed to the town for an enlargement of the cemetery the strip of land lying easterly of the dashes 26: 9: 1669, in accordance with a vote passed by the town 9: 1 mo: 1668-9: " Bought of Edward Grove all that peell of land of his lying next our Comon Burringe place neare Jno pickman on the East, for and in Consideration of twenty pounds in hand paid.† This strip of land early belonged to John Friend of Salem, carpenter, and he conveyed it to Edward Prescott of London, merchant, July 15, 1652.‡ Capt. Richard Moore of Salem, mariner, brought suit against Mr. Prescott in 1658, judgment was obtained and execution sued out thereon. In satisfaction of the judgment, this lot was assigned to Captain Moore, who conveyed it to Edward Grove of Salem, sailmaker, Jan. 17, 1667.§

That part of the cemetery bounding on Liberty street was purchased of Samuel Pickman for an entrance to the burial place from Liberty street, 26: 6: 1669: "Agreed with Samll pickman Marinr that for a quantitie of land of his that Runeth by a streight line by ye land wee ex-

*Town Records, book II, page 31.
†Town records.
‡Essex Registry of Deeds, book 1, leaf 13.
§Essex Registry of Deeds, book 3, leaf 27.

changed with Henry Bartholmew which is by vs Borowed of him for the towns vse all the land that Runeth to Jno. Pickmans fence next adjoyninge to his dwellinge house togeether with the priuieledge of the highway next to his land."*

The selectmen let to Mr. John Cromwell Feb. 24, 1680, "the hearbadge of the towns land at the Burying poynt for Seauen yeares from the Date hearof ; Improuing it for grasing to his Best Advantag Except Swine which wee alow not of. . . Always prouided that the towne hath the Same liberty for Buriall as before this Agreement."*

The cemetery was again enlarged immediately following the laying out of Charter street in 1767. The town bought, June 13, 1767, of William Lander of Salem, chairmaker, the southern end of the lot marked "John Pilgrim" on the map,† and of Joseph Mottey of Salem, mariner, the eastern two-thirds of the southern end of the lot marked "Estate of Timothy Lindall,"‡ being those parts of the lots lying between the new highway (Charter street) and the burial place.

This ancient burial place, used as early as 1637, was called ye burying place in 1652 ; ye common or burying place, 1667 ; the common burying place, 1669 ; ye burying point, 1679 ; the point burying place, 1794 ; the burying ground, 1807 ; and the burying ground point, 1820.

Estate of Eleazer Hathorne Lot. Major William Hathorne owned this lot as early as 1653. He conveyed it to his son Eleazer Hathorne of Salem, together with " my dwelling house standing thereon," Dec. 28, 1664.§ To carry out a certain marriage agreement, Eleazer Hathorne conveyed the house (which he called " my dwelling house") and lot to his wife Abigail, who was daughter of Capt. George Corwin of Salem, March 20, 1671.‖ Mr. Hathorne died, and his widow married, sec-

ondly, James Russell, esq., of Charlestown. The house was burned in the great fire of 1698. Mr. and Mrs. Russell and her children : William Hathorne and Sarah Hathorne, mariners, and Abigail, wife of John Rayner, mariner, all of Charlestown, conveyed the land, for eighty pounds, to Capt John Browne of Salem, merchant, June 11, 1702.*

William Hirst Lot. There was a dwelling house and shop upon this lot of land in 1651 ; and the land was owned by Alexander Field of Salem, cordwinder, as early as 1649. Mr. Field probably lived in this house ; and, for forty-five years, conveyed the house and land to William Venus 3 : 12 mo : 1651.† Mr. Venus lived in this house ; and, for a similar consideration, conveyed the house, shop, cellar and land " thereto belonging near the windmill field in Salem, to John Miller of Salem, tailor, 16 : 12 : 1652.‡ Mr. Miller lived here, and, for fifty pounds, conveyed the house and land to Mr. George Corwin of Salem, merchant, 29 : 6 : 1657.§ Captain Corwin sold the house and lot to Edward Grove of Salem, sailmaker, who paid him for the estate, though no deed passed. Mr. Grove conveyed the house and lot, for two hundred and ten pounds, to William Hirst of Salem, merchant, March 17, 1684-5.‖ Capt. Corwin had died that winter, without executing a deed of the premises ; and his administrator gave a deed of the estate to Mr. Grove and his heirs and assigns April 30, 1685.¶ The house was burned down in the great fire in 1698. Mr. Hirst continued to own the land until his decease, in 1717.

John Pilgrim Lot. This lot was the eastern half of the two-acre lot of a Mr. Webb of London, England. The whole lot came into the ownership of William Lord of Salem, cutler, before 6 : 6 : 1655,

*Town records.
†Essex Registry of Deeds, book 121, leaf 183.
‡Essex Registry of Deeds, book 121, leaf 184.
§Essex Registry of Deeds, book 2, leaf 93.
‖Essex Registry of Deeds, book 3, leaf 140.

*Essex Registry of Deeds, book 16, leaf 15.
†Essex Registry of Deeds, book 1, leaf 12.
‡Essex Registry of Deeds, book 1, leaf 18.
§Essex Registry of Deeds, book 3, leaf 70.
‖Essex Registry of Deeds, book 7, leaf 23.
¶Essex Registry of Deeds, book 3, leaf 32.

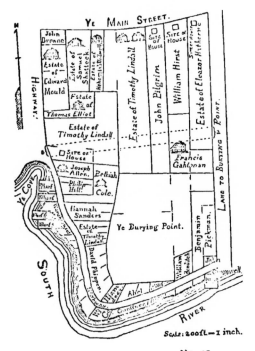

Scale: 200 ft — 1 inch.

PART OF SALEM IN 1700. No. 27.

when, for twenty pounds, he conveyed the entire lot of two acres to Robert Brett of Salem.[*] This part of the lot came into the possession of Henry Bartholmew of Salem, merchant; and he removed to Boston. In consideration of love, he conveyed it to his son-in-law, John Pilgrim of Salem, merchant, and his wife Elizabeth, Aug. 26, 1681.[†] Major Pilgrim erected upon the lot a dwelling house in which he lived until it was burned down in the great fire of 1698. He retained the land but a short time after the fire.

Estate of Timothy Lindall Houses. That part of this lot lying easterly of the dashes was the western part of the two-acre lot that belonged to a Mr. Webb of London, England. It came into the ownership of William Lord of Salem, cutler, before 6 : 6 : 1655, when, for twenty pounds, he conveyed the entire lot of two acres to Robert Brett of Salem.[*] Mr. Brett (or, Britt) called himself a planter, and, for seven pounds and ten shillings, conveyed this half of the lot to Henry Bartholmew of Salem 9 : 6 mo : 1655.[†] Upon this part of the lot Mr. Bartholmew, who was a merchant, erected a dwelling house before 1661. Mr. Bartholmew lived here until he removed to Boston, where he was also a merchant.

The small strip lying west of the dashes was a part of the house lot of John Holgrave very early. It subsequently came into the hands of Richard Prince, who conveyed it to Henry Bartholmew.

Mr. Bartholmew thus became the owner of the entire lot, and he conveyed the lot and house to Timothy Lindall of Salem, merchant, Feb. 7, 1679-80.[‡] The great fire of 1698 began in a warehouse situated at the northeasterly corner of this lot, where the Museum building now stands. The old house stood westwardly of it as shown on the map. Mr. Lindall was building a new house on the site of

the warehouse at the time of his death, Jan. 6, 1698-9. The other house was called "the old house" in the inventory of his estate, taken in the spring of 1699, and it was probably removed when the new house was completed. The estate remained in the possession of the widow of Mr. Lindall until her death Jan. 7, 1731-2. The estate was not divided until 1737. Samuel Barnard, esquire, and wife Rachel, Benjamin Morshed, mariner, and wife Sarah, widow Sarah Williams, and Edward Rose, mariner, and wife Mary, all of Salem, and Nathan Phippen of Boston, mariner, children and grandchildren of Timothy Lindall, deceased, conveyed their interests in the house and land around it to James Lindall, esquire, of Salem, a son of said deceased, Feb. 10, 1737.[*] James Lindall died May 10, 1753, intestate. The inventory of his estate shows that the house contained a kitchen, hall, hall chamber, hall chamber garret, parlor, parlor chamber, garret over the parlor chamber shops, shop chambers and shop chamber garrets. It was called his mansion house, being valued with the land that ran back to the cemetery at £476, 13s., 4d. In the division of the estate it was assigned to his son James Lindall. The son died the next year, Aug. 19, 1754, being also a merchant, without issue. In the division of his estate the house and land around it were assigned to his only brother Timothy Lindall of Salem, merchant. Mr. Lindall conveyed "my mansion house," barn and land to Joseph Mottey of Salem, mariner, June 18, 1763.[†] For four hundred and sixty-six pounds, thirteen shillings and four pence, Mr. Mottey conveyed the land and house, "in which Rev. Nathaniel Whitaker now lives," to John Gardner of Salem, gentleman, Feb. 24, 1772.[‡] Capt. Gardner died Jan. 15, 1784, intestate; and his administrator conveyed to George Peele of Salem, trad-

---

*Essex Registry of Deeds, book 1, leaf 28.
†Essex Registry of Deeds, book 6, leaf 18.
‡Essex Registry of Deeds, book 5, leaf 65.

*Essex Registry of Deeds, book 75, leaf 116.
†Essex Registry of Deeds, book 112, leaf 132.
‡Essex Registry of Deeds, book 131, leaf 6.

er, the two southwest rooms and the two chambers over them and part of the lot of land Nov. 25, 1786.* The remainder of the house was set off to the widow of the deceased, Mary Gardner, and in 1793 the house was occupied by Capt. George Smith and a Mr. White, a tallow chandler. Captain Gardner had two children living at the time of his decease. Mary Lemon, the daughter, apparently conveyed one-half of her half interest in the estate to her mother; and her brother, John Gardner, who inherited the other half, died possessed of it Oct. 27, 1805, having by his will devised it to his son Samuel P. Gardner. Mrs. Lemon and her husband, William Lemon of Boston, upholsterer, conveyed her remaining fourth interest to Samuel P. Gardner, esquire, of Salem, Feb. 7, 1814.† George Peele died possessed of his part of the estate in 1801, intestate; and it descended to his sister, the widow Mary Gardner, who had the dower interest in the remainder of the estate. She conveyed this part of the estate to John Andrew of Salem May 7, 1824;‡ and her other interests to Mr. Andrew on the same day.§ Samuel P. Gardner conveyed his interest in the estate to Mr. Andrew May 22, 1824.§ Mr. Andrew, for four thousand dollars, conveyed the land and buildings to The East India Marine Hall Corporation July 22, 1824.‡ The corporation removed the house immediately, and on its site erected the present home of the Peabody Academy of Science, commonly known as the Museum building.

Nehemiah Willoughby House. John Holgrave owned this house and lot in 1655. Richard Prince owed the estate, and conveyed it, probably, with the house thereon to Henry Bartholmew, sr., of Salem, merchant. For love, Mr. Bartholmew conveyed the estate to his son-in-law Nehemiah Willoughby of Salem, merchant, and wife Abigail, own daughter of Mr. Bar-

tholmew, Feb. 14, 1683.* Mr. Willoughby was then living in the house. He died Nov. 6, 1702; his wife, Abigail, having died two months previously. The house and lot descended to their eldest son Francis Willoughby of Salem, merchant, who, for one hundred and fifty pounds, conveyed the house, garden and land to Thomas Barton of Salem, apothecary, Feb. 6, 1710-1.† Colonel Barton took the old house down.

Estate of Samuel Shattock House. This house was occupied by John Bourne before 1655. William Browne of Salem, merchant, owned the house and land April 13, 1655, when, for thirty-six pounds, he conveyed the estate to Samuel Shattock of Salem.‡ Mr. Shattock lived here until his death, June 6, 1689, at the age of sixty-nine. From this house he was banished in 1660, and from it went to England and obtained from King Charles II., the mandate that caused the terrible Quaker persecution to cease. Mr. Shattock conveyed this house and lot to his wife Hannah Shattock for her life, and then to their children. She died Sept. 14, 1701, at the age of seventy-seven; and, Nov. 1, 1701, by agreement of the children the house and land became the estate of the son, Samuel Shattock. The house and land were then valued at forty-five pounds. The house was standing in 1721, and gone in 1723, when Mr. Shattock died possessed of the land.

John Browne Lot. Robert Gutch of Salem owned this land in 1655, and probably in 1651, when he mortgaged his estate to William Norton.§ He mortgaged his estate, a second time, to Mr. Norton Dec. 22, 1652;‖ and Mr. Norton assigned the mortgage to Nicholas Davison June 6, 1653.¶ Mr. Davison assigned it to Richard Gardner Nov. 26, 1656.¶ There

*Essex Registry of Deeds, book 146, leaf 172.
†Essex Registry of Deeds, book 201, leaf 295.
‡Essex Registry of Deeds, book 236, leaf 64.
§Essex Registry of Deeds, book 236, leaf 63.

*Essex Registry of Deeds, book 7, leaf 48.
†Essex Registry of Deeds, book 23, leaf 49.
‡Essex Registry of Deeds, book 1, leaf 55.
§Essex Registry of Deeds, book 1, leaf 12.
‖Essex Registry of Deeds, book 1, leaf 15; book 3, leaf 55.
¶Essex Registry of Deeds, book 3, leaf 55.

was a warehouse upon the lot in 1667 and 1669, when the estate was owned by William Browne. Mr. Browne died Jan. 20, 1687; and the estate descended to his son John Browne, who owned it in 1700.

Estate of Edward Mould House. Robert Gutch of Salem owned this house and lot in 1655, and probably in 1651, when he mortgaged his house and lot, to William Norton.* He mortgaged his house and lot, for forty pounds, a second time, to Mr. Norton Dec. 22, 1652.† For twenty-six pounds, Mr. Norton assigned the mortgage to Nicholas Davison June 6, 1653;‡ and Mr. Davison, for twenty-two pounds, assigned it to Richard Gardner Nov. 26, 1656.‡ Mr. Gardner was a mariner and lived in this house. He conveyed the house and lot as far south as the dashes, except "the new shop with the seller under it," to Edward Mould of Salem, fisherman, Aug. 25, 1667;§ and the house and whole of the lot, including the shop, May 5, 1669.‡ Edward Nichols of Clovelly, Devonshire, England, mariner, and his sister Mary Nichols, grandchildren and only surviving heirs of Elizabeth Nichols (alias Elizab. Baron), who was sister and heiress of Edward Mould of Salem, mariner and bonesetter, deceased, for fifty pounds conveyed this "old wooden cottage or dwelling house" and lot to Stephen Ingalls of Salem, tailor, Feb. 1, 1721-2.‖ Mr. Ingalls took the house down before 1725.

Estate of Thomas Elliot House. Nathaniel Pickman owned this lot as early as 1655. He was a house-carpenter and built a house upon it for his step-son Anthony Dike, a seaman, and Mr. Dike lived in the house when Mr. Pickman conveyed the house and lot to him, July 10, 1670.¶ Mr. Dike died in or before 1679, possessed of the estate, which was then valued at fifty pounds. His widow Margery married, secondly, John Polin in 16 , and by order of court the house and l became the property of his son Anthony Dike of Salem, tailor. For forty-one pounds and ten shillings, Mr. Dike conveyed the estate to Col. Bartholmew Gedney of Salem Dec. 16, 1689.* For forty-six pounds and ten shillings, Colonel Gedney conveyed the house and lot to Thomas Elliot of Salem, mariner, July 6, 1693.† Mr. Elliot died in 1694, when the house and land were appraised at forty pounds. His widow and administratrix, Hannah Elliot, and her son (?) Francis Elliot, husbandman, for twenty-five pounds, conveyed the house and land to widow Mary Lindall of Salem May 19, 1703.‡ The house probably stood but a short time after that date, being gone before 1737.

Estate of Timothy Lindall Lot. Nathaniel Pickman of Salem, house-carpenter, owned this house and lot as early as 1655. He died in 1684, possessed of the estate, which was then valued at sixty pounds. The house was occupied by his son Nathaniel Pickman, and to him and his children the arbitrators, whom the children of the deceased, namely, Nathaniel Pickman, John Sanders, Mary Hodges, Bethiah Hill and Edmo: Feveryeare, appointed to make a division of the estate, conveyed the house and land within the dashes Jan. 31, 1687-8.§ The arbitrators conveyed the remainder of the lot to Timothy Lindall of Salem, merchant, March 25, 1689.‖ Mr. Pickman, the son, apparently died, and his children, John Baker and wife Tabitha, and Elizabeth Pickman, singlewoman, all of Boston, Nathaniel Pickman, mariner, of Salem, and Joseph Pickman, Benjamin Pickman, Isannah Pickman, Hannah Pickman, Mary Pickman and Abigail Pickman, for thirteen

---

*Essex Registry of Deeds, book 1, leaf 12 .
†Essex Registry of Deeds, book 1, leaf 15; book 3, leaf 55.
‡Essex Registry of Deeds, book 3, leaf 55.
§Essex Registry of Deeds, book 3, leaf 20.
‖Essex Registry of Deeds, book 40, leaf 58.
¶Essex Registry of Deeds, book 3, leaf 106.

*Essex Registry of Deeds, book 8, leaf 144.
†Essex Registry of Deeds, book 9, leaf 144.
‡Essex Registry of Deeds, book 15, leaf 181.
§Essex Registry of Deeds, book 8, leaf 135.
‖Essex Registry of Deeds, book 8, leaf 149.

pounds and ten shillings, conveyed the " small old decayed dwelling house " and the land within the dashes to Mr. Lindall June 16, 1698.* The house was removed before the year was out. Mr. Lindall died Jan. 6, 1698-9 ; and the estate came into the hands of his widow, Mary Lindall, who owned it many years.

Joseph Allen House. This lot belonged to Nathaniel Pickman in 1655. Between 1689 and 1692, he conveyed the land to Zebulon Hill ; and Mr. Hill, who was of Salem and a cooper, for twenty pounds, conveyed the lot to Joseph Allen of Salem, joiner, April 15, 1695.† Mr. Allen erected a house on the lot ; and died April 19, 1710, possessed of the house and lot. He devised the estate to his wife Abigail for her life with power of disposal for her support, and then, if not sold, to his son Robert Allen. The house and lot were then appraised at one hundred and fifty pounds. The widow conveyed the house and lot to her said son, Robert Allen of Salem, joiner, June 5, 1749.‡ Mr. Allen probably removed the house some time before his death which occurred in 1780.

Philip Hill Lot. Nathaniel Pickman, sr., of Salem, carpenter, owned this land as early as 1655 ; and he died in the autumn of 1684. His administrator conveyed that part of the lot lying south of the dashes to John Hill of Salem, cooper, April 2, 1686 ;§ and he conveyed the remainder of the lot to Mr. Hill Feb. 15, 1686-7.|| Mr. Hill died in the spring of 1691, having devised this lot, with a shop and wharf, to his wife, Priscilla Hill. The land and buildings were then valued at thirty pounds. Mrs. Hill conveyed the same estate to Philip Hill of Salem, cooper, Nov. 22, 1692 ;¶ and Mr. Hill owned it in 1700.

Bethiah Cole House. Nathaniel Pickman, sr., of Salem, carpenter, owned this

lot as early as 1655. He conveyed it, as a gift, to his daughter, widow Bethiah Silsby Feb. 2, 1679-80.* Her dwelling house then stood upon the land. She married Alexander Cole before Sept. 17, 1683, when her father conveyed to her, "for the conveniences of a wharf," the strip of land down to the water as shown on the map.* Mr. Cole died June 27, 1687 ; and after the decease of Mrs. Cole the estate descended to their son Abraham Cole, a mariner, who removed to Boston before Dec. 12, 1710, when, for ninety pounds, he conveyed the house and lot, with the twelve feet passage to the highway and water, to Mighill Bacon of Salem, shipwright.† Mr. Bacon mortgaged the house and lot to his wife's father, Samuel Shattock of Salem, feltmaker, March 6, 1710-1.‡ Mr. Shattock evidently foreclosed the mortgage ; though he permitted the Bacon's to live there. Mr. Shattock died early in 1723 ; and he devised the house and land to his daughter, Mrs. Margaret Bacon, who still lived there. He had built a barn upon the lot ; and the house, barn and land were then appraised at one hundred and fifty pounds. The administrator of Mr. Shattock's estate, conveyed the land and buildings, for sixty-nine pounds, to John Higginson of Salem, shopkeeper, Nov. 30, 1726.§ For a similar consideration, Mr. Higginson conveyed the estate to Mr. Shattock's son John Shattock of Salem, mariner, who was the administrator, March 13, 1727.|| Mr. Shattock, for one hundred and twenty pounds, conveyed this " my dwelling house " and land to Mihill Bacon and Samuel Bacon, both of Salem, shipwrights, Feb. 21, 1733.¶ Samuel Bacon apparently conveyed his interest in the estate to his brother Mihill (they being sons of the former owner) before Feb. 19, 1749, when Mihill Bacon, for four hundred and twenty-

---

*Essex Registry of Deeds, book 13, leaf 142.
†Essex Registry of Deeds, book 10, leaf 151.
‡Essex Registry of Deeds, book 95, leaf 26.
§Essex Registry of Deeds, book 7, leaf 67.
‖Essex Registry of Deeds, book 8, leaf 3.
*Essex Registry of Deeds, book 9, leaf 58.

*Essex Registry of Deeds, book 6, leaf 92.
†Essex Registry of Deeds, book 22, leaf 208.
‡Essex Registry of Deeds, book 37, leaf 37.
§Essex Registry of Deeds, book 47, leaf 163.
‖Essex Registry of Deeds, book 46, leaf 230.
¶Essex Registry of Deeds, book 61, leaf 129.

six pounds, conveyed the estate to Benjamin Pickman of Salem, esquire.[*] Mr. Bacon then called the house " my now dwelling house." How much longer the house stood is not known.

Hannah Sanders Lot. That part of this lot lying northerly of the dashes belonged to Nathaniel Pickman, sr., of Salem, carpenter, as early as 1655. He conveyed this lot to his son-in-law John Sanders of Salem, mariner, and his wife Hannah Sanders, daughter of Mr. Pickman, as a gift, Dec. 31, 1681.[†]

That part of the lot lying southerly of the dashes was granted by the town of Salem and laid out to Abraham Cole 6 : 1 mo : 1661 ; and it came into the hands of Mr. Sanders soon afterward.

Mr. Sanders died June 9, 1694 ; and his widow was the owner of the land in 1700.

Estate of Timothy Lindall Lot. This lot originally constituted four lots, as shown on the map, being separated by the dashes, and all granted by the town of Salem and laid out 6 : 1 mo : 1661, as follows : the northern one to Henry Bartholomew, the next to John Browne, the ruling elder, the next to Mr. Price, and the next to Zebulon Hill for a shop. Mr. Bartholomew removed to Boston before Feb. 7, 1679-80, when he conveyed his warehouse, wharf, etc., to Timothy Lindall of Salem, merchant.[‡] John Browne gave his lot to his son James Browne, who died before a deed was passed, and John Browne then sold it to John Marston, who sold it to John Pilgrim of Salem, merchant, but no deed had yet passed. Mr. Browne gave a deed of it to Mr. Pilgrim Nov. 26, 1680.[§] Mr. Pilgrim apparently conveyed it to Mr. Lindall soon afterward. The other lots came into the hands of Mr. Lindall, but the deeds have not been found. Mr. Lindall died Jan. 6, 1698-9, possessed of the entire lot, it being valued, with the wharf and warehouse, at one hun-

dred pounds. The property remained his estate until 1737, when it was divided.

David Phippen Lot. This lot originally constituted four lots, separated on map by the dashes, all having been granted by the town of Salem and laid out 6 : 1 mo : 1661, as follows : the northern one to William Lake, the next Samuel Williams, the next to Edmund Batter and the next to John Brown (son of Mr. William Browne). No deeds have been found from William Lake and John Browne to Mr. Phippen of Salem, shipwright, but they were evidently conveyed very early ; Samuel Williams conveyed his lot to him in or before 1679 ; and Mr. Batter, for fifty shillings, conveyed his lot to Mr. Phippen May 3, 1679.[*] Mr. Phippen owned these lots in 1700.

William Gedney Lot. This lot was granted by the town of Salem and laid out to John Gedney for a warehouse 6 : 1 mo : 1661. Mr. Gedney died possessed of it Aug. 5, 1688, and it descended to his grandson William Gedney, who owned it in 1700.

Abel Gardner Lot. This lot was granted by the town of Salem and laid out 6 : 1 mo : 1661, to Samuel Gardner and his brother Capt. Joseph Gardner. Capt. Gardner was killed in King Phillip's war Dec. 19, 1675, and his interest in the lot was probably released to his brother Samuel Gardner, who died in 1689, possessed of it. The lot descended the latter's son Jonathan Gardner, who died about four years later, having devised the lot to his brother Abel Gardner of Salem, yeoman. Abel Gardner owned it in 1700.

William Hirst Lot. That part of this lot lying westerly of the dashes was granted by the town of Salem and laid out 6 : 1 mo : 1661, to Serg. John Porter. Sergeant Porter died Sept. 6, 1676, and his wife, who was the executrix of his will, conveyed this lot to her son-in-law, Lt. Thomas Gardner of Salem, June 15, 1680.[†] Mr. Gardner died Nov. 16, 1695 ; and his

*Essex Registry of Deeds, book 93, leaf 243.
†Essex Registry of Deeds, book 7, leaf 7.
‡Essex Registry of Deeds, book 5, leaf 65.
§Essex Registry of Deeds, book 5, leaf 95.

*Essex Registry of Deeds, book 14, leaf 219
†Essex Registry of Deeds, book 5, leaf 77.

son-in-law, Capt. William Bowditch of Salem, mariner, was the administrator of his estate. Captain Bowditch and his wife Mary, for fifty shillings, conveyed the lot to William Hirst of Salem, merchant, Dec. 31, 1698.*

That part of the lot lying easterly of the dashes was granted by the town of Salem and laid out to Maj. William Hathorne 6 : 1 mo : 1661. He died in 1681, possessed of it, and it then came into the possession of his son John Hathorne of Salem, merchant, who, for five pounds, sold it to Mr. Hirst Feb. 16, 1691, but no deed passed until Sept. 8, 1716.†

Mr. Hirst owned the entire lot for many years after 1700.

William Bowditch Lot. Feb. 14, 1680-1, the selectmen of Salem leased to Capt. William Bowditch of Salem, merchant, "all that lower end of that land the Towne purchased of mr. Edw. Grove att or by the burreing place viz. from the bank downwards to low watter marke or soe low as the order & custome of the Towne is and According as thay allow vnto others that border vpon the water er River."‡ Captain Bowditch owned the lot in 1700 apparently.

John Cromwell Lot. This lot was a part of the lot that Samuel Friend of Manchester conveyed to Samuel Pickman of Salem, mariner, Dec. 24, 1657.§ Mr. Pickman conveyed this part of it to William Bowditch of Salem, merchant, May 23, 1676.‖ Mr. Bowditch conveyed it with his warehouse, cellar, and wharf thereon to Philip Cromwell of Salem, slaughterer, Nov. 20, 1679.¶ Mr. Cromwell died possessed of the property March 30, 1693, and it descended to his son John Cromwell, who died, possessed of it, Sept. 30, 1700. The warehouse was then called " old," and the wharf still there.

Benjamin Pickman Lot. This lot belonged to Samuel Friend of Manchester very early ; and he conveyed it to Samuel Pickman of Salem, mariner, Dec. 24, 1657.* For six pounds Mr. Pickman conveyed that part of the lot at the southeast corner within the dashes to John Pickman of Salem, seaman, May 7, 1661.† John Pickman died in the winter of 1683-4, apparently without issue, and this part of the lot was released to his nephew Benjamin Pickman. The remainder of the lot was owned by Samuel Pickman until his death in 1691 ; and his heirs apparently conveyed it to Benjamin Pickman, who thus became the owner of the whole lot, which he died possessed of after 1700.

Francis Gahtman House. That part of this lot lying easterly of the dashes belonged to Samuel Friend of Manchester very early. Dec. 24, 1657, he conveyed it to Samuel Pickman of Salem.*

That part of the lot lying westerly of the dashes, with the house thereon, belonged to William Goult, who died in the winter of 1659-60, possessed of the property. The administratrix of his estate, for twenty-four pounds, conveyed the house and lot to Mr. Pickman June 12, 1660.‡ The southern end of this lot may have been a part of the lot that Edward Grove conveyed to the town for an enlargement of the cemetery, and a part of which was conveyed to Mr. Pickman for the piece of land they had of him for the same purpose, etc.

Mr. Pickman died in 1685, and the administratrix of his estate conveyed the house and entire lot to Dr. Francis Gahtman of Salem March 8, 1689.§ The house was standing and owned by Doctor Gahtman in 1750 ; but how much longer it stood has not been learned.

*Essex Registry of Deeds, book 15, leaf 219.
†Essex Registry of Deeds, book 31, leaf 60.
‡Town records.
§Essex Registry of Deeds, book 1, leaf 35.
‖Essex Registry of Deeds, book 7, leaf 59.
* Essex Registry of Deeds, book 6, leaf 22.

*Essex Registry of Deeds, book 1, leaf 35.
†Essex Registry of Deeds, book 8, leaf 2; and book 9, leaf 131.
‡Essex Registry of Deeds, book 2, leaf 55.
§Essex Registry of Deeds, book 22, leaf 265.
See, also, book 18, leaf 102.

IPSWICH COURT RECORDS AND FILES.

Continued from page 28.

Court, March 25, 1656.
Judges: Mr. Symon Brodstreet, Mr. Samuell Symonds, Maj.-gen. Denison, Mr. Will: Hubbard, and Mr. Rich: Dummer.

Trial jury: Mr. Jo. Apleton, Tho: Loe, Will: Addams, jr., Will: ffellows, Jacob Perkins, Jo: Trumble, Tho: Teney, Tho: Abbott, Dan. Thurston, Antho: Cumerby, Jo: Bartlet and Jacob Towne.

Henry Archer v. John Caldwell. Debt.

ffrances Johnson v. Peetr Palfree. For withholding money from Rich: ffoxwell.

Will: Wyld v. William Evans. For not returning a steer he hired.

[Lt. William Hudson of Boston certified that he sent a parcel of tobacco by Edward Woollen to carry it to Newfoundland and dispose of it. He chose Mr. Benjamin Guillam and Jno. Huson to end the matter of a dispute about it. Dated Salem, Jan. 12, 1654. Wit: John Manning. Also signed by the mark E. W. of Edward Woollen. Award signed by Jno. Huson and Ben. Gillum. Dated Jan. 31, 1655.

Deposition of Nathaniell Pittman and his wife Tabitha that they heard Mr. Henry Cowes say that he had bought Mr. Gifford's dun horse and the horse was here at Salem at Mr. Gednyes, etc. Sworn in court 28 : 4 : 1655, before Elias Stileman, clerk.

John Ballae, aged twenty-one years, deposed that when he was his brother Jenckes' servant he worked in that boat of Joseph Armitage's which was cast away subsequently, being employed by Capt. Thomas Savage. Sworn in court 29 : 4 : 1655, before Elias Stileman, clerk. — *Files.*]

Nath: Stow v. Tho: Smith, William Marchent and Richard Shatswell. For injury to his corn by cattle.

[Henry Kimball deposed that he saw the steers of Mr. Smith in Nathaniel Stowse corn and he went to get them out and he leaped over the five railed fence of Alexsander Knight's. Sworn in court 26 : 1 : 1656, before Robert Lord.

Walter Roper testified that he called with Nathaniell Masterson to see some harm that was done in Nath. Stow his corn this last summer, so that twenty-five bushels were destroyed by cattle. At the same time we viewed Henry Kimball's harms. Sworn to Daniel Denison March 24, 1655.

Samuel Younglove witnessed that he helped to bring fifty head of cattle of Henry Kimball's corn and Nath: Stow's, four of Richard Shatswell's, two of old Kimball's, two of goodman Marchent's, three of goodwife Cooks, a stear of Mr. Smith's; and, also, I saw a post down and two lengths of rails they saw some of the cattle go in there. the tracks of others. Sworn in court 1 : 1656, before Robert Lord, clerk.

William Dello deposed that there were two oxen of Tho: Smith, two steers Richard Setchwell and two cows of William Marchent in Nathaniel Stow's corn two days before the general training at Ipswich. Sworn in court as above.

Robert Lord, jr., deposed that he saw one steer of Thomas Smith in Nathan Stow's corn and two cows of John Newman at four several times. Sworn Ipswich court 25 : 1 : 1656.

See files.
—*Files.*]

Henry Kemball v. Thomas Smith, William Marchent, Richard Shatswell, John Newman. Injury to his corn by cattle.

[See files above.]

Robert Smyth deposed that about a week or fortnight before the last general training he was going by the outfence joining to the general field where Henry Kemble's corn was destroyed, and the fence was down. Sworn in court, Ipswich 1st mo : 1656.

Alexander Maxsy deposed that the outside fence of his master Richard Kimball was a sufficient fence when the damage was done. Sworn in Ipswich court 1 : 1656.

John Gage deposed that his fence was , sufficient one before the damage was ; ne in Henry Kimball's corn. Sworn as : ove.

Jeremiah Jowit testified that the fence i our common field against Henry Kim-...ll's lot or corn field was down in two ;:ces before Indian harvest. Sworn as :'ove.

Walter Roper testified that he viewed :.e harm in Henry Kimball's corn ~:th Nathaniel Masterson. Sworn before :aniel Denison March 24, 1655.

William *Parker* deposed that he saw ..ttle of John Numan, Thomas Smith, ki:h: Kemball, Aron Pengrye and Wil-.m Merchant in Henry Kimball's corn. ~vorn in Ipswich court March 25, 1656.

Mary, wife of Robert Smith, and Mary :'arcker testified that Nathaniel Stow said :. our house before many folks about s::ne corn he and Henry Kimball had :.ad spoiled that the fences were insuffi- ent. Sworn in Ipswich court 26 : 1 : :556.

Daniel Gag testified that he saw Rich-::d Kimball's oxen in Henry Kimball's :rn and the fence was down.

Robert Smith, Samuel Gage and Dan- :.l Gage testified that the fence was :wn.

Robert Smith testified that he and .:odman Simons' son saw cattle in Henry A::nball's corn, and four of them were ':. Norton's, others were old goodman ::rnbal's and his son Richard's, about :·dian harvest.

Robert Punill and Goodwife Newman ·:stified that Henry Kimball said that he ': :ght his father and his brother Richard ~ ·:ld undo him for their oxen had eaten :·. his corn.

Joseph Browne testified about the corn. ~vorn in Ipswich court 25 : 1 : 1656.

John Newman testified. Sworn as ..:ove.

—Files.]

Mordicha Larcum and wife Elizabeth, ·'e widow of William Clarke v. Corne- ~ Waldo. For making use of a dwell- ~ house built by William Clarke.

Elias Stileman v. Christopher Latimer. For withholding what he was to pay Mr. Stratton in fish.

Richard Kent v. John Pyke. Case.

Richard Kent v. John Cheny. For fencing part of the town common, which is a highway.

ffrancis Ingalls v. Mr. John Beax & Co. Debt.

[John Belknap deposed that the price of the oxen that William Robinson (in ye name of Mr. Jeffard) bought of ffrancis Inggales was £18. Sworn before Rob. Bridges 27 : 1 : 1655.

Writ: ffrancis Ingalls v. Mr. Jo" Beckes & company, etc., Mr. John Giffard, agent; dated 30 : 9 : 1655; by ye court, Elias Stileman. Attached ye slitting mill and one-half of the corn mill and iron works, and served upon Jemy Hagg and John Anchenter, and a warehouse in Bos-ton, 31 : 10 : 1655, by Samuel Archard, marshall. Ri: Wayte, marshall, committed Mr. John Gifford to prison 20 : 1 : 1656.

Bills of particulars on file.

Thomas Look deposed that the two oxen that William Robinson bought of ffrancis Ingalls by Mr. Gifford's order were killed at the Iron works for the company. His + mark. Sworn before Rob. Bridges 27 : 1 : 1655.

Richard Hood testified the same. Au-tograph signature. Sworn as above.

—Files.]

Joseph Armitage, attorney to ffrances Perry v. Mr. John Beax. Debt.

John ffrances v. Mr. John Beax & Co. Debt.

[Writ: Jo" ffrancis v. Mr. Jo" Beckes & company, etc., Mr. John Giffard, agent; dated 30 : 9 : 1655; by the court, Elias Stileman. Served as above writ.—*Files.*]

Thomas Wiggen v. Mr. John Beax & Co. Debt.

Robert Coker sworn constable for New-bury.

John Emry sworn clerk of the market for Newbury.

The deacons of Rowley, administrators of the estate of Henry Smith, in 1655, bought in an inventory of £8. It was

apportioned to the two children who are to be disposed of and cared for by them.

Mr. Henry Sewall, sr., late of Rowley, died intestate, leaving an estate of about £300, and his son and heir, Mr. Henry Sewall, is in England, the latter having made Henry Short of Newbury his attorney, administration is granted to Mr. Short who is ordered to lease or use the house and land.

John Suderland, being attached by Nath: Kirtland and goodman Barker, and the case not entered, is allowed costs.

Elias Stileman appeared to answer two actions commenced by Mordecha Cravett v. Mr. Walter Prisc. Phillip Cromwell witnessed that said Stileman was Mr. Prise's attorney; and the latter was allowed costs.

Elias Stileman, sr., of Salem licensed to sell strong waters.

Thomas Stace of Ipswich made free.

Henry Short of Newbury was discharged from ordinary training, paying a bushel of wheat annually to the use of the company.

Mordicha Larcum having sued Mr. Waldo, Mr. John Coggswell and William executor to John Cogswell, jr., chose George Giddings and Moses Pengry, and the court named Mr. John Appleton as a third man, arbitrators.

The remainder of Joseph Rowlinson's fine remitted.

Mr. Edward Woodman, Nicolas Noyse and Lt. John Pyke sworn commissioners for Newbury to end small causes.

William Bingley and Elizabeth Preston, for fornication, to be whipped, he twenty stripes and she twelve, or pay fine. Then to be carried to the post and stripped ready to be whipped, but the smart to be taken off. John Bartlet, Nicolas Noyse, John Emry and Lt. John Pike undertake for the fine.

Richard Hutcheson, being attached by William Blanton, writ not entered, allowed costs.

John Smith discharged of his bond for good behavior.

William White released from ordinary training.

Richard Holmes and his wife c charged of their presentments.

Topsfield is ordered to have a po and stocks by the next court.

Robert Smith and his wife Mary f. for incontinency before marriage.

Robert Long and James Jackson pointed administrators of the estate Henry Faye. The estate is to be disp of to his brothers in England.

The Lynn bridge being nearly done, pay costs and £200.

The bridge at Ipswich, being defect to be repaired.

John Mighill fined twenty shillings his presentment at last court.

Jonathan Platts, Henry Ryley a John Acee fined on their presentment last court.

24 : 2 : 1656.

John Browne fined for taking away neighbor's wood. [Wit. Thomas Pars and Samuel Pod.—Files.]

Maj. William Hathorne, being presed by the Salem military company to their commander-in-chief, and Lt. T Lathrop, their lieutenant; both were c firmed, their former commissions to sta in force.

Humphrey Griffin [presented, Ma —, 1656, for being drunk, appearing his gestures, evil words, falling off horse twice and his breath scenting m of strong liquors. Wit: Edward Ch man and wife, Mrs. Wade, Jonat Wade and Willm Dane.—Files] fo not drunk but admonished as to drink

John Averill fined [for striking Jo Grigs several times in the meeting ho in time of the public ordinance on Sabbath day. Wit: Mordica Larcom a John Loc.—Files].

John Tillison admonished [for abus his wife on Sabbath day morning throwing a bowl of water upon her, being sick in bed, chaining her to the post with a plow chain, to keep her un duress. Wit: John Houching, W Houching and George Little.—Files].

The two younger children of w Elitrop to be paid their portions into

...ls of John Wyldes. John Pickard, ...ecutor of Thomas Elitrop, brought the ...eipt from John Wyldes and the widow, ...d the two elder children therefor, and ...court discharged him.

Joseph Mussye fined for uncivil words ...d carriages to several maids on the ...bbath day, and to pay witness fee of Mary Elsye. [He was, also, presented for ...ofaning the Sabbath day by the same ...ds and acts. Wit: Sary Wodman, Mary Elsly and wife of Joseph Plumer. --Files.]

Francis Vrsselton's bond to bring his ...fe to next court at Ipswich to answer ...er presentment. [Sara Barnes, now wife ...f Francis Vsselton of Wenham, present-...d March —, 1656, for speaking re-...roachfully against the minister and peo-...le at Wells, saying that Mr. Syth Flech-...r, their said minister, upon the Sabbath ...ay in time of the public ordinance when ...e had set the Psalm, that while the peo-...'e were singing, Mr. Flecher did take ...bacco in the public meeting house, and ...hile he was preaching the people would ...ake tobacco in the public meeting house. Wit: Wife of George Dunker, wife of John Redington and wife of Abra: Redington. --Files.]

Goodwife Bachelour did not appear, to be attached. [Wife of Henery Batchi-...r was presented March —, 1656, for ...sence from public ordinances upon the ...bbath days at Rowley. Wit: The ...randjurymen of Ipswich.—Files.]

Zacheous Goold presented for absence ...m meeting on the Lord's day. Proved. ...acheus Gould of Rowley presented ...atch —, 1656, for not frequenting the ...blic ordinance upon the Sabbath days. Wit: Grandjurymen of Rowley.—Files.]

John Wild brought receipt of Thomas ...thop's children, and was discharged.

[Presentments (part), March —, ...56 :—

Willm Dugles, for taking £19 of Shor-...tne Wilson, his late servant, for nine ...nths' time, which we think tends to ...ression. Wit: Isaac Comings, sr., ...d Rob: Bridges.

Willm Young, for speeches, wishing them to be hanged that made that order of whipping, etc. Wit :. Willm Ballard and Andrew Alling.

p. William Bartholomew

in the name of ye rest.

Will of John Ward proved in the Ips-wich court March 25, 1656, by Mr. Rob-ert Payne. This will is printed in full in The Antiquarian, volume VI, page 114.

Inventory of the goods of John Ward, late deceased, taken by Robert Lord and Mathew Boyce. Amount, £308, 7s., 3d. It was filed and sworn to in the court at Ipswich by Mr. Robert Payne 25 : 1 : 1656. Debts were due from Mr. Chute, Mr. Epps, John Davis, Humfry Griffin, Thomas Lowe of Boston (mortgage of a wharf), Thomas Spaule of Boston, Mr. Phillips of Boston, Thomas Haukins of Boston, Simon Tomson of Ipswich, John Annibooll of Ipswich, John John-son of Ipswich, Joseph Medcalfe of Ipswich, Robert Gutch of Salem, Samuell Podd of Ipswich and Mr. Powell of Bos-ton. A surgeon's chest with books be-queathed to Thomas Andrus of Ipswich and a chest of linen to Nath. Ward.

Will of John Friend proved in Ipswich court 26 : 1 : 1656, by Edmund Grover and Henry Hericke before Edmond Bat-ter, commissioner. Allowed 27 : 1 : 1656. This will was printed in full in The Anti-quarian, volume VI, page 157.

Inventory of the goods of Henry Smith of Rowley, deceased, taken 1 : 16 : 1654-5, by Richard Swan and John Smith. Amount, £14, 3s. Due to Joseph Jewet, Richard Swan, Edward Hassen, Thomas Burtby, John Smith, Mr. Ezekiel Rogers, John Dresser, John Bointon, Thomas Dickinson, Daniell Roffe, John Pearson, William Acy, Maximillian Jewet, Nicholas Jackson and Benjamin Scott.

Inventory of the estate of Mr. Shewell taken by Joseph Jewett, Mathew Boyes and John Tod. Amount, £339, 17s.,4d.; real, £214; personal, £115, 17s., 4d. Due to goody Bradstreete, Mr. Carlton, Joseph Jowett, Mathew Boyse, Richard Swan, Ld. Reminton and John Tod. He

had two traps for wolves, valued at fourteen shillings. Filed March —, 1656.

Inventory of · the estate of ffrancis Parrat of Rowley, lately deceased, taken by Mr. Joseph Jawet, Max Jawet, Ezekiel Northine and John Smith. Amount, £357, 5s.; real, £197; personal, £160, 5s.

— *Files.*]

Court, Sept. 30, 1656.

Judges: Mr. Symon Brodstreet, Mr. Samuell Symonds, Maj.-gen. Denison, Mr William Hubart and Mr. Richard Dummer.

Trial jury: Joseph Medcalfe, Tho: Bishop, Audr: Hodges, John Denison, John Addams, James Barker, Edw. Hassen, John Smith, Will: Ilsly, Rich: Dole, Hugh Marsh and ffran: Pabody.

Grand jury: George Gidding, Richard Jacob, Symon Tompson, Moses Pengry, Edward Bragg, Robert Day, John Cheeny, Will: Moody, Tho: Smith, Lt. Remington, Will Hobson, Will: Law, Jo: Steuens and Will: Evans.

Walter Roper v. Stephen Kent, attorney of William Wakefield. Review.

Samuell Graves v. John ffullar and wife Elizabeth. Slander done his wife in her name.

James Adams v. Samuell Bennett. For taking away a cart and pair of wheels.

James Adams v. Nicolas Pinion. Debt.

Daniell Clarke v. Allan Perley. For non-performance of work by his son.

Daniell Clarke v. Mr. William Bartholmew. For not supporting a division-fence.

Daniell Clarke v. Mr. William Bartholmew. For a heifer promised to his wife.

John Averill v. Mr. Daniell Epps. For not returning a cow which the latter had to winter.

Robert Tucker v. James Walker. For getting away Jonathan Brigg, etc.

John Hathorne, assignee and attorney of Nicholas Pinion v. Henry Lenourd.

John Vinton, being attached, and writ not entered, allowed costs.

John Hathorne v. Nicolas Pinion.

William Evans v. Evan Morice. Slander.

William Evans and wife Agnes v. Evan Morice. Slander.

Richard Kimball in behalf of his son Caleb v. Thomas Parsons. Slander.

Richard Shatswell v. Richard Kimball, sr., and Richard Kimball, jr. Debt.

Richard Shatswell v. Henry Kimball. For striking his maid.

Thomas Rowell in behalf of his daughter Abigail Ossgood v. ffrances Leech. Slander, saying his daughter was with child.

Elias Parkman, being attached by John Williams, acknowledged judgment.

Corp. John Andrews licensed to keep an ordinary at the White Horse.

John Trumble allowed clerk of the writs for Rowley.

Tho: Dorman fined for not warning the freeman to meet to nominate magistrates.

Silvester Evely fined for neglect of carrying the votes of the freemen of Gloucester to the shire town.

Freemen of Wennam fined for not sending their votes for nomination of magistrates to their shire town.

County tax to be levied.

Witnesses in the case of William Bingley and Elizabeth Preston to be paid by him.

Hackaliah Bridges, accused by Sarah ffrench of his getting her with child, bound over, being brought by Sergent ffrench.

Allen Perley released from ordinary training, paying ten shillings yearly to the use of the company.

Robert Long and Rich: Browne, both of Newbury, released from ordinary training, paying eight shillings each year to the use of the company.

Stephen Webster released from training for one year.

Richard Loell fined for offering violence toward the body of Jane Boulton tending to uncleanness. [Richard Lowle of Newbury presented 30: 7: 1656. Wit: Jane Boulton.— *Files.*]

Caleb Johnson of Andover died intestate. Administration on his estate was

granted to Henry Ingalls. Amount of the inventory of the estate £20, 8s.

John ffargason to be whipped for uncleanness breaking, prison and lying.

Sarah ffrench to be whipped fifteen stripes.

[John ffargison and Sarah ffrench, both of Ipswich, presented, 30 : 7 : 1656, for uncleanness, together.—*Files*.]

Henry Kimball licensed to keep an ordinary and draw wine and strong water at Wennam.

Nathaniell Stow, attached by Rich : Shatswell, and the writ not entered, allowed costs.

John Cogswell and Phillip ffowlar consent to an assignment of said John of his servant Thomas ffowlar unto his uncle Phillip ffowlar.

Ordered that Mr. Willson take care to set up a fence at the house of correction and impowered to warn men to the work.

[Presentments (part) made 30 : 7 : 1656 :—

John ffargison, for purloining his master's goods, as malt, wool and stockings. Wit : John Andros, sr., Samuel Ingalls and Ester Dicks.

John ffargison, for several lies about borrowing a horse. Wit : John Andros, sr., and Edward Bridges.

Humphrey Griffin, for profaning the Sabbath in unloading a load of barley before sundown. Wit : Thomas ffouler and Anne Sawer.

Edward Bridges of Andiver, for lying in saying he had got 100 rails for Shawshin bridge. Wit : Hon. Mr. Broadstreet, William Ballard and Robert Barnard. Also, for saying that he had a letter from his father to his master. Wit : Henry Ingalls and Thomas Varnum.

Evin Moris of Topsfield, for reviling the ordinance of God, and such as are in the church fellowship, " saying when some was together keeping a day of Humiliation that they were Howling like wolues and lifting up there paws for there Children saying the gallows were built for members and members Children and if

there had beene noe members of Churches there would haue been noe need of gallows." Wit : James How, jr., John How, John Pearly and Mary How.

Signed by George Giddinge in the name of the rest.

Rowley vital records, 1656 :—

Sarah Philips, daughter of Samuell and Sarah, born 1 mo : 7.

John Palmer, son of John and Margarit, born 1 : 15.

Martha Clarke, daughter of Richard and Alice, born 1 mo : 10.

Joseph Jewit, son of Joseph and Ann, born 2 mo : 1.

Sarah Tenny, daughter of William and Katherin, born 7 : 20.

Mary Spofard, daughter of John and Elesabeth, born 9 mo : 1.

John Wood, son of Thomas and Ann, born 9 mo : 2.

Samuell Kilbourne, son of George and Elesabeth, born 9 mo : 11.

Mary Plats, daughter of Jonathan and Elesabeth, born 9 mo : 11.

John Burkbie, son of Thomas and Martha, born 9 : 16.

Hannah Jonson, daughter of John and Hannah, born 9 : 20.

Sarah Scot, daughter of Benjamin and Margaret, born 11 mo : 1.

Sarah Pickard, daughter of John and Jane, born 1 : 1.

Henry Ryley married Mary Eletrope, 8 mo : 12 : 1656.

Nicholas Jackson married Elesabeth Chaplin Dec. 9.

Henry Sewell buried 1 mo : 1656.

Signed by John Trumble.

Newbury vital records, 1655 :—

Joseph, son of Will Richardson, born May 18, 1655.

Sarah, daughter of John Poore, born June 5, 1655.

Christopher, son of Christopher Bartlet, born June 11, 1655.

James, son of James Jackman, born June 22, 1655.

John, son of Richard Bartlett, born June 22, 1655.

Timothy, son of Nicholas Noyes, born June 23, 1655.

John, son of George Little, born July 28.

Elizabeth, daughter of John Bishop, born Aug. 1, 1655.

Sara, daughter of William Ilsly, born Aug. 13, 1655.

Mary, daughter of William Bolton, born Sept. 25, 1655.

Sara, daughter of John Pike, born Sept. 13, 1655.

Hester, daughter of John Bond, born Sept. 3, 1655.

Ephraim, son of John Davis, born Sept. 29, 1655.

Elizabeth, daughter of John Knight, born Oct. 18, 1655.

Sara, daughter of Stephen Grenleafe, born —— 18, 1655.

John, son of Aquila Chase, born Nov. 2.

Debora, daughter of Tristram Coffin, born Nov. 10, 1655.

Ruth, daughter of Edw: Richardson, born Nov. 23, 1655.

Sara, daughter of James Ordway, born Jan. 14, 1655.

Elizabeth, daughter of Stephen Swett, born Jan. 17, 1655.

William, son of William Sawyer, born Feb. 1, 1655.

Abigail, daughter of David Wheeler, born Feb. 2, 1655.

John, son of John Webster, born Feb. 11, 1655.

Hanna, daughter of Samuell Plumer, born Feb. 16, 1655.

Sara, daughter of Mr. James Noyes, born March 21, 1655.

Henry Fay died June 30, 1655.

John Wallington died Feb. 6, 1655.

Thomas Silver died March 3, 1655.

Elizabeth Morse died March 18, 1655.

Elizabeth Bishop died March 11, 1655.

John Tilletson married Jane Evans May 24, 1755.

Daniell Thurston married Anna Pell Oct. 20, 1655.

p^r Anthony Somerby.

—*Files.*]

To be continued.

WILL OF THOMAS FLINT.

The will of Thomas Flint was proved in the court at Salem June —, 1663. The following copy is transcribed from the original on file in the office of clerk of courts at Salem, volume IX, leaf 16.

Dated Aprill the first 1663.

This present writing doth declare that I Thomas fflint being one my sicke bed, doe leaue this as my Last will & testament. To my wife I giue fiftie Acres of emproved Land & my meadow & housing. To my fonne Thomas I Giue thirtie acres of vpland one my ffarme next to Mr Gardners as hee fees fit not entrenching one his mothers meadow or broken land as alfo ten pounds in Corne or Cattell all which he is to enjoy at age: As *alfo after* my wiues deceafe to enjoy two thirds of my farme i bought of which was Mr Higginsons & Goodman Goodall, & in cafe his mother doth marrie then that he shall enjoy the one halfe of the emproved Lands & meadow & housing. To my fonnes George & John, I give all my Land I bought beyond the River, to enjoy equally devided to them when they are at age or at theire mothers deceafe yf fhee die before, it is my will that yf George die without feed, then my fonne John to enjoy his part, & yf John die without feed then my fonne George to enjoy his parte. To my fonne Joseph I give the other third part of my Land which was Mr Higginfons & Goodman Goodalls, It is provided that my fonne Joseph enjoy it at his mothers deceafe, & yf my fonne Thomas die without feed vnmarried then his part to fall to my fonne Joseph & Contratiwife yt my fonne Joseph die without feed then his part to fall to Thomas & foe to pafs from one to another yf hee that enjoyes it die without ifsue. To my daughter Elizabeth I Giue thirtie pounds at marriage in Corne & Cattell, & I doe appoint my fonne Thomas when he enjoyes his two thirds as abouefaid then to pay to my Daughter Elizabeth & in cafe the farme fall into Josephs hands before he is of age or after he to pay her the faid ten pounds I doe

appoint my wife whole executor, I en-
treate my Two freinds M⁏ William Browne
Senio⁏ & Goodman Moulton to bee my
overseers, to see this my will & testament
pformed, & this I Leaue at my Last will
and Testament. In witnefs wheareof I set
to my hand

Testes ⎨ Robert Moulton   T. F.
     Joseph Pores marke
     Job Swinerton Juner

my will is that my wife at her death
giue the estate fhee leaues to my children
whome shee will

my defire is that my freind Job Swinerton Junior be joined with m⁏ Browne &
Goodman moulton.

SUFFOLK COUNTY DEEDS.

VOLUME III.

The following are abstracts of all records
in volume III of the Suffolk county registry of deeds relating to Essex county
persons and property, when parties are
given as residing, or property is mentioned
as being located in Essex county. The
records in this volume are from 1656 to
1661.

Joseph Armitage of Lynn, for £26,
mortgaged to Capt. Thomas Savage "two-
thirteenth shares in y⁏ Condit neare y⁏
Dock & house of" grantee, which shares
were granted to me on execution by court
at Boston June 25, 1656, against the
estate of Mr. Jn⁰ Bex and Company
undertakers of ye Iron workes at Lynn
and Brantry, by Sam⁏ Archer, marshall,
July 13, 1656.—*Page* 3.

Samuel Bennet of Lynn conveyed to
George Wallis, gent., a farm house in
Boston, called Rumly Hall, and barn and
land, lying on Lynn bounds; and eight
acres over the creek in Lynn opposite the
said house; and by this bond Mr. Wallis
bound himself to pay Mr. Bennet £200,
Dec. 3, 1656.—*Page* 4.

Joseph Armitage, assignee of Mr. Samuel Bennet of Lynn and Daniel Salmon,
administrator of the estate of Joseph
Boovy recovered judgment against Mr.

John Becks & Company and Mr. John
Giffard, agent for said John Becks & Company, formerly undertakers for ye Iron
workes at Lynn, Joseph Armitage for
£102, 9s., 9d., and Daniell Salman for
£11, 15s., 3d., and several parcels of land
in Brantry, of or belonging to the furnace
in Brantry, were set off to said judgment
creditors, who now convey to William
Pen of Brantry 300 acres in Brantry May
13, 1657.—*Page* 30.

Raph Upcraft of Norwich, ropemaker,
appointed his son-in-law Abraham
Catesse of Norwich, feltmaker, his attorney to recover of John Geddney, now or
late of Salem, worsted weaver, £7, 10s.,
Feb. 9, 1656.—*Page* 59.

John Holwey of Bristol, England, and
John Richbell of Charlestown, merchants,
bond to William Browne of Salem, merchant, Dec. 15, 1657, conditioned to pay
£60 in sugar at 3d. per pound to be put
aboard a ketch in ye Barbadoes.—*Page* 81.

At court in Boston Sept. 14 and 15,
1653, several creditors of the undertakers
of the Iron works sued the estate of Mr.
John Bex and company of undertakers,
as aforesaid, recovered judgment for
£3,658, 13s., 4d., including bill of
Henry Webb of Boston, merchant,
William Payne of Boston, merchant,
mortgaged the Iron works at Lynn and
Brantry to Mr. Webb to secure him for
his £1,300, payable in twenty-five tons of
bar iron delivered at Boston in the dock,
Feb. 3, 1657.—*Page* 137.

Jane, the now wife of Richard Tare, late
of Boston, heretofore the widow of John
Parker, late of Boston, deceased, with
Thomas Parker, her son, for love, gave to
her children, Jn⁰, Thomas and Noah
Parker, for their education and maintenance, 15:5:1646, after her death, her
house and land in Boston, and forty acres
at Muddy river; said Jane Tare and
Thomas her son, for £50, conveyed to
Stephen Greenlefe of Newbury, blacksmith, said house and some land Oct. 14,
1656.—*Page* 148.

In general court, in suit of Mr. Jn⁰ Gifford, attorney to Mr. Jn⁰ Bex & Company,

Capt. Savage and others May 25, 1658, was ordered to be recorded the letters of attorney from several of the company to Mr. Bex and to Mr. Gifford.

Certificate of Sr. Rob' Tichborne, knight, Lord Major of the city of London, and the aldermen or senators of London, that, in the Chamber of the Guild hall of London, John Gifford of the parish of Allhallowes Barking, London, merchant, aged about 34 years, ffrancis Wiseman of the precinct of the White Fryers, London scrivenir, aged about 61 years, and Thomas Wiseman, son of said Francis Wiseman, aged about 16 years, men of credit, made oath that said John Gifford and ffrancis Wiseman deposed that had been showed to them a deed or letter of attorney dated July 16, 1657, said to have been made by Thomas ffoley, Nicholas Bond, Walter ffrost, John Pococke, George Sharpulus, William Greenhill, William Hegcocke and William Beeke, adventurers and copartners, with others in Iron works at Lynn and Brantrey, appointing John Beck of London, merchant, one of the company, their attorney and agent, Sept. 1, 1657. Signed by Jo: Bigge.

Above said partners, for the further managing and carrying on said works, employing divers servants both of ye English and Scottish nation belonging to said adventurers, appoint John Beck their attorney July 16, 1657.

Another copy of said letter of attorney, dated Aug. 25, 1657, to Capt. Robert Bridges of Lynn, Capt. William Ting of Boston, Henry Webb and Joshua ffoote of Boston, Capt. Rob' Keayne and Josias Winslow of Boston, Aug. 25, 1697.
—*Pages* 155-161.

Samuell Bennet of Boston, yeoman, for £23, conveyed to John Otway of Boston, husbandman, land in Boston and Lynn, bounded by land of William Merriam, Capt. Robert Bridges, Lt. Thomas Marshall, etc., Nov. 10, 1657.—*Page* 161.

Symon Bradstreete of Andover, gent, agreed to ship in several vessels to Barbadoes beef and pork to Charles Richards

of Barbadoes, merchant, Niccolas Morri etc., Oct. last, 1657.- *Page* 169.

Thomas Broughton of Boston, merchant and wife Mary, he being indebted to th amount of £4,000, to Henry Shrimpte and Lt. Richard Cooke of Boston, merchants, and Walter Price of Salem, merchant, and also to Anthony Stoddard John Checkley and others, conveyed to them land and buildings in Boston April 19, 1659. Possession of Noddle's island etc., given to Walter Price for himself and the others the next day.—*Pages* 228-230

Thomas Broughton of Center Haven in Boston, merchant, shipped aboard the good ship Hope now riding in Piscataqua river pine boards and staves, for Barbadoes, conveyed one-fourth of the cargo to John Croad of Salem, merchant, and threefourths to Hezekikiah Usher of Boston, merchant, April 20, 1659.—*Page* 233.

Thomas Broughton of Boston, merchant, for £120, to Lt. Richard Cooke of Boston and Walter Price of Salem, merchant, the good ketch Amitie, Robert Lemon, master, being twenty-five tons, etc., May 2, 1659.—*Page* 237.

Henry Shrimpton reconveyed to Thomas Broughton a moiety of the real estate conveyed as above (page 228), June 23, 1659.—*Page* 248.

Thomas Broughton of Centre Haven, in Boston, merchant, who conveyed to Richard Cooke of Boston and Walter Price of Salem, merchants, and others April 20, 1659, certain land and ship Hope, conveys to said Cooke and Price said property, land at Salmon Falls, Noddle's island, vessel, etc., June 23, 1659.—*Page* 250.

Agreement made in 1647, between Robert Paine, William Paine, John Whittingham, John Whiple, Jonathan Wade and William Bartholomew to carry on a trade at Ipswich for five years, which expired Jan. 24, 1652, the stock was then divided by Mr. Samuell Symonds, Mr. Daniell Dennison and Robert Lord of Ipswich. Now William Paine of Boston, merchant, releases to said Robert Paine of Ipswich, merchant, any claim against

him, by reason of said agreement, etc., April 12, 1660.—*Page* 357.

Salem, Aug. 17, 1657, Will Sheares orders his friend Mr. John Checkley to pay to Mr. Edmond Batters £15.—*Page* 371.

Edward Rawson, heretofore of Gillingham, Dorsetshire, England, now of Boston, New England, gentleman, before his marriage with Rachell, daughter of Richard Perne of Gillingham, gentleman, who agreed to give said Edward Rawson £300 as a marriage portion, and Edward promised to add £600 of his own estate to it to purchase lands for a jointure for himself and wife for their lives and then to their heirs, but Richard Perne died before the contract was carried out; Edward and his wife removed to New England, and agreed with the widow of Mr. Perne that he (Edward) would carry out the agreement if she would pay balance of the £300 remaining unpaid, he (Edward) would make over land and buildings in England to friends for the sole use of said Rachel his wife and her heirs by Edward to the value of three hundred pounds. Edward received of Rachell Perne, widow of said Richard, the balance about 1642. Now said Edward conveys to Thomas Danforth of Cambridge, gentleman, Edmond Batter of Salem, merchant, and Samuel Torrey of Hull, clerk, friends in trust for said Rachell Rawson certain chattels and dwelling house and land in Boston, Dec. 21, 1660. Cancelled May 10, 1664, by a new deed.—*Page* 414.

Robert Nash of Boston, butcher, for £250, conveyed to William Bartholmew of Ipswich, merchant, buildings and land in Boston, July 26, 1659.—*Page* 438.

Evan Thomas of Boston, vintner, and wife Alice promise to pay to her four daughters (by her former husband Phillip Catlin of Lynn, merchant, deceased), Mary Catlin, Sarah Catlin, Susanna Catlin, and Hannah Catlin, £20 each, at date of their marriage; and the real estate in Lynn to be Mrs. Thomas' and after her decease her son Ebenezer Catlin's, Nov. 8, 1659.—*Page* 447.

Evan Thomas of Boston, vintner, to William Bartholmew of Boston, merchant, and Oliver Purchase of Lynn, friends in trust on account of the late Alice, relict of Philip Kirtland of Lynn, now wife of said Evan Thomas, for her and her children (Mary Kirtland, Sarah Kirtland, Susannah Kirtland, Hannah Kirtland and Ebenezer Kirtland) house and land known by the name of the King's Armes, Ebenezer to have the real estate at twenty-one years of age, etc., April 12, 1661.—*Page* 483.

Lt. William Philips of Boston, for £78, 15*s.*, mortgaged to Richard Dummer of Ipswich, gentleman, land in Boston Oct. 28, 1659.—*Page* 512.

THE OLD ROCKING CHAIR.

BY T. C. HARBAUGH.

It stands over there in the corner alone,
Its varnish is cracked and one rocker is gone;
What's left of its tidy is dusty and brown
And scattered and silent its fringes hang down;
No songster appeareth to warble its praise,
When we were but children it saw its best days;
And many a face that was rosy and fair
Reposed after play in the old rocking chair.

How often in it in the winter nights cold
The tales of the fairies by nurses were told;
How often we listened with kiss-bedewed brow
To lullaby strains that we hear even now;
Aye, far in the past with its sunshine and shade
I hear the sweet sounds that the old rockers made;
And now as I listen I willingly share
The loves of the years with the old rocking chair.

She rests where the roses their love vigils keep
Who fondly and tenderly rocked me to sleep;
But still, when I look in the corner, I trace
Within the old rocker a well-cherished face;
The years that have vanished no more to return
But deeper the joys of a childhood inurn,
And thus doth the past with a halo most fair
Re crown with its beauty the old rocking chair.

No longer to music now fast and now slow
At morning and evening it moves to and fro;
No more from its depths where sweet memories throng
With an angelic touch comes a lullaby song;
'Tis covered with dust, but the dust cannot hide
The prints of the hands that will ever abide
Upon the old arms so reposeful and fair,
When memory turns to the old rocking chair.

SOLDIERS AND SAILORS OF THE REVOLUTION.

Continued from page 41.

CHARLES BOWDEN of Salem; seaman, ship "Rhodes," com. by Capt. Nehemiah Buffington; descriptive list of officers and crew dated Aug. 14, 1780; age, 22 years; stature, 5 ft., 7 in.; complexion, light; residence, Salem.

EDWARD BOWDEN of Cape Ann; drummer, Capt. Joseph Roby's co., Col. Moses Little's (17th) reg.; co. return [probably Oct., 1775]; age, 28 years; enl. June 6, 1775; *also*, Capt. Bradbury Saunders' (2d) co.; enl. Jan. 16, 1776; rolls made up to Aug. 31, 1776; service, 7 mos., 15 days, at Gloucester; *also*, list of men mustered in Suffolk co. by Nathaniel Barber, mustermaster, dated Jan. 8, 1777; Capt. Abraham Hunt's co., Col. John Patterson's reg.

ELIAS BOWDEN of Marblehead; priv., Capt. John Selman's (8th) co., Col. John Glover's (21st) reg.; muster roll dated Aug. 1, 1775; enl. May 25, 1775; service, 2¼ mos., 5 days; *also*, co. return dated Cambridge, Oct. 9, 1775; *also*, order for bounty coat dated Marblehead, Jan. 3, 1776.

FRANCIS BOWDEN of Lynn; Capt. Ezra Newhall's co., Col. Mansfield's reg.; order for advance pay dated Cambridge, June 8, 1775; *also*, priv.; muster roll dated Aug. 1, 1775; enl. May 3, 1775; service, 3 mos., 5 days; *also*, co. return dated Oct. 6, 1775; *also*, Capt. Newhall's co.; Col. Israel Hutchinson's (19th) reg.; order for bounty coat dated Winter Hill, Nov. 4, 1775.

FRANCIS BOWDEN of Marblehead; Capt. John Selman's (8th) co., Col. John Glover's (21st) reg.; receipt for advance pay dated Cambridge, June 27, 1775; *also*, priv.; muster roll dated Aug. 1, 1775; enl. May 25, 1775; service, 2¼ mos., 5 days; *also*, co. return dated Cambridge, Oct. 9, 1775; reported on furlough; *also*, order for bounty coat dated Marblehead, Jan. 3, 1776.

FRANCIS BOWDEN of Marblehead; return of men enl. or drafted into Continental Army from Col. Jonathan Glover (5th Essex co.) reg.; dated Nov. 2, 1777; residence, Marblehead; enl. to Marblehead; drafted for 8 mos.

FRANCIS BOWDEN of Marblehead; descriptive list of officers and crew of the ship "Jack" (privateer), com. by Capt. Nathan Brown, dated July 1, 1780; age, 35 years; stature, 5 ft., 6 in.; complexion, dark; residence, Marblehead.

FRANCIS BOWDEN of Salem; mate, ship "Rhodes," com. by Capt. Nehemiah Buffington; descriptive list of officers and crew dated Aug. 14, 1780; age, 30 years; stature, 5 ft., 8 in.; complexion, light, residence, Salem.

JOHN BOWDEN of Marblehead; Capt. Courtis' co., Col. John Glover's reg.; receipt for advance pay dated Cambridge, June 27, 1775; *also*, serg., Capt. John Glover's co., Col. John Glover's reg.; muster roll dated Aug. 1, 1775; enl. May 10, 1775; service 2 mos., 26 days.

JOHN BOWDEN of Marblehead; Capt. John Selman's (8th) co., Col. John Glover's (21st) reg.; receipt for advance pay dated Cambridge, June 27, 1775; *also*, priv.; muster roll dated Aug. 1, 1775; enl. May 25, 1775; service, 2¼ mos., 1 day; *also*, corp.; co. return dated Cambridge, Oct. 9, 1775; *also*, order for bounty coat dated Marblehead, Jan. 3, 1775.

SAMUEL BOWDEN of Marblehead; drummer, Capt. William Courtis' (1st) co., Col. John Glover's (21st) reg.; co. return [probably Oct., 1775]; reported present, sick; *also*, order for bounty coat dated Cambridge, Dec. 21, 1775.

SAMUEL BOWDEN of Marblehead; serg., Capt. Francis Felton's co.; receipt for advance pay dated Marblehead, Sept. 26, 1775; *also*, same co.; enl. July 17, 1775; service to Dec. 31, 1775, 5 mos., 28 days; co. raised and stationed in Marblehead; *also*, same co.; enl. Jan. 4, 1776; service to Nov. 15, 1776, 10 mos., 13 days.

SAMUEL BOWDEN of Marblehead; return of men enl. into Continental Army

from Col. Jonathan Glover's (5th Essex co.) reg., dated Nov. 7, 1777 ; residence, Marblehead ; enl. for Marblehead for 3 years.

SAMUEL BOWDEN of Marblehead ; quartermaster, ship " Rhodes," com. by Capt. Nehemiah Buffington ; descriptive list of officers and crew dated Aug. 14, 1780; age, 35 years; stature, 5 ft., 7 in.; complexion, dark; residence, Marblehead.

SAMUEL BOWDEN, JR., of Marblehead ; priv., Capt. Francis Felton's co.; enl. Jan. 8, 1776; service to Nov. 15, 1776, 10 mos., 9 days.

SIMEON BOWDEN (also given Simpson), JR., of Marblehead; priv., Capt. Francis Felton's co.; enl. July 17, 1775; service to Nov. 1, 1775, 3 mos., 23 days; co. raised and stationed at Marblehead ; *also*, same co.; service from Oct. 31, 1775, to Dec. 31, 1775, 2 mos., 5 days.

THOMAS BOWDEN of Marblehead ; 2d lt, Capt. Samuel Trevett's co., Col. Richard Gridley's (artillery) reg.; muster roll dated June 21, 1775; enl. May 8, 1775; service, 1 mo., 16 days; *also*, Capt. William Hooper's co.; receipt for advance pay dated Salem, Sept. 26, 1775; *also*, same co.; enl. July 13, 1775; service to Dec. 31, 1775, 6 mos., 2 days; *also*, 2d lt., Capt. Hooper's (2d) co.; list of sea coast officers stationed at Marblehead ; commissioned Jan. 6, 1776; *also*, same co.; enl. Jan. 4, 1776; dis. Nov. 15, 1776; service, 10 mos., 13 days.

THOMAS BOWDEN of Marblehead; return of men enl. into Continental Army from Col. Jonathan Glover's (5th Essex co.) reg., dated Nov. 7, 1777 ; residence, Marblehead ; enl. for Marblehead ; enlistment, 1 year.

WILLIAM BOWDEN of Salem ; drummer, Capt. Thomas Barnes' co., Col. Mansfield's (later Hutchinson's) reg.; muster roll dated Aug. 1, 1775; enl. May 20, 1775 ; service, 2 mos., 16 days.

BENJAMIN BOWDON of Lynn ; priv., Capt. Daniel Galusha's (10th) co., Col. Ruggles Woodbridge's (25th) reg.; co. return [probably Oct., 1775]; *also*, list of men who served at Concord battle and else-

where [year not given], belonging to Lynn, now called Lynn, Lynnfield and Saugus.

JOHN BOWDON of Marblehead ; 1st serg., Capt. John Glover, jr.'s (10th) co., Col. John Glover's (21st) reg.; co. return [probably Oct., 1775].

SAMUEL BOWDON of Marblehead; drummer, Capt. William Courtis' co., Col. John Glover's reg.; muster roll dated Aug. 1, 1775; enl. May 10, 1775; service, 2 mos., 27 days.

JOSHUA BOWDWELL of Methuen ; Capt. John Popkin's co., Col. Richard Gridley's (artillery) reg.; order for bounty coat dated Winter Hill, Jan. 2, 1776.

JOSHUA BOWDWELL of Methuen; matross, Capt. John Popkin's co.; Col. Richard Gridley's (artillery) reg.; muster roll dated Aug. 1, 1775 ; enl. June 7, 1775; service, 1 mo., 27 days.

EDWARD BOWEN of Lynn ; Capt. Addison Richardson's co., Col. John Mansfield's reg.; order for advance pay dated Cambridge, June 8, 1775 ; *also*, priv.; muster roll dated Aug. 1, 1775 ; enl. May 20, 1775 ; service, 2 mos., 16 days ; *also*, Capt. Richardson's co., Col. Israel Hutchinson's (19th) reg.; receipt for wages for Sept., 1775, dated Camp at Winter Hill ; *also*, order for bounty coat dated Camp at Winter Hill, Oct. 27, 1775.

MICHAEL BOWEN of Marblehead (also given Manchester, Rutland and Beverly) ; return of men in Col. Gerrish's reg. stationed at Chelsea and Brookline dated Aug. 3, 1775; reported ill with dysentery at Chelsea ; *also*, fifer, Capt. Richard Dodge's (3d) co., Col. Loammi Baldwin's (late Gerrish's) 38th reg.; return dated Chelsea, Sept. 1, 1775; *also*, co. return dated Chelsea, Oct. 2, 1775 ; reported enl. May 1, 1775 ; *also*, return of men enl. into Continental Army from 1st Beverly co., Essex co. reg., dated Feb. 13, 1778; residence, Beverly; enl. for town of Beverly; joined Capt. Fairfield's co., Col. Wigglesworth's reg.; enlistment, 3 years ; reported mustered by Esquire Cushing ; *also*, fifer, Capt. Fowle's co., Col. Calvin Smith's (13th) reg.; Continental Army pay ac-

counts for service from Jan. 1, 1780, to Dec. 31, 1780; *also*, descriptive list of enl. men dated West Point, Jan. 29, ·781; Capt. Daniel's co,, Lt.-col. Smith's reg.; age, 22 years; stature, 5 ft., 8 in.; complexion, light; hair, dark; eyes, light; residence, Rutland; enl. Nov., 1779, by Lt. Levi Holden; rank, fife major; enlistment, during war; *also*, fife major, Capt. Japheth Daniel's co., Lt.-col. Calvin Smith's (6th) reg.; return for wages, etc., for Jan., 1781—Dec., 1782; reported transferred to field and staff March, 1782; *also*, order for wages for service in 1781 and 1782, dated Beverly; *also*, Col. Thomas Nixon's (6th) reg.; return of men entitled to gratuity for serving during the war; *also*, certificate dated Boston, March 5, 1805, stating that he is entitled to land on account of service in the 13th reg.

NATHAN BOWEN of Marblehead; priv., Capt. Nathaniel Lindsey's co.; service from Dec. 10, 1776 to March 18, 1777, 3 mos., 9 days; co. raised in Marblehead to reinforce Continental Army.

WILLIAM BOWER of Amesbury (also given Scarborough); return of men enl. into Continental Army from Capt. William Ballard's co., Essex co. reg., dated Amesbury, April 18, 1778; residence, Amesbury (also given Scarborough); enl. for Amesbury; joined Capt. William Scott's co., Col. Handly's (also given Col. Hanley's) reg.; enlistment, 3 years.

JOHN BOWERS of Topsfield; priv., Capt. Joshua French's co., Col. Edward Wigglesworth's reg.; pay abstract for mileage from Albany home, dated Jan. 30, 1777.

MICHAEL BOWIN of Manchester; fifer, Capt. Richard Dodge's co., Col. Loammi Baldwin's (late Gerrish's) 38th reg.; muster roll dated Aug. 1, 1775; service, 13 weeks, 1 day; *also*, order for county coat dated Chelsea, Dec. 27, 1775.

EDWARD BOWING of Lynn; priv., Capt. Addison Richardson's co., Col. Mansfield's (19th) reg. under com. of Lt.-col. Israel Hutchinson; co. return dated Oct. 6, 1775.

CHARLES BOWLES of Salem; Capt. Micajah Gleason's co., Col. John Nixon' reg.; receipt for advance pay dated Jun. 10, 1775; *also*, priv.; muster roll dat Aug. 1, 1775; enl. April 23, 1775; service, 3 mos., 16 days; *also*, co. return dated Sept. 30, 1775; Capt. Gleason's (3d) co., Col. Nixon's (4th) reg.; return of men in service Sept. and Oct., 1776, dated North Castle; *also*, receipts for wages for Sept. and Oct., 1776, dated Camp Winter Hill; *also*, receipts for wages for Nov. and Dec., 1776; *also*, return of men who engaged to serve the month of Jan., 1777, dated Springfield, Jan. 25, 1777.

JOHN BOWLES of Beverly; priv., Capt. Micajah Gleason's co., Col. John Nixon's reg.; muster roll dated Aug. 1, 1775; enl. May 1, 1775; service, 3 mos., 8 days; *also*, co. return dated Sept. 30, 1775; *also*, receipt for wages for Sept., 1775, dated Camp Winter Hill.

JOHN BOWLES of Beverly (also given Ipswich); priv., Capt. Porter's co., Col. Benjamin Tupper's reg.; Continental Army pay accounts for service from Feb. 1, 1777, to Dec. 31, 1779; *also*, Capt. Billy Porter's co., Col. Tupper's reg.; muster roll for Jan., 1779, dated West Point; *also*, Capt. Samuel Page's (light infantry) co., Col. Tupper's (15th) reg.; muster roll dated West Point, April 5, 1779; enl. Feb. 1, 1777, for 3 years.

JONATHAN BOWLES of Beverly (also given Ipswich); priv., Capt. Ebenezer Francis' co., Col. Mansfield's reg.; muster roll dated Aug. 1, 1775; enl. May 4, 1775; service, 3 mos., 5 days; *also*, Capt. Billy Porter's co., Col. Ebenezer Francis' reg.; subsistence from date of enlistment, Feb. 1, 1777, to time of arrival at destination, 52 days; marched to Bennington March 12, 1777; *also*, corp., Col. Benjamin Tupper's (10th) reg.; service from Jan. 1, 1781, to Jan. 1, 1782.

JONATHAN BOWLES of Beverly; descriptive list of enlisted men; age, 25 years; stature, 5 ft., 4 in., complexion, light; hair, brown; occupation, cordwainer; birthplace, Ipswich; residence, Beverly;

enl. for Boston, March 24, 1781 ; joined Capt. Benjamin Heywood's co., 6th reg.; enlistment, 3 years ; *also*, priv., Col. Benjamin Tupper's (10th) reg.; service from Feb. 1, 1782, to Jan. 1, 1783, 11 mos. ; *also*, Capt. T. Francis' co., 10th reg.; return for provisions, etc. [year not given]; *also*, Capt. Benjamin Heywood's co., Lt.-col. Calvin Smith's (6th) reg. ; return for wages, etc., for June-Dec., 1782 ; reported joined from 10th reg. Dec. 17, 1782 ; *also*, Capt. Heywood's (4th) co., Col. Tupper's (6th) reg. ; muster rolls for Jan., March and April, 1783.

REUBEN BOWLES of Ipswich ; priv., Capt. Elisha Whitney's co. of minute-men, which marched on the alarm of April 19, 1775, from Ipswich Hamlet to Mystic ; and also marched from Ipswich Hamlet to Cambridge May 1, 1775 ; service, 16 days.

JONATHAN BOWLS of Ipswich (also given Beverly); Lt. Billy Porter's co., Col. Mansfield's reg. ; order for advance pay dated Cambridge, June 8, 1775 ; *also*, priv., Capt. Ebenezer Francis' co., Col. Mansfield's reg.; co. return dated Oct. 6, 1775; *also*, Capt. Francis' co., Col. Israel Hutchinson's reg.; order for bounty coat dated Camp at Winter Hill, Oct. 26, 1775 ; *also*, return of men enlisted into Continental Army from 2d Beverly co. ; Essex co. reg., dated Feb. 13, 1778 ; residence, Beverly; enl. for Beverly; joined Capt. Billy Porter's co., Col. Francis' reg.; enlistment, 3 years ; *also*, corp., Col. Benjamin Tupper's (10th) reg. ; service from Jan. 1, 1782, to Jan. 1, 1783, 12 mos.

REUBEN BOWLS of Ipswich ; priv., Capt. Richard Dodge's co., Col. Loammi Baldwin's (late Gerrish's) reg.; muster roll dated Aug. 1, 1775 ; enl. May 12, 1775 ; service, 7 weeks, 4 days ; *also*, co. return dated Chelsea, Oct. 2, 1775 ; reported discharged July 4, 1775.

GEORGE BOYCE of Salem ; priv., Capt. William Warner's co., Col. Josiah Whitney's reg.; pay abstract for travel allowance, etc., dated Camp at Hull, June 18, 1776.

SAMUEL BOYES of Newburyport ; seaman, brig " Julius Cæsar," com. by Capt. Nathaniel Bently ; descriptive list of officers and crew dated June 21, 1780 ; age, 16 years, 2 mos.; stature, 5 ft., 2 in. ; complexion, light ; residence, Newburyport ; roll sworn to before naval officer at port of Falmouth.

BENJAMIN BOYNTON of Cape Ann ; priv., Capt. Joseph Roby's co., Col. Moses Little's (17th) reg.; co. return [probably Oct., 1775]; age, 36 years ; reported enl. May 29, 1775.

JOHN BOYLS of Beverly ; priv., Capt. Robert Dodge's co., Col. Jonathan Titcomb's reg.; marched April 25, 1777 ; service, 2 mos., 2 days, at Rhode Island. Roll dated Warren.

ASA BOYNTON of Rowley ; priv., Capt. Richard Peabody's co., Col. Edward Wigglesworth's reg. ; pay abstract for travel allowance from Ticonderoga home in 1776.

BENJAMIN BOYNTON of Cape Ann (also given Gloucester) ; priv., Capt. Joseph Roby's co., Col. Moses Little's reg.; order for bounty coat dated Dec. 11, 1775 ; *also*, list of men enl. into Continental Army [year not given]; residence, Gloucester ; enl. for Gloucester.

ENOCH BOYNTON of Newbury; descriptive list of men enl. from Essex co., 1779, to serve in the Continental Army ; age, 52 yrs. ; stature, 5 ft., 6 in. ; complexion, light ; residence, Newbury ; delivered to Lt. William Storey ; *also*, return of men mustered by John Cushing, muster master for Essex co., to join the Continental Army for 9 mos. dated Boxford, Dec. 8, 1779 ; enl. for Newbury; *also*, priv. Capt. Thomas Mighill's co., Col. Nathaniel Wade's (Essex co.) reg.; enl. July 5, 1780 ; dis. Oct. 10, 1780 ; service, 3 mos., 18 days ; enlistment, 3 mos.; co. raised to reinforce Continental Army.

JAMES BOYNTON of Boxford ; priv., Capt. William Perley's co. of minute-men, Col. James Frye's reg., which marched on the alarm of April 19, 1775 ; service to April 25, 1775, 7 days ; enl. Feb. 16, 1775 ; *also*, receipt for advance pay dated

Cambridge, June 22, 1775 ; *also*, muster roll dated Aug. 1, 1775 ; enl. April 26, 1775 ; service, 2 mos., 8 days; *also*, co. return [probably Oct., 1775]; reported died June 28, 1775.

JONATHAN BOYNTON of Andover ; priv., Capt. Benjamin Ames' co. of minute-men, Col. James Frye's reg., which marched on the alarm of April 19, 1775 ; service, 7 days ; *also*, return of men in camp at Cambridge, May 17, 1775 ; *also*, co. return dated Oct. 6, 1775 ; *also*, order for bounty coat dated Cambridge, Nov. 14, 1775 ; *also*, list of men enl. into Continental Army [year not given] ; residence, Andover ; enl. for Andover.

JOSEPH BOYNTON of Gloucester ; priv., Capt. John Baker's co., Col. Moses Little's (17th) reg.; co. return [probably Oct., 1775]; age, 50 yrs. ; reported enl. Aug. 1, 1775.

JOSHUA BOYNTON of Newbury; priv., Capt. Silas Adams' co., Col. Titcomb's reg.; service, 2 mos.; roll dated June 29, 1777.

MOSES BOYNTON of Andover; corp., Capt. Benjamin Ames' co. of minute-men, Col. James Frye's reg., which marched on the alarm of April 19, 1775 ; service, 7 days ; *also*, return of men in camp at Cambridge, May 17, 1775 ; *also*, corp., co. return dated Oct. 6, 1775 ; *also*, order for bounty coat dated Cambridge, Nov. 14, 1775.

MOSES BOYNTON of Rowley; priv., Capt. Eliphalet Spofford's co. of minute-men, Col. Samuel Gerrish's reg., which marched on the alarm of April 19, 1775, from Rowley (West parish) to Cambridge ; returned April 23, 1775 ; service, 6 days; *also*, Capt. Joseph Ilsley's co., Col. Cogswell's reg.; enl. Sept. 28, 1776 ; dis. Nov. 16, 1776 ; service, 2 mos., 2 days; roll dated Newcastle.

THOMAS BOYNTON of Andover ; serg., Capt. Benjamin Ames' co., of minute-men, Col. James Frye's reg., which marched on the alarm of April 19, 1775 ; service, 7 days ; *also*, return of men in camp at Cambridge, May 17, 1775 ; *also*, return of men who served in battle at Charlestown, dated Cambridge, June 19, 1775 ; *also*, co. return dated Oct. 6, 1775 ; *also*, order for bounty coat dated Cambridge, Nov. 14, 1775.

SAMUEL BRADBRY of Haverhill ; priv., Capt. Ebenezer Colby's co. of minute-men, Col. Johnson's reg., which marched on the alarm of April 19, 1775, to Cambridge ; service, 4 days ; *also*, Capt. Samuel Johnson's co., Col. Titcomb's reg.; service from date of arrival at Providence, R. I., April 27, 1777 ; to date of dis., June 27, 1777, 2 mos., 10 days ; roll dated Bristol.

WILLIAM BRADBRY of Haverhill ; priv., Capt. Ebenezer Colby's co. of minute-men, Col. Johnson's reg., which marched on the alarm of April 19, 1775, to Cambridge ; service, 2 days.

EBENEZER BRADBURY of Haverhill ; descriptive list of men enl. from Essex co. in 1779, to serve in the Continental Army ; age, 17 years ; stature, 5 ft.; complexion, light; residence, Haverhill ; delivered to Capt. L. Bailey.

To be continued.

NOTES.

Sarah Bowry married Charles Woodier Feb. 13, 1728-9.

Elizabeth Bowry married John Rose Jan. 20, 1733-4.

Joseph Bowery married Ann Tayner Nov. 19, 1702.

Elizabeth, Joseph and Sarah Bowry baptized June 3, 1716.

Grace, daughter of Charles and Sarah Bowry, and Joseph, son of Joseph Bowry, baptized Nov. 9, 1729.
—*Marblehead records.*

Mrs. Mary Bowiger married Capt. Christopher Clark, both of Salem, Dec. 12, 1695.—*Salem town records.*

Mary Boo (also Boos), daughter of Archibald Ferguson of Marblehead, 1726.

Mary Bowes alias Mary Grimes, single-woman, Sarah Brawden, widow, John Jackson, fisherman, and wife Sarah, all of Marblehead, 1745.

Piam Bowhow (Indian?), aged about seventy-seven in 1681.

Joel Bowker of Salem, blacksmith, 1796, 1797.

Robert Bow of Marblehead, cordwainer, and wife Mary, only heir of Archibald Ferguson of Marblehead, deceased, 1746. She had a daughter Patience Graham.

James Bowler of Lynn, baker, 1778, 1785; wife Betsey, 1785.

Thomas Bowler of Lynn, baker, 1786, 1796.

Thomas Bowler of Lynn, yeoman, 1789. —*Registry of deeds.*

Richard Bowland of Marblehead, 1668. —*Court files.*

Thomas Bowland published to Anna Twist, both of Salem, June 7, 1777.— *Salem town records.*

David Bowler (also Boler) of Lynn, 1753-1793 (was deceased in 1797); yeoman; wife Abigail (Fuller?), 1768-1793; child: David, lived in Marblehead, baker; married Sarah ———— before 1797; both living in 1798.—*Records.*

James Bowler of Marblehead, baker, 1781-1799; married Elizabeth Collins of Lynn May 19, 1781; administration was granted on his estate May 6, 1799, to Widow Sarah Bowler of Marblehead (surety, James Bowler of Marblehead, baker); estate was insolvent.—*Records.*

Widow Ruth Bowler of Haverhill appointed administratrix of estate of Oglando Bowler of Haverhill, seaman, Aug. 22, 1778.—*Probate records.*

S A L E M, July 18.

Wednesday died at Newbury-Port, Mrs. ELIZABETH GREENLEAF, Consort to BENJAMIN GREENLEAF, Esq; and eldest Daughter to the Rev. Dr. CHAUNCY of Boston.

July 17, 1769, Cadwallador Ford of Wilmington advertised for his indented servant lad Robert Kilby, who had run away. He was of short stature, well set, of a light complexion, brown hair, nearly eighteen years old. He wore when he went away, a brownish colored camblet coat, lined with red, striped linen and woolen jacket, double-breasted, green worsted plush breeches, blue seamed stockings, thick pumps, brass buckles, tow shirt, tow trousers, and felt hat. There was with him Joseph Ross, who was supposed to have run away from Ipswich, and to have said Robert to go with him. They had with them two brownish dogs each about as big as a fox.

BEVERLY, June 24, 1769.

THIS Evening the Remains of the second Wife of the Reverend Mr. CHIPMAN, of the Town, were decently interred, who died in the Morning of the 21st.

His first Wife was sister to the late Col. HALE, of Beverly; a Woman respectable for her Piety, an Ornament to her Sex, a Pattern to her Family, and a Crown to her Husband. By her he had his children, viz. eight Sons, and seven Daughters; three only of which Sons, and five of the Daughters, yet survive.

This his second Wife was sister to the late Reverend Mr. WARREN, of Wenham; a Woman of excellent Knowledge, especially in the sacred Oracles, and full of Goodness even as the other. Upon her coming into Family, she soon taught the younger Children to esteem and reverence her Person; and by her prudent and constant Exertions for their best Good, fixed them in a steady Course of chearful and filial Obedience to her, to the End; yea, excited their Gratitude to that Degree, that they seemed ready to expend their own Life for her Relief, in the Time of her Distress.—The Neighbourhood were moved with Grief, as her last Sickness came on. The Gentle women of her Acquaintance, both elder and younger, treated her with the Compassion due to a Sister or Mother in Adversity; sparing no Cost, no Labour, which might minister to her Ease or Comfort. Dying of a Dropsy, her Sufferings were constant, without Intermission, and very tedious for more than six Weeks. She patiently endured them, being animated with a lively Hope of her being present with the Lord as soon as she should be absent from the Body.

—*Essex Gazette, July* 11-18, 1769.

Henry Bowen of Marblehead published to Miss Mary Holliday of Newburyport Feb. 10, 1776.—*Newburyport town records.*

The blurred line on page 165 of volume X reads: "-hain, Feb. 8, 1705-6,‡ and Gerrish," and on page 168: "Enfield, Jan. 18, 1727."

Ambrose Bowden (No. 3, page 45) married Lydia ———, who was born about 1666.

Richard Babson (No. 9, page 1, volume V, of *The Antiquarian*) married Mary Dolliver before 1696.

Nathaniel Andrews married Eunice, only child of John & Eunice Bowles, 1803. The mother, Eunice, was daughter of Daniel Malloon of Salem, miller, who died in 1783.

—Ed.

Children of James and Fanny Bradburn: Fanny, born Jan. 9, 1798; Nancy, born Sept. 25, 1799.

Benjamin, son of Joseph and Mercy Blashfield, born Jan. 12, 1761.

—Beverly town records.

Prudence Braden married John Clinton July 6, 1752.—*Danvers town records.*

James Bowler married Lydia Burrill, both of Lynn, Feb. 25, 1779.

Thomas Bowler married Lydia Newhall, both of Lynn, Dec. 16, 1784; children: Thomas, born Jan. 3, 1786; John, born July 17, 1789; Nathaniel, born May 4, 1792; Samuel, born June 7, 1794.

—Lynn town records.

David Bowler married Sally Williams of Lynn July 5, 1789.

David Bowler published to Mary Procter Aug. 16, 1794.

David Bowler published to Sarah Johnson Dec. 19, 1795.

Nellie Bowler married Charles Hutchings of Penobscot Nov. 10, 1797.

William Bowler married Elizabeth Gordon April 18, 1794.

Lydia Burrill, daughter of James and Lydia Bowler, baptized Dec. 5, 1779.

—Marblehead records.

Christopher Bowles (also, Bouls) of Ipswich, 1691, 1711; yeoman, 1711.

Thomas Bowlin of Salem, mariner, 1796.

William Bowman of Haverhill, husbandman, 1750.

—Registry of deeds.

John Bowley[1] (also Bowlan) married Hannah Hadlock, both of Newbury (published March 21, 1718-9); children, born in Newbury: 1. Mary[2], born Dec. 13, 1719; 2. John[2], born Jan. 31, 1720; lived in Methuen; married Elizabeth Courser Dec. 7, 1744, in Newbury; children, born in Methuen: 1. Sarah[3], born May 31, 1746; married Samuel Chase of Newbury July 6, 1769; 2. Hannah[3], born Oct. 8, 1749; 3. John[3], born Aug. 31, 1752; 4. Oliver[3], born May 25, 1755; died Nov. 12, 1756; 5. Elizabeth[3], born April 21, 1758; 6. Lucy[3], born March 8, 1761; 7. Samuel[3], born July 16, 1764; 3. Hannah[2], born July 5, 1724; 4. Oliver[2], born July 25, 1726; married Anna Weed of Amesbury Feb. 28, 1744-5; 5. Abigail[2], born Dec. 31, 1728; 6. James[2], born Aug. 21, 1730; died young; 7. James[2], born July 14, 1737; married Martha Sergeant Aug. 11, 1763.—*Records.*

William Bowley married Abigail Goodridge, both of Newbury, March 13, 1791; and their daughter Abigail was born Jan. 16, 1792.—*Newbury town records.*

Ebenezer Bowman of Gloucester, 1741-1748; probably removed to Cambridge, when he was living in 1752; blacksmith, 1741-1752; married Elizabeth Sanders Nov. 23, 1741, in Gloucester; children, born in Gloucester: John, born Dec. 19, 1744; Elizabeth, born Dec. 26, 1746; John.—*Records.*

John Bowles, jr., married Lydia Wallis Oct. 9, 1788.

George Bowman of Ipswich married Mary Russell of Boston Sept. 21, 1737.

—Ipswich town records.

Thomas Bowlin married Anna Twiss, both of Salem, Dec. 12, 1784.

James Bowman married Mary Palmer, both of Salem, Oct. 5, 1773.

John Bowman married Violet Pike, negroes, Oct. 23, 1786.

John Bowman married widow Hannah Wilson, both of Salem, negroes, Oct. 20, 1793.

Betsey Bowman married Andrew Ward, 3d, both of Salem, Nov. 18, 1798.

Mary Bowman published to John Byrne, both of Salem, Sept. 2, 1797.
—*Salem town records.*

John Bowman of Bedford married Hannah Frye of Andover Sept. 19, 1781; lived in Andover; children, born in Andover; John, born Feb. 22, 1784; Jonathan, born Feb. 28, 1786; Isaac, born July 16, 1789; Sarah, born May 27, 1792; Philip Farrington, born Sept. 25, 1794; Hannah, born Jan. 25, 1797; Mary, born Aug. 21, 1799.—*Andover town records.*

Anna Bowman married Peter Nesey Sept. 18, 1775. Both were formerly residents of Boston.—*Haverhill town records.*

James Bowtell of Lynn, 1655, 1661.—*Court files.*

Children of James Bowman, baptized in Episcopal church in Salem: Mary, Oct. 22, 1775; Betsey, July 26, 1778; Lydia, Sept. 19, 1779; James and Richard, twins, Aug. 11, 1782.

James, son of —— Bowman, baptized May 23, 1784.

John Bowman, negro child, baptized March 19, 1792.

Jenny and Henry, children of John Bowman and wife, negroes, baptized Sept. 13, 1796.

Widow Unice Bowles baptized Jan. —, 1796.

Unice, aged ten years, and Maria, aged seven years, children of Capt. and Unice Bowman, baptized Jan. —, 1796.
—*Episcopal church (Salem) records.*

William Bowman of Lynn published to Abigail Sprague of Charlestown April 10, 1708.—*Lynn town records.*

Thankful Boyce married George Doyle (resident in Danvers) Nov. 24, 1779.—*Danvers town records.*

Children of Jonathan and Anna Boyce: Charlotte, born Sept. 28, 1797; Jona-than, born Aug. 1, 1799.—*Lynn town records.*

Widow Judith Boies published to Thomas Jenkins, both of Newburyport, Oct. 13, 1770.

Judith Boice published to Josiah George, both of Newburyport, Nov. 13, 1776.
—*Newburyport town records.*

William Boyes married Judith Ingersoll Nov. 28, 1754.—*Gloucester town records.*

John Boies married Hannah Gragg Sept. 1, 1768.—*Andover town records.*

David Boyce, cordwainer and shoemaker, lived in Salem as early as 1777; married Hannah Lang of Salem July 27, 1777; she was his wife in 1789, and was dead in 1825; he died in Salem Aug. 20, 1838, apparently leaving no issue. His brother Joseph Boyce was deceased in 1825, leaving a son David Boyes.

Christopher Boyce of Salem died before July 10, 1738, when administration was granted upon his estate. He was a seaman. His sister Frances Boys married Anthony Manual in Marblehead Dec. 26, 1725.
—*Records.*

John Coles was appointed administrator of the estate of widow Joan Boyce of Salem March 16, 1719.—*Probate records.*

Margaret Boice married Jonathan Trask Feb. 23, 1709-10.

Sarah Boice married Jonathan Harwood Aug. 18, 1726.

Eleanor Boyce married Samuel Thomas, both of Salem, Dec. 15, 1735.

Esther Boyce of Salem married George Edmonds of Lynn Nov. 3, 1747.

Anna Boyce married Absalom Harwood, both of Salem, Sept. 22, 1748.
—*Salem town records.*

Judith Boyce married Jona. Merrill March 2, 1777, Newburyport.

Judith Boyce married John Smith Jan. 21, 1779, Newburyport.
—*Court records.*

Children of William and Jane Boyce: James, baptized Aug. 2, 1730; died April 23, 1731; Jane, baptized March 26, 1732.—*Wenham records.*

Samuel Boyd, cordwainer, lived in Topsfield, 1720-1736; wife Margaret, 1736; children, baptized in Topsfield: Eliezer, March 11, 1721-2; Ann, John and Samuel, Dec. 16, 1733; Mary, July 27, 1735.

Matthew Boyes, born about 1611; yeoman; came from Yorkshire, England, with Rev. Ezekiel Rogers, to Rowley, in 1638, and lived in Rowley until 1655, when he removed to Ipswich, where he lived in 1655 and 1656, and returned to Leeds, Yorkshire, England, the next year. He was living in Leeds, a clothmaker in 1661. He was representative from Rowley to the general court four years. His wife was Elizabeth. Children : Samuel, born 7 mo : 10 : 1640; Hannah, born 4 : 16 : 1642; Matthew, born 1 : 23 : 1644; Elizabeth, born 3 : 20 : 1646; Grace, born 3 : 23 : 1648; Elkanah, born 1 : 25 : 1650; Mercy, born 2 : 26 : 1650; John, born 5 : 23 : 1651; Nathaniel, born 7 mo : 1 : 1653; Faith, born 10 : 28 : 1654.
—*Records.*

Abraham Boyd married Olive Pool Dec. 10, 1789.

Jane Boyd married Joseph Day Dec. 7, 1719.

Abraham Boyd married Peggy Haskins (recorded Sept. 22, 1798).
—*Gloucester town records.*

Abraham Boyd of Gloucester, gentleman, 1792.

Adam Boyd of Ipswich, tradesman, 1793.
—*Registry of deeds.*

Administration on the estate of James Boyd of Salem, mariner, was granted Aug. 5, 1771.—*Probate records.*

Joseph Boyed of Marblehead, 1663.—*Court records.*

Margaret Boid baptized at Topsfield Aug. 22, 1725.—*Wenham church records.*

Mary Boyd married Stephen Story, jr., Dec. 29, 1785.

Adam Boyd married Lydia Burnham Dec. 18, 1788.
—*Ipswich town records.*

John, son of Joseph and Sarah Boyd, baptized Dec. 1, 1728.

John Boyd married Rebecca Peck at Salem, Dec. 11, 1738; children : John, baptized Sept. 7, 1740; Rebeckah, baptized June 12, 1743; George, baptized July 28, 1745.

Joseph Boit married Mary Seal Feb. 20, 1766; children : Joseph and Mary, twins, baptized Oct. 18, 1767.

Sarah Boit married Rowland Maugier Dec. 6, 1733.

Rebeckah Boit married Abraham Mullett, jr., Jan. 28, 1762.
—*Marblehead records.*

James Boyd (called "esquire" in 1770) married Susanna Coffin, in Newbury, Aug. 11, 1757; children : Robert, born Nov. 13, 1758, in Newbury; Joseph Coffin, born July 23, 1760, in Newbury; Margaret, born Jan. 25, 1762, in Newbury; John Parker, born Dec. 21, 1764, in Newburyport; Frances, born Aug. 14, 1766, in Newburyport; Ebenezer Little, born July 6, 1768, in Newburyport; Charles Coffin, born Feb. 3, 1770, at "20 m. past 10 a. m." in Newburyport; died Aug. 19, 1770, in Newburyport; William, born March 20, 1776, at St. Andrews; Mary Lee, born Jan. 22, 1778.—*Newbury and Newburyport town records.*

Elizabeth Boyd published to Isaac Bullock, both of Salem, Aug. 21, 1776.

James Boyd married Mary Leach, both of Salem, Sept. 22, 1784.

Martha Boyd published to Thomas Kendale, both of Salem, Dec. 15, 1781.

John Boyd published to Polly Neal, both of Salem, March 15, 1796.

Peggy Boyd married Thomas Smothers, both of Salem, April 25, 1797.

William Boyd married Patty Frank, both of Salem, Aug. 10, 1798.
—*Salem town records.*

Children of William and Martha Boyd baptized : John, Jan. 13, 1799; Rachel, Aug. 17, 1800; George, July 30, 1802.—*Episcopal church, Salem, records.*

Hannah Boyd married Ezekiel Collins June 27, 1782.

Hannah (Molly—*publishment*) Boyd married Ezekiel Collins Nov. 27, 1793.
—*Salisbury town records.*

Thomas Boyes of Marblehead, mariner, and wife Mary, who was granddaughter of Ruth Gatchel, 1781.—*Registry of deeds.*

Children of Patrick and Mary Boyles baptized: Daniel, June 16, 1728; Sarah, Dec. 28, 1729.

Mary, daughter of Thomas and Elizabeth Boyles baptized March 20, 1742-3.

Children of John and Lydia Boyles baptized: Lydia, Sept. 30, 1744; John, March —, 1745-6.

Thomas, son of Thomas Boyles, baptized Oct. 28, 1744.

—*Marblehead church records.*

Elizabeth Boyles married Michael Poor Aug. 8, 1756.

John Boyles married Lydia Gale July 31, 1744.

Eunice Boyles of Beverly married Joseph Pedrick Sept. 29, 1763, at Beverly.

Mary Boyles married Edward Hilyar April 26, 1764.

—*Marblehead records.*

Elisha, son of Elisha and Mildred Boyle (or Boyles), born Jan. 20, 1757.—*Danvers town records.*

Charles Boyles married Hannah Eveleth Jan. 17, 1726-7; children: Hannah, born April 13, 1728; Abigail, born Aug. —, 1730; Charles, born Jan. 21, 1732.

—— Boyles published to Nathaniel Roberts April 22, 170-.

Mary Boyles married William Manning April 1, 1723.

—*Gloucester town records.*

Charles Boyles married Sally Stacy (Story—*publishment*) Oct. 21, 1792.—*Ipswich town records.*

Mary Boyles married Samuel Woodberry, Feb. 7, 1771.—*Manchester town records.*

Elizabeth Boyden married John Taly 7: 10 mo: 1676.

Jeremiah Boyle published to widow Hannah Lampereel, both of Salem, March 24, 1796.

—*Salem town records.*

William Boysen, a resident of Beverly, married Huldah Butman May 8, 1798, and had children born in Beverly, 1800-

1808. She died Dec. 21, 1805.—*Beverly town records.*

Hannah Boynton of Newbury married Francis Worcester of Sandwich Oct. 28, 1741.

Hannah Boynton married Thomas Tenney, both of Newbury, Feb. 3, 1745-6.

Caleb Boynton married Mary Shackford Aug. 30, 1762.

Susanna Boynton of Newbury married Charles Welch, resident in Newbury, Oct. 29, 1776.

David Boynton married Susanna Richardson, both of Newbury, Feb. 8, 1783.

—*Newbury town records.*

Nathaniel Boynton married Hannah Collins, both of Salem, Dec. 24, 1796.—*Salem town records.*

Bridget Boynton married Samuel Scott, both of Rowley, March 13, 1751-2, in Rowley.—*County records.*

Martha Boynton published to David Sawyer Aug. 16, 1746.

Mary Boynton published to Moses Dresser Sept. 3, 1774.

Abigail Boynton married Andrew Elwell, jr., Nov. 2, 1773.

Benjamin Boynton married Anne Fear Jan. 5, 1772.

Mary Boynton married Samuel Elwell, jr., Jan. 7, 1759.

Jerusha Boynton married Bennett Hodgkins, recorded Feb. 10, 1786.

Benjamin Boynton published to widow Abigail Hodgkins Jan. 17, 1754.

—*Gloucester town records.*

Administration on the estate of Joseph Boynton of Newburyport, housewright, was granted Dec. 30, 1793.—*Probate records.*

David Boynton published to Miss Sarah Goodhue, both of Newburyport, Oct. 24, 1767.—*Newburyport town records.*

Widow Jemima Bointon, "an aged Woman, died very suddenly" March 27, 1770.—*Topsfield church records.*

Joseph Boynton of Gloucester, tailor, bought house and land in Marblehead in 1725 and 1727; and sold land in Marblehead in 1727, 1728, 1732 and 1733.

Jonathan Boynton of Newbury house-wright, 1730-1.

Damaris, wife of Joseph Boynton of Rowley, 1699.

John Boynton of Rowley, yeoman, 1725-1740.

David Boynton of Newburyport, joiner, and wife Sarah, 1781.

David Boynton of Rowley, 1779-1789; yeoman, 1779-1787; wife Susanna, 1779-1787.*

David Boynton of Rowley, cordwainer, 1769-1784; wife Susanna, 1784.*
—*Registry of deeds.*

David Boynton of Rowley married Susanna Woodman of Bradford Jan. 7, 1773.

Boston, a negro belonging to Haverhill, married Lucy, a negro woman of Bradford, June 17, 1781.
—*Bradford town records.*

QUERIES.

Queries are inserted for one cent a word.
Answers are solicited.

468. What was a "iugg," which was used as a measure of land in the early settlement of the county? W. F.

469. Grant Webster married Hannah —— about 1747, apparently at Haverhill or Salisbury. She appears by deeds and names of children to have been connected with Pecker or Wainwright family. Wanted, her ancestry and date of marriage. T. M. JACKSON.
215 *Montague St., Brooklyn, N. Y.*

470. Susannah Beale married Richard Pattee before 1715. *Antiquarian* of January, 1904, page 46. Wanted, names of parents and grandparents of said Susannah Beale. B.

ANSWERS.

358. Some years ago I tried to find out where Benjamin Jones of Enfield, Conn., came from, but failed. I ook up

*Probably lived in Meredith, N. H., yeoman, 1794.

the work again this year, and found that he came from Gloucester, Mass. He was born in 1651, and died in 1718. The inventory of his estate, dated July, 1718, mentions children, Thomas, Benjamin, Ebenezer, Eleazer and also an heir, John Howard. The settlement by the heirs mentions wife Elizabeth, and states that it does not include any land that belonged "to the estate of the deceased that is in Gloucester." In that way I found that he came from Gloucester. The History of Enfield gives the family record in that town.—*R. H. J.*

358. The family record of Benjamin and Elizabeth (Wildes) Jones is given in the Historical Collections of the Essex Institute, volume XLII, page 150.—*Ed.*

465. Elizabeth, wife of Aaron Waite of Ipswich, was daughter of Capt. Elias Lowater of Ipswich. Her mother was Elizabeth, daughter of Capt. Stephen and Mary (Eveleth) Perkins of Ipswich, where she was baptized Oct. 18, 1713. Aaron Waite was baptized in Ipswich Dec. 20, 1724. His mother was Ruth, daughter of Joseph Fellows of Ipswich.—*Ed.*

NEW PUBLICATIONS.

VITAL RECORDS OF LYNN, MASS. Salem, 1906, 1907. The Essex Institute has completed the copying, arrangement and printing of the births, baptisms, intentions of marriages, marriages and deaths in Lynn before 1850. The first volume, containing the births and baptisms, was issued last year, and the second volume, which includes the marriages and intentions and deaths, has just been finished, and is now for sale. The two volumes aggregate 1,050 pages, and are sold, bound in cloth, for $10.95 postpaid. In this work as heretofore are records from gravestones, church records and family bibles. In these volumes are included the Quaker records of the Monthly meeting which includes Salem and other towns, and was begun in the early Quaker days. The address of the Essex Institute is Salem, Mass.

ii

An Ill

Tl
1809,
tiona,
(. a.
pl ted
.og in

Uni

Vol. 1.
" 10
5

Oi

Tl
proclass

J 10.

Gen.l.
1.
Anti,
C.

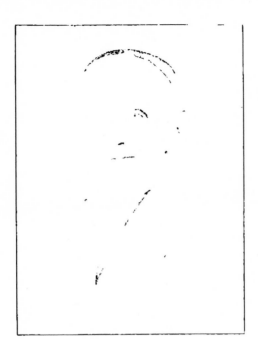

MRS. EVELINA (BRAY) DOWNEY.

THE ESSEX ANTIQUARIAN.

Vol. XI.   SALEM, MASS., JULY, 1907.   No. 3.

EARLY PLANTED CROPS.

THE early settlers of Essex county found here in a wild state several varieties of fruits and vegetables that were new to them. There were also many kinds that were like those cultivated in the fields and gardens in England, though here they were less developed than there. The planters brought their own English seeds, and planted them in the untried soil of New England, proving that the new world was capable of producing crops equal to those of the homeland. The wild plants and fruit-bearing shrubs and trees were improved by cultivation, and made to minister to the needs of the immigrants.

The Indians of this section of America were apparently not as nomadic as has been supposed. The localities of their abodes were fixed and certain, the tribes having occupied a somewhat definite territory. They dwelt in settled villages, and cultivated the soil, sometimes on a considerable scale and for a long time on the same spot.

They gathered and used the wild fruits, nuts, grapes, plums, berries, etc., but probably cultivated none of them.

The most important cultivated planted crop of the Indians was maize, or, as the settlers called it, Indian corn, and in our own time known simply as corn. It was raised generally throughout the country; and was indeed of great importance and value to the aborigines. No other cereal or fruit or vegetable was so well adapted to their necessities. The hard hull prevented it from spoiling, and it could be readily carried about their persons. Its parching quality gave it a further advantage, and they did not tire of its flavor. Its cultivation was easy, and increase great.

In our ancient pastures and forests corn-hills may still be seen. While many of these were made by our forefathers, frequently will be found those of the Indians of three hundred years ago. The little hillocks of earth are about three feet apart, and in rows. Only about four stalks were grown in a hill; and the method of cultivation by the Indian was adopted by the English settler. The corn-cribs, or houses, set on posts, which are still to be seen upon farms in various parts of Essex county, was, it is said, the Indian method of preserving their grain from small animals. However this may be, it is certain that the supply of corn on hand not needed for immediate consumption was preserved in holes in the ground. The holes were about the size of an ordinary hogshead, and the corn was kept from contact with the earth by being placed in baskets made of rushes and osiers with mats above and under them. The early English settlers sometimes bought corn of the Indians, being supplied from this source.

The latter fertilized their corn, generally with fish, and sometimes with manure and probably seaweed and vegetable compost. The cultivation of the ground devolved upon women; and the squaws bore the brunt of the exposure and labor from the burning over the ground, to destroy the weeds before the soil was dug up with their hoes made of large clam shells, till the harvest.

Indian corn immediately became the staple crop of the white settlers, who

adopted the aboriginal methods in its cultivation, and in the course of centuries have modified them but little. Instead of the ground being slightly stirred by the clam-shell hoe, the English immediately used the iron-strapped wooden plow, and later the sub-soil plow. Fertilizing was increased and hoeing was more thorough and often, the cultivator later on adding to the deeper stirring of the soil. Probably the Indians had no use for the stalks, but the English fed them to cattle.

Husking parties may have been enjoyed among the Indians, and certainly they soon became occasions of great merriment among the colonists.

Shelling corn by hand during the long winter evenings was hard work at any period, whether it was upon the edge of an inverted shovel blade, on the long handle of a frying pan, or a long knife blade set in the edge of a piece of wood. The cobs were used as fuel, in curing hams, giving a delightful flavor to the smoked shoulder.

The settlers also learned from their dusky friends how to pulverize their corn, by pounding in a mortar or grinding between stones. The mortar was a section of the trunk or stump of a tree a foot or more in diameter and three feet in height, hollowed out by burning. The top of the wooden pestle, which was used for pounding the grain, was fastened to the top of a bent young tree, which formed a spring to raise the pestle. This was called a samp mill. Corn was also cracked and broken in this manner. The grist-mill, similar to the modern kind, was soon instituted, not only to grind Indian corn, but wheat, rye, and other grains. Windmills were adopted a little while before the water mills, though both appeared very early in the settlements of the early colonists. The Indians ate their corn green as well as ripe. They boiled or roasted the green ears, probably of the sweet variety, with the husks still on; a practice which might be desirable in our own time. From their methods of cooking the ripened grain, we have received ash-cake, hoe-cake, Johnny cake, succotash, samp, hominy, parched corn and hasty pudding.

Parched or popped corn then became known for the first time to the children of the settlements here. Governor Winthrop wrote about 1630 that when corn was parched it turned inside out and was " white and floury within."

Then became known to our forebears the Indian pudding boiled in a bag, and the rye and Indian bread; and hasty pudding, as we know it, was entirely novel.

The Indians also raised cucumbers (or cow-cumbers, or cow-combers), water and musk melons (or, millions, as they were then called), and squashes, which Higginson called " squanter squashes." They also cultivated gourds, the shells of which were employed for storage and carrying or water jugs, dippers, spoons and dishes, for mixing bowls, masks, etc.

They also had pumpkins called by them " pompions." The English settlers cultivated them, planting them among the corn, as the Indians had done, a practice which is still continued here. This vegetable was fruitful, easily grown, easily cooked, and kept well. In the early days they were important as a food supply, being used for sweetening, and dried and ground made into bread. Johnson, in his Wonder-working Providence, called it " A fruit which the Lord fed his people till corn and cattle increased;" and rebuked the colonists for their lack of its appreciation. A colonial poet shows how necessary it was, in his couplet:

" We have pumpkins at morning and pumpkins at noon,
   If it were not for pumpkins we should be undone."

Pumpkins were dried in the sun and kept for winter use by both Indians and colonists. They were eaten stewed, and the old-fashioned " pumpkin pie " is still cooked, but the squash has nearly supplanted it.

Beans were abundant and raised by the Indians amongst their corn. These they

shelled and preserved dry, as at the present day by their successors. They baked them in earthen pots and the colonists and their descendants have continued the custom ever since. The Indians also had peas, and these, too, have ever been popular with all the residents of New England, whether cooked green or dry. "Pease" are often mentioned in the early records but under this designation beans were probably included.

The Indians had several varieties of edible roots, as turnips, parsnips and carrots; and also onions. There was wild hemp, from which they obtained fibre for cordage and cloth.

Besides all these plants which were growing wild and those which were cultivated by the natives, seeds of various others were brought from England for sowing in our soil, as well as seeds of improved species like those that were American. Most of the new varieties succeeded, being soon adapted to the changed conditions of soil and climate.

The Massachusetts Bay Company provided to be sent to Salem in the winter following the arrival of Endecott a hogshead each, in the ear, of wheat, rye, barley and oats, beans, peas, woad seed, saffron heads, liquorice seed, madder roots and seed, potatoes, and hemp and flax seed. The potatoes were probably of the sweet variety, which had been introduced into England from the southern American colonies, the officers of the company in England evidently being ignorant that the climate and soil of Salem was hardly adapted to this vegetable of a warmer region.

The general court passed a law May 13, 1648, that no wheat, rye, barley or Indian corn should be transported into any foreign parts, or put aboard any vessel with that intention, under penalty of twenty shillings per bushel, one-half of the penalty to go to the informer. The exportation of corn was again forbidden in 1662. Corn was received for taxes at the following rates per bushel: in 1650, three shillings, 1654, two shillings and

eight pence, and in 1655, two shillings and six pence. In 1650 and 1654, wheat and barley were received for taxes at the rate of five shillings per bushel, and rye and peas at four shillings. In 1655, wheat and barley were received at four shillings and six pence, rye at three shillings and six pence, and peas at four shillings per bushel. May 23, 1655, the general court authorized towns to appoint men to measure corn, in cases of dispute that might arise.

John Goffe of Newbury, who died Dec. 9, 1641, had seven bushels of Indian corn on hand, valued at seventeen shillings, and one bushel of wheat, valued at four shillings. Hugh Churchman of Lynn, when the inventory of his estate was taken July 4, 1644, had twenty bushels of wheat, four bushels of Indian corn, two bushels of barley, and corn on the ground. Isabel West of Salem, when her estate was appraised Dec. 30, 1644, had sixteen bushels of Indian corn and five bushels of pease. Robert Pease of Salem, when he died in 1644, had one acre each of wheat, barley, pease and Indian corn; and he was a small farmer. John Talbey of Salem, when the inventory of his estate was taken in January, 1644-5, had twenty bushels of Indian corn, valued at two shillings and six pence a bushel, and three pecks of naked oats, appraised at seven shillings. John Gaines of Lynn, when his estate was appraised, Jan. 14, 1644-5, had thirty bushels of Indian corn, valued at four pounds, and also, oats, white peas, beans, hemp and flax. Widow Margaret Pease of Salem, who died in 1644, had wheat, Indian corn and rye. John Pride of Salem, whose estate was appraised in February, 1647-8, then had on hand wheat, barley, pease and Indian corn, together valued at three pounds. Edmund Ingalls of Lynn, at the time that he was drowned in March, 1648, had hemp and flax in his barn valued at one pound. When the estate of Hugh Burt, jr., was appraised Oct. 8, 1650, he had wheat and other English grain, valued at one pound and one shilling, and

thirty bushels of Indian corn, valued at four pounds and ten shillings. Edmund Lewis of Lynn, at the time his estate was appraised, Feb. 12, 1650-1, had ten bushels of wheat, valued at two pounds and ten shillings, ten bushels of oats, valued at five pounds and seven shillings, and sixty bushels of Indian corn, valued at ninety pounds. The inventory of the estate of John Osgood, sr., of Andover, taken Nov. 25, 1651, shows that he had sixty bushels of barley, valued at thirteen pounds, fifty bushels of pease, valued at eight pounds and fifteen shillings, and rye sowed twelve pounds. When the estate of William Stevens of Newbury was appraised, June 13, 1653, he had four acres of rye, wheat and barley growing, valued at eight pounds, and three acres of Indian corn, valued at four pounds. In the inventory of the estate of Thomas Trusler of Salem, taken March 5, 1653-4, is mentioned four bushels of Indian meal, valued at twelve shillings, twenty pounds of hemp, valued at ten shillings, two bushels of seed barley, valued at ten shillings, and two bushels of seed pease, valued at eight shillings. In the inventory of the estate of John Balch of Salem, taken in 1648, is mentioned nine acres of wheat, valued at nine pounds six acres of Indian corn, valued at six pounds, one acre of oats, valued at one pound, and twelve bushels of Indian corn, valued at one pound and sixteen shillings. Thomas Mighill of Rowley, who died early in the summer of 1654, had a large farm, and in the inventory of his estate is mentioned corn meal and malt, corn measures, one breaking-up plow with "her" irons, valued at one pound and two shillings, three other plows, valued at one pound and one shilling, seven and one-half acres of wheat and barley, valued at eight pounds and five shillings, four and one-half acres of corn, valued at five pounds and eight shillings, three acres of Indian corn, valued at three pounds and twelve shillings, four acres of wheat and Indian corn, valued at four pounds, and corn at the pen, valued at three pounds. John Porter, sr.,

of Salem, who died Sept. 6, 1676, was a more extensive farmer than Mr. Mighill. In the inventory of his estate is mentioned forty-six sheep, fourteen lambs, eight oxen, fifteen cows, eleven calves, nine two-year olds, eight yearlings, two steers, one bull, fourteen swine, eleven shoats, six mares, five horses, two colts, twelve acres of barley, valued at twenty-seven pounds, two acres of pease, valued at three pounds, one acre of wheat, valued at thirty-two shillings, and twelve acres of Indian corn, valued at twenty-four pounds.

In the earlier inventories of estates of deceased persons is no mention of roots, turnips, parsnips, carrots, onions, squashes melons, etc. Probably these were produced in small quantities, as they were more perishable than the hard grains.

The flail and the floor were the means of threshing out the grain by the early settlers; and in the inventory of the estate of Edmund Lewis of Lynn, Feb. 12, 1650-1, is mentioned a "fan", which was probably an instrument to separate the grain from the chaff.

NOTES.

Miss Anna Bragdon married James Hodgskins, both of Newburyport, Oct. 5, 1787 (published April 1, 1786).—*Newburyport town records.*

The words "Captain More" in line thirty-six, second column, page 18, should read "Mr. Osgood."—*Ed.*

Administration upon the estate of Alexander Brabender of Wenham was granted Nov. 29, 1678, to Charles Gott, with whom said Brabender had boarded for ten weeks next prior to his death. The date of his death was 22: 8: 1678. His estate was appraised at £5, 3s.—*Probate records.*

Alexander Brabinger of Lynn, 1657, 1658.

Alexander Brabiner of Lynn, aged about fifty years, 1663.

—*Court records.*

DESCENDANTS OF THOMAS BRAY OF GLOUCESTER.

THOMAS BRAY[1] lived in Gloucester as early as 1646, being a ship-carpenter. He married Mary Wilson 3 : 3 : 1646 in Gloucester; and died in Gloucester Nov. 30, 1691. His estate was valued at £133, 5s. He devised his homestead to his son John Bray. His wife survived him; and died, his widow, in Gloucester March 27, 1707, being "aged."

Children, born in Gloucester :—

2—I. MARY[2], b. Jan. 16, 1647; m. John Ring of Ipswich Nov. 18, 1664; and she was his widow in 1712.
3—II. THOMAS[2], b. March 31, 1649; d. Aug. 12, 1653.
4—III. SARAH[2], m. James Sawyer; and she was his widow, of Gloucester, in 1712.
5—IV. THOMAS[2], b. May 16, 1653; d. young.
6—V. JOHN[2], b. May 14, 1654; lived in Gloucester; yeoman; m. Margaret Lambert Nov. 10, 1679, in Gloucester; he d. in Gloucester Sept. 25, 1714; his estate was valued at £190, 10s.; his wife survived him, and d., his widow, in Gloucester, Jan. 28, 1725, aged seventy. They were apparently childless.
7—VI. NATHANIEL[2], b. June 21, 1656. See below (7).
8—VII. THOMAS[2], b. Jan. 19, 1658-9. See below (8).
9—VIII. HANNAH[2], b. March 21, 1661-2; m. John Roberts of Gloucester Feb. 4, 1677; and she was his wife in 1712.
10—IX. ESTHER[2], b. April 13, 1664; m. Philip Stanwood of Gloucester Oct. 30, 1683; and she was his wife in 1712.

7

NATHANIEL BRAY,[2] born in Gloucester June 21, 1656. He was a yeoman, and lived in Gloucester. He married Martha Wadin (or Waden) Jan. 22, 1684; and died May 2, 1728, in Gloucester. She survived him.

Children, born in Gloucester :—

11—I. MARTHA[3], b. Sept. 21, 1685; m. William Botham Dec. 7, 1715; lived in Gloucester; he was lost on a fishing voyage near the Isle Sables Aug. —, 1716, at the age of twenty-five; and she d. in Gloucester, his widow, in 1757. They had one child,

12—II. MARY[3], b. May 31, 1688; lived in Gloucester; and d., unmarried, her will, dated May 29, 1759, being proved April 21, 1760.
13—III. NATHANIEL[3], b. June 15, 1690. See below (13).
14—IV. HANNAH[3], b. April 20, 1693; m. John Huse Oct. 10, 1735; and she was living in 1759.

8

THOMAS BRAY[2], born in Gloucester Jan. 19, 1658-9. He was a yeoman; and lived in Gloucester. He married Mary Emerson Dec. 23, 1626, in Ipswich; and she was his wife in 1722. He had a wife in 1732. His will, dated April 10, 1732, was proved April 11, 1743.

Children, born in Gloucester :—

15—I. THOMAS[3], b. Oct. 9, 1687. See below (15).
16—II. JOHN[3], b. Sept. 7, 1689. See below (16).
17—III. DANIEL[3], d. May 14, 1696.
18—IV. NATHANIEL[3], b. May 19, 1694. See below (18).
19—V. MOSES[3], b. Nov. 26, 1696. See below (19).
20—VI. AARON[3], b. July 2, 1699. See below (20).
21—VII. MARY[3], b. March 23, 1702; m. William Ring Jan. 25, 1719-20; and she was his wife in 1732.
22—VIII. SARAH[3], b. March 31, 1706; d. May 23, 1706.
23—IX. ABIGAIL[3], b. Aug. 6, 1707; m. Humphrey Woodbury Jan. 13, 1725-6; and she was his wife in 1732.

13

NATHANIEL BRAY[3], born in Gloucester June 15, 1690. He was a husbandman and lived in Gloucester until 1741, perhaps removing from town. He married Sarah Davis (published Dec. 11, 1714) : and she was his wife in 1741.

Children, born in Gloucester :—

24—I. ISAAC[4], b. June 30, 1716. See below (24).
25—II. SARAH[4], b. Sept. 4, 1718; d. June 4, 1720, aged one year and ten months.
26—III. NATHANIEL[4], b. June 20, 1727. See below (26).

15

DR. THOMAS BRAY[3], born in Gloucester Oct. 9, 1687. He was first, a cordwainer, and then a physician; and lived in Gloucester. He married Eleanor Dodge of

Beverly (published Dec. 28, 1716); and died before Jan. 14, 1744-5, when administration was granted upon his estate. She survived him, and was his widow in 1763.

Children, born in Gloucester:—

27—I. ELEANOR⁴, b. May 15, 1719; m. Joshua Haskell March 31, 1741.
28—II. THOMAS⁴, b. March 11, 1721. *See below (28).*
29—III. MARY⁴, b. March 31, 1723.
30—IV. EDWARD⁴, b. March 15, 1725; m. Sarah Woodberry May 25, 1748, in Gloucester.
31—V. ABIGAIL⁴, b. July 4, 1727.
32—VI. EBENEZER⁴, b. April 18, 1732. *See below (32).*

16

JOHN BRAY³, born in Gloucester Sept. 7, 1689. He was a weaver, and lived in Gloucester as late as 1747. He married Susanna Woodbury Dec. 19, 1716; and she was his wife in 1736.

Children, born in Gloucester:—

33—I. ANN⁴, b. May 19, 1721; living in 1747.
34—II. JOHN⁴, b. August 19, 1725. *See below (34).*
35—III. HUMPHREY⁴, b. March 27, 1728. *See below (35).*
36—IV. ENOCH⁴, b. July 20, 1730. *See below (36).*
37—V. SUSANNA⁴, b. April 6, 1732; m. Nehemiah Somes (pub. Nov. 8, 1755).
38—VI. SARAH⁴, b. June 9, 1736; living in 1747.

18

NATHANIEL BRAY³, born in Gloucester May 19, 1694. He was a cordwainer, and lived in Gloucester. He married Sarah Haskell Nov. 22, 1733; and they were both living in Gloucester in 1763.

Children, born in Gloucester:—

39—I. SARAH⁴, b. Jan. 25, 1735.
40—II. NATHANIEL⁴ (twin), b. March 2, 1737.
41—III. DANIEL⁴ (twin), b. March 2, 1737.
42—IV. ——EL⁴ (son), b. March 14, 1739.
43—V. ——N⁴ (son), b. July 7, 1741.
44—VI. ——⁴ (dau.), b. Nov. 21, 1743.
45—VII. ——RON⁴ (son), b. Jan. 19, 1746.
46—VIII. ——RY⁴ (dau.), b. Oct. 25, 1748.
47—IX. ——⁴ (son), b. Dec. 26, 1750.
48—X. ABIGAIL⁴, b. Dec. 8, 1753.
49—XI. BENJAMIN⁴, b. June 28, 1756.

19

MOSES BRAY³, born in Gloucester Nov. 26, 1696. He was a yeoman, shipwright and carpenter, and lived in Gloucester.

He married Mary Woodberry Nov. 21, 1717, in Beverly. He conveyed his house and land in Gloucester to his son Moses in 1767; and probably died soon afterward. She was his wife at that time.

Children, born in Gloucester:—

50—I. MOSES⁴, b. April 25, 1719; d. May 14, 1719.
51—II. SAMUEL⁴, b. Oct. 25, 1720. *See below (51).*
52—III. NICHOLAS⁴, b. Jan. 18, 1723. *See below (52).*
53—IV. ABIGAIL⁴, b. Feb. 15, 1728.
54—V. MARY⁴, b. Sept. 27, 1730.
55—VI. MOSES⁴, b. Oct. 4, 1737; "captain;" mariner; lived in West Gloucester; m. Lucy Goodrich (pub. March 31, 1759); administration was granted on his estate Sept. 28, 1773; his estate was valued at £200, 5s., 9d.; and she d., his widow, in 1799, aged sixty-two.

20

AARON BRAY³, born in Gloucester July 2, 1699. Ha was a yeoman, and lived in Gloucester. He married, first, Elizabeth Davis Dec. 28, 1727; and she died in 1744. He married, second, Ruth Winter (published Nov. 24, 1744); and died before June 30, 1772, when administration was granted on his estate, which was appraised at £206, 8s., 3d. His wife Ruth survived him, and was non compos after his death. For his dutiful carriage " towards " his parents, they deeded some lands to him in 1722.

Children, born in Gloucester:—

56—I. ELIZABETH⁴, b. Jan. 15, 1729; m. Nehemiah Parsons Feb. 11, 1752.
57—II. SARAH⁴, b. Dec. 21, 1731; m. Thomas Witham March 14, 1756.
58—III. LOIS⁴, b. Dec. 1, 1733; m. John Witham Jan. 11, 1753.
59—IV. EUNICE⁴, b. May 13, 1736; m. Samuel Varrel (pub. Dec. 21, 1754).
60—V. ABIGAIL⁴, b. Aug. 24, 1738.
61—VI. AARON⁴, b. May 10, 1742. *See below (61).*
62—VII. JUDITH⁴, b. April 30, 1744.
63—VIII. MARK⁴, b. Sept. 19, 1745; lived in Gloucester; yeoman; m. Hannah Bray March 10, 1768; and was living in 1786 in Gloucester.
64—IX. EDWARD⁴, b. Aug. 24, 1749; blacksmith, of Gloucester, 1772.
65—X. THOMAS⁴, b. May 24, 1751.

24

ISAAC BRAY[4], born in Gloucester June 30, 1716. He lived in Gloucester; and married Abigail Averill July 22, 1748. They were living in Gloucester in 1761.

Children, born in Gloucester :—

66—I.   ISAAC[6], b. June 14, 1749.   *See below* (66).
67—II. ABIGAIL[5], b. Aug. 28, 1751; probably m. John Morgan Oct. 29, 1772.
68—III. SARAH[5], b. Sept. 7, 1753; probably m. William Newman May 20, 1772.
69—IV. ANDREW[5].
70—V.   MARY[5], b. Nov. 13, 1758.
71—VI. BENJAMIN[5], b. Oct. 2, 1759.
72—VII. SUSANNA[5], b. Nov. 24, 1761.

26

NATHANIEL BRAY[4], born in Gloucester June 20, 1727. He was a fisherman and mariner, and lived in Gloucester until 1760 when he sold his house and land near Little river in Gloucester and settled in Newbury. He married Ruth Riggs June 10, 1755, in Gloucester. They were living in Newbury in 1767.

Children :—

73—I.   RUTH[6], b. Oct. 19, 1756, in Gloucester.
74—II. NATHANIEL[5], b. April 1, 1763, in Newbury.
75—III. WILLIAM[6], b. July 20, 1767, in Newbury.

28

THOMAS BRAY[4], born in Gloucester March 11, 1721. He was a husbandman, and lived in Gloucester. He married Judith Sargent Jan. 16, 1746; and they were living in Gloucester in 1770.

Children, born in Gloucester :—

76—I.   THOMAS[5], b. Oct. 3, 1746.
77—II. JUDITH[5], b. June 12, 1748.
78—III. THOMAS[5], b. March 26, 1750.
79—IV. ANDREW[5], b. July 23, 1751.
80—V.   ABIGAIL[5], b. Feb. 26, 1753.
81—VI. JOHN[5], b. Jan. 5, 1770; probably m. Nabby Poland Nov. 21, 1796.

32

EBENEZER BRAY[4], born in Gloucester April 18, 1732. He was given by the town, Nov. 6, 1760, seven pounds "towards helping him to the Latting Tongue ;" and he was a schoolmaster in Gloucester for many years. He married Judith Bennet April 19, 1762 ; and they were both living in Gloucester in 1777.

Children, born in Gloucester :—

82—I.   BETTY BENNET[5], b. April 30, 1764.
83—II. STEPHEN BENNET[5], b. April 2, 1766.
84—III. MARY HOOK[5], b. Sept. 1, 1770.

34

JOHN BRAY[4], born in Gloucester Aug. 19, 1725. He was a yeoman, and lived in Gloucester. He married, first, widow Mary Brown April 16, 1750 ; and she died Feb. 18, 1768. He married, second, Abigail Row Oct. 20, 1768.

Children, born in Gloucester :—

85—I.   SUSANNA[5], b. Feb. 25, 1751.
86—II. BETTY BROWN[5], b. April 24, 1758.
87—III. BENJAMIN ROW[5], b. Feb. 21, 1770; m. Abigail Brookins Nov. 7, 1793.
88—IV. JOHN[5], b. Dec. 4, 1771.
89—V.   WILLIAM WISE[5], b. Feb. 1, 1774.

35

HUMPHREY BRAY,[4] born in Gloucester March 27, 1728. He was a mariner ; and lived in West Gloucester. He married Lydia Woodbury June 22, 1749 ; and she died Sept. 14, 1779, at the age of fifty-four years and three months. He died before May 1, 1786, when administration was granted upon his estate.

Children, born in Gloucester :—

90—I.   LUCY[5], b. Sept. 2, 1750; probably m. Jacob Procter of Ipswich (pub. Dec. 9, 1775).
91—II. EDWARD[5], b. Nov. 29, 1751; mariner; lived in Gloucester; and m. Edith Doane (pub. Nov. 19, 1774).
92—III. ABIGAIL[5], b. Jan. 9, 1754.
93—IV. HUMPHREY[5], b. Oct. 18, 1757.   *See below* (93).
94—V.   RUTH[5], b. Oct. 17, 1760.
95—VI. SARAH WOODBERRY[5], b. Aug. 18, 1763.
96—VII. SILAS[5], b. Aug. 14, 1765; m. Sally Bray March 12, 1793.

36

ENOCH BRAY,[4] born in Gloucester July 20, 1730. He was a yeoman, and lived in Gloucester. He married Hannah Bray of Rowley May 10, 1753 ; and they were living in Gloucester in 1765.

Children :—

97—I.   HANNAH[5], b. Dec. 22, 1755, in Gloucester.
98—II. ELIZABETH[5], b. Dec. 21, 1757, in Rowley.
99—III. ENOCH[5], b. Dec. 21, 1762, in Gloucester; probably m. Lucy Day of Damariscotta July 21, 1786.

100—IV. LOIS⁶, b. Dec. 22, 1763, in Gloucester.
101—V. DANIEL⁵, b. Oct. 21, 1765, in Gloucester. *See below (101).*

51

SAMUEL BRAY⁴, born in Gloucester Oct. 25, 1720. He was a yeoman ; and lived in Gloucester. He married, first, Abigail Grover June 13, 1743, in Gloucester ; and she died Sept. —, 1764. He married, second, Elizabeth Choate May 14, 1765 ; and they were living in Gloucester in 1798.

Children, born in Gloucester :—
102—I. TABITHA⁵, b. May 5, 1744; m. William Allen, 3d (pub. Nov. 29, 1770).
103—II. SAMUEL⁵, b. March 19, 1746; yeoman; lived in Gloucester; m. Mary Herrick (pub. Dec. 21, 1770); and they were living in Gloucester in 1791.
104—III. MOSES⁵, b. April 8, 1756.

52

NICHOLAS BRAY⁴, born in Gloucester Jan. 18, 1723. He was a yeoman, and lived in Gloucester. He married widow Anne Ring May 29, 1747, in Gloucester ; and died before Jan. 21, 1760, when administration was granted upon his estate, which was appraised at £62, 9s., 8d. She died, his widow, before Jan. 25, 1768, when administration was granted upon her estate.

Children, born in Gloucester :—
105—I. HANNAH⁵, b. Jan. 27, 1748; probably d. unmarried, in Gloucester, July 7, 1829, aged " eighty-four."
106—II. NICHOLAS⁵, b. about 1753; living in 1769.
107—III. ELIZABETH⁵, b. about 1756; living in 1770.

61

AARON BRAY⁴, born in Gloucester May 10, 1742. He was a sailmaker ; and lived in Marblehead, Manchester, Newbury and Newburyport respectively. He married Hannah Davis April —, 1768, in Gloucester ; and she was his wife when he was living in Newbury. He was living in Newburyport in 1793.

Children, born in Manchester :—
108—I. HANNAH⁵, b. March 26, 1771; m., when of Newburyport, Smith Adams of Newbury Oct. 5, 1794.
109—II. AARON⁵, b. April 9, 1773; d. May 12, 1773.

110—III. AARON⁵, b. May 15, 1774; d. July 1774.
111—IV. MARK⁵, b. Nov. 17, 1775.
112—V. NABBY⁵, bapt. July 1, 1777 (daughter of " Mr. Bray").
113—VI. WILLIAM⁵, b. June 15, 1783, in Newbury; d. in Newburyport Aug. 1802.

66

ISAAC BRAY⁵, born in Gloucester June 14, 1749. He was a mariner, and lived in Gloucester. He married Sarah Killam Jan. 20, 1771 ; and they were living in Gloucester in 1791.

Children, born in Gloucester :—
114—I. SALLY⁶, b. July 17, 1779.
115—II. ISAAC⁶, b. March 30, 1781.
116—III. SUSY⁶, b. June 4, 1783.
117—IV. LUCRETIA⁶, b. Aug. 4, 1785.
118—V. SOLOMON⁶, b. July 31, 1787.
119—VI. ISSACHER⁶ (twin), b. Dec. 27, 1791.
120—VII. DOLLY⁶ (twin), b. Dec. 27, 1791; m. Theophilus Herrick before 1814.

93

HUMPHREY BRAY⁵, born in Gloucester Oct. 18, 1757. He married Molly Bray (published Dec. 22, 1776). They were living in Gloucester in 1789.

Children, born in Gloucester :—
121—I. EPES⁶, b. Aug. 24, 1787.
122—II. ELIA⁶ (son), b. Oct. 18, 1789.

101

DANIEL BRAY⁵, born in Gloucester Oct. 21, 1765. He married Sally Jaques Dec. 24, 1792 ; and lived in Gloucester.

Children, born in Gloucester :—
123—I. JEREMIAH PARSONS⁶, b. Jan. 4, 1793.
124—II. DANIEL⁶, b. Oct. 8, 1796.
125—III. SIMON THURLA⁶, b. Nov. 8, 1799.
126—IV. AMOS⁶, b. Feb. 6, 1802.

NOTES.

John Brabrook of Watertown by wife Elizabeth had children : Elizabeth, born Nov. 4, 1640 ; John, born April 12, 1642 ; and Thomas, born May 4, 1643 ; first was at Hampton, 1640, removed to Newbury, where he lived with his uncle Henry Short, and died June 28, 1662. (Coffin

William Brabrook of Lynn removed to Sandwich in 1637, says Lewis.

—*Savage.*

DESCENDANTS OF ROBERT BRAY OF SALEM.

ROBERT BRAY[1] lived in Salem as early as 1668. He was a fisherman, and was lost at sea about 1692. His wife was Thomasine ——.

Children :—

2—I. MARGARET[2],* m. James Wilkins of Salem April 20, 1684.
3—II. ROBERT[2]. *See below* (3).
4—III. PRISCILLA[2],* m. David Hillard Aug. 15, 1689.
5—IV. DANIEL[2], b. Nov. 29, 1673. *See below* (5).

3

ROBERT BRAY[2]. He was a mariner, and lived in Salem. He married Christian Collins of Salem Nov. 5, 1685 ; and died between 1693 and 1702. She was his widow in 1724.

Children, born in Salem :—

6—I. JOHN[3], b. Sept. 4, 1686; supposed to have been drowned from the ketch "Dragon," Capt. William Brown, bound from Virginia, lost on Cape Cod, Dec. 23, 1705.
7—II. ROBERT[3], b. Dec. 22, 1688. *See below* (7).
8—III. PRISCILLA[3], b. March 11, 1689-90; m. Jonathan Webb of Salem, cordwainer, March 23, 1713-4; and was his wife in 1743.
9—IV. BENJAMIN[3], b. Sept. 27, 1692. *See below* (9).
10—V. CHRISTIAN[3], b. March 19, 1694; m. William Cash, jr., of Salem, mariner, June 1, 1715-6; and was living in 1724.

5

CAPT. DANIEL BRAY[2], born in Salem Nov. 29, 1673. He was a master-mariner, and lived in Salem. He married Hannah Brown Aug. 28, 1701; and he died Dec. —, 1717. She was his widow in 1728.

Children, born in Salem :—

11—I. HANNAH[3], b. Dec. 20, 1702; m. William Mansfield of Salem, fisherman, Nov. 2, 1722; and she was living in 1757.
12—II. MARY[3], b. Dec. 31, 1704; m. Thomas Lisbell (or, Lisbril) of Salem Feb. 27, 1727-8.

*Margaret and Priscilla are assumed to belong to this family, though there is no positive proof of it.

13—III. EUNICE[3], b. March 9, 1706-7 ; m. Thomas Stevens of Salem, joiner, March 13, 1728-9; and was living in 1768.
14—IV. ELIZABETH[3], b. Oct. 10, 1710; m. John Ingersoll, jr., of Salem Nov. 27, 1740; and d. Aug. 5, 1768, aged "fifty-six."
15—V. PRISCILLA[3], b. May 11, 1713; d., unmarried, in Salem, Sept. —, 1768. She had a pew in the East meeting house; and her estate was valued at £214, 8s., 9d. In her will, she bequeathed to Elizabeth Suddel a pair of large silver buckles, a pair of gold buttons, a pair of gold ear-rings, a gold ring, etc.

7

ROBERT BRAY[3], born in Salem Dec. 22, 1688. He was a fisherman, and lived in Marblehead. He married Alice Gifford of Marblehead Feb. 6, 1711-2 ; and she died there in 1753.

Children, born in Marblehead :—

16—I. SARAH[4], bapt. Aug. 29, 1714 ; m. Joseph Homan Sept. 17, 1730.
17—II. JOHN[4], bapt. Sept. 12, 1714. *See below* (17).
18—III. ALICE[4], bapt. June 9, 1717; m. Thomas Gale Dec. 25, 1735.
19—IV. MARY[4], bapt. March 13, 1720; m. William Cruff Nov. 27, 1738.
20—V. ELIZABETH[4], bapt. July 16, 1727; m. Andrew Stacey June 20, 1751.

9

BENJAMIN BRAY[3], born in Salem Sept. 27, 1692. He was a fisherman and mariner, and lived in Salem. He married Hannah Lander of Salem Nov. 8, 1717 ; and she died Oct. 12, 1785. He probably survived her.

Children, born in Salem :—

21—I. HANNAH[4], b. 26 : 8 : 1718; m. Capt. Thomas Poynton of Salem Sept. 8, 1743. He was a native of England; and sailed hither in his own vessel as hostilities began; and remained there. She d. in Salem, his widow, Aug. 1, 1811, aged nearly ninety-three.
22—II. BENJAMIN[4], b. Dec. 21, 1720. *See below* (22).
23—III. JOHN[4], b. Dec. 29, 1723. *See below* (23).
24—IV. ROBERT[4], b. Jan. 3, 1726-7; mariner; d., unmarried, in 1748-9, on a cruise on His Majesty's ship *Elizabeth*, sailing from Jamaica, being impressed into its service.

25—V. SARAH⁴, bapt. July 6, 1729; m. Capt.
Michael Driver of Salem (pub. Dec.
8, 1753); he d. Aug. 28, 1785; and
she was his widow in 1795.

26—VI. DANIEL⁴, b. July 17, 1735. *See below*
(*26*).

17

JOHN BRAY⁴, baptized in Marblehead
Sept. 12, 1714. He was a shoreman, and
lived in Marblehead. He married Jean
Elkins Feb. 6, 1738-9; and died before
Feb. 2, 1773, when administration was
granted upon his estate. She was living
in Marblehead, his widow, in 1793.

Children, born in Marblehead :—

27—I. JOHN⁵, bapt. Oct. 5, 1740. *See below*
(*27*).

28—II. ELIZABETH⁵, bapt. July 14, 1745; m.
Samuel Chinn Dec. 11, 1764.

29—III. ALICE⁵, bapt. Oct. 11, 1747.

30—IV. JEAN⁵, bapt. Aug. 27, 1758; m. Samuel
Thompson June 15, 1779.

31—V. ROBERT⁵, bapt. Dec. 28, 1760.

22

BENJAMIN BRAY⁴, born in Salem Dec.
21, 1720. He lived in Salem; and married Sarah Driver of Salem July 11, 1746.
He died a few years later; and his widow
married, secondly, John Webb.

Child :—

32—I. SARAH⁵, bapt. Oct. 9, 1748; m. Robert
Hale Ives of Salem March 20, 1766;
and d. in Beverly Sept. 27, 1782.

23

JOHN BRAY⁴, born in Salem Dec. 29,
1723. He was a cordwainer, and lived
in Salem. He married Elizabeth Driver
of Salem April 8, 1750; and died Nov.
19, 1803. She was living in 1769.

Children, born in Salem :—

33—I. JOHN⁵, bapt. June 2, 1751; m. Eunice
Becket of Salem Nov. 29, 1774.

34—II. ROBERT⁵, bapt. Dec. 22, 1751; d.
young.

35—III. BENJAMIN⁵, bapt. July 28, 1754; d.
young.

36—IV. HANNAH⁵, bapt. Jan. 28, 1759; m.
Capt. Benjamin Webb of Salem (pub.
May 24, 1783).

37—V. ROBERT⁵, bapt. Nov. 16, 1760. *See
below* (*37*).

38—VI. ELIZABETH⁵, bapt. June 12, 1763.

39—VII. THOMAS POYNTON⁵, bapt. Sept. 30,
1764; probably d. unmarried.

40—VIII. BENJAMIN⁵, bapt. June 14, 1767. *See
below* (*40*).

41—IX. DANIEL⁵, bapt. Oct. 22, 1769; of Salem
clerk, 1804 ; and d., unmarried, Nov.
30, 1849.

26

CAPT. DANIEL BRAY⁴, born in Salem
July 17, 1735. He was a master-mariner, then called a rigger in 1788, and
yeoman in 1795, and lived in Salem.
He married Mary Ingalls May 15, 1760,
and died June 24, 1798, aged nearly
sixty-three. She survived him, and died
his widow, Sept. 28, 1805, aged sixty-
eight.

Children, born in Salem :—

42—I. MARY⁵, b. June 25, 1763; m. Capt.
Benjamin Henderson of Salem June
11, 1785; and d., his widow, Sept.
25, 1853.

43—II. ELIZABETH⁵, b. Nov. —, 1766; m.
John Willis of Salem May 17, 1789;
and d. March 20, 1859.

44—III. HANNAH⁵, b. May —, 1769; m. Robert
Barr Aug. 18, 1791; and d. in Salem
June 7, 1804.

45—IV. SALLY⁵, b. Nov. —, 1772; m. George
Batchelder of Salem Oct. 29, 1795;
and d. March 5, 1859.

46—V. ABIGAIL⁵, b. April —, 1774; m. Josiah
Richardson July 13, 1796.

47—VI. DANIEL⁵, b. Nov. —, 1775; m. Mary
Hodgdon Oct. 30, 1802; and d. Feb.
24, 1850.

48—VII. BENJAMIN⁵, b. Oct. —, 1780.

27

JOHN BRAY,⁵ baptized in Marblehead
Oct. 5, 1740. He married Mary Lewis
Dec. 28, 1766 ; and lived in Marblehead.

Children, born in Marblehead :—

49—I. JOHN⁶, bapt. March 29, 1767.

50—II. MARY⁶, bapt. April 14, 1771 ; m. Edmund Lewis Aug. 17, 1790.

51—III. JANE⁶, bapt. Sept. 12, 1773; probably
m. Abel Gardner July 24, 1815.

52—IV. BENJAMIN⁶, bapt. Jan. 11, 1775. *See
below* (*52*).

53—V. ROBERT⁶, bapt. Dec. 29, 1776.

37

ROBERT BRAY⁵, baptized in Salem Nov.
16, 1760. He married Sally Ropes of
Salem March 25, 1792.

Children :—

54—I. RUTH⁶; d., unmarried.

55—II. SARAH⁶, m. —— Parnell of Andover.

56—III. ROBERT⁶; d., unmarried.

57—IV. ELIZABETH⁶; d., unmarried.

40

BENJAMIN BRAY5, baptized in Marblehead June 14, 1767. He lived in Salem,
and married Margaret Hill Ellison of
Salem March 2, 1794.

Children, born in Salem :—

i—1.   JOHN6, bapt. April 12, 1795, in East
        church.
2—11. BENJAMIN6, b. in 1796; d. Jan.19, 1798,
        aged fifteen months.
3—111. ALBERT6, d. Jan. 1, 1808, aged seven
        months.
4—IV. JOHN6, bapt. Dec. 31, 1807.

52

CAPT. BENJAMIN BRAY6, baptized in
Marblehead ; Jan. 11, 1775. He lived in
Marblehead, and was "Drowned off
Braces Cove in a gal of Wind comeing in
from India, Vessell & Cargo lost," recorded Feb. 28, 1807 (gravestone says he died
March 1, 1807, aged thirty-two years and
eighteen days). He married Sally Waitt
Sept. 30, 1798; and she died Feb. 11,
1801, aged twenty-two years and seven
months.

Children, born in Marblehead :—

1—1. JOHN WAITT7, bapt. May 19, 1799; m.
        Nancy Brown March 9, 1824.
2—11. SALLY WAITT7, bapt. Dec. 11, 1803;
        m. John Roundy Nov. 22, 1825.

WILL OF WILLIAM CANTLEBURY.

The will of William Cantlebury of Salem was proved in the court held at Salem
3: 5 mo: 1663. The following copy is
taken from the original instrument on file
in the office of the clerk of courts, volume
IX, leaf 22.

whereas the lord our god hath ap-
poynted his servants to set there houses in
order, to the prayse of his name, the comfort of their owne soules and the peace of
their famelyes.

Therefore I Willyam Cantlebery of Sa-
em though weake in body yet in perfect
memory in obedience vnto christ my sau-
ior do commit my body to earth in its
mation : hopinge when christ who is my
life shal appeare : to be brought agayne
with him in glory.

And for my outward estate I doe thus
dispose thereof makinge this my last will
& testament

Inprimis, I giue vnto Beatrice my wife,
my house and orchard, & the land lyinge
betweene the land of Richard Leach &
John Rowden : the which house and land
I giue to her & to be at her dispose.

Item : I giue vnto Beatrice my wife :
all my moueable goods, all my Catle :
both younge and old, & horse and mares

All the which foresayed house and land :
mouable goods and Catle I giue vnto
her frely, & to be at her dispose : Prouided, that in case my wife should marry
to another husband : my children be not
depriued, of what my wife shal leaue at
her deceafe.

Item : I giue vnto my son John : the
3 quarters of the farme. I bought of mr
George Corwine (the 20 acres excepted,
that I disposed of to Job Swinnerton)
only Inioyninge him, to pay as legacyes
out of the same, twenty pounds to my
Daughter Ruth, & twenty pounds to my
Daughter Rebbecca & her children.

Item : my will is in case my son John
shal depart this life, or shal not come to
take possession of the sayd farme, I giue
vnto him, for that is my will that he shal
come in person to take possession : or else :
If he depart this life, or doe not come to
take possession thereof I giue then the
sayd farme bought of mr George Cor-
winne as aforesayd, vnto my daughter
Ruth : Inioyninge her to pay as a legacy
vnto my ‖daughter‖ Rebbeca, thirty
pounds, & in case my daughter Ruth :
shal by gods providence, be disposed of in
marriage, the profit of the sayd farme shal
be hers, vntil, my son John shal take pos-
sesson as aforesayd : the legacyes beinge
payd, both the wth forefayd legacyes ar
to be payd vpon the entry vpon the farme.

Item I constitute & apoynt Beatrice my
wife to be sole executrix of this my last
wil and testament

Item : I Constitute, and appoynt my
louinge ffreinde mr John Croade ouerseer
of this my last wil and testament

That this is my laft wil & teftament
witnes my hand & feale
Dated the 2th of April
      1661   fignum
            WILLYAM O CANTLEBERY
Sealed & delinered
In the prefence of
         vs
John Porter fen
Nathaniel ffelton

SALEM IN 1700. NO. 28.
BY SIDNEY PERLEY.

The map on page 111 represents that
part of Salem which is bounded by Essex,
Washington, Front and Central streets.
It is based on actual surveys and title
deeds, and is drawn on a scale of two
hundred feet to an inch. It shows the
location of all houses that were standing
there in 1700.

Essex street was one of the original
streets of the settlement. It was called
a street in 1660; street passing to the
meeting house, 1664; the main street
whereon the meeting house standeth,
1664; the main street, 1689; Main
street, 1690; Street from ye meeting
house to ye East end of ye town, 1694;
street or highway, 1698-9; and Essex
street as early as 1796.

Central street was an original way to
the water front. It was called the lane
or way that goes to the water side and
wharf whereon the warehouse of William
Browne standeth in 1664; lane or way
that goeth down along by the warehouse
of Benjamin Browne to the South river,
1690; highway to river, 1693; street or
highway that leads down to Major
Browne's wharf, 1714; the highway, 1733;
the lane leading to the water, 1782;
lane or street leading from Main street
to South river, 1785; Hanover street
leading from the main street to the South
river, 1790; Market street 1809; and
Central street, 1821.

Front street was one of the ancient
ways along the water front. It was called
the water side in 1662; highway, 1682:

highway leading by the sea, 1716; W
street, 1784; the street leading by
South river, 1787; Water street, 1
and Front street, as early as 1853.

Washington street was originally
out four rods wide, but the space ar
reserved on this side of Essex street
about seven rods wide. For a year c
after Endecott came this space rem
unoccupied. The first part that be
private land was that part defignate
the map as the lot of Elizur Ke,
which evidence indicates was the s
the house of Rev. Francis Higginson.
jail was erected here, and grants
made to John Horne, Mary Chiche
Henry West and Thomas Tuck.
second meeting house was located in
space also. That part westerly of
Elizur Keysor house was called the t
land or street in 1698; street lea
from the Court house to the wha:
1760; highway leading from the c
house in Salem to Marblehead, 17:
"road leading to Marblehead or e
where", 1785; road leading from Mar
head to Capt. William Orne's store
wards the new court house, 1794;
Washington street in 1810. East of
Elizur Keysor house the way was call
highway in 1665; town land or st
1693; lane or way leading from ye t
house down to the sea, 1746; lane lea
from the great meeting house to the a
house wharf, 1762; lane between the
of Edmund Henfield and land of Aba
Cabot and Hannah Smith,1770; and a
in 1810. On the south side of the L
Keysor lot, it was called the town lan
street in 1693; highway in 1760;
common land in 1770 and 1810. On
north side of the Elizur Keysor ho:
the land was called the town land
street in 1693; and highway in 1;
One of these lanes was popularly ca
"Shirk alley" nearly a century ago.

The lane on the east side of the J
Orne lot was called a highway in 1665
street or highway, 1703; way from
main street, 1726; lane, 1747; high
1762; and lane or way, 1791. This

polished on the widening of Washington street in 1839.

The short way, of about five rods in length, at the corner of what was originally the broad street and the street to the south of the premises was called a highway in 1695; highway or common land, 1747; town land, 1786; way leading to Cabot's wharf and to wharves to the eastward of it, 1792; a road, 1794; and short street, 1827.

The way on the south side of the meeting house was called a highway in 1665; a street or highway, 1693; and highway by the south side of the great meeting house, 1762.

The way on the east side of the meeting house was called a street, in 1674; street or highway, 1693; a lane between the meeting house and shop of William Driver, 1702; and ye highway as late as 1734.

The cove which came up into the street was called a creek in 1736. This was filled about a hundred years ago.

The South river was called the river in 1660; South river, 1664; and the sea in 1746. It was filled along the street about a century ago.

The meeting house lot was taken from the lot of William Lord before August, 1635. The first meeting house, built prior to that date, stood on the vacant lot east of the meeting house shown on the map. For the history of the first meeting house, see Essex Institute Historical Collections, volume XXXIX, page 329. The meeting house was taken down in August, 1672; and its timbers were used in the construction of a town, school and watch house a few yards westerly of the meeting house shown on the map, two years later. It was not finished in 1677, when it was removed to the middle of Washington street opposite to what is now known as the Brookhouse estate. The meeting house shown on the map was built in 1671, sixty feet long, fifty feet and twenty feet posts. This edifice stood until 1718. After the first meeting house was removed its site was known

and used as a market place. When the second meeting house was erected in 1671, the prison, which then stood upon that site, was removed to the west, into what was then the garden of Benjamin Felton; and there the prison remained until the new jail on St. Peter street was built in 1684.

In the sketches that follow, after 1700, titles and deeds referred to pertain to the houses and land adjoining and not always to the whole lot, the design being after that date, to give the history of the houses then standing principally.

David Phippen House. This lot was early owned by William Browne of Salem, merchant. For thirty-two pounds, he conveyed the northern part of it and the dwelling house thereon to Thomas Cromwell of Salem, tailor, 20: 2: 1664.* Mr. Cromwell died March 17, 1686-7; and his widow, Ann Cromwell, and son-in-law Jonathan Pickering and wife Jane, and son-in-law David Phippen and wife Ann, all of Salem, for sixty-five pounds and seventeen shillings, conveyed the house and northern part of the lot to Benjamin Browne of Salem, merchant, Oct. 21, 1690.† Benjamin Browne's stable stood upon the southern part of the lot, and he probably received his title from William Browne who owned the stable and land in 1664, but no conveyance has been found. Benjamin Browne apparently conveyed the entire lot with the house and stable to David Phippen of Salem, shipwright, before 1693. The latter died in 1703, intestate. The house and lot were then valued at ninety-five pounds. Mr. Phippen's widow, Anne Phippen, and the surviving children of Mr. Phippen, viz.: Thomas Phippen, mariner, William Furneux, rope maker, and wife Abigail, Benjamin Ropes, cordwainer, and wife Anne, and John Webb, seaman, and wife Elizabeth, all of Salem, for eighty pounds, conveyed the house and lot to Capt. John

*Essex Registry of Deeds, book 6, leaf 97.
†Essex Registry of Deeds, book 8, leaf 170.

Brown of Salem, merchant, May 27, 1714.* The house was gone apparently before Captain Brown's death, which occurred in the spring of 1719.

George Felt House. Elias Stileman owned this lot very early: and July 4, 1693, when he was of Portsmouth, N. H., for fourteen pounds and ten shillings, conveyed it to George Felt of Salem, blockmaker.† Mr. Felt built a house upon the lot, in which he lived until his death, which occurred Feb. 24, 1729. The house, shop, barn and land were then appraised at three hundred and twenty pounds. Four children survived Mr. Felt, Mary, wife of William Bartoll of Falmouth, Me., shipwright, Jemima Ashby, widow of Jonathan Ashby of Salem, shipwright, Bonfield Felt of Salem, blockmaker, and Benjamin Felt of Salem, coaster. Bonfield Felt conveyed his interest to his brother Benjamin Felt Feb. 18, 1733 ;‡ and Mrs. Ashby conveyed her interest to her brother Bonfield Felt May 1, 1734.§ Mr. and Mrs. Bartoll conveyed the latter's interest to her brother Bonfield Felt in June, 1736.‖ Feb. 2, 1749, a partition of the estate (the mother having died) took place between Bonfield and Benjamin, and Bonfield received the northern half of the lot and western half of the house,¶ and Benjamin the southern half of the lot and eastern half of the house.** May 12, 1760, when Bonfield Felt was living in his end of the house, he conveyed that part of the house and the land to his brother Benjamin ;†† and April 15, 1763, he released his interest in the entire estate to his brother Benjamin.‡‡ Benjamin Felt lived in the house, and died March 1, 1769, having devised the house and land under and adjoining to his son Benjamin. Benjamin Felt, jr., was a

coaster, and lived in the house. For : hundred and forty pounds, he conveyed the western half of the house and under and to the westward of it to w. Bethiah Trask of Salem Dec. 19, 17·· She lived in the house, and, for one h dred and twenty pounds, conveyed · same estate to Edward Augustus Holy esq., of Salem July 25, 1793.† Mr. i. yoke, for four hundred and fifty Spa milled dollars, conveyed the same pro ty to Edward Russell of Salem, coas May 3, 1798.‡ Benjamin Felt had c: veyed the eastern end of the house . land under and next easterly of it to ' Russell March 11, 1790.§ Mr. R· moved the house to the rear part of : lot ; and died Jan. 14, 1815, having : vised the estate to his wife Sarah. 'I house was then valued at one hund: dollars. She died Oct. 12, 1843, hav devised it to Sarah Baxter Safford a Edward Barker Russell. The latter liv in Brunswick, Me., and was a mari. He conveyed his half of the estate to : rah Baxter Safford, who lived in Sale being the wife of Joshua Safford, Aug. : 1845.‖ Mrs. Safford took the ho down. It was a small one-storied ga brel-roofed house, standing end to : street, and having the front door in t middle of one side. There was one w dow on either side of the front door, a dormer windows in the roof.

Benjamin Browne Lot. This lot ! longed to William Browne quite early, he died possessed of it Jan. 20, 168· This also included an interest in : wharf at the southeast corner which w granted to him by the town of Salem A 29, 1681. It descended to his son Be jamin Browne of Salem, a merchant, w owned it until his death in 1708.

John Cromwell Houses. This lot land originally belonged to Rev. Sam Skelton, and to Mr. Philip Cromwell

*Essex Registry of Deeds, book 25, leaf 273.
†Essex Registry of Deeds, book 9, leaf 157.
‡Essex Registry of Deeds, book 62, leaf 142.
§Essex Registry of Deeds, book 64, leaf 178.
‖Essex Registry of Deeds, book 72, leaf 271.
¶Essex Registry of Deeds, book 95, leaf 264.
**Essex Registry of Deeds, book 95, leaf 265.
††Essex Registry of Deeds, book 107, leaf 105.
‡‡Essex Registry of Deeds, book 112, leaf 125.

*Essex Registry of Deeds, book 142, leaf 3·
†Essex Registry of Deeds, book 156, leaf ?·
‡Essex Registry of Deeds, book 163, leaf 1·
§Essex Registry of Deeds, book 148, leaf 2·
‖Essex Registry of Deeds, book 358, leaf 2·

PART OF SALEM IN 1700. NO. 28.

SCALE: 200ft. = 1 inch.

1647. In 1660, there was only one house upon it. Mr. Cromwell apparently erected another house upon the lot some years later. He laid out a passage to it twelve feet wide and seventy feet long, and died possessed of the estate March 30, 1693. It descended to his son, John Cromwell, who died possessed of the lot and both houses Sept. 30, 1700. The house nearest the street had been occupied by Edward Cox, and the other by a Mrs. Bartholomew. Under the will of Mr. Cromwell, his widow, Hannah Cromwell of Salem conveyed the estate to Florence Maccarty of Boston, slaughterer, Nov. 28, 1701.* Mr. Maccarty evidently took down the old house immediately, and died in 1712. His estate was divided Jan. 18, 1723, when the houses were both gone.

Florence Maccarty House. This lot originally belonged to Rev. Samuel Skelton, and to Mr. Philip Cromwell as early as 1647. There was then a house upon the lot, and the latter died possessed of the estate March 30, 1693. The estate descended to his son John Cromwell of Salem, slaughterer, who built a shop and slaughter-house. For one hundred and twenty pounds, he conveyed the house, shop, slaughter-house and land to Florence Maccarty of Boston March 17, 1698-9.† Mr. Maccarty died in 1712, possessed of the estate, and the house was gone before 1723.

William Browne House. That part of this lot lying easterly of the dashes originally belonged to Rev. Samuel Skelton, whose house stood at the southern end of the lot. Mr. Skelton came to Salem in 1629, and was the first pastor of the church in Salem. He died Aug. 2, 1634; and the estate came into the hands of his son-in-law Nathaniel Felton of Salem. Mr. Felton sold the "old" house and land to Mr. William Browne, sr., of Salem in 1643, though no deed was passed in confirmation of the sale until Nov. 26, 1668.‡ "The ould houfe In Salem which

once was mr Skeltons being in Eminent Danger of prefent falling to the endangering of the lives of Children & Cattell and others" the county court ordered that it be taken down within ten days 27: 6: 1644, and it was so removed probably.*

The remainder of the lot belonged to Hugh Laskin very early, and he lived in the house at the southern end of the lot, which was called "an old house" in 1647. The two houses and the land were owned by Richard Stilman of Salem, when he conveyed the estate to Samuel Sharp, elder of ye church of Salem, and Elias Stilman, sr., feofees in trust, for the use of his son Samuel Stilman and his heirs forever; reserving his dwelling house thereon for eighteen years at the rent of five pounds a year, "Provided if by Casualtie of fire the houses be destroyed the Rent to be abated accordinglie, and in case the sd Samuell dyeth before he be at adg of 21 years then the whole Estat to Returne to ye said Richard & his heires." This instrument is dated Aug. 9, 1647.† Samuel Stilman probably died a minor, as his father, who had removed to Portsmouth, N. H., conveyed the houses and land to his cousin Elias Stileman, esq., of Portsmouth, April 12, 1660.‡ The old house was gone before July 23, 1694, when Elias Stileman, for one house and twenty pounds, conveyed one house and the lot to Maj. William Browne, esq., of Salem, merchant.§ Mr. Browne lived here, and died in February, 1715-6, possessed of the entire estate. In his will he devised this his homestead, with the house, land, etc., to his son Samuel Browne. Col. Samuel Browne was a judge, representative and one of the largest merchants of the town in his time. He removed the house before 1731.

Estate of William Driver House. This little lot of fifteen feet square was a part of the homestead of William Lord as early as 1635. The town voted, 22: 0

*The Essex Antiquarian, volume V, page 25

*Essex Registry of Deeds, book 15, leaf 7.
†Essex Registry of Deeds, book 13, leaf 213.
‡Essex Registry of Deeds, book 3, leaf 45.

*Essex Registry of Deeds, book 1, leaf 3.
‡Essex Registry of Deeds, book 2, leaf 15.
§Essex Registry of Deeds, book 11, leaf 183.

1635, that a committee " should consider of some convenient place for shops yt may be wth the owners consent ;" and suggestions for shops at this corner were made. Benjamin Felton had a shop on the lot in 1647 ; and at a meeting of the selectmen, 3 : 6 : 1659, " Leave was given to Richard Horne Taylour to mend vp the little house Joyning to the meeting house & make vse of it for a shopp at the Townes pleasure."* The town gave liberty to Thomas Hale " to build a shopp adoyinge to the meetinge houfe were the felect men shall apoynt it : & to enioy it at the Towns pleafure."† Edward Wharton owned the lot, with the house thereon, in 1660. Capt. George Corwin, the merchant, subsequently owned it ; and with the two-story shops and cellar theron conveyed the estate to Joseph Stacey. Mr. Stacey owned " the house of shops" in 1689. He died Oct. 15, 1690, and the house and lot were then appraised at forty-five pounds. Orally, in the presence of John Marston and Hannah Harby, he gave everything he had to his mother the night he died. His mother, Susannah Stacey of Salem, with the consent of her sons William Stacey and John Stacey, who join in the deed, conveyed the estate to William Driver of Salem, chandler, Jan. 3, 1690-1.‡ Mr. Driver died the same year; and his son William Driver of Salem, cordwainer, for ten pounds, released the shop and lot to his step-father, Daniel Grant of Salem, chandler, April 30, 1702.§ Daniel Grant had married Mr. Driver's widow and also continued the chandler business at the old stand. Mr. Grant, as administrator of Mr. Driver's estate, for forty-seven pounds and ten shillings, conveyed the house and land to Daniel Caton of Salem, tailor, March 3, 1709-10.‖ For seventy-five pounds, Mr. Caton conveyed the house and land to Samuel Browne of Salem, merchant, Oct. 21, 1734.¶ Mr.

Browne died possessed of it in 173-, and the house stood some years after 1742, but was gone before 1784.

Samuel Phillips Houses. That part of this lot lying north of the dashes was originally a part of the homestead of Hugh Laskin, and early came into the hands of Richard Stilman, who owned it in 1647. He removed to Portsmouth, N. H., after that date, and he conveyed it to his cousin Elias Stileman of Portsmouth April 12, 1660.* The latter, for ten pounds, conveyed it to Samuel Phillips of Salem, goldsmith, May 25, 1689.† Mr. Phillips built a house upon this lot ; and conveyed the house and land, "where I now dwell," one-fourth to his wife Sarah, one-fourth to his daughter Patience, and one-half to his son John Phillips, stationer, May 3, 1722.‡ Mr. Phillips was then sick probably and died before Nov. 14, 1722, when a division of his estate was made, and this house and lot were assigned to the widow and Patience as their half of the estate.§ For ninety-five pounds, they conveyed the house and lot to Richard Bethel of Salem, tailor, Nov. 17, 1722;‖ and, for sixty pounds, Mr. Bethel conveyed the estate (in mortgage) to Col. Samuel Browne of Salem, esquire, July 12, 1731.¶ Colonel Browne died possessed of it in 173-. The house was standing in 1742, but was probably gone some years later.

That part of the lot lying westerly of the dashes was also a part of the William Lord lot, and was owned, with the house thereon, by Edward Wharton as early as 1660 and in 1671. It belonged to Lt. Thomas Gardner of Salem subsequently, and he died possessed of it in 1682. A suit at law was brought against his estate, and judgment therein was obtained July 31, 1683. In satisfaction of the execution, which was issued upon the judgment, this part of the lot was set off to the judgment creditor, the executor of the

*Town Records, volume I.
†Town Records, volume II, page 1.
‡Essex Registry of Deeds, book 8, leaf 184.
§Essex Registry of Deeds, book 17, leaf 127.
‖Essex Registry of Deeds, book 22, leaf 70.
¶Essex Registry of Deeds, book 62, leaf 281.

*Essex Registry of Deeds, book 2, leaf 15.
†Essex Registry of Deeds, book 8, leaf 173.
‡Essex Registry of Deeds, book 38, leaf 237.
§Essex Registry of Deeds, book 39, leaf 177.
‖Essex Registry of Deeds, book 50, leaf 13.
¶Essex Registry of Deeds, book 55, leaf 239.

will of Hezekiah Usher of Boston, merchant, deceased, by the sheriff, Nov. 18, 1684.* The said executor conveyed the house and this part of the lot to Samuel Phillips of Salem, goldsmith, Oct. 26, 1698.† The house was then occupied by Stephen Ingalls, the widow of Lt. Thomas Gardner having lived there until her decease in or before 1695. Mr. Phillips conveyed the house and land to his wife Sarah, his daughter Patience and his son John Phillips of Boston, stationer, May 3, 1722.‡ Upon the division of the estate, Nov. 14, 1722, this house and lot were assigned to his son John Phillips.§ It was then called "an old house." Two days later, for ninety-five pounds, John Phillips conveyed the land and "old house or end of a house" to Richard Bethel of Salem, tailor;‖ and Mr. Bethel conveyed the house and lot to Col. Samuel Browne of Salem, esquire, July 12, 1731.¶ Colonel Browne probably took the house down.

That part of the lot lying within the dashes at the southeast corner of the lot was a part of the lot originally owned by Hugh Laskin, and later by Richard Stileman. Mr. Stileman removed to Portsmouth, N. H., before April 12, 1660, when he conveyed it to his cousin Elias Stileman, esq., also of Portsmouth.** For a parcel of glass, Mr. Stileman conveyed this small lot to Edward Wharton of Salem, glazier, Aug. 31, 1668.†† It came into the ownership of Lt. Thomas Gardner of Salem, and it belonged to him at the time of his death, in 1682. Upon the execution already mentioned this lot was assigned to the executor of the will of Hezekiah Usher of Boston, merchant, deceased, Nov. 18, 1684.* The executor conveyed it to Samuel Phillips of Salem, goldsmith, Oct. 26, 1698 ;† and Mr. Phillips owned it until 1722.

*Essex Registry of Deeds, book 7, leaf 18.
†Essex Registry of Deeds, book 13, leaf 47.
‡Essex Registry of Deeds, book 38, leaf 237.
§Essex Registry of Deeds, book 39, leaf 177.
‖Essex Registry of Deeds, book 42, leaf 175.
¶Essex Registry of Deeds, book 55, leaf 239.
**Essex Registry of Deeds, book 2, leaf 15.
††Essex Registry of Deeds, book 5, leaf 45.

Susanna Lyde Lot. This lot was owned by Capt. George Corwin as early as 1660, and his "upper" warehouse, measuring 18½ x 44½ feet, stood upon it. He died Jan. 3, 1684-5, and by agreement of the heirs, July 4. 1684, it was assigned to his daughter Susanna, wife of Edward Lyde of Boston, merchant, but the agreement was not put into writing until Dec. 1, 1701.* She owned it after that date. It is stated that Captain Corwin bought the lot of Edward Beacham and Edward Norrice.

Walter Price Lot. This lot was a part of the homestead of William Lord as early as 1635. He died about 165-, and his widow and executrix, Abigail Lord, for forty pounds, conveyed this lot and part of the dwelling house, "adjoining to the row of houses I now live in to that part," to Edmund Berry of Salem, weaver, Oct. 1, 1674.† Mr. Berry lived in this house. and, for his life support conveyed the lot and house to his son-in-law Mark Haskell of Beverly, carpenter, Sept. 13, 1684.‡ The house was gone April 5, 1693, when Mr. Haskell conveyed the lot to Sarah Price of Salem, "gentlewoman."§ She died in 1698, and the lot descended to her only child, Walter Price of Salem, merchant, who owned it in 1701.

Josiah Wolcott Lot. This was a portion of the homestead of William Lord as early as 1635 ; and he died possessed of it in 165-. His widow and executrix, Abigail Lord of Salem, for love, conveyed it, with the eastern half of the dwelling house thereon, containing the "upper and lower room," to Samuel Gray and his wife Abigail, her daughter and son-in-law, Oct. 1, 1674.‖ Mrs. Lord then occupied part of the house. This part of the estate belonged to Mrs. Gray's nephew, Joseph Lord who conveyed it to his father, William Lord. The latter gave it to his son Jeremiah Lord of Ipswich, weaver, who.

*Essex Registry of Deeds, book 14, leaf 279.
†Essex Registry of Deeds, book 4, leaf 89.
‡Essex Registry of Deeds, book 7, leaf 6.
§Essex Registry of Deeds, book 9, leaf 121.
‖Essex Registry of Deeds, book 4, leaf 104.

for five pounds, released it to Josiah Wolcott of Salem, merchant (the house being gone), July 13, 1693.* Mr. Wolcott owned it in 1700.

Samuel and Abigail Gray Lot. This was a part of the homestead of William Lord as early as 1635. He died possessed of it in 16—; and his widow and executrix, Abigail Lord, for love, conveyed the land and house, except the eastern end of the house, comprising the upper and lower rooms, in which she then lived, and the use of the old barn, well, etc., which she reserved for her life, to her daughter Abigail and the latter's husband Samuel Gray Oct. 1, 1674.† The house was gone before 1700, when the lot still belonged to them.

Deliverance Parkman House. That part of this lot lying northwesterly of the dashes was owned by William Lord as early as 1635; and, for ten pounds, he conveyed it to Stephen Haskett of Salem, soapboiler, April 6, 1664.‡ For a similar consideration, Mr. Haskett conveyed it to Edward Wharton of Salem, glazier, Oct. 3, 1671.§ Mr. Wharton died before Nov. 26, 1678; and, for twelve pounds, the administrator of his estate conveyed it to Hilliard Veren of Salem, scrivener, April 8, 1682.‖ Mr. Veren, for thirteen pounds, conveyed the lot to Deliverance Parkman of Salem, mariner, March 25, 1683.¶

The remainder of the lot was owned by William Lord as early as 1635. For six pounds, he conveyed it to John Cole of Salem, cooper, " for a house plot," March 19, 1662.** Mr. Cole built a house thereon, and, for twenty-eight pounds, conveyed the house, shop, wharf and lot to Robert Wilkes of Salem, shipwright, Feb. 22, 1675-6.†† He was taken sick while on a voyage from Bristol to New England in the autumn of 1677, and died on the

voyage, having devised this house, outhouses and land to his wife Mary for her life, and then to his niece Mary Woodbury. The estate was then appraised at fifty pounds. Mrs. Woodbury and her husband, Isaac Woodbury, sr., and their daughter Mary Woodbury, all of Beverly, for thirty pounds, conveyed the house, shop and land to Mr. Parkman (who owned the remainder of the lot) Feb. 19, 1693-4.* Mr. Parkman thus became the owner of the entire lot, and died in 1715, possessed of it, with the warehouse, " small old dwelling or work house " and wharf thereon. The estate was then valued at sixteen pounds. The house was probably gone soon after.

Edmond Batter Lot. That part of this lot lying easterly of the dashes was a part of the homestead of William Lord as early as 1635. He died possessed of it in 165—; and by his request his executrix conveyed it to his daughter Margaret Lord. Her brother-in-law William Godsoe of Salem, mariner, had built a dwelling house partly on this part of the lot and partly on the other part which he bought of Reuben Guppy; and Obadiah Rich lived in it in the winter of 1673-4, and Edward Winter in 1674. Miss Lord conveyed her part of the land to Mr. Godsoe July 1, 1682.†

That part of the lot lying westerly of the dashes was granted by the town to Mr. Godsoe by order of Reuben Guppy of Salem March 6, 1678-9.‡ The grant was of "a house lot to the southward off will Lords present dwelling house, bounded, with the land of mr Resolued white on the East & the house and land of Wm Lord on the north & wth the townes land on the West & South to Lay forty two fott longe from within Six foott from william Lords house Southerly & twenty two fott & halfe in Breadth East & West." Mr. Guppy conveyed it to Mr. Godsoe Dec. 14, 1678.§

*Essex Registry of Deeds, book 9, leaf 120.
†Essex Registry of Deeds, book 4, leaf 104.
‡Essex Registry of Deeds, book 6, leaf 19.
§Essex Registry of Deeds, book 5, leaf 89.
‖Essex Registry of Deeds, book 6, leaf 46.
*Essex Registry of Deeds, book 6, leaf 82.
**Essex Registry of Deeds, book 9, leaf 40.
††Essex Registry of Deeds, book 4, leaf 130.

*Essex Registry of Deeds, book 11, leaf 136.
†Essex Registry of Deeds, book 6, leaf 104.
‡Town Records, volume 11, page 208.
§Essex Registry of Deeds, book 5, leaf 54.

Mr. Godsoe lived in the house. It was gone before Oct. 20, 1694, when it had passed to Madam Elizabeth Corwin, widow of Capt. George Corwin, who on that date, for eighteen pounds, conveyed the land to James Gillingham of Salem, sawyer.* Mr. Gillingham conveyed it to Edmon Batter of Salem, tanner, Oct. 18, 1695,† and Mr. Batter owned the lot in 1700.

Joseph Lord House. The selectmen of Salem granted to Mary, wife of William Chichester, 24 : 1 : 1662-3. "a fmall plott of grounde belowe Rich : Harveyes houfe to fet a dwellinge houfe : 25 foote in lenght and 18 foote in breadth provided fhee build on it within two yeares elce to returne to the towne."* A house was built upon the lot immediately. John Mastone, jr., of Salem, carpenter, conveyed the house and land to Ankias Horsman of Salem, seaman, Dec. 26, 1667;§ and, for fifty pounds, Mr. Horsman conveyed the estate to William Lord, sr., and his wife, Abigail Lord, Feb. 3, 1667-8.‖ The house was then unfinished, and in the last-mentioned deed was agreed to be finished according to a covenant between Mr. Henry Bartholomew and John Norton, sr., dated 12: 11 mo: 1663. John Norton was probably the contractor. John Guppy lived in this house in 1674. Isaac Stearns of Salem conveyed the estate to Joseph Lord of Salem, mariner, before 1692 ; and Mr. Lord removed to Boston, where he was living in 1700. The house was probably gone soon after that date.

John Orne House. This lot was granted by the town of Salem to John Horne (Orne) 18 : 9 : 1661, and described as "in the gutt between Wᵐ Lord fen & Helyard veren houfe : 18 foote broad & 40 foot in length."§ He evidently conveyed it to Richard Harvey of Salem, tailor, who immediately built a house

upon it ; and, for thirty pounds, Mr. Harvey conveyed the house and lot to Mr. Horne June 17, 1665.* Deacon Horne conveyed the estate to his son John Orne of Salem, cordwinder, as a gift, Nov. 4, 1684.† The grantee was then living in the house, and he continued to occupy it. He removed to Boston, and died there possessed of the estate. The executor of his will, for ninety pounds, conveyed the land and house "with an old end of a dwelling house adjoining to it" to Zechariah Birchmore of Salem, mariner, April 24, 1724.‡ Mr. Birchmore, for seventy-five pounds, conveyed the house and land to Abraham Cabot of Salem, fisherman, Oct. 14, 1732.§ For forty pounds, Mr. Cabot conveyed the house, well and land to George Smith of Salem, mariner, Jan. 18, 1762.‖ Mr. Smith apparently removed the house soon afterward.

Elizur Keysor House. By an agreement made in London April 8, 1629, with the governor and company of the Massachusetts Bay, Rev. Francis Higginson, the first teacher of the church in Salem, was to have a house built for him. Mr. Higginson arrived here June 29, 1629 ; and in just a year thereafter he died, leaving a widow and eight children. The house and land was apparently given to his widow. In this house lived Roger Williams ; and at the time of his banishment, at the request of Mrs. Higginson (who had removed to Charlestown), he conveyed the estate to John Woolcott of Salem. Mr. Woolcott conveyed it, with two bedsteads, table, forms and shelves in the house, and all the fences about it, to William Lord of Salem Nov. 9, 1635. The following is an exact copy of the deed, which is unrecorded and is found in the files of the county court at Salem for March 30, 1669 :—¶

*Essex Registry of Deeds, book 10, leaf 115.
†Essex Registry of Deeds, book 20, leaf 157.
‡Town Records, volume II, page 45.
§Essex Registry of Deeds, book 3, leaf 24.
‖Essex Registry of Deeds, book 3, leaf 35.
¶Town Records, volume II, page 22.

*Essex Registry of Deeds, book 43, leaf 55.
†Essex Registry of Deeds, book 7, leaf 53.
‡Essex Registry of Deeds, book 59, leaf 33.
§Essex Registry of Deeds, book 61, leaf 235.
‖Essex Registry of Deeds, book 107, leaf 215.
¶Court Files, volume XIV, leaf 15.

In Salem, the — of the 8th month caled octobr 1635

Memorandu that I John Woolcott of Salem have Bartered and Sould vnto William Lord

all and euery part of my houfe and mifteed in Salem (formerlie in the occupation of mr Roger williams, & from him by order from mrs Higenfon fould vnto me, as by a quittance vndr mr wms hand doth appear; as alfo all the out houfing, wth 2 bedfteads Table formes & fhelues in the forefaid dwelling houfe, with all the ffences about it, or wt els vnto belong vnto it. Alfo all the Intereft mrs Higenfon of Charles Towne, & fo my felf, had or ‖now‖ haue in a Tenn Acre Lott of ground on the fouth fyde; flor, & in Confideration of the fome of ffifteene pounds Tenn fhillings to me in hand paid, (according to an order of Arbitermt mad by mr Throckmorton. & John woodbury, in differently chofen by vs both for that purpofe,) in full fatiffaction of the premifes, wth faid fome &c the faid John Woolcott doth acknowledg him felf fully contented and paid and therof acquitteth the fd wm Lord his heirse & affigns for euer In witnes wherof I haue hearvnto put my hand feale this 23th of the 9th mo: caled Novebr anno 1635.

Sealed Signed and
delivered in prfence   Jon
  of   woollcott (SEAL)
Raph flogg sr
The mark
of Elizabeth Turner

This deed is on file among the papers in the case of William Lord against John Horne, which relates to the title of the land to the westward of William Lord's land as shown on the map. This deed could not have referred to William Lord's homestead as he owned it some time before the date of this deed of the Higginson house. As the deed conveyed "all the fences about it," the conclusion is that no part of the fences belonged to any other person, that is, that there were no adjoining owners, Mr. Hilliard Veren, who appears as its owner in 1659, was a public man, and a man worthy to succeed to such a prominent and historic residence. Mr. Lord and the Veren family had many real estate transactions together.

Hillard Veren owned the estate May 2, 1659, when the town granted to him "Roome before his now dwellinge house to make a Porch."* He died Dec. 20,

*Town Records.

1683, at the age of sixty-three; and the estate, which was then valued, with the house and barn thereon, at one hundred pounds, descended to his two daughters, Mary, wife of Samuel Williams of Salem, and Abigail, wife of Benjamin Marston of Salem. They divided the house and lot, Mary taking the western, and Abigail, the easterly part. Mr. Williams died, and his widow, Mary Williams, with the consent of her son Samuel Williams, for forty-three pounds, conveyed her half of the house and lot to John Woodwell of Salem, glover, April 6, 1693.* Mr. Marston, for forty pounds, conveyed his wife's half of the lot and house, with the leanto, to Mr. Woodwell Nov. 14, 1693.† For forty-five pounds, sixteen shillings and eight pence, Mr. Woodwell conveyed the house, barn and land to Elizur Keysor of Salem, tanner, May 11, 1698.‡ Mr. Keysor conveyed the same estate to Florence Maccarty of Boston April 7, 1707.§ Mr. Maccarty, for twenty-eight pounds, conveyed it to Peter Windet of Salem, currier, May 8, 1707.‖ Mr. Windet evidently removed the old house soon afterward.

NOTES.

John Brobrooke lived in Newbury at the time of his death, June 28, 1662. He had a mother and an uncle Short. He had an estate in England, and interest in a house and lot in Watertown, evidently his father's as his mother had an interest in it also. His estate here was appraised at £117, 3s., 3d. He had brothers and sisters Samuel, Joseph, Elizabeth, Sarah, Rebecca, Rachel and Thomas living in 1662.—*Records.*

Mary Brabrook of Salem, 1742.

James Brace of Salem, mariner, 1794, 1796.

—*Registry of deeds.*

*Essex Registry of Deeds, book 12, leaf 143.
†Essex Registry of Deeds, book 12, leaf 144.
‡Essex Registry of Deeds, book 13, leaf 2.
§Essex Registry of Deeds, book 20, leaf 27.
‖Essex Registry of Deeds, book 20, leaf 28.

IPSWICH COURT RECORDS AND FILES.

Continued from page 86.

Court, March 31, 1657.

Judges: Mr. Symon Brodstreet, Mr. Samuell Symonds, Major-general Denison and Mr. William Hubbert.

Trial jury: Lt. Samuell Appleton, Serg. Tho: ffrench, Tho: Safford, Sam : Youngloue, John West, John Trumble, James Barker, John Lambert, Willm Morse, James Packman (Jackman?), Robert Lord, Tho: Dorman, Will : Howard, Jo: Pike, Ez: Northen, Hen: Skerry and Rich : Kent.

Rich : Doall sworn constable for Newbury, and John Dane for Ipswich.

Nicolas Noyse and John Pike sworn commissioners for Newbury.

Joseph Noyse and Joseph Mussey of Newbury and George ffarough of Ipswich made free.

[Mary Pareker, aged about twenty years, testified that Henry Kimball never agreed with her for the stripes he gave her until Robert Whitman went to her master's house a few days before April 23. Sworn before Daniel Denison 9 : 24 : 1656.

Ezekiel Mighill and Philip Nelson deposed that they heard Mr. Shepard say to John Asy (Acie) that he had better let John Pickard alone and not sue him for he would win out.

Rebecca Black testified that "Willm, Goodm Harradenys man," came into her master, Wm. Cogswell's house when people were going to meeting on the Sabbath day, and asked her where James was. She said, "He is gone to meeting." Then he took a stool and sat down before her. Then he rose from the stool and sat in her lap, kissing her. She strove with him, and he went to a door and locked it. He would not let her go forth. She then went to the cradle to see how the child was to get away from him, and he took her by the shoulders, throwing her against the table board ; etc. She strove so hard with him that she sweat, and she had much ado to keep herself from him,

etc. He threw her upon a chest that stood near; and she said, "Let me go and look to our children ;" etc.

Joseph Porter aged about nineteen years and John Glover, aged about twenty-one years, deposed that the colt that was Mr. Cowes was wintered at their farm two years, etc. Sworn to 25 : 2 : 1656, before William Hathorne.

—*Files.*]

Mr. Richard Dummer v. Phillip Nellson. Review of a case tried at Salem last June. The question was whether the children mentioned in the memorandum meant the children of their two bodies.

Phillip Nelson v. Mr. Richard Dumer, executor to Mr. Thomas Nelson. For giving a false account of his father's estate at Salem court. Verdict for the plaintiff, money damages and two-fifths of the saw-mill irons, etc.

Verdict in Nelson's case. Signed by Elias Stileman, clerk.

Writ: Mr. Richard Dumer v. Mr Philop Nelson. Review, concerning an account as executor of the estate of Mr. Thomas Nelson, deceased ; dated 7 : 1 : 1656-7 ; by the court, William Howard. Served by Edward Browne, marshall of Ipswich, March 25, 1657, by attachment of a gray mare, a black mare colt with a gray tail and a reddish mare with a black tail, branded with R. D.

List of articles further demanded, being delivered to Mistress Nelson after her husband's death and before the will was proved ; and land at mill. More was due to Mr. Thomas Dumer in England.

"mr Dumer there is due from mr Nelfons farme at Crane meadow 2ll 4f 10f of which ‖we‖ defier you to pay St to Brother fwan to Brother Dickinfon 8s 10d and ye remainder which is 1ll 8th 0d to Brother Tod

"from thofe which laid it out
"William Hobfon
Thomas Dickanfon
in the name of the ref"

Richard Dumer's bill of charges in the review against Mr. Philip Nelson.

Account: personal estate in Old England and New England. For the fence at the warehouse. Philip Nelson is creditor for clothing and education. Money from Mr. Jewitt, John Pickard and Goodm Spaford, and many cattle. Old saw-mill fence.

Account of the estate of Mr. Thomas Nelson, deceased, presented to Salem court by Mr. Richard Dumer June —, 1656, upon suit of Philip Nelson, rectified. The mill and all that belonged to it, appertaining to Mr. Nelson's widow from Aug. 1, 1648, the time of her husband's death. Rent of ground in the pond field; land at the mill and meadow. A piece of stuff sent to the widow by her father for a gown, wrongly inventoried. Repairs on the mill. Money paid the widow in England given her by will. A silver bowl to the widow, a choice mare and four of the best cows paid in England. A jointure by bond to the widow, payable in August, 1648. Charges in England, from Southampton to Yorke and Hull, which is four hundred (eighteen days), time of three horses, two men and expense. Voyage into England. Money due on balance of account as agent under the hands of the worshipful Mr. Symonds and Captain Bridges, a committee of the general court, of the amount paid in England. Paid to Francis Parrat, Goodm Boise (breaking up land in the house field), Good^m Longhorne (making rail fence; thatching the house; laying out the farm at Crane meadow). Arbitration with Goody Crosse. Executor's six years' salary. Due to Mr. Thomas Dumer in England. Plate to Philip and Thomas.

Copy of will of Thomas Nelson dated 6:6: 1648, proved March 31, 1657. (This will was printed in full in *The Antiquarian*, volume III, page 187.)

Copy of statement relating to a marriage contract of Joane Dumer of Newbury with Thomas Nelson of Rowley, gent. Bond of Thomas Nelson, for two hundred pounds, to Richard Dumer of Newbury in trust for said Joane; and said Joane Nelson states that her husband died, leaving certain estate for her in his will, which she received near Southampton, in Old England; dated July 1, 1654. Witnesses: Tho: Dumer, sr., Tho: Dumer and Hester Dumer.

The following is from a copy on file:—

"february 20th 1654

"Reced of my vnckle Richard Dumer by the hands of coufen Thomas Dumer thefe sumes hearafter mentioned for & toward the mayntenance of my two children Samuell Nelfon and marfy Nelfon being monyes iffueing out of the Intrest of their portions *first the* som of Twenty eight pounds and feaventeene pounds and Twenty pounds being in all sixty five pounds which is all I haue receiued since my hufband dyed I saye 65^l o^s o^d.

"Witneffes   Jone Nelfon
Tho: Dumer
Hest^r Dumer"

Statement by the executor of grounds for review. A boy was sold for eight pounds.

Copy of a statement of Philip Nelson. Account: to William Jackson for work, Goodman Bradstreet, William Boynton, Philip Nelson, Mr. Rogers, for teaching the children, Robt Heaselington, things for the children, to Mathu Boyse, for fence at Pencorkitt, Humfry Rayner, cutting the children's hair, clothing for the two boys, Tho: Miller, Mark Prime for the mill dam, Joseph Juitt for books, etc., for the children, Mr. Brock for teaching the two boys, Goodman Parrit, Ed: Calton, Rich: Longhorne, Tho: Nelson, Mr. Johnson for teaching the children, Mr. Gadden for teaching the children, John Spaford for work, Franc Paritt for diet, Philop Nelson, shoes, sent thirty pounds into England for the release of Mrs. Nelson and her children by the consent of Mr. Bellinger. Auditor: Samuel Symonds and Robert Bridges. Dated 25:8: 1649.

List of disbursements by Mr. Rich: Dumer on account of Mr. Tho: Nelson, Dec. 6, 1645,—Sept. 30, 1649: Paid

to John Remington, passage to England, five pounds. Cloth, shoes and stockings for John Johnson. Paid to Joseph Juitt, Mr. Showell, Georg Gouldwyre, Edward Carlton and Mrs. Cutting. For Mrs. Nelson and her children when they went to England. Carrying down the goods to Boston. To Rich: Lighton, Will Scales, Willm Law, Anthony Sumersby, John Dresser, John Trumble, Willm Boynton, James Barker, John Boynton, firewood for the school, Tho: Millerd, Sara Glover, shoes and inkhorns for the children, to the deacons and Robt Hunter, Rich: Swan, Richard Longhorne, Isaac Cossens, Ez: Norden, John and Robt Hasslington, John Tod, Will: Tennee, Humfery Rayner for tanning hides, and John Spaford.

Copy of contract of marriage of Thomas Nelson and Joane Dumer, dated 12: 15: 1641. (This was printed in *The Essex Antiquarian*, volume I, page 67.)

Richard Swan deposed that he bought a couple of oxen of Mr. Dummer about two years Mr. Nelson went unto England that were Mr. Nelson's oxen. Sworn to in Ipswich court 31: 1: 1657.

Joseph Jewett deposed that he gave to Richard Dummer after the rate of ten per cent for eighty pounds, which said Dumer should use for Mr. Nelson's children for one year. Sworn as above.

John Pickard* and Richard Longhorne* certified that the seven acres of meadow at Rowley mill is worth fifteen shillings a year, and the little field by the dam's side at ye mill was worth as much, as when we rented both with ye farm, and ye three acres called pond field.

"The Testimony of Daniell Elly aged *aged* about 23 or 24 years :: Concerninge what I [in margin "London"] remember of Mr Nelsons estate at either by sight or circumstance, I beinge his servant I am priuie to some things, as one hogshead of yorkeshire woolen cloath, and the payment for four passengers, and earnest giuen for some apparrell, and tools for his trade of sope boilinge, and for two

*Autograph.

feather beds ; and I hope he had wherewith to pay for them and likewise at home, some other feather beds fitted, with the prouision for the uoige, and my master liinge some time, before the ship was redy, the hogsheade of cloath was fetched of abord againe, and ten pounds of the passage payed to my mrs and halfe a passage by one that came hither, and for my selfe eight pounds :

"Taken upon oath this 9th of the 4th month before mr Ri : Bellingha dep' gov' —1656 [in margin: "London "] in the margent was on the oath before my subscription : Ri : Bellingham this beinge a true coppy of the original in my hand."

Richard Longhorne deposed that there were ten oxen left unto Mr. Richard Dummer his disposing at Mr. Nelson's when Mrs. Nelson went to England; which oxen of Mr. Thomas Nelson's he took into his possession. Sworn in Ipswich court 31 : 1 : 1657.

John Pickard and Richard Longhorne deposed that the homefield was let to Ezekiel Northern for twelve shillings an acre a year; also that the warehouse lot was let. Sworn to by John Pickard as above.

Writ : Philip Nellson v. Mr. Richard Dumer, executor of Mr. Thom Nelson ; £200 ; dated March 19, 1656-7 ; for giving in a false account of his father's estate at Salem court; signed, by the court, Robert Lord. Served by Edward Browne, marshall of Ipswich, March 23, 1656-7.

Answer to Mr. Richard Dummer's objections : The widow did not have her two hundred pounds which were allowed her, etc.; the party being dead, the power of attorney is of no force; that he was Mr. Nelson's servant, and that Dummer acknowledged the same ; the money was given the widow to build a house with, which she never did, therefore neither principal nor profit due.

Copy of power of attorney, signed by Joane Nelson, of the parish of North-Stoncham, in the county of South D——, widow of Thomas Nelson, late of Rowly, gent., deceased, appointing her uncle

Richard Dumer of Newbury falls in New England, gent., her attorney, to obtain one-third of land, etc., of said Thomas Nelson's estate as dower, and what was bequeathed by will to three of the children of me and my said husband, deceased, viz: Marcy Nelson, John and Samuel Nelson. Dated March 26, 1650. Witnesses; Christr Walleston, mayor of Soughton, Roger Poiblsy and Tho: Dumer. Copied from the original May 2, 1757, by Robert Lord, clerk.

Estate of Mr. Thomas Nelson of Rowley, deceased, who left an estate of £1,131, 15s., 5d. Improvements on the land since 1649 until 1655, for the farm at Rowley and his mill, etc. To Lt. Remington for work at the mill and going to the Bay. To Goodman Pecker fourteen days' work about the cellar. To Goodman Cousins for mending maling bills and other work about the mill. For millstone burs and plaister and bringing them from England, and from Boston to Rowley mill. To Marke Prime; Francis Parrot, marchant Jewet for white leather about the mill. To "goodman funnell for makinge the millstones and for diet and for stronge beare for those that help him 13-6-3." To Goodman Law work about the stones. To Goodman Prime, the same: "for the maintenance of the widow and sent into England for the children 69-4-6." To Goodman Boyes and Richard Longhorne. Farm at Crane meadow. Recording the mill in England. Legacies paid to Philip Nelson, Thomas Nelson and Mrs. Matson(?). Received of Goodwife Crosse. Copy made by Samuel Archard,* marshall.

Land due to Philip Nelson by will, estate in England and New England. By Goodwife Crosse.

Received by Mr. Richard Dumer out of Mr. Thomas Nelson's estate from 6: 10 mo: 1645 to last of 7th mo: 1649. Received of Mr. Sparhoake, part of the vessel which was sold; of Mag Gibings, household stuff sold to Job Clemens; of

*Autograph.

Jemmy Northend, house and land sold to John Palmer; of John Newmash, for land at the mill; and of Joseph Juitt, John Remington, Good: Reiner, Mathu Boyse, Good: Parrit, John Dresser, Rich: Clark, Isaac Cossens, Goodman Swan and Goodm Goffe; of Rich: Longhorn and Rich: Holmes, for rent; of Hugh Chaplin and James Bayley; of Ezek: Norden, Willm Law and John Spoffor, for rent; and of Ezek: Northren.

Copy of lease of Richard Dumer of Newbury, gent., to John Pearson of Rowley, carpenter, one-half of the corn-mill of Rowley and one-half of the land belonging to the mill and two cow commonages for ten years; and if either of the stones shall break, except through neglect of the lessee, Dumer is to pay one-half for the mending the same. Five pounds in corn annually for rent. Dated 1 : 5mo: 1654. Not signed, but witnessed by Joseph Jewett and William Howard.

Ezekiell Northen deposed that Mr. Richard Dummer told him that Mr. Joseph Jewet and Thomas Barker were willing to allow eight pence a rod for ye fence, but nothing for carting it, etc. Sworn to before Dan el Denison March 31, 1657.

Mark Prime deposed that the last year before Mr. Nelson went away, on an accounting he asked me what one-half of the profits of the mill came to, and I agreed to keep it on the same terms for Mr. Richard Dumer, etc. Sworn to before Samuel Symonds; and copy by Samuel Archard, marshall, 23 : 4 : 1656.

John Person deposed that for the first quarter of a year after I bought one-half of the mill of Mr. Dumer, I hired Marke Prime to keep her. The income was £25, 14s., that year. Sworn and copied as above 23 : 4 : 1656.

Eze: Nordon deposed about a brown ox of Nelson's; that he rented the Pond field in Rowley, etc., and Mr. Dumer had hay off of it, etc. Sworn in Ipswich court 31 : 1 : 1657.

—*Files.*]

John ffullar and Mr. Nathaniell Rogers assignees of Zerobabell Phillips v. Isaack

Comings. Debt. [Zerobabell Phillips assigned to Mr. Nathaniel Rogers and others a debt due from Isaac Cumings, sr., and a cow in the hands of John Rise of Dedham, as security for said Z. P.'s appearance at court; dated Oct. —, 1656. Witness : Daniel Denison.

Writ : John ffuller and Mr. Nathaniel Rogers, assignee of Zerobabell Phillips v. Isaac Commings; served by Edward Browne, marshall, March 23, 1656-7.

Thomas Averiell deposed that he heard goodman Cumings acknowledge that he delivered some money to Zerobabell Philips for his son Isaac.

4 : 8mo: 1656, Zerobabell Philips acknowledged that he owed Rob : Crosse, and to deliver it at Mr. Barthollmews' in Ipswich. Witnesses : Will Perkins and John Cummings.

Bondsmen of Zerobabell Phillipps empower John ffuller to sue for him ; signed by William Smyth, Nathaniel Rogers, Humphrey Griffin (his H mark), John ffuller, John Caldwell, March 30, 1657.

John Cumins deposed that being with John Fuller and the other eight at the house of Zerobabell Phillips, I heard them say that they had appointed my father to pay some money to Mr. Hubbard, etc. Sworn at Ipswich court.

Thomas Averill deposed that before Zerobabell came to answer before Mr. Symonds, Robert Crose met Zer¹, etc., and that it be paid Isaac Cummings, etc.

Reasons of appeal by John ffuller* March 25, 1657. Received by Samuel Symonds.

William Moare, sr., deposed that he had seen ten or twelve of John Fuller's hogs and shoats in the Indian corn of Isaac Cummings, sr. John Fuller had a woman servant.

Isaac Cummings, jr., deposed that his father sent him, etc., 1656.

Richard Nicolls and John Leigh, sr., deposed about hogs in corn. Thomas Preston deposed that he was keeping sheep on the common, and so was John

* Autograph.

Fuller's son. Goodman Cummings' gⁱ told him that Mr. Hubbert's horse had broken down the fence.

Edward Bragg, Samuel Moare, Ephraiⁿ Fellows, John Choate, Ralph Dix, Samuel Younglove, Widow Haffild, Katherⁱⁿ Brimmengen, Nathaniel Lummas, Samuel Heires and Thomas Low deposed about the hogs. Good Burnam and John Fuller's wife also deposed.

Copy of town order concerning swine
—Files.]

Robert Lord v. James Howe.

ffrancis Johnson v. Mr. Roger Connatt, Peeter Palfry and Nath : Pittman. Review of a case tried at Salem in November, 1655. Plaintiff appealed to the next court of assistants at Boston ; bond, £100.

[Copy of record in case of Mr. Roger Conant, Peter Palfrey and Nathaniel Pickman (also, Pitman) v. Mr. Francis Johnson. For detaining beaver and otter. 27 : 9 : 1655, Elias Stileman, clerk.

Declaration of Francis Johnson : About twenty-four or twenty-five years ago there was a co-partnership between Mr. Roger Conant, Peter Palfry, Anthony Dike and myself for a trade to the eastward, to be managed by me, both buying and selling. At end of three years I sold to Mr. Rich : ffoxwell all the interest in the house and debts due from the Indians, etc. In the beginning of this winter came one Mr. Richard Tucker with an order from Mr. ffoxwell to end the business. Two or three days afterward Mr. Conant, Peter Palfry and Nathaniel Pittman went to Boston and put it to arbitration.

Two briefs for the court.

Copy of letter from ffrances Johnson to Mr. ffoxwell, dated at Newtowne May 6, 1635. Copied by Samuel Archard, marshall.

Copy of receipt signed by Mr. Abraham Shartt, merchant, dated June 13, 1635, for beaver, received of Richard Foxwell, for Mr. Johnson. Witnesses : Robert Knight and James Radestue. Copied by Samuel Archard, marshall.

Copy of acknowledgment of indebtedness to Francis Johnson and his partners, by Richard ffoxwell, merchant, dated July 16, 1633. Witnesses: Edward Gibones and Elias Mavericke. Copied by Samuel Archard, marshall.

Copy of two letters signed by ffrancis Johnson to Mr. ffoxwell. P. S. " pray rememb my love to yor wife." Sir: Dated Feb. 12, 1635. Yours of Dec. 8th and 12th by Mr. Richard Tucker received. Mr. Gardner will not accept of it. Beaver to Mr. Comer.

Moses Maverick testified that Mr. Roger Conantt and partners said in my hearing that there were three bills from Mr. ffoxwell delivered to Peter Palfry to keep; and that they had put all their power into Mr. Johnson's hand for them; Anthony Dike being only to sail the vessel, and do as Mr. Johnson should tell him. Sworn in Ipswich court March 25, 1657.

Amos Richardson testified that being chosen arbitrator with Capt. William Hathorne about a business between ffrancis Johnson, Mr. Conant, Peter Palfery and Nathaniell Pittman, on the part of Mr. Richard ffoxwell, found two bills due. Sworn 24: 1: 1655-6, before Natha: Duncan, commissioner.

Richard Collicutt, aged fifty-two years, deposed that about January last he heard Mr. Rich: ffoxwell say that many years since he bought a plantation and trading house at ye eastward of Mr. ffrancis Johnson of Marblehead, etc.; that the French dispossessed him of said house and lands. Sworn to 21 : 1 : 1655 6, before Edward Tynge, commissioner.

Georg Tayler deposed that about eighteen years ago, I dwelt with Mr. Cleeves in Casco bay, and Mr. Richard Tucker and I were going to Boston ward, and at Sako we met with Mr. Richard ffoxwell. He desired us to carry some beaver and otter for him to Mr. ffrancis Johnson, and we delivered it to him in the bay. Sworn to June 18, 1654, before John West and Robert Booth, commissioners of Saco. Copied by Samuel Archard, marshall.

Samuel Archer testified about the same as Moses Maverick above. Sworn to 22: 1 : 1655-6, before William Browne, commissioner.

Mr. Richard Tucker deposed that about a fortnight since he met Mr. Francis Johnson of Marblehead at Boston, and he had some order from Mr. Richards of Blu poynt near Sacoe to end the difference betwixt him and Mr. Foxwell. Sworn to 20: 9: 1655, before Mr. Richard Parker, commissioner. Copy.

Lott Conant testified that about seven years since he was going to the eastward, and desired to carry a letter by Nathaniell Pickman to Mr. Richard ffoxwell of Blue Poynt; that after said Foxwell read it, he said he owed said Pickman nothing, but what he owed was to Mr. Johnson and Anthony Dike, for goods he had of them at ye trading house. Sworn to 14: 1: 1654, before John Endecott, Dep.-gov. Copy.

Richard ffoxwell by his bill made July 16, 1633, was indebted to Francis Johnson and partners, etc.

Acknowledgement of indebtedness by Richard Foxwell, merchant, Sept. 14, 1634, to ffrancis Johnson and his partners. Copy by Samuel Archard, marshall.

John Pickard testified that he advised the widow Melody to go to Boston with her son. She answered that she would never go from Ipswich. Sworn to 31 : 1 : 1656, in Ipswich court.

Tabitha Pittman testified that at my husband Dike's last going away from me he was taken away at Cape Cod by the hard winter. His last words to me were that he had paid Peter Palfrey, etc. Sworn to 1 : 1657, before Edward Batter, commissioner.

Lott Conant deposed that his father went to Boston. Sworn to 24 : 1 : 1655-6, before Moses Mavericke, commissioner.

Samuel Archard, marshall, deposed about this matter in Ipswich court April 2, 1657.

Richard Tucker deposed that there is a difference between Mr. ffrancis Johnson of Marblehead near Salem and Mr. Rich-

ard ffoxwell of Blew point concerning some beaver and otter, which Mr. ffoxwell delivered to me in my boat, eighteen or twenty years ago. I delivered them to Mr. Johnson. Sworn to July 1, 1654, before Edw. Richworth, recorder. Copy by Samuel Archard, marshall.

John Roads and Thomas Ward testified that being at ye eastward with Mr. ffrancis Johnson last October, said Johnson was desirous of going to Blew Poyntt to speak with Mr. ffoxwell, but we could not go in on account of the wind. Sworn to 24 : 1 : 1655-6, before Moses Mavericke, commissioner.

Dorothy Norice testified that when she was at Marblehead at her brother Johnson's house, about three or four years since, there came a man from ye eastward who said to Mr. Johnson that Mr. ffoxwell was poor, and had nothing to pay with. Sworn to 22 : 1 : 1655-6, before William Browne, commissioner.
—*Files*.]

John Severns v. Job Nesetance. Debt.
[Bond of Job Neasentans (his S mark), sagamore of Agowam, commonly so called, to John Severnes of Salsberry, for eight pounds ; that he appear at Ipswich court last Tuesday in March, 1657. Witness : Theophilus Wilson.

Statement of Job *Nesohtans*, as to indebtedness, 19 : 5 : 1656.

Theophilus Wilson deposed that said Job acknowledged the indebtedness to John Severance, in my house. Sworn in Ipswich court 31 : 1 : 1657.
—*Files*.]

William Thomas v. Thomas Seers. Concerning an acre of land bought of said Seers, who refuses to deliver it.

Town of Ipswich v. Issaack Coussens, For bringing an old woman and leaving her in the town without providing for her. Continued for advice of the general court.

Thomas Davis v. Benjamin Swett. For taking away plaintiff's servant, Stephen Dow. The boy to be returned ; and plaintiff confessed that he was to teach Stephen to read and write and the trade of a stone mason according to the capaci-

ty of the boy and the employment of place where he lives.

[Bill of charges of Thomas Davis.

Bartholmew Heth, aged forty-one ye deposed that Steven Dow was a very and weak creature to look upon and of very low stature according to ye age he was said to be when he came to with Thomas Davis ; that said Davis n corrected him ; that the provision in house was as good as that of men estate ; that the boy ate the same kin food as his master ; heard some dis between said Davis and the defendant cerning the boy, and Davis asked Swe prove his title to the boy before indiff ent judges. Swett refused to arbitra This was at Newbury. On coming la from Newbury later we saw said S coming home from Haverhill with the riding. Sworn to before Robert Cleme

John Williams, sr., deposed that heard the boy speak well of his ma and dame, viz. : Thomas Davis and wife, that they used him well, and the fared as well as most in ye town. taught him his book, he was well dress and was not abused. Sometimes he away without cause.

John Bartlett testified that Thom Dowe, father of Steven Dow, at his ret from Haverhill, said that he had left boy with the plaintiff until he was eight years old, to teach him to read and wr and the trade of a stone mason, etc.

Richard Littlehale and wife Mary posed that they saw at Thomas Davis' kind and tender usage of the boy,— parents. When the boy first went the about eight and a half years ago, he w poor helpless child, of small statu Sworn before Robert Clement.

Robert Clement, jr., deposed that remembered an agreement by Benjam Swett of Newbury and Thomas Davis Haverhill, about evidence of their title the boy. Sworn to before Robert Cle ent.

Thomas Eyer deposed that a little fore Thomas Dow died he was at w with me, and we had some conversat

about his son dwelling at Thomas Davis'. He said he had not bound him to him. Sworn to before Robert Clements.

Robert Hazeldine deposed: I saw Benjamin Swett with Steven Dow in my canoe over ye river at Haverhill when I asked said Swett where they were. He answered, "I am going to carry him to his right owner." Swett helped the boy up his horse and went away. Sworn to before Robert Clements.

Judith, wife of Samuell Gild, deposed that when the boy came to live with said Davis he was a very weakly child and meanly clothed; and Davis was to have him twelve and a half or thirteen years. Sworn to as above.

Samuel Gild deposed that he first had Steven Dow for a week, but the boy's father wanted Thomas Davis to have the boy, and so took him there. He was a poor helpless child, likely to be a burthen and no benefit, very hard to learn his book, very meanly apparrelled, and not able to put on and off his own clothes. Sworn to as above.

Joanna, wife of George Corlis, deposed that it was a good while before the boy could eat his master's food, this is, meat and milk, or drink beer, saying he did not know it was good because he was not used to eat such victuals, but to eat bread and water porridge and drink victuals. Sworn to as above.

Steven Swett deposed that at ye ordinary in Newbury he heard Benjamin Swett demand of Thomas Davis of Haverhill whether he would deliver the boy to his mother. Davis replied that he would not, etc. Sworn to March 31, 1657, before John Pike, commissioner for Newbury.

Phebe Dow, mother of the boy, testified that Thomas Davis was to teach him the trade of a stone mason. Stephen came to my house, and there was willing to abide, but said Davis pulled him away with violence, to our great grief. Signed by her p mark.

Christopher Bartlet, aged thirty-three years, deposed that Thomas Dow told him that he had placed his son with Thomas Davis till he was eighteen years of age, etc.

James Davis, sr., and wife deposed that they were very much troubled when their son-in-law Samuel Gild was about taking of Steven Dow to be his servant as he was such a poor helpless child and likely to be a burthen to him and little benefit. Sworn to before Robert Clement.

Ephraim Davis deposed that Thomas Dow said it was much to his joy and comfort that Thomas Davis had taken his son. Sworn as above.

George Corlis deposed that Steven Dow was a very weakly child, and of a low stature, when he came to live with Thomas Davis. Sworn as above.

Tristram Coffin, jr., deposed about the same as Steven Swett did, as above. Sworn in court.

—*Files.*]

Mr. John Ward v. John Procktor. For not delivering thirty-five bushels of Indian corn, etc. Withdrawn.

John Hathorne, assignee to William Bridgewatter v. Edward Hutcheson. For unjustly detaining a ton of bar iron.

[Writ: Mr. Edward Hutchinson, sr. v William Bridgwater; dated 24 : 4 : 1656; signed by the court, Jonathan Negus. Addressed to the marshall, etc., of Boston. Served by attachment of bar iron in the hands of Edw Hutchinson in his warehouse, and three cow hides, delivered to Henry Brigam, Hugh Deney, constable of Boston. Copy, by Edward Rawson, recorder.

Mr. William Bridgwater* assigned to John Hathorne, both in New England, a ton of bar iron, in hands of Mr. Edward Huchinson of Boston, and Company now of the Iron Works in New England, Jan. 12, 1656. Witnesses: Phillip Cromwell* and Samuel Archard.*

James Robinson, aged about thirty-eight years, testified that about three months ago, about the bar iron, etc. Sworn to 26 : 1 : 1656, before Nathan : Duncan, commissioner.

*Autograph.

Antony Hacker, aged forty-eight years, and Samuel Davice, aged thirty-three years, testified about the bar iron, helping to hand it in about three months ago to Mr. Edward Huchison's warehouse in Boston, as Joseph Armitage's boat was cast away and Whitwell brought it ashore in his boat, etc. Sworn to 26 : 1 : 1657, before Natha : Duncan, commissioner.

Robert Burges, aged about thirty-six years, deposed that Mr. Oliver Purchase weighed the iron at the iron house unto Mr. William Bridgwater, and that John Clarke marked the bars with a cold chisel; and when the boat was cast away at Pullen Point, etc. Sworn to March 30, 1657, before Thomas Marshall, commissioner of Lynn.

Joseph Armitage, aged about fifty-five years, deposed that he heard Oliver Purchase, clerk of the Iron works, say that he had an order from Mr. Edward Huchinson to deliver to him one and one-half tons of iron, etc. Sworn to 30 : 1 : 1657, before Thomas Marshall, commissioner of Lynn.

—Files.]

Mr. William Perkins v. Jacob Towne, in behalf of the town of Topsfield. For detaining his maintenance due to him for his labors in the ministry. Withdrawn.

Richard Kent v. Lancelott Granger. For not permitting him to reenter upon his farm, cattle, etc., and for not performing an award. Houses, farm and cattle to be delivered to the plaintiff within three days, as mentioned in the lease, etc.

Lancelott Granger v. Richard Kent. Replevin. Two cases.

[Writ: Richard Kent v. Lancelot Granger. On arbitration, to deliver his farm to Richard Kent again; dated Dec. 23, 1656; by the court, Anthony Somerby, Served by Robard Coker, constable of Newbury, by attachment of sixteen cows and four oxen, Dec. 23, 1656, and attachment of two heifers, a bull and steer, 14 : 1 : 1656.]

William Howard deposed that he was one of four arbitrators in the case between these parties, etc.

John Chater and Rich : Doole wi nessed to the same. All sworn in co March 31, 1657.

James Brading testified that, Dec. 1656, Richard Kent and his servants w over to his farm and cleaned his cowls and at night he spoke to one to de Lancilot Granger to show him how to up the cattle. He answered, I am to to my brother, and will come back gs ently and tie them up for you. Rich Kent carried out muck with the cattle nine days; and Dec. 20, 1656, Rich Kent sent over his servants to fetch for the cattle. Mr. Granger refused let them take away hay, saying that would not abide by the award of the a bitrators. He bade me speak to r uncle, to fetch away the cattle he ha bought of his brother, etc. Sworn in I swich court 31 : 1 : 1657.

Daniel Thurston deposed that Mr Granger told, the next day after the awar was made, that he had delivered the far etc., to Mr. Kent and he was to remain the farm house a short time to thresh some corn he had in the barn; etc.; th Goodman Gould was engaged for it part and his father Addonis or Goo Chater for the rest; and he had so thought of going to England, etc. Swo to in Ipswich court 31 : 1 : 1657.

Award dated Dec. 10, 1656, by Zac eus Gould, Richard Dole and John Ch (his I mark). Witness : William Howe

Original lease of Richard Kent of Ne bury, yeoman, to Lancelot Granger Newbury, of his great island or farm a part of Goodale's island, and housi barn, etc.; dated July 11, 1654; witne es : Nicholas Noyes, Anthony Somer and mark R of Robert Adams.

Another original of the lease, in du cate.

—Files.]

Thomas Nelson chose, in court, M Joseph Jewett to be his guardian.

The freemen of Manchester fined f not appearing at the last court.

Hugh Chapline, deceased, left a w which was not proved within twe

months, the widow forfeits one hundred pounds by the law. [Will of Hugh Chaplin of Rowley proved March 31, 1657. This will is printed in full in *The Antiquarian*, volume VII, page 17.

Will of Antony Newhall proved before Thomas Marshall, commissioner, by John Fullar and Mathew Farington. This will was printed in full in *The Antiquarian*, volume VII, page 21.

Inventory of estate of Antony Newhall; due from Edward Richards; house, barn, land, etc., deceased had devised to his two children; sworn to by Richard Hood March 31, 1656. Land at John Hawthorn's house, by Jonathan Hudson's.
'.   —*Files*.]

William Chandlour allowed to be a packer at Newbury for searching and packing fish and flesh.

Robert Roberds acknowledged judgment to Mr. William Payne.

George Smith acknowledged judgment to William Payne.

William Symons acknowledged judgment to Mr. William Payne.

Thomas Robins and Henry Skerry bound for the appearance of Elizabeth Robins when the court shall call for her.

Administration granted to Marke Bachelour on the estate of his father. Referred to Salem court for further orders.

Richard Window released from ordinary training, paying a bushel of corn per annum to ye use of ye company.

John Roe released from ordinary training paying eight shillings per annum to the use of the company.

Administration upon the estate of Anthony Newhall granted to Richard Hud, to settle it according to an intended will, which he left. Administration bond. Overseers approved the court : Mathew Farrington, John ffullar and Nathaniell Kertland.

John Trumble sworn clerk of the market for Rowley.

Edmund Clarke of Gloucester allowed to be clerk of the writs.

The constables of Newbury made a motion for a penny in the bushel and demurrage to remain till Mr. Batter be spoken with.

John Stephens admonished for a battery.

The constable of Marblehead fined ten shillings and fees. Mr. Johnson undertook for its payment.

William Young, for contempt of, and slanderous speeches against, authority, to acknowledge his great offence in a public meeting at Andover and be whipped at next court, unless he shall bring a certificate under the hands of six of the principal men of the town to the next court that he is of good behavior.

John Hathorne fined for disorder in his house, suffering persons to sit tippling in his house and for suffering two persons at several times to be drunk.

[Oliver Purchase and George Darline, at Iron works, deposed that in February last, 1656, in the moonlight we went to Lynn town, Mr. Purchase going to the ordinary about Iron works business. They found a great store in ye house drinking, some being full of drink, particularly Sergeant Eldridge of Maldin, who had been there the greater part of the day before, as we heard. In one room was one Muzzy and his wife,—she sitting on one side of the table between two men and her husband on ye other table merrily singing to ye rest. Katherine Lary testified to the same. Allester Munduggle also testified.

Jane Armitage and Thomas Boal, both of Lynn, testified that Oliver Purchase, clerk of the Iron works, spoke to Thomas Wiggins, employed at ye Iron works, about drinking in Mr. John Hathorne's house on ye Lord's day. Sworn to 30 : 1 : 1657, before Thomas Marshall, commissioner of Lynn.

James Axey*, commissioner of Lynn, and Bray Wilkins, constable of Lynn, testified that Hugh Alley of Lynn was taken by said Wilkins about a fortnight before and brought before the commissioners of Lynn for being drunk at John Hathorn's, and said Alley acknowledged his offence before said Axey.

*Autograph.

Oliver Purchis and Alexander Bruldiner testified that Thomas Kelton, a Scotsman, being at a difference with some of the colliers at ye Iron works about a bargain made as they claimed with Henry Tucker on the Sabbath while drinking at Mr. Jnº Hathorn's house. Sworn to 31 : 1 : 1657, before Thomas Marshall, commissioner of Lynn.

George Darline and wife Kate deposed that last winter all Sabbath day there were several persons sitting and drinking at Mr. Jnº Hathorn's house. They saw Jnº Divan of ye Iron works and Ralph Russell in ye house overgone with drink. Mr. Bridgwater was also seen drunk in ye house sometimes. Sworn to as above.

Oliver Purchis, clerk at ye Iron works, deposed March 31, 1657, that he has seen several persons in the house of Mr. Jnº Hathorne of Lynn, drinking; and not able to speak or go. Sworn to in Ipswich court.

—*Files.*]

Theophilus Willson, constable, to be paid for setting up a fence about the house of correction.

Georg Bunker allowed two shillings and sixpence for his wife in boarding a witness in a criminal case.

William Browne, for divers miscarriages, to lie in prison one week and be fined twenty marks and pay costs to Thomas Prince, etc.

[William Vincent acquaints the court with the practice of William Browne in speaking disgracefully against Mr. Blinman, Mr. Pkins and Mr. Millet "for the day before that William Browne frighted goodwife Prince hee sayed mr. Blinman was naught, and Pkins was starke naught and millet was worse than Perkins." Edmund Clarke and George Ingersol also heard it. Sworn in court April 2, 1657.

Jan. 19, 1656, William Browne bound in forty pounds, and Samuel Delabar and Richard Beeford with him, to answer at next court at Ipswich for his misdemeanor towards Goodwife Prince, and to good

behavior towards Thomas Prince and his wife. Copy, made by Daniel Denison.[*]

30 : 1 : 1657, Susanner Eveleuth, fifty years, deposed that she was at goodwife Prince's labor with the midwife at delivery of the child, it was found dead, apparently having been dead for some time, and when we came to cut the naval string we found it to have no blood in it. Sworn to before Sylvester Eveleth and William Vinson, commissioners for Gloucester.

Grace Duch, Elinor Jo——, Joane Collins, Sarra Vinson deposed that they were with Goodwife Prince when the child was delivered, Saturday night. We thought that she would die. They mention William Browne's wife, etc. Sworn to in Ipswich court April 2, 1657.

Debrow Skilling, aged thirty-four years, deposed that she came to Goodie Prince's house and found her trembling and shaking, saying that Browne had been there and spoken such words to her " that her time was but short and the deuce would fech her Away spedily," etc. Sworn to 30 : 1 : 1657, before Silvester Eveleth and William Vinson, commissioners of Gloucester.

Hannah Verrie deposed that she sent to Steven Glover's and there was Browne and he said to said Glover something about Prince's wife. Sworn as above.

Abigall Sargainte testified 30 : 1 : 1657, that William Browne and Thomas Prince were at Steven Glover's house, and he said " Prince, you wil go to thy house and tell thy wife that you are at Steven's kissing of mother Kettell and mother Sargent;" and Prince made answer, etc. Sworn as above.

Steven Glover, aged about thirty years, deposed as above. Sworn as above.

Sarah Venson testified that Hannah Verrie and Abigall Sargen said in my hearing that they were at Goody Balson's when Goody Prince came in with yarn in her hand, and she began to relate what William Browne did say unto her, etc. Sworn to in Ipswich court March 31, 1657.

[*] Autograph.

Mary Millett, sr., testified that, etc. It was spoken in mother Babson's house. Sworn as above.

Goodwife Margaret Prince, wife of Thomas Prince of Gloucester, testified that Goodman Browne came into my house and asked me if I had done well to set my hand to that writing, and I told him I thought I had, etc. He called me one of Goodwife Jackson's imps, etc, I went out weeping to an ancient woman, my neighbor. Taken in presence of William Bartholmew and William Vincent (his T mark). Sworn to in Ipswich court April 2, 1657.

Her husband, Thomas Prince, testified also. Sworn to Jan. 29, 1656, before Daniel Denison.

Wife of Elias Parkman, saith that she was at Thomas Prince's house, etc. Sworn to 30 : 1 : 1657, before William Stevens and Robert Tucker, commissioners of Gloucester.

Wife of John Kettell testified that she was at the harbor, and saw Goodee Prince come with a pailful of clay on her head, and I went home along with her. I told her she did wrong in carrying clay at such a time ; she said she had to, her husband would not, and her house lay open. Sworn to as above.

Further complaint of Thomas Prince and his wife against William Browne, being at Stephen Glover's house, etc., as Abigail Sargent testified above.

John Kittell, aged about thirty-two years, testified that he saw Thomas Prince's wife daubing her husband's house two or three weeks before she was in travail with her last child. She reached up over the door to daub with clay. Sworn to before William Stevens and Robert Tucker, commissioners of Gloucester.

Wife of Thomas Jons testified, etc. Sworn as above.

Wife of Richard Window testified that the wife of Thomas Prince hired her daughter for a fortnight to help her when she did lie in, etc. Sworn as above.

Stephen Glover and Goodie Sargen deposed that William Browne came to Steven Plumer's house and Goodwife Verie came in ; Mr. Browne asked Mrs. Verie if she had got her husband's supper ; and told that goodman Vinson, etc. Sworn to 30 : 1 : 1657, before William Vinson and Sylvester Eveleth, commissioners of Gloucester.

Isabell Babson, midwife, aged about eighty years, deposed that she lived near house of Thomas Prince, and told of what Brown said to Goody Prince, as she told her, about the ministers, etc. Sworn to March 30, 1657, as above. She signed the deposition.

Abigail, wife of William Seargant, testified that she went to Prince's house, and saw his wife spinning, etc. Sworn as above.

Hana, wife of Thomas Very, testified that she was at widow Babson's house, etc. — Files.]

Thomas Robins bound to bring his wife Isbaell Robans to next court at Salem to answer suspicion against her.

Benjamin Woodrow confessed that he consulted with Thomas Wast to run away together, and that he was at the meeting at Jonath. Bullock's house, where there was great quantities of wine and strong liquors drunk in the night to disorder, etc. The court found two burglaries committed by Thomas West, one on the Lord's day. He also stole malt, wheat, a pistol, and tobacco pipes. To be whipped, etc. Bond to appear at next court at Salem or general court ; Osmound Traske, surety.

Warrant to be issued against Henry Bulocke of Salem for disorderly meetings in the night at his house by many young persons, when great quantities of wine and strong waters were drunk.

Edmond Bridges fined for lying.

The constable of Manchester fined.

Theophilus Willson, keeper of the prison, to have three pounds a year and five shillings for every person committed into the prison, the prisoners before being released to pay their charges for food and attendance ; others to be allowed only bread and water.

Humphry Griffin fined for unloading barley on the Sabbath day before sunset.

William Tittcombe discharged of his presentment.

Adjourned to

April 9, 1657.

James White, jr., confessed that his father struck him for some fault, and he held up an andiron at him, and when his father asked him what he would do said he should know by and by, etc. To be whipped.

Robert Punell fined and to be whipped for lying.

William Linkhorne, for abusive carriages to Rebecca Blake, to be whipped in Rebecca's presence.

John Perley to be whipped or fined for lying.

[George Abbott, aged about forty years, testified that Oct. 3 last John Perley and John How came into Andover, Perley upon a colt and How upon a mare, both apparently tired. Perley said he bought the colt but lately, and had not fully broken him.

Mary Holt, aged eighteen years, and Thomas Farnam, aged twenty-four years, testified.

Stephen Osgood, aged about forty-eight years, testified that the colt was the bay that Anthony Potter fetched from Andover, and that the mare was goodman Cooper's.

Elizabeth Holt, aged twenty, George Abbott, jr., aged twenty-six, Henry Ingolls, aged twenty-seven, and his wife, and Edw. Bridges and his brother Hackeliah, also testified. All sworn Nov. 18, 1656, before Simon Bradstreet.

—Files.]

Andrew Creeke fined for lying.

John Chote fined for lying.

[Samuel Mighell deposed that in the summer of 1656 he went to Ipswich with John Chote, who said his master, John Andrews, made a fool of Samuel Younglove, and at night fetched Hannah Day and Hanna Portar to Goodman Androws' house, and there they were in his parlor with goodwife Androues and Thomas

Androus, and the musician was there w. his music. John Chote kept the doo: keep out Samuel Younglove, and w they had spent as much of the night they pleased the maids were carried h. Also, he said the major-general was ti e: Sworn in Ipswich court April 9, 1657.- Files.]

Mordcha Larcum fined for lying.

William Tittcombe fined for lying.

[William Tidcom presented for lying. ye general town meeting when they ve: for governor, etc.; and in ye ordinar and at Mr. Noyes' house, Richard Brow: told William Tidcom that his brot. Steven Greenlefe was troubled with testimony that he gave before the arbi: tors. Witnesses: Richard Browne, Hen: Jaquish, John Knight, Captain Gen: Niclas Noic, Richard Knight, Atony S: marbye and Henry Lunt.

John Emery, sr., John Bartlet, Joh: Hutchins, John Rolfe, John Mussewi: John Cheney, Samuel Plumer, Richa: Dole, Joseph Plumer, Niclos Batt, france Plumer, Robert Coker, Archelaus Wee: man, John Mehell, Christopher Bart: Steven Swett, William Sayer, Thon: Blomfeild, John Emery, jr., and John Po certified to court that to our great gr: our neighbor William Titcombe we under stand is complained of. We can test: that we have known him years, and o: served him to be honest and christian!: in his conversation, and not a liar, e: Sworn to in Ipswich court April 9, 165:

Henry Jaquis testified, etc. Sworn : above.

Hugh March* also testified.

—Files.]

Hackaliah Bridges fined or to !: whipped for lying, and to pay Josias He: bard for his gloves. [John Young!: and Samuel Belcher deposed that the: inquired of Hackiliah Bridges one nig: this week concerning a pair of glove with black fringes, which Nehemiah Je: ett took from Edmun Bridges, lay: claim unto in his brother Josiah He: bard's name, and Hackiliah said that !:

*Autograph.

bought them of John Smith of Rowley for two shillings. Sworn in Ipswich court April 9, 1657.—*Files.*]

Andrew Tarvarse and Michaell, the Irishman, to acknowledge their offence at the next lecture at Ipswich or to pay a fine.

Edmond Bridges fined for writing a note in Rowley meeting house in lecture time to John Tod for five shillings in his father's name.

James Barker freed from ordinary training, paying five shillings yearly to the use of the company.

May 26, 1657.

In the case of Mr. Richard Dummer of Ipswich v. Phillip Nelson, the words "there children" meant all the children. Plaintiff appealed to next court of assistants.

Court, 29 : 7 : 1657.

Judges : Mr. Brodstreet, Mr. Symonds, Major-general Denison, Major Hathorne and Mr. Will Hubbard.

Trial jury: Mr. Jo: Appleton, Ensign Howlett, John Perkins, John Ayres, And: Hodges, Dan: Thurston. John Cheney, Rbt Addams, John Tod, James Bayley, John Smith and ffran: Pabody.

Grand jury : Joseph Medcalfe, Tho : Tredwell, Phillip ffowlar, Tho : Bishop, Dan: Houey, Jo: Bartlett, Hen: Lunt, Will: Assye, James Barker, Tho: Leuer, Tho: Browneing and Robert Barnerd.

Mr. Robert Payne, executor to Mr. John Ward v. Anthony Loe, executor to his father John Loe. Withdrawn.

Richard Kent v. John Cheney. For denying him a way where it is laid out. John Chenye is to make the way laid out by the town sufficient, as Mr. Nicolas Noyse and Henry Short should judge, etc.

Lt. John Pike v. Richard Kent. For cutting grass upon his lot at Plumb Island and carrying it away under pretence of trying the title.

[Richard Dole testified that he heard Richard Kent own the cutting of grass at Plum Island, by his boys, on the sev-

enth lot. Signed and sworn to in Ipswich court 2 : 7 mo : 1657.

John Webster testified that being at Plum Island he saw Richard Kent, John Kent, and Josias Parker carry the cocks of hay on the seventh lot and stack it on the sixth lot. Sworn to 29 : 7 : 1657, in Ipswich court.

John Emery testified that Richard Kent told John Pike that his boys cut hay, etc. Signed by John Emuerry. Sworn as above.

Copy of order of town of Newbury about parting the common, May 12, 1641, and Dec. 7, 1642, made by Anthony Somerby.

Copy of orders of town of Newbury May 5 and June 25, 1656, as to division of Plum Island grass. By Anthony Somerby.

The selectmen of Newbury and the three commissioners, with Richard Knight chosen March 1, 1651, to stint common. Copy by Anthony Somerby.

Copy of record of the general court, 2 : 3 : 1649, of receipt of petition from Newbury for confirmation of Plum island to them, voted that it be divided into five parts, two to Ipswich two to Newbury and one to Rowley. Copy by Wm. Torrey, clerk, 14 : 3 : 1657.

Special verdict : Common land in Plum Island belonging to Newbury is divided amongst the freeholders.
—*Files.*]

John West v. John Marshall. Case.
John West v. Thomas White. Debt.
John Smith v. Thomas Perry.
Jonathan Platts v. Thomas Perry. Debt.
Benjamin Baker v. Thomas Wetherell. Debt.

Mr. Stephen Biles v. John Bryden. For withdrawing from the ship to his great damage. To return to the ship.

Mr. Stephen Byles v. Julious Croft. For withdrawing from the ship to his great damage. To return to the ship.

[Stephen Biles* of the city of London, mariner, commander of ship Eve of Lon-

*Autograph.

don appointed his friend Arnold Elhey of the city of London, merchant, his attorney, to implead Julius Crofte and Jo⁰ Braiden, both shipped by me; dated Sept. 29, 1657. Witnesses: John Gedney* and Thomas Cromwell.*

Matt: James Mansfild; *boatswain:* Rogers Trenum; chirurgeon: John ffrewen; gunner: Humphrey Seale; carpenter: Edmon Soel, certified last of September, 1657, at Salem, that they were shipped at London by Mr. Stephen Bylls, commander of ship Eve of London to proceed thence to this country, from hence to Pheroe or any port in the ffrench king's dominions, we being entertained at Mr. Mencell Sallaire for the voyage, and so into England. Witnesses: Edmo: Batⁱ ter* and John Gedney.*

Deposition of John Fruen: who saith the ship Eve of London was bound for New England, and thence for Farough in Portinggall or any part of France, and the voyage was known at Boston before the ship came out. Sworn to in Ipswich court 29 : 7 : 1657.

—*Files.*]

Edmund Bridges, jr. v. Mary Quilter. Slander. Withdrawn.

General court moderated fines of Nicolas Jackson and John Trumble for not proving the wills of their wives' (?) former husbands, viz : Hugh Chaplin and Mighill Hobkinson.

Rebecca Brodstreet chose Joseph Jewett to be her guardian, and he acknowledged that he had received her portion of the estate of her father Humphrey Bradstreet given to her in his will from her mother Bridget Broadstreet, executrix of the will.

Robert Elwell being attached by Elias Parkman, and the writ not entered, was allowed costs.

John Redington, chosen by Topsfield as clerk of the writs, is allowed.

William Gibbs, complained of by Myghill Emerson, upon suspicion, etc., to pay charges of complaint.

*Autograph.

[Anne, wife of Francis Thorley, testified that William Gibs came to our log the day the jacket of Michael Emers was lost. He asked me what two hen those were in the bottom and great har upon the hill, and I told him Goodn… Charters.

Francis Thorley testified the same, et (Short hand on back.)

William Gibs acknowledged hims…. bound to appear at next court at Ipsw: to answer complaint of Michael Emers for suspicion of stealing a coat; take July 14, 1657. Copy by Daniel Deniso:

Examination of William Gibbs : H said he went into a swamp Saturday la near half a mile above Goodman Tharil to cut a pole and that he saw not Goodman Chatter's barn nor any coat hange near the barn, and on his return he me four Indians in ye path towards Good man Therril's. Taken by Daniel Denison.

—*Files.*]

Margaret Scott was appointed administratrix of the estate of her late husband Thomas Scott.

William Dellow fined for pilfering, etc. and bound to good behavior.

[William Dellow acknowledged that he took a beetle and wedges from John Caldwells, and then denied it.

Robert Collings swore that Will Dellow denied both forks, but confessed he took one. Confessed he took Goodman Symond's plow.

—*Files.*]

Edmond Bridges, for fornication, etc. to be severely whipped and bound to good behavior. Mary Browne, for suffering it, to stand by and see him whipped.

[Samuel Younglove, aged twenty years, testified that Edmond Bridges was mowing with him, and Bridges told him about his undue relations with Mary Browne and Mary Quilter, and John Allen with Mary Browne; and he had been persuading Thomas Gittins and others, etc. Sworn to in Ipswich court 29 : 7 : 1657.

Simon Stacey deposed that he met Edmon Bridges on lecture day, and asked

Bridges if he had heard of the story around town of him (Bridges) and two wenches. I said, No. He said he told Samuel Younglove about it, and the simple went and told Thomas Fowlar. Bridges confessed it in court.

John Allen deposed that he saw Edward Bridges at Mr. Hubbard's house two or three times this summer; and saw his unseemly carriage toward Mary Browne; etc.

—Files.]

Hackaliah Bridges to be severely whipped for fornication; to give bond of good behavior and to secure the town about bringing up the child.

Mary Quilter to be severely whipped for fornication.

[John How deposed that last Michaelmass, going over the new bridge he overtook Hack: Bridges, who asked him to go with him (Bridges) to Mr. Rogers, where he said he had a wench, Mary Quilter, and boasted of his relations with her. I went with him as far as William Avrey. Then I parted to my vncle Danes, and he went to Mr. Rogers. I spoke to him of this business in the prison, and he bid me hold my peace, for he had resolved to deny it, and knew they could not whip him, unless they could prove it, or I confess. Sworn in Ipswich court 29 : 7 : 1657.—*Files.*]

Edmond Bridges bound to good behavior, especially towards Mary Quilter.

An Trumble appointed administratrix of the estate of her late husband John Trumble. There were eleven children, of three sorts. The estate is ordered to be divided, to four of Mighill Hobkinson's, five of John Trumble's before he married her, two of his and hers, viz.: to Jonathan Hobkinson, £25, Jeremiah Hobkinson, £18, John Hobkinson, £18, Caleb Hobkinson, £18; to John Trumble, £15, Hannah Trumble, £8, Judah Trumble, £8, Ruth Trumble, £8, Joseph Trumble, £8; and to Abigail Trumble and Mary Trumble (children by him and her), £20 each. The rest of the estate to the widow, £55.

[Inventory of estate of John Trumball of Rowley, deceased, appraised by Joseph Jewett, Maximillian Jewit, Thomas Dickinson and John Pickard. Amount, £225, 17s., 10d.; real, £62; personal, £163, 17s., 10d. Sworn to by his widow Ann Tromble in Ipswich court 29 : 7 : 1657.— *Files.*]

Humphrey Griffen allowed common packer of beef and pork for Ipswich.

Adjourned to

Nov. 19, 1657.

Newbury, presented for defect in highways, being now mended, discharged.

Ned Acockett, an Indian, acknowledged judgment to Jeremiah Belchar.

Ned Acocket acknowledged judgment to Zacheous Gould.

Reginall Foster and Thomas Emerson of Ipswich made free.

Daniell Wycome fined.

John Chattour to pay fees, etc.

[William Morse deposed about John Cheater and the value of the beast, appraised by Anthony Morse and Benjamin Sweate.

William Trotter deposed that he was at work at goodman Cheatter's with his man Francis Waker, and he asked Waker about the beast now in controversy with John Poore being the same his master had.

Joseph Noyes and Roberd Saveri deposed that it is Mr. Noyes' steer. Sworn in Ipswich court 19 : 9 : 1657.

Peter Godfrey* testified about the steer. Sworn as above.

Goodwife Barbara Ilsly deposed that twelve months ago when John Chater brought a beast to his father Emery to be killed, etc.

Francis Waker deposed that his master Chater branded the letters.

Nicholas Browne (servant to John Chater) testified that the steer came to my master Chater's and I branded him. Sworn in Ipswich court 19 : 9 : 1657.

William Trotter deposed. Mistress Noise (a party).

Alis, wife of John Chater, deposed.

*Autograph.

John Chater's two children deposed.

Steeven Webster, aged about twenty years, deposed.

Mary Emery deposed.

Francis Walker deposed before Shubael Dumer.

Nicholas Noyes* and Joseph Noyes* deposed. Sworn in Ipswich court 19 : 9: 1657.

Jeremiah Elsworth states that upon his marriage with Mary Smith he binds himself to Thomas Dickanson, John Pickard and Deacon Jewett, in the sum of two hundred pounds; bond dated 26 : 9: 1657; witnesses : Joseph Jewett, Thomas Dickanson and John Tod; conditioned to pay their portions to Hugh Smith's children, viz. : Samuel, Mary, Sara, Hannah, Marthay and Edward Smith.

Petition of Peter Harvi,* Richard Palmer,* Richard Comer* and Moses Eborn* for the four daughters and husbands of Humphrey Gilbert, deceased, Jan. 20, 1657, to appoint the four husbands, the petitioners, administrators on said Gilbert's estate of six acres of fresh meadow. They were appointed.

Vital records of Newbury March 25, 1656, to March 25, 1657 :—

Peter Godfry married Mary Browne May 13, 1656.

Samuell Moore married Mary Ilsly Sept. 12, 1656.

Nathaniel Weare married Elizabeth Swayne Dec. 3, 1656.

John Roafe married Mary Scullerd Dec. 4, 1656.

Robert Savory married Mary Mitchell Dec. 8, 1656.

Thomas Seeres married Mary Hilton Dec. 11, 1656.

Mr. James Noyes died Oct. 22, 1656.

Edmund Moores died Nov. 8, 1656.

Mary Bolton died Dec. 6, 1656.

William Richardson died March 25, 1656.

Rebecca, daughter of William Titcomb, born April 1, 1656.

*Autograph.

Rebecca, daughter of Thomas Blonfeild, born May 4, 1656.

Moses, son of Capt. Will: Gerish, born May 9, 1656.

Edward, son of Samuel Poore, born May 22, 1656.

Elizabeth, daughter of Edward Woodman, jr., born July 11, 1656.

Elizabeth, daughter of Francis Tharly, born June 3, 1656.

William, son of William Pilsbury, born July 27, 1656.

Benjamin, son of Benjamin Swett, born Aug. 5, 1656.

John, son of John Allen, born Aug. 28, 1656.

Sara, daughter of Soloman Keyes, born Aug. 24, 1656.

Sara, daughter of Lyonell Worth, born Oct. 12, 1656.

Lidia, daughter of John Poore, born Dec. 5, 1656.

Hugh, son of Hugh Marsh, born Nov. 3, 1656.

Benjamin, son of Joseph Plumer, born Oct. 23, 1656.

Jonathan, son of John Bishop, born Jan. 11, 1656.

Nicholas, s. of Nicholas Wallington, born Jan. 2, 1656.

Susanna, daughter of Robert Long, born Nov. 14, 1656.

Hanna, daughter of James Mirick, born Feb. 6, 1656.

Anthony, son of Peter Godfry, born March 3, 1656.

Benjamin, son of Willi Richardson, born March 13, 1656.

By Anthony Somerby.

Rowley vital records, 1657 :—

Mr. Phillip Nellson married Sariah Jewitt June 24.

John Brocklbank married Sariah Woodman Sept. 26.

Jeremiah Elsworth married Mary Smith, sr., Dec. 2.

Nathaniell Elithorp married Mary Batt Dec. 16.

Thomas Teney married widow Elizabeth Parrat Feb. 24.

John Smith married Faith Parrat, sr., Feb. 24.

John, son of Thomas Burkbee, buried July 15.

John Trumble buried July 18.

An, wife of Thomas Teney, buried Sept. 26.

Samuell, son of James Bally, buried Nov. 28.

Elizabeth, wife of Lt. John Remington, buried Dec. 24.

Thomas, son of Richard Longhorne, born the last of June.

Jonathan, son of Thomas Leaver, born Aug. 28.

Mary, daughter of William Law, born Oct. 15.

Timothie, son of John Harris, born Nov. 1.

Robert, son of Robert Hesseltine, born Nov. 7.

Francis, son of John Palmer, born Dec. 4.

Jonathan, son of Lenord Harryman, born Dec. 5.

Thomas, son of Edward Hassen, born Jan. 20.

Ezekiel, son of Richard Lighton, born 8 : 12 mo.

Samuel, son of Mr. Samuel Philips, born March 13.

Sariah, daughter of Maxemilian Jewit, born March 17.

Arthur Parker testified that Edword Brogis, doing some work for me, his father not being at home, I must pay him in wheat next time I came to Ipswich with my cart. I did so, and met Edword Bregis in the street by goodman Cosens' shop. He said pay it to goodman Tod of Rowly, etc. Sworn to 9 : 2mo : 1657, before Simon Bradstreet.

Shoreborne Willson deposed that in the meeting house at Rowley lecture in February last he saw Ed : Bridges in sermon time get a piece of paper of Daniell Warner, jr., and write on it, and over his shoulder read these words : "Goodman Tod I would intreate you ;" and he gave it to Tod after the lecture, and said his father sent it, etc. Sworn to April 9, 1657, in Ipswich court.

Thomas Varnham, aged twenty-five, deposed that he heard that Edward Bridges was gone from his master's to Ipswich without his master's consent. I met him going home ; he said he had a letter from his father to his master. He showed me a letter directed to Mr. Bradstreete. Sworn to April 2, 1657, before Daniel Denison.

Samuel Lumas testified as Willson above. Sworn to April 2, 1657, in Ipswich court.

Daniel Warner, jr., deposed about the piece of paper. Sworn as above.

Writ : to replevy eight pewter dishes of Mr. Samuel Symonds distrained by Edward Browne ; dated June 22, 1657; by the court, Robert Lord. Served by Theophilus Wilson, constable.

Notice, by Robert Lord, of an attachment by Mr. William Payne, assignee of Joseph Armentage, to Nathaniell Boulter ; dated March 17, 1657.

Attested copy by Edward Rawson, secretary of court of assistants, at Boston Sept. 2, 1657. Case of Richard Pitfold accused by Ruben Guppy of beastiality. Deferred to Salem court.

Marye Lynard, aged about thirty-two or thirty-three, deposed that Indian harvest last was seven years Indian harvest was gathered at the Iron works before John Smith went away from the Iron works. Sworn to in court 25 : 9 : 1657, per Wm Hathorne.

—Files.]

John Boynton admonished.

Humphry Griffen fined.

John Tilison sentenced to the house of correction, but released and bound to " good behaviour & to liue with his wife & pvyde for her acording to his place as a husband ought to doe."

Ned Acockett to be severely whipped, and returned to house of correction until he give bond of good behavior, and to keep the child. Such security as the magistrates and Mr. Hubart shall see fit.

Sarah Jordon to be severely whipped.

Thomas Perry testified that he had not concealed any part of his estate, etc.

The young men summoned to court about not going to service to appear before the selectmen,

Dec. 3, 1657.

Humphrey Ned's brother John, Old William's son and Jeremy Netecot bound to good behavior of Ned and to pay six pounds yearly towards the keeping of the child as long as the court sees meet.

To be continued.

BRADSTREET NOTES.

Capt. Elijah Bradstreet (No. 83, page 56) married Phebe Ingalls of Andover June 8, 1790; removed to Greenfield, Mass., and after 1800 to Pelham, N. H., where he lived on a farm on Gage hill. She died July 20, 1847, aged seventy-eight; and he died at Pelham Dec. 2, 1850, aged eighty-three. Children: 1. Elizabeth Ingalls, born in Andover May 28, 1791; married Capt. Caleb Wheeler Dec. 12, 1815; lived in Andover and Methuen; and died April 21, 1828. 2. Elijah, born Dec. 15, 1792; married Hannah —— April 1, 1824; she died Feb. 20, 1875; he died June 29, 1882; they had four children. 3. Stephen Ingalls, born in Greenfield, Mass., Oct. 27, 1794; graduated at Dartmouth college; studied theology; spent one year in Virginia as a missionary, and then went to Cleveland, O., where he established the first church there and was also active in the founding of the Western Reserve college; married Anna Dana Smith of Amherst, Mass., Aug. 5, 1824; he died in Cleveland, O., June -, 1837, aged forty-three; and she died there May 27, 1838; they had four children, one of whom is Edward Payson Bradstreet, esq., of Cincinnati, O. 4. Phebe, born in Greenfield, Mass., Sept. 29, 1796; married Artemas Herrick Dec. 27, 1827; and died Feb. 10, 1875; they had five children, one of whom is Rev. William Dodge Herrick of Amherst, Mass. 5.

Ruth Emerson, born in Greenfield, Mass., July 20, 1798; married William Wyman of Pelham, N. H., Oct. 15, 1827; and died at East Cambridge, Mass., Aug. 1886, aged eighty-eight. 6. Ruby, born in Greenfield, Mass., July 4, 1800; married Thomas Thaxter Sept. 25, 1877; and died June 21, 1843.—*Charles J. Fletcher, Perth Amboy, N. J.*

The wife of Humphrey Bradstreet was named "Bridget," instead of "Elizabeth" (page 57).

Samuel Bradstreet (No. 20, page 57) is probably son of Capt. Moses Bradstreet (No. 7, page 57).

—*Ed.*

John Bradstreet (No. 3, page 57), married Hannah Peach of Marblehead; and after his death she married, secondly, William Waters.

Capt. Moses Bradstreet (No. 7, page 57), married, secondly, Sarah (Platts), widow of Samuel Prime; and she was living in 1697. Moses' son John was born in December, 1662; Nathaniel, baptized Jan. 14, 1671-2; Hannah, baptized Nov. 9, 1673; Samuel, baptized Aug. 22, 1675; died in infancy; Bridget, baptized Dec. 3, 1676; Aaron, baptized Jan. 18, 1679-80; not mentioned in his father's will in 1690; Samuel, baptized May 14, 1682; died in infancy; Samuel, born May 4, 1687; not mentioned in his father's will in 1690; and Jonathan was baptized June 22, 1690.

Elizabeth Bradstreet (No. 18, page 58) was baptized in Rowley Jan. 28, 1693-4.

Hannah Bradstreet (No. 19, page 58) was baptized in Rowley Feb. 14, 1696-7.

Dorothy (Sewall), widow of Moses Bradstreet (No. 10, page 58), died June 17, 1752.

Moses Bradstreet (No. 24, page 58) was baptized Feb. 27, 1697-8; and married, first, Abigail Lunt of Rowley Nov. 10, 1720; she died July 11, 1723; and he died Feb. 15, 1727.

Moses Bradstreet (No. 10, page 58) had son John baptized April 21, 1700; died May 12, 1724, unmarried; and a son Nathaniel, baptized June 25, 1701;

died in infancy ; Jane, baptized Feb. 15, 1707-8 ; married John Manning July 2, 1728.

Nathaniel Bradstreet (No. 25, page 58) was baptized Nov. 18, 1705.

The first three children of Dr. Humphrey Bradstreet (No. 15, page 58) were born in Rowley.

Sarah Bradstreet (No. 39, page 58) married Josiah Porter of Salem Jan. 11, 1749.

Abigail Bradstreet (No. 42, page 59) was baptized Aug. 15, 1722 ; and married Moses Jewett of Ipswich May 13, 1741, dying Nov. 8, 1794.

Mary Bradstreet (No. 41, page 59) was baptized July 25, 1725.

Children of Lt. Nathaniel Bradstreet (No. 25, page 59) : John, baptized July 13, 1729 ; died young ; Hannah, baptized Nov. 9, 1730 ; died young ; Nathaniel, baptized Sept. 1, 1734 ; died young ; Ezekiel, baptized Oct. 25, 1735 ; died young ; Nathaniel, baptized July 31, 1737 ; died young ; Jane, baptized Feb. 25, 1738-9 ; Nathaniel, baptized June 20, 1740 ; married Phebe Jewett ; Elizabeth, baptized Sept. 15, 1743 ; John, baptized June 26, 1748 ; married Judith Hale of Newbury Feb. 14, 1771 ; and died in Palermo, Me., Aug. —, 1833 ; Mary, baptized June 24, 1750 ; married Nathan Pearson June 20, 1774 ; and died Nov. 18, 1810 ; Sarah, baptized Oct. 1, 1752.

Hannah Bradstreet (No. 45, page 59) married Richard Shatswell of Ipswich in 1751.

Moses Bradstreet (No. 43, page 59) married Lucy Pickard of Rowley Dec. 12, 1749 ; he died Oct. 29, 1811, and she died June 9, 1816, aged eighty-eight. Children : 1. Ezekiel, bapt. Aug. 26, 1750 ; married, first, Abigail Pearson ; she died Aug. 23, 1773 ; married, second, Jemima Nason, both of Biddeford, Jan. 12, 1775 ; 2. Moses, baptized Sept. 30, 1753 ; 3. Nathaniel, baptized Oct. 5, 1755, died Oct. 12, 1755 ; 4. Nathaniel, baptized Feb. 13, 1757 ; went to sea when about twenty-one years old, and was never heard from ; 5. Lucy, baptized May 4, 1760 ; married

George Todd of Rowley Feb. 4, 1779 ; 6. Hannah, baptized June 27, 1762 ; married Daniel Todd, jr., of Rowley (published Feb. 12, 1783) ; 7. Dolly, baptized Sept. 8, 1765 ; married Rev. Moses Bradford Nov. 2, 1788 ; and died June 24, 1792 ; 8. Jonathan, baptized April 10, 1768 ; not mentioned in his father's will.

Moses Bradstreet (son of above Moses), baptized Sept. 30, 1753 : married Sarah Mighill Jan. 26, 1775 ; lived in Rowley ; he died Oct. 23, 1829 ; and she died Sept. 8, 1851 ; children : Dorothy, born Jan. 5, 1776 ; married Richard Cresrey of Rowley March 24, 1795 ; Sarah, born March 27, 1777 ; died Jan. 10, 1849, unmarried ; Moses, born Dec. 1, 1779 : married Mary Kimball of Andover in 1808 ; he died May 11, 1846 ; she died Aug. 19, 1885, lacking two months less one day of being a century old ; they had seven children : Lucy, born Nov. 21, 1780 ; married John Saunders of Rowley in 1805 ; Nathaniel, born Dec. 18, 1782 ; married Charlotte Bradford ; Hannah, born May 6, 1786 ; died, unmarried, March 1, 1873 ; Rachel, born Nov. 2, 1788 ; married Amos Saunders of Rowley Nov. 20, 1832 ; and died June 17, 1842 ; Thomas, born March 10, 1791 ; died Oct. 9, 1793 ; Irene, born Feb. 15, 1793 ; married Daniel Hale of Rowley Sept. 17, 1820 ; and died Aug. 31, 1823 ; Thomas, born Feb. 19, 1795 ; died June 27, 1800.

Nathaniel Bradstreet (No. 47, page 60) married Phebe Jewett of Rowley Dec. 7, 1762 ; he died of dropsy March 27, 1806 ; and she died Dec. 18, 1814. Children : Elizabeth, married Aaron Jewett of Ipswich ; David, settled in Maine ; Daniel, lived in Bridgton ; Nathan, graduated at Dartmouth college in 1791 ; ordained in 1793, as colleague with Rev. Ebenezer Flag of Chester, N. H. ; and removed to Westford, Mass., in 1820 : married Phebe Dexter of Charlestown in August, 1797 ; and died June 29, 1827 ; Phebe, married John Cressey of Rowley Nov. 15, 1792 ; and died Oct. 20, 1849 ; Mary, baptized Feb. 18, 1776 ; married James Todd of Rowley March 3, 1829 ; and died Oct.

12, 1861; Nathaniel, baptized May 2, 1779; married Elizabeth Jewett; died July 2, 1844; Sarah, baptized Nov. 25, 1781; married John Lambert of Rowley Dec. 20, 1804; Hannah, married John White June 12, 1823.
—*George B. Blodgette, Rowley.*

Lt. Nathaniel Bradstreet (No. 25, page 58) was born Nov. 18, 1705.

Mary Bradstreet (No. 46, page 59) was baptized June 27, 1750, and married Nathan Pierson June 14, 1774. These were grandparents of my great-grandfather Nathan Jewett of Ipswich.
—*Herbert C. Varney, St. Paul, Minn.*

CAPT. EDMUND BRAY.

Capt. Edmund Bray married Sarah Pedrick Jan. 4, 1795; and lived in Marblehead, in the house now belonging to Francis Goodwin, on State street. His wife died, of consumption, April 10, 1814, at the age of forty. His mother, Mrs. Bray, died, of dysentery, Sept. —, 1822, at the age of seventy-four. Captain Bray's children were born in Marblehead, and were as follows: Mary, baptized May 9, 1796; Isabella, baptized June 11, 1797; Edmund, baptized, Nov. 6, 1798; buried at the Island of Java Aug. 20, 1835, aged thirty-six; John baptized May 13, 1804; died, of consumption, March 30, 1826; Knott Pedrick, baptized May 13, 1804; lived in Marblehead; master-mariner; married Mary E. Andrews Oct. 22, 1846; Sally, baptized Oct. 28, 1804, died, of consumption, July 28, 1826; Thomas Pedrick, baptized Dec. 14, 1806; Evelina, baptized March 24, 1814.

Evelina, the youngest child, is said to have been three or four years old at the time of her baptism. At the age of seventeen she attended Haverhill Academy, being a classmate of John Greenleaf Whittier, who was at that time two years older than she. They became deeply interested in each other; and Whittier visited her at her home in Marblehead. The following verses of his poem, entitled

"A Sea Dream," she acknowledge! relate to them:—

The waves are glad in breeze and sun;
The rocks are fringed with foam;
I walk once more a haunted shore,
A stranger, yet at home,—
A land of dreams I roam.

Is this the wind, the soft sea-wind
That stirred thy locks of brown?
Are these the rocks whose mosses knew
The trail of thy light gown,
Where boy and girl sat down?

I see the gray forts broken wall,
The boats that rock below,
And, out at sea, the passing sails
We saw so long ago
Rose-red in morning's glow.

Adverse circumstances forbade marriage. Both families opposed the match his family because they were Quaker and could not permit a marriage "out society," and her family because Whittier was poor. She rarely referred to her early acquaintance with the poet, though at the latter part of her life she remarked that during that youthful acquaintance with Whittier it seemed as if the devil kept whispering to her, "He is only a shoemaker!"

She was engaged with Catherine Beecher in educational work, and finally married an Englishman, Rev. William Downey, who was an evangelist. Mr. Downey made a crusade against Romanism, and his death was caused by wounds received from facing a New York mob. She had no children. As is well known, Mr. Whittier never married. In her widowhood she corresponded with the poet, and attended the reunion of the scholars of the old academy in 1885. At the reunion, as Rev. S. F. Smith said, in her more than seventy years, a black silk and white muslin veil, reaching over her silvered head and down below her shoulders, she looked just as if she were a Romish Madonna, who had stepped out from an old church painting. She survived Whittier but a short time. The frontispiece of this number of the *Antiquarian* is the best likeness of her

THE AMERICAN FLAG.

BY F. G. HALLECK.

When Freedom, from her mountain height,
  Unfurled her standard to the air,
She tore the azure robe of night,
  And set the stars of glory there;
She mingled with the gorgeous dyes
The milky baldrick of the skies,
And striped its pure celestial white
With streakings of the morning light;
Then, from his mansion in the sun,
She called her eagle-bearer down,
And gave into his mighty hand
The symbol of her chosen land.

Flag of the free hearts' only home,
  By angel-hands to valor given,
Thy stars have lit the welkin dome,
  And all thy hues were born in heaven.
Forever float that standard sheet!
  Where breathes the foe, but falls before us,
With Freedom's soil beneath our feet,
And Freedom's banner streaming o'er us?

WILL OF THOMAS ANTRUM.

The will of Thomas Antrum of Salem was proved in the court held in Salem 3 : 5 mo : 1663. The following copy is taken from the original instrument on file in the office of the clerk of courts at Salem, volume IX, leaf 24.

The Last Will and Testament of Thomas Antrum beinge of pfect Memory

Inprimis I giue to : Haack Burnape the fon of my daughter Burnape ten pounds at the age of twenty one years to be paid : if he dye before to be giuen to my fon Obadiah Antrum

Item I giue to Thomas Spooner my horfe Colt

Item I giue to Helyard Verin five pounds

Item I giue to Obadiah Antrum my fon all the Remaind^r of my eftate but in Cafe it should pleafe god to take away by death my fon before the will be proued : that then the Childe or Children of my daughter Hannah Burnape : (who hath hade her full porcon Already) shall haue the eftate devided amongft them at the age of eighteene years.

Morou I apoynte Edmond Batter my Executor for this my will and Thomas

Spooner and Helyard Veren my Ouerfeer as witnes my hand : this 24 of 11mo 1662

figne

Thomas + Antrum

Signed and deliuered
in the p^{r}fence of vs
  Thomas Spooner
  William Woodcocke

WILL OF THEOPHILUS SHATSWELL.

The will of Theophilus Shatswell of Haverhill was proved in the court held at Hampton 13 : 8 : 1663. The following is a copy of the original instrument on file in probate office at Salem.

The Last will of Theophelus Satswell : Datted ye twenteth day of ye fourth : m^o in ye yeare of o^r lord one thoufand six : hundred Sixty & thre

Memorandum : In ye name of ye Lord Amen.

I Theophelus Satswell being but weake in bodey, but of perfitt memory doe Bequeath my soull to god that Gaue it & in his time my bodey to ye graue in a chriftian & deasent maner of buriall & my goods to be : Dispozed of as followith viz: I giue to my eldist Daughter Mary dureing her life one hundered & tenu : Acers of Adishon to ye 3^d deuishon of upland with all privledges to it belonging, & one & thirty Acers of 2nd deuishon Adjoyneing to wilya : Deales Land & six : aceres of planting Land adjoyneing to his Land by ye great riuer And one partiell of y^o East meadow with a 3^d partt of my Salt marsh at Salsbury & hogghill meadow Also half of my 4th deuishon of vpland for quantity and quallity it being in ye whole thre hundred & 15 acers wth all Preuiledges therevnto belonging & a young gray hors & ye vse of a payer of bullocks two years ‖allready receiued‖ wth other things

Allso I giue unto my daughter Lidea : dureing her lif ‖y^t farme‖ beyond Spickitt riuer as it is bounded bettwen Steuen Kentt And Wilyam Simons & y^e meadow y^t lyeth out of y^e farme vpon y^e brook at y^e head of thomas Danises 3d Deuishon half y^o meadow being gourg corlis & half

mine not yett parted & a white mare & y^e
couts y^t cam of The mare calle[d] her
mothers mare with other things alreadey
receiued

Also I giue Hanill Clark my whole
pportion of hauks meadow & y^e 3d deuishon of vpland belonging To Sauages
Land Layed out beyond haukes meadow
vpon a chaing betwene Robertt Swan & I
& tenn pounds al. If he stay wth me or
mine untill he be one & twenty years of
age : ||or else null all|| And I make my
wif Susanah & my Daughter Hannah Executors & Administrato^s all my other
Lands houseing catle & all other herredi-
ments And at ye Death of my wif then
my will is y^t my Daughter Hannah shall
be sole Administratour & if hannah dye
then ye other sesters Adminestring, Also
my will is in all aboue written y^t my lands
after the desease of my daughters Shall
goe to there children by ye heade to part
alike & if any of my daughters dye leaue-
ing no child nor children Then her partt
so dyeing shall be to all ye lineing children alike pportion pseeding from her
other Sister Further I Desire my Brother
Wilyam Sargent : & my Kinsman Lefttent-
ent Philip challis To be my ouer Seers To
Se this my will fulfillid accord : to ye ten-
nor of it.

                          Theophelus
                          Shatswell
witnes : Jonathan Singltary
         Edward clarke

NOTES.

A full account of an event at Cape Ann
implicating one Samuel Fellows, who had
commanded a vessel belonging to a merchant there, is given in the *Essex Gazette* for July 18-25, 1769. Fellows had
behaved in such a manner in the West
Indies that it was difficult for him to render a fair and just account of his transactions. As an easier way of settlement
he informed the custom-house officers upon oath that more molasses had been
landed than was reported. The vessel was
thereupon seized ; and Fellows served

the favor of the officers of the custo
who rewarded him by giving him t
command of one of his majesty's ar
cutters of the coast guard, with the p
of making seizures. He commenced
tilities against the merchants, stopp
vessels and searching them, impres
men, etc. May 25, 1769, Deputy-she
Jacob Parsons of Cape Ann had in h
custody Josiah Merril as a prisoner ; an
Fellows, then in the harbor, with four o
his men with fire-arms, cutlasses, etc
came on shore in a boat, and asked Me
ril what he was doing there. Merril replied that he was in custody for debt;
and at Fellows' request Merril broke
away from the deputy and ran toward
Fellows. The deputy commanded, in h
majesty's name, several persons to assi
in seizing and stopping his prisoner,
whom they accordingly seized. Fellows,
being within four rods from the deputy
and his assistants, ordered his four men to
fire. Two of the four men leaped upon
the beach, ran toward the deputy, and
when within two rods of him and his assistants fired. The shot and ball scarcely
missed them, and entered a store within
a few inches of where they stood ; Merril
broke away and ran to the boat. Fellows'
men continued firing as they left the
shore in their boat, etc.

Thomas Jacques of Gloucester advertised that his negro man Titus, about
twenty-one years old, ran away on the
night of July 18, 1769. The negro was
of middling stature, stuttered conside:-
ably, and had lost part of one of his
great toes. He wore a striped jacket, a
striped woolen shirt and a pair of sheep-
skin breeches, but no hat, cap, shoes or
stockings.

John Lowell, esq., was nominated to be
a justice of the peace for the county of
Essex by the governor at Cambridge
July 12, 1769.

—*Essex Gazette, July* 18-25, 1769.

Thomas Bracey of Haverhill, mariner,
1795, 1798.—*Registry of Deeds.*

Thomas Bracy of Ipswich, 1635.—*Savage.*

Mary, wife of William Brackenbury, died Sept. 13, 1720, aged thirty-five.— *Inscription in ancient Ipswich burying ground.*

Joseph Braybrook of Newbury, aged twenty, 1669.

Rachel Brabrock of Newbury, aged twenty, 1669.

— *Court records.*

Samuel Brackenbury of Rowley, probably son of William, was a physician, who preached two years, but was not ordained yet, removed to Boston, and died of small pox, says Hull's diary, 11 (16?) Jan., 1678.—*Savage.*

Richard Brabrook of Jabeaque, in Ipswich, born in 1613, yeoman, 1644-1670; of Wenham, 1672-1680; wife (1653-1669) Joanna, 1669; his will, dated July 17, 1680, proved Nov. 23, 1681; he bequeathed six pounds to the college and six pounds to the minister of Wenham; John Bayer of Ipswich called him "uncle" in 1669; Mr. Brabrook's widow, Joanna, married Thomas Penny, in Gloucester, May 17, 1682; and she was living in 1693. Mr. Brabrook's daughter Mehitable (aged sixteen or seventeen in 1668, servant of Jacob Perkins) married John Downing of Ipswich, planter, 2 : 9 mo: 1669, and to the latter's children Mr. Brabrook's estate was given.

Samuel Brabrook of Salem, weaver, 1695-1722; made his will April 6, 1720, and it was proved April 2, 1722. He gave all of his estate to his wife Mary (1695-1720). She was his wife as early as 1681. He was son-in-law of Jeremiah Watts in 1680.

Richard Brackenbury of Beverly, born about 1600, came to Salem with Endecott in the Abigail, Sept. 6, 1628; yeoman; and died in 1684, at the age of eighty-four. His estate was appraised at £100. His wife was named Ellen. He had a son who had children, John and Katharin Phips, living in 1684; a daughter Elizabeth, living in 1684; a son Miles, living in 1685; a daughter Hannah, baptized June 1, 1651; and a daughter who married John Patch before 1684.

William Brackenbury married Abigail Heard, both of Ipswich, in Newbury, Sept. 3, 1707. Children, born in Ipswich: Abigail, born 3 : 4 : 1708; died Aug. 19, 1708; Mary, born 29 : 7 : 1709; William, baptized 2 : 1 : 1712.

William Brackenbury of Ipswich, tailor, married Mary Walcott of Salem Village (published Aug. 15, 1730); administration was granted upon his estate to his widow Mary Brackenbury Feb. 8, 1742-3. Children, born in Ipswich: Samuel, baptized 10 : 26 : 1731; died Jan. 6, 1731-2; Samuel, baptized June 2, 1734; Daniel, baptized Dec. 5, 1736.

— *Records.*

Mercy Brackenbury published to Samuel Harris 31 : 8 : 1719.

William Brackenbury published to widow Mary Cross 28 : 9 : 1719.

Mary Brackenbury married Joseph Burnam Oct. 20, 1731.

Mary Brackenbury published to Samuel Harris of Rowley Aug. 11, 1753.

Widow Brackett died June 2, 1790.

— *Ipswich town records.*

William Witty, son of John and Elizabeth Braaket, baptized Oct. —, 1749.

Mary, daughter of John and Mary Bracket, baptized Nov. 3, 1751.

Children of John and Elizabeth Brackett, baptized: Elizabeth, Sept. 24, 1727; and John, May 31, 1730.

— *Marblehead church records.*

Thomas Bracey published to Miss Hannah Pecker, both of Newburyport, Oct. 12, 1787.—*Newburyport town records.*

Samuel Brackenbury married Anne Smith March 13, 1758.

John Bradbrook died June 18, 1662.

— *Newbury town records.*

Thomas Brackett of Salem, husbandman, wife Alice, 1671-1673; she died, his widow, in Salem, in 1690; her will dated June 20, 1688, being proved Nov. 25, 1690; she called herself, in the will, "aged and sick;" and devised her estate to her grandson Thomas Ward, who then lived with her and had been helpful to her. Thomas' father was dead and he had a guardian in 1690. He had broth

ers Samuel and John and a sister Lydia.
—*Probate records.*

Zachariah Bracket of Ipswich (probably came from Falmouth some years before), yeoman, died July 25, 1755. Administration upon his estate was granted to his widow Mary. His estate was appraised at £253, 1s., 7d. Administration upon her estate was granted Dec. 2, 1793.
—*Records.*

Thomas Bracket (or Brocket) of Salem, 1658 (Quaker?), 1660, 1669 (Frenchman?) ; inventory of estate taken in 1668.
—*Court records.*

James Brackett of Beverly, freeman, 1675.

Thomas Brackett of Salem punished for attending Quaker meeting in 1658 ; had Thomas baptized Dec. 7, 1645 ; died at twenty-two years ; Mary, Feb. 4, 1649 ; and Joseph, June 15, 1651 ; died young, as also daughter Lydia.

Joseph Brade of Marblehead, 1668.

Moses Bradford of Salisbury, 1669, removed to Boston, and was drowned March 23, 1692.

James Brading of Newbury removed to Boston, 1659 ; married Hannah, daughter of Joseph Rock, Oct. 11, 1659 ; children : Elizabeth, married Edward Bromfield ; James, born in 1662 ; Joseph.

John Bradley of Salem died June —, 1642, at Dorchester, by will proved July 29, 1642, only wife and brother in-law William Allen mentioned.
—*Savage.*

Theophilus Bradbury, jr., of Newburyport published to Miss Harriet Hains of Concord, N. H., Aug. 20, 1795.

A child of Theophilus Bradbury, jr., died Sept. 24, 1799.
—*Newburyport town records.*

Samuel Bradbury of Newburyport, cooper, 1795.—*Registry of deeds.*

Children of William and Judith Blyth : Betsey, born Nov. 21, 1794; Sophia, born April 17, 1797 ; Eliza, born Dec. 10, 1801 ; Elizabeth and Judith King, baptized July 1, 1804 ; and Judith, born Dec. 5, 1804.

Charlotte, daughter of Betsy (Simonds), Blyth, born March 25, 1793.
—*Beverly records.*

Ephraim Bradbury published to Mary Waier of Hampton Feb. 13, 1773.

Elizabeth Bradbury published to Anthony Halley of Amesbury Aug. 7, 1773.

Sarah Bradbury published to David Osgood, jr., March 12, 1774.

John Bradbury published to Susanna Hutchens of Gilmantown June 1, 1776.

Jacob Bradbury married Mehitable Morrill Nov. 22, 1781.
—*Salisbury town records.*

Sarah Bradbury married Josiah Brown April 17, 1784.

Sally Bradbury married Austin George July 6, 1786.
—*Haverhill town records.*

Jabez Bradbury (No. 52, page 147, volume X of *The Antiquarian*) married Mary Merrill May 16, 1749, in Newbury.

Anne Bradbury (No. 56, page 147, volume X of *The Antiquarian*) married Samuel Greenleaf May 17, 1749, in Newbury.
—*County records.*

Joseph Bradley of Haverhill had a garrison at his house, which was surprised Feb. 8, 1704, when his wife, for the second time, was taken by the Indians and carried away, her infant child, born after her capture, dying of want. His son Abraham* lived in Concord, N. H., in 1754. Children, Joseph, Martha, and Sarah, had been killed March 11, 1697, by the Indians.

Joshua Bradley of Rowley, 1663.

Thomas Brand of Salem, cooper, came in the fleet with Higginson in 1629.

Peter Brateler (Brately?) of Salem, 1648 (Felt) : of Salem, mariner, 1683 (Felt).
—*Savage.*

Abigail Beynet married Richard French March 21, 1780.—*Gloucester town records.*

*Abraham Bradley was probably brother of Joseph Bradley.

QUERIES.

Queries are inserted for one cent a word.
Answers are solicited.

471. Wanted, date of death and name of wife of Nathaniel (baptized June 21, 1779, Salem), son of Capt. Jonathan and Mary (Hodges) Ingersoll. Also, date of birth of children.
Pontiac, Mich. L. D. A.

472. Was the Samuel⁴ Ingersol (John³, John², Richard¹) who married Elizabeth Wakefield, 1700, the same Samuel who married Sarah Hasket, 1702? Wanted, date of his birth and death and record of children. L. D. A.

473. Wanted, parentage of Elizabeth ―― who married John Becket, jr., March 9, 1774. L. D. A.

474. Was John Ingersoll who married Sarah Pratt, 1724, the son of Richard and Ruth of Beverly? And was his son John, baptized Aug. 9, 1730, Beverly, the same who married Lydia Cressy April 2, 1764? Did he live later (1778) in Windham, Me.? L. D. A.

474. Mrs. Lillian Drake Avery of Pontiac, Mich., is compiling the Ingersoll genealogy, and would like all of the family who have not sent their records to do so as soon as possible.

475. Wanted, parents of Isaac Johnson who married, 1761, Elizabeth Coffin. *Philadelphia.* C. H. C.

476. Wanted, parents of Oliver Knight who married, 1742, Sarah Coffin. C. H. C.

477. Wanted, parents of Joseph March, jr., of Salem, who married Elizabeth Coffin. C. H. C.

478. Wanted, parents of Elizabeth Coffin of Salisbury, and of Olive Fowler, who married, in 1729 and 1750, respectively, Joseph Coffin. C. H. C.

479. Wanted, parents of Joseph Smith who married, 1749, Elizabeth Coffin.
C. H. C.

480. Wanted, parents of Joseph Pilsbury who married, 1766, Eunice Coffin.
C. H. C.

481. Wanted, wife of Jonathan Woodman of Newbury whose daughter Miriam married Benjamin Coffin. C. H. C.

482. Wanted, parents of Richard Carr of Salisbury who married, 1778, Abigail Coffin. C. H. C.

483. FELTON. Twenty-five dollars reward is offered for the maiden name and parentage of Sarah, wife of Daniel Felton of Marblehead. At her death, May 4th, 1763, she was aged seventy-five years and four months. Her husband Daniel was born October, 1687, at Salem Farms, now Danvers, and removed to Marblehead probably when a young man, and thereafter made Marblehead his home. E. C. FELTON.
Haverford, Pa.

ANSWERS.

468. An example of the use of the word "lugg" as a measure of distance is found in the record of a grant of land in Newbury to Mr. Dumer, about 1650. By following down the title to this land it has been ascertained that a "lugg" and a rod are identical.—*Ed.*

469. Hannah (Wainwright) Webster was born Feb. 1, 1721-2, in Newbury, Mass., and died March 13, 1765. She was the daughter of John and Hannah (Redford) Wainwright. Grant Webster when appointed administrator to the estate of Redford Wainwright of Newbury, June 9, 1746, is called brother to said Wainwright. Grant and Hannah were married May 31, 1739. Grant Webster had no relatives of the name of Webster. He was the only son of John Webster and Mary (Smith) Webster who married and left children. John, in turn, was the only son of Henry and Esther Webster. Henry Webster came to Boston April 15, 1679, in the ship Robert from Barbadoes. He was the son of John Webster of Bar-

badoes who died about 1666. There is now living only one descendant of this Henry Webster bearing the name of Webster. The last male of the name was Prof. John White Webster, who was executed for the murder of Doctor Parkman. A number of descendants in the female lines are still living. I published a full account of this family in the Genealogical Magazine, June, 1905, page 97. They are in no ways, so far as I know, related to the other Websters of Essex county. Grant Webster was a graduate of Harvard college.—*S. P. Sharples, Cambridge.*

NEW PUBLICATIONS.

CHARLES BROOKS AND HIS WORK FOR NORMAL SCHOOLS. *By John Albree.* Medford, 1907. This was a paper read before the Medford Historical Society May 5, 1906. Mr. Albree, with his customary care, thoroughness and taste, has prepared and printed this valuable and interesting pamphlet of thirty-one octavo pages, having added to the text four portraits of Rev. Mr. Brooks (1795-1872), the subject of the paper, who was the pastor of the Third church in Hingham, but a native of Medford. The engravings show Mr. Brooks as he looked at several ages. Mr. Albree has done well in letting the public know the kind and extent of the effort put forth by Mr. Brooks in his efforts to advance the cause of education by having teachers trained to teach, and finally the institution of the Normal school system.

GENEALOGY OF THE STIMPSON FAMILY OF CHARLESTOWN, MASS., and Allied Lines. *By Charles Collyer Whittier.* Boston, 1907. This volume contains the genealogical record of the descendants of Andrew Steavenson or Stimson of Cambridge, whose son Andrew Stimson removed to Charlestown about 1678. The larger part of the book consists of most of the descendants of the daughters, owing to the fact that in each of the first four generations only one male member married

and had issue. There are now livin only twenty-eight male descendants of Andrew Steavenson, who bear the name of Stimpson.

The volume is embellished by twelve half-tone engravings, ten of which are portraits. One index of names of persons and another of places is given. It is bound in cloth, contains two hundred and six octavo pages, and is sold for $3 by the author, whose address is 374 Blue Hill Avenue, Roxbury, Mass. The book is well printed, and everything in its appearance indicates carefulness and accuracy.

A GUIDE TO MASSACHUSETTS LOCAL HISTORY. *Compiled by Charles A. Flagg.* Salem, 1907. This is a volume of 25 large octavo pages, two columns to page, printed in small type. It is a bibliographic index to the literature of the towns, cities and counties of the state, including books, pamphlets, articles in periodicals and collected works, books in preparation, historical manuscripts, newspaper clippings, etc.

Mr. Flagg is in the Library of Congress in Washington, and has an excellent chance to know what there is in the way of local literature. He has, also, been in correspondence with people who could anyway assist in making the work complete.

After the sources of information relative to the whole state is given, the work is divided into counties and county authorities given, then each county taken up by towns alphabetically. There are certain kinds of books and references that are not included, as town records, church records, and biographies of single subject and genealogies devoted to one family, as the existence of such are can be readily known to the inquirer. In this work are included references to unpublished manuscripts in the possession of private persons.

The volume is published by The Salem Press Company, Salem, Mass., and neatly and strongly bound in cloth; it will be sent postpaid for $6.20.

Volume XI.   October, 1907.

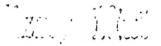

An Illustrated Quarterly &c.

Devoted to the

Biography, Genealogy, History

of

Essex County, Massac

SIDNEY PERLEY, *Editor*.
GEORGE FRANCIS DOW, *Business A.*

CONTENTS.

ONE DOLLAR PER ANNUM. SINGLE COPIES, T.
FOREIGN SUBSCRIPTIONS, EXCEPT FROM CANADA AND M.

SALEM. MASS.
The Essex Antiquaria

ii

An Illust

The
rious p
to any
(2d and
of the each
time in t

Uniformly

Vol. I,
" II,

Sub

T

A

OFFICIAL

The pub
province of t

C

Publishe
Genealogical
Each nu
Antiquities, e
Comme
began in janu
Terms:
sent single co
Read't

GEORGE PEABODY.

BREED GENEALOGY.

THIS name was spelled *Bread* with few exceptions until after 1700. Since that date *Breed* has been the general spelling. The ancestor of the American family is

ALLEN BREED[1].* He was born in 1601; and settled in Lynn as early as 1630. He was a farmer, and lived near the junction of what is now Summer street and the turnpike. He was one of the Long Island settlers, but returned to Lynn before 1646; and was a selectman and constable of Lynn. He married, first, ——— ———; and, second, Elizabeth, widow of William Knight, 28: 1: 1656. He was called "Old Allen Breed;" and died March 17, 1690-1, at about ninety years of age. His wife Elizabeth had probably died before him.

Children:—

2—I. ALLEN[2]. *See below* (2).
3—II. ELIZABETH[2]; m. William Merriam about 1653; and lived in Lynn.
4—III. JOHN[2]. *See below* (4).

2

ALLEN BREED[2], was a husbandman, and lived in Lynn. He married Mary ——— before 1660; and she died 30: 9: 1671. His will, dated in 1704, was proved Feb. 11, 1707. His estate was appraised at £232, 15s.

Children, born in Lynn:—

5—I. TIMOTHY[3]. *See below* (5).
6—II. JOSEPH[3], b. about 1658. *See below* (6).
7—III. ALLEN[3], b. 30: 6: 1660. *See below* (7).
8—IV. JOHN[3], b. 28: 11: 1662; living in 1704.
9—V. MARY[3], b. 24: 6: 16—; m. ——— Lewis before 1704.

*Allen Breed was probably born in Westoning parish, Bedfordshire, England. See Essex Institute Historical Collections, volume XL., pages 147-153.

10—VI. ELIZABETH[3], b. 1: 9 mo: 1667; m. Thomas Burrage Nov. 16, 1687.
11—VII. SAMUEL[3], b. 25: 7: 1669. *See below* (11).

4

JOHN BREED[2], was a resident of Lynn. He married, first, Sara Hathorne 28: 10: 1663; and she died about Nov. 22, 1676. He married, second, Sarah Hart March 4, 1677-8; and died June 28, 1678. His wife Sarah survived him, their wedded life continuing only three months. His estate was appraised at £267, 9s.

Children, born in Lynn:—

12—I. JOHN[3], b. June 7 (Nov. 15?), 1664. *See below* (12).
13—II. SARAH[3], b. Dec. 28, 1667; m. John Hood of Lynn, husbandman, before 1728; and she was of Lynn, his widow, in 1735.
14—III. WILLIAM[3], b. 18: 3: 1671; probably d. young.
15—IV. EPHRAIM[3], b. 16: 10: 1672; mariner; m. Martha Glass; lived in Charlestown; had children; he d. before 1728; and she was his widow in 1744.
16—V. EBENEZER[3], b. April 15, 1676; master-mariner; lived in Lynn, 1704; and settled in Charlestown; m. Hannah Carey Dec. 4, 1712; and had children.

5

TIMOTHY BREED[3], was a resident of Lynn. He married, first, Sarah Newhall March 3, 1679-80; and she was buried Nov. 27, 1693. He married, second, Sarah Bran Feb. ———, 1693-4; and died before Jan. 2, 1717-8, when administration was granted upon his estate. His last wife survived him. His estate was valued at £346, 12s., 6d.

Children, born in Lynn:—

17—I.   JOSEPH⁴, b. Oct. 18, 1681. *See below* (*17*).

18—II. TIMOTHY⁴, b. March 31, 1683 ; ship-wright ; lived in Boston ; m. Eunice Souther, in Boston, June 24, 1708. They were living in Boston, 1738.

19—III. SAMUEL⁴, b. July 1, 1686 ; probably d. before 1718.

20—IV. THOMAS⁴, b. Jan. 14, 1694-5 ; d. young.

21—V.   SARAH⁴ (twin), b. Aug. 14, 1696 ; m. Samuel Larrabee of Lynn Jan. 14, 1717-8 ; and was living in 1738.

22—VI. MARY⁴ (twin), b. Aug. 14, 1696 ; d. Aug. 28, 1696.

23—VII. THOMAS⁴, b. Sept. 21, 1698 ; husband-man ; lived in Lynn ; m. Miss Sarah Farr Oct. 25, 1726 ; and d. June 5, 1754 ; she d., his widow, June —, 1769.

24—VIII. JONATHAN⁴, b. Jan. 29, 1699-1700. *See below (24).*

6

JOSEPH BREED³, born in Lynn about 1658. He was a coaster and yeoman, and lived in Lynn. He married Sarah Farrington Sept. 27, 1683 ; and died Nov. 25, 1713, at the age of fifty-five. She survived him, and died, his widow, April 2, 1752, at the age of eighty-eight.

Children, born in Lynn :—

25—I.   MARY⁴, b. July 4, 1684 ; m. Ralph Lindsey (pub. July 30, 1709) ; and was his wife in 1713.

26—II. JANE⁴, b. Oct. 19, 1687 ; m. Elisha Newhall Feb. 27, 1710-1 ; and was his wife in 1713.

27—III. SARAH⁴, b. July 16, 1689 ; m. Andrew Mansfield Dec. 16, 1712.

28—IV. JOSEPH⁴, b. "last of June," 1691. *See below (28).*

29—V.   RUTH⁴, b. Sept. 13, 1693 ; d. young.

30—VI. ELIZABETH⁴, b. Oct. 6, 1695 ; m. Ebenezer Newhall (pub. Nov. 8, 1718).

31—VII. MATTHEW⁴, b. Nov. 22, 1697 ; d. Jan. 25, 1697-8.

32—VIII. MATTHEW⁴, b. Jan. 31, 1698-9. *See below (32).*

33—IX. MARCY⁴, b. July 20, 1701 ; m. Robert Potter Nov. 29, 1721.

34—X.   MEHITABLE⁴, b. Dec. 21, 1704 ; m. Jacob Eaton (pub. Oct. 29, 1727).

35—XI. ALLEN⁴, b. March 16, 1706-7. *See below (35).*

7

ALLEN BREED³, born in Lynn 30 : 6 : 1660. He was a yeoman and wheel-wright ; and lived in Lynn. His grand-father, Allen Breed, conveyed by deed certain property to him, who " Hath dis-bursed money upon my estate, And man-ageth all my work for mee, done & pformed for mee," Dec. 13, 1689. He married Elizabeth Ballard, at Charlestown May 22, 1684 ; and died in Lynn Dec. 27, 1730, at the age of seventy. She was his wife in 1730 ; " Old widow Allen Breed " was buried 26 : 5 : 1743.

Children, born in Lynn :—

36—I.   NATHANIEL⁴, b. Aug. 24, 1685 ; live in Boston ; m. Sarah Davise March 31, 1709, in Boston ; and had chil-dren.

37—II. ELIZABETH⁴, b. Jan. 24, 1687-8 ; m. Samuel Witt of Marlboro (pub. Dec. 2, 1716) ; and was his wife in 1730.

38—III. JOHN⁴, b. Oct. 10, 1689. *See below (38).*

39—IV. MARY⁴, b. March 21, 1691-2 ; m. Dan-iel Newhall (pub. Nov. 20, 1713) ; and was his wife in 1730.

40—V.   REBECCA⁴, b. Jan. 26, 1694-5 ; m. Eb-enezer Witt of Marlboro (pub. Sept. 30, 1715) ; and was his wife in 1730.

41—VI. HEPZABETH⁴, b. June 19, 1697 ; m. Edmund Lewis Jan. 8, 1723-4 ; and was his wife in 1730.

42—VII. JOSIAH⁴, b. Jan. 2, 1700-1 ; probably d. young.

11

SAMUEL BREED³, born in Lynn 25 : 7 : 1669. He was a husbandman and weaver, and lived in Lynn. He married Anna Hood Feb. 5, 1691-2 ; and she was his wife in 1745. His father devised his homestead to him. He died Feb. —, 1755, being buried on the fifteenth of the month. His estate was appraised at £358, 8s., 4d.

Children, born in Lynn :—

43—I.   SAMUEL⁴, b. Nov. 11, 1692. *See below (43).*

44—II. AMOS⁴, b. July 20, 1694 ; was living in 1745, probably in Boston.

45—III. JAMES⁴, b. Jan. 26, 1695-6. *See below (45).*

46—IV. ABIGAIL⁴, b. Sept. 7, 1698 ; d. before 1745.

47—V.   NATHAN⁴, b. Jan. 3, 1702-3. *See below (47).*

48—VI. KEZIAH⁴, b. Oct. 16, 1704 ; m. Samuel Newhall, jr., Dec. 8, 1721.

49—VII. ANNA⁴, b. July 28, 1706 ; m. Ebenezer Hawkes of Marblehead (pub. April 11, 1725).

50—VIII. EBENEZER⁴, b. May 1, 1710. *See below* (50).
51—IX. RUTH⁴, b. March 10, 1711-2; m. Daniel Purinton of Salem, potter, March 1, 1736; and was living in 1745.
52—X. BENJAMIN⁴, b. July 4, 1715. *See below* (52).

12

CAPT. JOHN BREED³, born in Lynn June 7 (Nov. 15?), 1664. He was a husbandman; and lived in Lynn. He married Miss Mary Kertland April 28, 1686; and he died in Lynn Dec. 14, 1728, aged sixty-four. He went to Port Royal. His estate was valued at £2,037, 19*s.*, 5*d.* In h's will he gave thirty pounds to the First Church of Christ in Lynn for furnishing the Lord's table; and to his pastor, Rev. Nathaniel Hinchman, fifty pounds and his "colash." Captain Breed had brought up the wife of Rev. Mr. Hinchman from a child, and treated her as such; and also other children. He also bequeathed a sum of money to the poor widows of the First parish of Lynn, to be distributed by the deacons of the First church, and to his nephew, John Breed, he gave his great bible. Probably no more elaborate funeral ever occurred in Lynn, according to the accounts on file in the probate office; and the allowance of the bills was objected to by the heirs. Mrs. Breed survived him; and was his widow in 1743.

Child, born in Lynn:—
53—I. SARAH⁴, b. July 15, 1687; d. Jan. 28, 1687-8.

17

JOSEPH BREED⁴, born in Lynn Oct. 18, 1681. He lived in Marblehead, and was a cooper. He married Anna Rolls Dec. 1, 1709; and died in 1738. She was his wife in 1738.

Children, born in Marblehead:—
54—I. TIMOTHY⁵, bapt. Oct. 8, 1710.
55—II. MARY⁵, bapt. May 31, 1713; pub. to Benjamin Huchason June 22, 1735, but his father forbade the marriage two days later.
56—III. JOSEPH⁵, bapt. March 13, 1714-5; shipwright; lived in Charlestown, 1750, 1751.
57—IV. JOHN⁵, bapt. Dec. 2, 1716.

58—V. SAMUEL⁵, bapt. Nov. 16, 1718; living in Boston, mariner, in 1750, 1751; m. Abigail Brown (pub. July 24, 1743).
59—VI. AMOS⁵, bapt. Dec. 4, 1720; living in 1738.
60—VII. ELIZABETH⁵, bapt. March 28, 1725.
61—VIII. ANNA⁵, bapt. Aug. 11, 1728; m. Mathew Lindsey Dec. 1, 1747.

24

JONATHAN BREED³, born in Lynn Jan. 29, 1699-1700. He lived in Marblehead; and married Ruth Haynes (Hooper—*church*) June 1, 1725, in Marblehead. He died about 1730; and his widow married, secondly, William Mors of Marblehead Dec. 22, 1731. She was his wife in 1762.

Children, born in Marblehead:—
62—I. SARAH⁴, bapt. Feb. 20, 1725-6; m. Timothy Goodwin May 18, 1753; and was living in 1762.
63—II. RUTH⁴, bapt. July 16, 1727; m. Ivory Witt Dec. 1, 1747, in Lynn; and was living in 1762.
64—III. JONATHAN⁴, bapt. Aug. 31, 1729; lived in Marblehead: m. Elizabeth Dolliber Nov. 22, 1759; he d., childless, before May 11, 1761, when administration was granted upon his estate, which was appraised at £407, 2s., 3 1/2*d.*; he had a fishing schooner named Breed; his wife survived him, and probably m. Capt. William Courtis Feb. 18, 1766.

28

JOSEPH BREED⁴, born in Lynn the "last of June," 1691. He was a coaster, and resided in Lynn. He married Miss Susannah Newhall of Lynn July 16, 1717; and they were living in Lynn in 1738.

Children, born in Lynn:—
65—I. THEOPHILUS⁵, b. Aug. 2, 1719. *See below* (65).
66—II. RUTH⁵, b. Sept. 31, 1721; m. John Stocker March 17, 1742-3.
67—III. SARAH⁵, b. Feb. 6, 1723-4.
68—IV. JOSEPH⁵ (twin), b. Sept. 7, 1726; d. Sept. 27, 1726.
69—V. SUSANNA⁵ (twin), b. Sept. 7, 1726; d. Aug. 4, 1740, aged thirteen.
70—VI. LYDIA⁵, b. Oct. 18, 1729; d. July 12, 1740, aged ten.
71—VII. JOSEPH⁵, b. Jan. 1, 1731-2. *See below* (71).
72—VIII. MARY⁵, b. Jan. 6, 1733-4; m. Josiah Breed Dec. 18, 1755; and d. May 7, 1767, aged thirty-three.

73—IX. EPHRAIM⁵, b. May 26, 1736. *See below (73).*

32

MATTHEW BREED⁴, born in Lynn Jan. 31, 1698-9. He was a cooper and coaster, and lived in Lynn. He married Mary Stocker Dec. 11, 1723, and died April 17, 1767, aged sixty-eight. His estate was valued at £243, 19s., 6d. She survived him.

Children, born in Lynn :—

74—I. MARY⁵, b. Oct. 10, 1724; m. Benjamin James March 4, 1742; and was living in 1765.

75—II. SARAH⁵, b. Aug. 23, 1726.

76—III. MEHITABEL⁵, b. March 12, 1728-9; m. Samuel Hallowell Sept. 22, 1747; and d. before 1765.

77—IV. HANNAH⁵, b. Jan. 18, 1730; m. Samuel Bacheller March 6, 1755; and was living in 1765.

78—V. MATTHEW⁵, b. Aug. 16, 1733; d. Sept. 8, 1733.

79—VI. RUTH⁵, b. Aug. 1, 1734; m. Joseph Breed (71) Jan. 26, 1758.

35

ALLEN BREED⁴, born in Lynn March 16, 1706-7. He was at first a house carpenter, became a coaster and cooper, and subsequently returned to his trade of a housewright. He married Huldah Newhall June 2, 1728; and they were living in Lynn in 1765.

Children, born in Lynn :—

80—I. JOSEPH⁵, b. June 3, 1729; blacksmith; lived in Lynn, 1751, and in Marblehead, 1754-1774; m. Rebecca Merriam Nov. 1, 1750. He d. before April 4, 1774, when administration was granted upon his estate. She survived him.

81—II. LOVE⁵, b. Aug. 16, 1731; m. Alen Newhall March 29, 1750.

82—III. JERUSHA⁵, b. Sept. 3, 1733; m. Henry Batcheler April 4, 1758.

83—IV. HULDAH⁵, b. Sept. 10, 1736; m. Nehemiah Lindsey Dec. 30, 1755.

84—V. ABIGAIL⁵, b. Sept. 8, 1739; d. Sept. 16, 1740, aged one year.

85—VI. ABIGAIL⁵, b. Nov. 7, 1741; m. Richard Richards Dec. 2, 1761.

86—VII. ALLEN⁵, b. April 19, 1744. *See below (86).*

87—VIII. HEPSEBAH⁵, b. Dec. 15, 1746.

88—IX. ELIPHALET⁵, b. June 4, 1750; shipwright; lived in Lynn; m. Mary Johnson Dec. 10, 1772.

89—X. FREDERICK⁵, b. Aug. 20, 1755. *below (89).*

38

JOHN BREED⁴, born in Lynn Oct. 1689. He was a yeoman and coaster, and lived in Lynn. He married Lyd Gott of Wenham Jan. 2, 1717-8, in Lynn, and died April 16, 1774, aged eighty-four. She died, his widow, Aug. 1, 17.. aged ninety.

Children, born in Lynn :—

90—I. ALLEN⁵, b. Oct. 26, 1718; d. Aug. 2 1757, aged thirty-eight.

91—II. JOHN⁵, b. Sept. 13, 1720; living 1768; probably m. Jane Newhall June 13, 1743.

92—III. NATHANIEL⁵, b. July 22, 1728; living in 1768.

93—IV. JOSIAH⁵, b. Dec. 16, 1731. *See below (93).*

94—V. DELIVERANCE⁵, b. Oct. 17, 1736; m. William Haskell of Marblehead Oct. 24, 1758.

43

SAMUEL BREED⁴, born in Lynn Nov. 11, 1692. He was a yeoman, and lived in Lynn, in that portion known as Nahant being at the time of his purchase of Dr. John H. Burchstead, Dec. 18, 1718, the only inhabitant. He built a house where the Whitney hotel lately stood, and was an innholder in 1738 and 1739. He was small in stature, and was generally called "Governor Breed." He married Mrs. Deliverance Basset of Lynn Jan. 1719-20; and died "at Nahant" May 14, 1768, aged seventy-five. His house became the property of his son Nehemiah. His estate was appraised at £747, 6s., 10d.

Children, born in Lynn :—

95—I. ANNA⁵, b. March 20, 1726; m. James Purinton, cordwainer, Oct. 10, 17..; and was living in 1760.

96—II. SARAH⁵, b. Sept. 29, 1729; living in 1760; m. Samuel Silsbe, shipwright, March 11, 1755.

97—III. HULDAH⁵, b. May 13, 1731; m. Eben Breed (110) Aug. 29, 1757.

98—IV. NEHEMIAH⁵, b. Sept. 19, 1736. *See below (98).*

99—V. WILLIAM⁵, b. March 22, 1738-9.

45

JABEZ BREED⁴, born in Lynn Jan. 1695-6. He was a yeoman and house

wright, and lived in Lynn. He married Desire Bassett (published Nov. 17, 1723); and she was his wife in 1774. He died in 1778, being "aged." His will, dated 13 : 8 : 1774, was proved Oct. 5, 1778. His estate was valued at £2,126, 0s., 2d.

Children, born in Lynn :—

100—I. ISAIAH⁵, b. Oct. 25, 1724. *See below (100).*
101—II. NATHAN⁵, b. Oct. 7, 1726. *See below (101).*
102—III. AMOS⁵, b. Aug. 14, 1728. *See below (102).*
103—IV. MARY⁵, b. Jan. 11, 1730; m. Joseph Hill of Kittery Jan. 12, 1749-50, in Lynn; and lived in Kittery and Berwick, Me. She was his wife in 1774.
104—V. ABIGAIL⁵, b. Aug. 29, 1732; m. Daniel Farrington Aug. 29, 1757.
105—VI. THEODATE⁵, b. Dec. 6, 1734; m. Pharoah Newhall April 24, 1764; and was living in 1774.
106—VII. ——⁵, buried 27: 5: 1748.
107—VIII. DEBORAH⁵, b. June 3, 1738; m. Samuel Alley July 16, 1758; and was living in 1774.

47

NATHAN BREED⁴, born in Lynn Jan. 3, 1702-3. He was a cordwainer, and lived in Lynn. He married Miss Mary Basset Oct. 28, 1728; and died Feb. 26, 1755, aged fifty-two. She survived him, and died, his widow, in Lynn, in 1793; her will, dated March 14, 1782, being proved Aug. 6, 1793. His estate was appraised at £7,481, 4s., 6d. (old tenor).

Children, born in Lynn :—

108—I. HANNAH⁵, b. July 20, 1729; d. Aug. 18, 1730.
109—II. HANNAH⁵, b. May 30, 1731; m. John Mower of Lynn, husbandman, Nov. 11, 1754; and was living in 1796.
110—III. EZRA⁵, b. March 16, 1733. *See below (110).*
111—IV. ABIGAIL⁵, b. March 13, 1735; m. Nehemiah Breed (98) Jan. 2, 1759.
112—V. ZEPHANIAH⁵, b. March 10, 1737. *See below (112).*
113—VI. JOHN⁵, b. May 8, 1739; d. July 1, 1740.
114—VII. DANIEL⁵, b. July 9, 1742; cordwainer and mariner; lived in Lynn; m. Miss Elizabeth Phillips of Boston Feb. 25, 1773; and probably d. before 1796.

115—VIII. ALICE⁵, b. Sept. 22, 1744; m. Ezra Newhall of Salem before 1782. She was his wife in 1796.
116—IX. ANNA⁵, b. Sept. 17, 1746; m. Ezra Burrill of Salem, cordwainer, Feb. 22, 1770; and was living in 1782. She d. before 1796.
117—X. MARY⁵, b. Aug. 4, 1748; m. Philip Sawyer of Newbury, cordwainer, April 22, 1773; and removed to Weare, N. H., in 1788.

50

EBENEZER BREED⁴, born in Lynn May 1, 1710. He was a housewright, and lived in Lynn. He married Rebecca Phillips of Boston Nov. 29, 1737; and died Sept. 26, 1762, aged fifty-two. She survived him. His estate was valued at about £772.

Children, born in Lynn :—

118—I. RICHARD⁵, b. Sept. 11, 1738. *See below (118).*
119—II. AMOS⁵, b. Nov. 4, 1739. *See below (119).*
120—III. EBENEZER⁵, b. May 1, 1741. *See below (120).*
121—IV. REBECCA⁵, b. Dec. 29, 1742; probably m. Enoch Collins at Hampton Jan. 4, 1764.
122—V. SAMUEL⁵, b. April 10, 1747. *See below (122).*
123—VI. JAMES⁵, b. April 19, 1749. *See below (123).*
124—VII. ELIZABETH⁵, b. March 19, 1751; m. Jedediah Purinton, cordwainer, April 27, 1773; and was living in 1817.
125—VIII. WILLIAM⁵, b. Feb. 20, 1753; lived in Lynn, cordwainer; and d. Oct. 28, 1817, probably unmarried.
126—IX. SIMEON⁵, b. Sept. 13, 1755. *See below (126).*
127—X. RUTH⁵, b. about 1758; m. Micajah Alley of Lynn, cordwainer, April 29, 1778; and was living in 1818.

52

BENJAMIN BREED⁴, born in Lynn July 4, 1715. He was a cordwainer and husbandman, and lived in Lynn. He married Ruth Allen of Mendon Nov. 27, 1747; and died 7 : 6 mo : 1798. She died in Lynn April 11, 1811, aged eighty-six years and six months.

Children, born in Lynn :—

128—I. JABEZ⁵, b. Dec. 7, 1748. *See below (128).*

129—II. KEZIAH⁵, b. Aug. 14, 1750; m. Abner
Hood 11: 6 mo: 1783.

130—III. ABRAHAM⁵, b. April 8, 1752. *See below (130)*.

131—IV. RUTH⁵, b. Feb. 18, 1754; m. Matthew
Hawkes of Philadelphia, cordwain-
er, 1: 6 mo: 1774; d. Aug. 19,
1776.

132—V. NATHAN⁵, b. Feb. 19, 1756.

133—VI. BENJAMIN⁵, b. Feb. 23, 1758. *See
below (133)*.

134—VII. ANNA⁵, b. Nov. 26, 1761; d. Nov. 14,
1763.

135—VIII. EBENEZER⁵, b. May 12, 1766. See
the History of Lynn, edition of
1865, page 519.

65

THEOPHILUS BREED⁵, born in Lynn
Aug. 2, 1719. He was a cordwainer,
coaster and yeoman, and lived in Lynn.
He married, first, Martha Newhall Dec.
10, 1745; and she died April 17, 1749,
aged twenty-six. He married, second,
Mary Newhall Dec. 12, 1751; and she
was his wife in 1782. He conveyed all
his estate to his sons, Joel and Joseph, in
1784; and died Nov. 17, 1811, aged
ninety-two.

Children, born in Lynn :—

136—I. LYDIA⁶, b. Aug. 17, 1746; m. Benjamin Johnson Jan. 27, 1774.

137—II. MARTHA⁶, b. Jan. 17, 1748-9; m.
Ebenezer Newhall Aug. 23, 1783;
and she was his wife in 1820.

138—III. JOEL⁶, b. Jan. 28, 1755; yeoman;
lived in Lynn; and d., probably unmarried, Jan. 12, 1825, aged nearly
seventy.

139—IV. JOSEPH⁶, b. April 30, 1763; yeoman;
lived in Lynn; d. Aug. 4, 1816.

71

JOSEPH BREED⁵, born in Lynn Jan. 1,
1731-2. He lived in Lynn; and married
Ruth Breed (79) Jan. 26, 1758.

Children, born in Lynn :—

140—I. MATTHEW⁶, b. Oct. 27, 1758. *See
below (140)*.

141—II. JONATHAN⁶, b. May 15, 1761; cordwainer and mariner; lived in Lynn.

142—III. RUTH⁶, b. Feb. 24, 1763; d. Aug. 24,
1765.

73

EPHRAIM BREED, ESQ.⁵, born in Lynn
May 26, 1736. He was a chairmaker
and yeoman, and lived in Lynn. He was
called " esquire " in his later years, and

was a town officer. He married Susan
Mansfield Nov. 22, 1762 ; and she d.
Sept. 22, 1806, at the age of seve..
one. He died April 4, 1812, aged s:
enty-five.

Children, born in Lynn :—

143—I. ——⁶, buried Nov. 3, 1763.

144—II. ——⁶, buried Nov. 3, 1763.

145—III. ABIGAIL⁶, b. Nov. 28, 1765; pro..
m. Thomas Chever, jr., Ma,
1797 (6?).

146—IV. JOSEPH⁶, bapt. June 5, 1768; d. y
buried Aug. 29, 1769.

147—V. SUSANNA⁶, b. May 8, 1768; prob..
m. William Newhall Nov. 9, 17

148—VI. MARY⁶, b. May 6, 1770; prob...
Daniel Rust Witt Nov. 18, 176.

149—VII. JOSEPH⁶, b. Dec. 18, 1771. *Se.
(149)*.

150—VIII. SARAH⁶, b. July 19, 1773; pr...
m. John Massey Feb. 19, 1795.

86

ALLEN BREED⁵, born in Lynn April 1.
1744. He was a yeoman, and lived
Lynn. He married Abigail Lin...
March 4, 1766; and they probably
moved about 1777 to Merrimack, N. H.
where they were living in 1780.

Children, born in Lynn :—

151—I. NEHEMIAH⁶, b. March 24, 1767;
Abigail Blaney of Chelsea Ju.. ..
1793.

152—II. ALLEN⁶, b. Feb. 7, 1773. *See i..
(152)*.

153—III. LOVE⁶, b. Jan. 11, 1775 ; m. M..
Shorey Aug. 26, 1797.

89

COL. FREDERICK BREED⁵, born in L...
Aug. 20, 1755. He was a cordwainer
trade ; and was called "gentleman" ..
"esquire." He married, first, Hephz...
Cox May 25, 1775; and she was his w..
in 1778. He married, second, Sa.
Mansfield April 13, 1780; and she d...
of consumption Aug. 23, 1803, age:
fifty-five. He married, third, Mary R...
ardson of Lynnfield (published Dec.
1804) ; and died June 17, 1820, a: ..
age of sixty-four. She died, his wido..
Oct. 19, 1820, aged sixty-two.

Children, born in Lynn :—

154—I. BETSEY⁶, b. March 16, 1778; m. J..
than C. Hill before 1816.

155—II. JOSEPH⁶, b. Jan. 19, 1781; living
1816.

156—III. FREDERICK[5], b. July 1, 1782; living in 1816.

157—IV. WILLIAM[6], b. March 26, 1784; living in 1816.

158—V. MARY[6], b. Nov. 29, 1785; d., of bilious fever, Oct. 9, 1803, aged seventeen.

159—VI. SALLY[6], b. June 28, 1787; m. James Burrill Jan. 5, 1806.

160—VII. ALLEN[6], b. March 6, 1789; living, 1816.

93

JOSIAH BREED[5], born in Lynn Dec. 16, 1731. He was a cordwainer, and lived in Lynn. He married, first, Mary Breed Dec. 18, 1755; and she died May 7, 1767, aged thirty-three. He married, second, Hannah Batchelder June 30, 1768; and died Dec. 12, 1790, aged fifty-eight. His wife Hannah survived him, and was distracted in her mind from the time of his death to her own decease, which occurred Aug. 16, 1805, at the age of seventy-six.

Children, born in Lynn:—

161—I. MEHITABLE[6], b. Jan. 8, 1757; m. Theophilus Bacheller Nov. 18 (28?), 1791 (2?); and d. before 1806.

162—II. ALLEN[6], b. July 14, 1759; housewright; probably lived in Peckersfield, N. H., in 1791; was living in 1806.

163—III. NATHANIEL[6] (twin), b. Aug. 31, 1761; d. between 1792 and 1806.

164—IV. CHARLES[6] (twin), b. Aug. 31, 1761. See below (164).

165—V. JOSEPH[6], b. March 29, 1764. See below (165).

166—VI. MARY[6], b. April 29, 1772; m. Elijah Downing April 7, 1799.

98

NEHEMIAH BREED[5], born in Lynn Sept. 19, 1736. He was a yeoman, and lived in Lynn. He married Abigail Breed (111) Jan. 2, 1759; and died March 23, 1809, aged seventy-two. She died at Nahant, being buried Sept. 2, 1763.

Child, born in Lynn:—

167—I. WILLIAM[6], b. Sept. 21, 1759. See below (167).

100

ISAIAH BREED[5], born in Lynn Oct. 25, 1724. He was at first a cordwainer, and subsequently a yeoman. He married

Miss Hannah Estes April 12, 1748; and she died in Lynn 30: 7: 1808, aged eighty-eight years, ten months and one day. He died in Lynn 13: 4: 1809, aged eighty-four.

Children, born in Lynn:—

168—I. DESIRE[6], b. Feb. 16, 1748-9; was "Desire Breed" in 1801.

169—II. LOIS[6], b. July 10, 1750; m. James Alley of Lynn, cordwainer, April 25, 1769; and was living in 1801.

170—III. HANNAH[6], b. Jan. 24, 1751; d., unmarried, 14: 1: 1835, in Lynn.

171—IV. EUNICE[6], b. Nov. 4, 1753; m. Benjamin Chase, from Swansea, cordwainer, Nov. 17, 1773; and was living in 1801.

172—V. JAMES[6], b. Jan. 24, 1755. See below (172).

173—VI. MARY[6], b. July 18, 1757; m. Richard Holder, late of Nantucket, cordwainer, 14: 4: 1784; and was living in 1801.

174—VII. MOSES[6], b. Nov. 23, 1758; killed with a cart 13: 11: 1769.

175—VIII. EBENEZER[6], b. May 12, 1763; d. Sept. 13, 1763.

101

NATHAN BREED[5], born in Lynn Oct. 7, 1726. He was a cordwainer and yeoman, and lived in Lynn. He married, first, Keziah Buxton of Danvers Oct. 3, 1754; and she was his wife in 1765. He married, second, Sarah Alley Oct. 27, 1774; and she was his wife in 1797. He died in 1803; his will, dated 24: 7: 1797, being proved Oct. 10, 1803.

Children, born in Lynn:—

176—I. JAMES[6], b. Aug. 26, 1754; d. young (?).

177—II. ABIGAIL[6], b. June 20, 1757; was "Abigail Breed" in 1797.

178—III. JAMES[6], b. Feb. 1, 1759. See below (178).

179—IV. KEZIAH[6], b. April 10, 1761; d. young.

180—V. BUXTON[6], b. May 7, 1763.

181—VI. KEZIAH[6], b. 1: 12 mo: 1765; m. Rufus Newhall of Lynn, cordwainer, 26: 12: 1787; and was living in 1797.

182—VII. ELIZABETH[6], youngest daughter; m. Nehemiah Silsbe of Lynn, cordwainer, 18: 3: 1795.

102

AMOS BREED[5], born in Lynn Aug. 14, 1728. He was a mariner and fisherman, and lived in Lynn. He married Ruth

Newhall Oct. 1, 1754; and she was his wife in 1771 being deceased in 1798. He died in Lynn 5 : 5 : 1776.

Children, born in Lynn :—

183—I. AMOS[6], b. Aug. 31, 1755; d. in 1775.
184—II. ELIZABETH[6], b. June 7, 1758; probably m. Zachariah Attwell July 16, 1778.
185—III. AARON[6], b. March 7, 1761. *See below* (*185*).
186—IV. BENJAMIN NEWHALL[6], b. June 11, 1763. *See below* (*186*).
187—V. THEOPHILUS[6], b. Aug. 11, 1765. *See below* (*187*).
188—VI. JAMES[6], b. July 15, 1768. *See below* (*188*).
189—VII. MARY[6], b. Jan. 16, 1771; m. Ezra Allen of Lynn March 19, 1789.

110

EZRA BREED[5], born in Lynn March 16, 1733. He was a cordwainer and yeoman, and lived in Lynn. He married Huldah Breed (97) Aug. 29, 1757; and she died Oct. 5, 1817, aged eighty-six. He died Aug. 23, 1821, aged eighty-eight.

Children, born in Lynn :—

190—I. ELEANOR[6], b. July 4, 1758; d. —: 2 mo: 1793.
191—II. NATHAN[6], b. Oct. 13, 1760; yeoman and cordwainer; lived in Lynn; wife Mary, 1823; d. in Lynn Dec. 30, 1823, aged sixty-three, probably childless; devised his house, barn, etc., to his nephew William E. Breed; and bequeathed one thousand dollars to the Preparative Meeting of Friends, the income to be used for the support of the poor Friends of the Meeting of Friends in Lynn.
192—III. SARAH[6], b. July 10, 1762; m. Samuel Johnson of Newbury 11 : 4 mo: 1783; and d. 9 : 2 mo: 1798.
193—IV. SAMUEL[6], b. May 22, 1764; d. June 13, 1775.
194—V. ALICE[6], b. May 12, 1766; d. 3 : 8 mo: 1819.
195—VI. WILLIAM[6], b. May 13, 1768. *See below* (*195*).

112

ZEPHANIAH BREED[5], born in Lynn March 10, 1737. He was a saddler and yeoman, and lived in Lynn until 1776, when he removed to Weare, N. H., settling at the "Centre," where he kept a tavern. He married, first, Miss Ruth Phillips April 27, 1762; and she was his wife in 1777. He married, second, Abigail —— and she was his wife in 1792. He d. in the summer of 1792 : his will, d —: 16 : 7 : 1792, being proved Aug. 2 1792.

Children :—

196—I. ABIGAIL PHILLIPS[6], b. Jan. 21, 1763 in Lynn; m. Edmund Johnson Deering, N. H., yeoman in 1793
197—II. MARY[6], b. in 1763; m. Edmund of Weare, yeoman, before 1792.
198—III. ELIZABETH[6], living in 1796.
199—IV. DANIEL[6], b. April 9, 1765; lived Weare and Unity, N. H.; first wright; m., first, Mary Chase 1794; she d. in 1796; m., Abigail Hodgdon in 1799; she 1802; m., third, Mary Austin Rochester, N. H.; she d. in 18— m., fourth, Betsey Peaslee in 1— he d. in 1852; she d. April 10, 18— he had eight children.
200—V. ZEPHANIAH[6], b. in 1771; yeoman lived in Weare in 1796.
201—VI. CORNELIA[6], b. Feb. 18, 1774; Enoch Page of Weare, yeoman, before 1796.
202—VII. JONATHAN[6], b. Nov. 29, 1776; Lydia Johnson of Unity, N. H.; d. Dec. 22, 1859. They had children.

118

RICHARD BREED[5], born in Lynn Sept 11, 1738. He was a housewright, and lived in Lynn. He married Anna —— in or before 1767 : and died June 28 1789, at the age of fifty. She died, his widow, in Lynn, Nov. 9, 1822, aged seventy-eight. She was born 25 : 12 1742-3.

Children, born in Lynn :—

203—I. REBECCA[6], b. Oct. 16, 1767; d. Dec. 4, 1788.
204—II. ANNA[6], b. Sept. 17, 1771; d. Sept 23, 1790.
205—III. AMEY[6], b. Feb. 13, 1774; under guardianship; d., unmarried, Feb 3, 1834, aged nearly sixty.
206—IV. SARAH[6], b. July 30, 1776; m. Samuel Silsbe, jr., 19 : 11 : 1794; and was livi g in 1823.
207—V. RICHARD[6], b. Aug. 3, 1778; lived in Lynn; m. Comfort —— before 18—
208—VI. JUDITH[6], b. Oct. 30, 1781; d. Oct. 7 1800, aged nearly nineteen.
209—VII. ALICE[6], b. 10 : 17 : 1784; m. Jonathan Conner of Lynn (from Kensington N. H.) 18 : 2 : 1807.

119

AMOS BREED[5], born in Lynn Nov. 4, 1739. He was a cordwainer, and lived in Lynn, being a Quaker. He married Miss Ruth Estes April 30, 1766 ; and she died March 1, 1787. He died Aug. 19, 1821, aged eighty-one.

Children, born in Lynn :—

210—I. WILLIAM[6], b. Feb. 3, 1767; d. Feb. 17, 1767.

211—II. DEBORAH[6], b. April 24, 1768; d. April 12, 1772.

212—III. AMOS[6], b. Aug. 19, 1771; cordwainer; lived in Lynn; and d., of dysentery, Aug. 26, 1848, aged seventy-seven.

213—IV. WALTER[6], b. April 1, 1774; d. April 28, 1774.

214—V. DEBORAH[6], b. Nov. 23, 1775; d., unmarried, 2: 6 mo: 1801.

215—VI. RUTH[6], b. July 30, 1778; d. June 22, 1793.

216—VII. HANNAH[6], b. Feb. 16, 1781; m. Ebenezer Burrill, jr., March 27, 1809; and was living in 1834.

217—VIII. REBECCA[6], b. June 17, 1784; unmarried in 1834.

120

EBENEZER BREED[5], born in Lynn May 1, 1741. He lived in Weare, N. H.; and married, first, Lydia Basset Sept. 3, 1763 ; and, second, Mary Green.

Children :—

218—I. EBENEZER[6], b. April 17, 1764; m. Martha Peaslee of Newton, N. H.; and d. in 1848.

219—II. ENOCH[6], b. Jan. 23, 1766; cordwainer; lived in Lynn with an uncle until 1780, when he returned to his father in Weare; m., first, Martha Mower Oct. 15, 1794; and, second, Lydia Frye of Bolton.

220—III. STEPHEN[6], b. May 8, 1768; m. Rhoda Chase; and d. in 1827.

221—IV. CONTENT[6], b. Oct. 27, 1769; m. Daniel Gove.

222—V. LYDIA[6], b. April 12, 1776; m. William Breed (195) of Lynn.

223—VI. REBECCA[6], b. Nov. 26, 1777; m. Josiah Gove.

224—VII. ISAIAH[6], b. Oct. 24, 1779; m. Sally Gove; farmer; and d. March 17, 1849.

225—VIII. RUTH[6], b. May 26, 1782; m. Isaac Bassett of Lynn 21: 4: 1802.

226—IX. WILLIAM[6], b. June 8, 1784; m. Sally Dixy of Salem.

227—X. MARY[6], b. July 3, 1786; m. Ezekiel Estes of Lynn 23: 10: 1805.

228—XI. MICAJAH[6], b. Oct. 20, 1788; lived in Weare, Hamilton and Unity; m. Ruth Gove in 1811.

229—XII. ANNA[6], b. Feb. 1, 1791; m. Elisha Parker of Lynn.

230—XIII. PHEBE[6], b. April 6, 1793; m. Abner Jones; lived in Great Falls and Lynn; she d. in 1856.

231—XIV. SAMUEL D.[6], b. June 12, 1795; m. Elizabeth H. Maddock; lived in Philadelphia, Pa.

122

SAMUEL BREED[5], born in Lynn April 10, 1747. He lived in Lynn ; and married Miss Theodate Puritun April 13, 1771. He died Jan. 21, 1821 ; and she died Sept. 14, 1836.

Children, born in Lynn :—

232—I. CHARLOTTE[6], b. 8: 3 mo: 1772; d. 13: 3: 1772.

233—II. CHARLOTTE[6], b. April 4, 1773; m. Gamaliel Wallis Oliver of Salem Oct. 28, 1807.

234—III. ANNA[6], b. July 16, 1775; m. Jonathan Boyce of Danvers, cordwainer, 26: 10: 1796.

235—IV. SAMUEL[6], b. Nov. 18, 1778; lived in Lynn; m. Susanna Morrill of Falmouth, Me., 20: 1: 1813; d. Oct. 22, 1826, aged forty-seven.

236—V. EBENEZER[6], b. March 18, 1786; d. March 2, 1831.

237—VI. DELIA[6], b. April 20, 1789; m. John Newhall, jr., 26: 11: 1817.

123

JAMES BREED[5], born in Lynn April 19, 1749. He was a blacksmith, and lived in Lynn, being a Quaker. He married Miss Rebecca Basset 21: 4: 1773 ; and died Jan. 1, 1810. She survived him, and died, his widow, Oct. 30, 1829, aged seventy-five.

Children, born in Lynn :—

238—I. EUNICE[6], b. Jan. 26, 1774; m. Joseph Fuller of Lynn, cordwainer, 18: 3: 1795.

239—II. REBECCA[6], b. Nov. 12, 1777; d., unmarried, April 6, 1837, aged fifty-nine.

240—III. JAMES[6], b. 3: 25: 1780; d. March 28, 1795, aged fifteen.

241—IV. HANNAH[6], b. June 16, 1782; d. March 6, 1790.

242—V. WILLIAM BASSETT[6], b. Sept. 11, 1791; lived in Lynn; m. Miss Urania Chase of Somerset 15: 6: 1814; and d. June 21, 1833, leaving children.

126

SIMEON BREED[5], born in Lynn Sept. 13, 1755. He lived in Lynn, being a heel-maker, and married Lois Gould Dec. 22, 1783. He died March 21, 1829; and she died, of palsy, Nov. 6, 1845, at the age of eighty-seven.

Children, born in Lynn :—

243—I.   LYDIA[6], b. Oct. 27, 1784.
244—II. ASA[6], b. Oct. 14, 1786; d. Aug. 13, 1813.
245—III. SIMEON[6], b. Nov. 19, 1788; d. Sept. 21, 1790.
246—IV. ANNA[6], b. Sept. 9, 1790.
247—V.   SIMEON[6], b. Nov. 9, 1792; d. Aug. 26, 1813.
248—VI. ABIGAIL[6], b. June 27, 1794; d. Aug. 15, 1794.
249—VII. ABIGAIL FARRINGTON[6], b. April 11, 1797.
250—VIII. BENJAMIN ALLEY[6], b. Feb. 22, 1799; d. Sept. 9, 1813.
251—IX. RICHARD[6], b. May 18, 1800; d. Nov. 3, 1803.

128

JABEZ BREED[5], born in Lynn Dec. 7, 1748. He was a cordwainer and hus-bandman, and lived in Lynn. He mar-ried Miss Mary Bassett 19 : 4 : 1775 ; and she was his wife in 1791. He died Oct. 13, 1814, aged sixty-five.

Children, born in Lynn :—

252—I.   BASSETT[6], b. Oct. 24, 1775 ; m. Nan-cy Nichols April 26, 1807.
253—II. RUTH[6], b. Jan. 24, 1780.
254—III. ASA[6], b. Feb. 23, 1783; lived in Lynn; m. Betsey Nichols (pub. May 7, 1809); she d. May 19, 1830, aged forty-one; and he d. Oct. 27, 1841, aged fifty-eight.
255—IV. CONTENT[6], b. April 15, 1785.
256—V.   FRANCIS[6], b. Jan. 7, 1789.

130

ABRAHAM BREED[5], born in Lynn April 8, 1752. He was a cordwainer, and lived in Lynn. He married Miss Sarah Bassett in or before 1783 ; and died Nov. 26, 1831. She survived him about a month, and died Dec. 30, 1831.

Children, born in Lynn :—

257—I.   JOSEPH BASSETT[6], b. Sept. 30, 1783; m. Miss Mary Johnson 23: 9: 1807; and d., of consumption, Oct. 17, 1844, aged sixty-one.
258—II. EUNICE[6], b. May 22, 1788.

259—III. ANNA[6], b. Feb. 6, 1791; m. Fran. Johnson 23: 7: 1817.
260—IV. SARAH[6], b. Sept. 20, 1798; m. J. B. Chase Dec. 10, 1815.

133

BENJAMIN BREED[5], born in Lynn Feb. 23, 1758. He lived in Lynn, and mar-ried Abigail Alley Jan. 17, 1788 ; and she died 15 : 9 : 1840. He died July 2, 1843.

Children, born in Lynn :—

261—I.   DEBORAH[6], b. May 6, 1788.
262—II. EBENEZER[6], b. Dec. 27, 1789; d. Jan. 15, 1790.
263—III. RUTH[6], b. Feb. 9, 1791.
264—IV. GEORGE P.[6], b. Dec. 13, 1792; d. Feb. 26, 1796.
265—V.   LYDIA[6], b. Jan. 26, 1795; m. Asa Skelton of Burlington 25: 9: 1819.
266—VI. LUCINDA[6], b. Feb. 21, 1797; d. Nov. 23, 1814.
267—VII. BENJAMIN[6], b. March 24, 1799.
268—VIII. ENOS ALLEY[6], b. Aug. 25, 1800. He m. Lucy B. Pope, who d. Feb. 12, 1840, aged thirty-five; lived in Lynn; cordwainer; d. of bowel complaint and fever Aug. 30, 1848, aged for-ty-seven.
269—IX. KEZIA HOOD[6], b. Nov. 21, 1804; m. Amos Walden Nov. 28, 1827.
270—X.   HARRIET[6], b. Dec. 27, 1806.
271—XI. AMOS ALLEY[6], b. Sept. 6, 1809; d. 15: 9: 1840, on the day his mother died.

140

MATTHEW BREED[6], born in Lynn Oct. 27, 1758. He lived in Lynn ; and mar-ried Miss Sarah Farrington Nov. 7, 1782. She died Feb. 13, 1829; and he died July 29, 1832, aged seventy-three.

Children, born in Lynn :—

272—I.   SALLEY[7], b. Nov. 18, 1783.
273—II. JOSEPH[7], b. June 19, 1785; shoemaker, d., of consumption, May 5, 1844.
274—III. MATTHEW[7], b. Oct. 13, 1786.
275—IV. RUTH[7], b. Sept. 2, 1788.
276—V.   POLLEY[7], b. March 15, 1792.
277—VI. NATHANIEL[7], b. Feb. 28, 1792.
278—VII. EPHRAIM[7], b. June 17, 1794.
279—VIII. JONATHAN[7], b. April 8, 1796.
280—IX. SUSANNA[7], b. Nov. 24, 1798.
281—X.   JOHN[7], b. May 27, 1800.

149

JOSEPH BREED[6], born in Lynn Dec. 18, 1771. He was a yeoman, and lived in Lynn. He married Mary (Polly) Sweet-ser Nov. 17, 1794 ; and died Sept. 30,

1834, at the age of sixty-two. She survived him.

Children, born in Lynn :—

282—I. JOSEPH[7], b. March 28, 1795; cordwainer; and lived in Lynn in 1834.
283—II. POLLY[7], b. Aug. 20, 1797.
284—III. SUSANNA[7], b. Oct. 21, 1799.
285—IV. LYDIA[7], b. Sept. 16, 1802.
286—V. ABIGAIL[7], b. Nov. 23, 1804.
287—VI. HANNAH[7], b. Aug. 22, 1807.
288—VII. EPHRAIM[7], b. March 1, 1810; d. Jan. 1, 1811.
289—VIII. SALLY[7], b. Nov. 20, 1811.
290—IX. LUCY HEADING[7], b. Sept. 10, 1815; m. Josiah B. Stiles May 5, 1842.
291—X. NANCY[7], b. March 5, 1818.

152

ALLEN BREED[6], born in Lynn Feb. 7, 1773. He married Priscilla Southwick (published in Danvers July 2, 1796).

Child, born in Lynn :—

292—I. ALLEN BLANEY[7], bapt. July 9, 1797.

164

CHARLES BREED[6], born in Lynn Aug. 31, 1761. He lived in Lynn, and married Tamer Chever Nov. 1, 1789. He died Feb. 14, 1809.

Children, born in Lynn :—

293—I. MARY[7], b. Aug. 25, 1790; d., of dysentery, Sept. 23, 1795, aged five.
294—II. LYDIA[7], b. Aug. 6, 1792.
295—III. DANIEL CHEVER[7], b. Aug. 17, 1794.
296—IV. NATHANIEL[7], b. Sept. 2, 1796.

165

JOSEPH BREED[6], born in Lynn March 29, 1764. He was a blacksmith alias yeoman, and lived in Lynn. He married (when of Peckersfield, N. H.). Mary Haskell of Lynn Jan. 19, 1789 ; and died Dec. 26, 1806, aged forty-two. She died, his widow, Feb. 2, 1817.

Children, born in Lynn :—

297—I. JOHN[7], b. Nov. 24, 1789; laborer; lived in Lynn ; pauper; d., of consumption, April 9, 1846, aged fifty-six.
298—II. JOSIAH[7], b. March 27, 1791; m. Jane Cragg of Lynn (pub. Sept. 19, 1819); and lived in Lynn.
299—III. DELIVERANCE[7], b. July 13, 1793; m. Joseph Skinner Feb. 13, 1812.
300—IV. HASKEL[7], b. Jan. 2, 1796; d. April 20, 1796, aged three months.
301—V. HASKEL[7], living in 1806.

167

WILLIAM BREED[6], born in Lynn Sept. 21, 1759. He was a yeoman, and lived in Lynn. He married Miss Hannah Bassett 22 : 9 : 1784 ; and she was his wife in 1796. He (" formerly resident at Nahant ") died May 7, 1819, aged fifty-nine.

Children, born in Lynn :—

302—I. NEHEMIAH[7], b. Oct. 14, 1785; lived in Lynn; m. Miss Miriam Alley 15 : 4 : 1812.
303—II. DANIEL[7], b. Jan. 14, 1788; m. Abigail Newhall 18 : 10 : 1820.
304—III. NABBY[7], b. Sept. 1, 1792; d. Aug. 26, 1809.

172

JABEZ BREED[6], born in Lynn Jan. 24, 1755. He was a cordwainer, and lived in Lynn, being a Quaker. He married Miss Lydia Mower April 15, 1778 ; and died 2 : 7 mo : 1780. His estate was appraised at £199, 4s., 6d. She survived him, and married, secondly, John Pratt of Lynn, cordwainer, 19 : 3 : 1783.

Children, born in Lynn :—

305—I. MOSES[7], b. 19: 10: 1778; cordwainer; lived in Lynn, 1797.
306—II. JABEZ[7], b. 15: 8: 1780, posthumous; living in 1809.

178

JAMES BREED[6], born in Lynn Feb. 1, 1759. He was a cordwainer, and subsequently a tallow chandler, and lived in Lynn. He married Miss Hannah Alley 22 : 9 : 1784 ; and she died July 13, 1802. He died, of dropsy, Sept. 18, 1848, aged eighty-nine.

Children, born in Lynn :—

307—I. SARAH[7], b. July 6, 1785; m. John Mower of Lynn 14: 9: 1803.
308—II. ISAIAH[7], b. Oct. 21, 1786; lived in Lynn; state senator; shoe manufacturer; m., first, Mary Blake of Amherst, N. H., 22 : 11: 1809; and, second, Sally P. Moore; and d. May 23, 1859.
309—III. KEZIA[7], b. April 21, 1788; m. Daniel Carter Jan. 5, 1806.
310—IV. LYDIA[7], b. May 20, 1789; m. Daniel Smith 18: 12: 1811.
311—V. CONTENT[7], b. Feb. 13, 1792; d., unmarried, Feb. 5, 1841, aged nearly forty-nine.

312—VI. NATHAN³, b. Jan. 28, 1794.
313—VII. HANNAH³. b. Nov. 8, 1795; d. June 26, 1796.
314—VIII. HANNAH³, b. April 14, 1797; m. Jonathan Buffum, jr., of Salem 15: 5: 1816.
315—IX. JAMES³, b. May 17, 1799; d. Sept. 8, 1825, aged "thirty-five."
316—X. HULDAH³ (twin), b. Dec. 18, 1800; d. Sept. 7, 1801.
317—XI. MARY³ (twin), b. Dec. 18, 1800; d. Sept. 10, 1801.

185

AARON BREED⁶, born in Lynn March 7, 1761. He was a cordwainer, and lived in Lynn. He married, first, Sarah Attwell Oct. 2, 1781; and she died Dec. 26, 1804. He married, second, Mrs. Mary Filebrown, at Groton, Nov. 10, 1805; and he died, of apoplexy, in Lynn, Dec. 23, 1817, aged fifty-six. His wife Mary survived him, and died, his widow, April 30, 1841, aged sixty-five.

Children, born in Lynn :—

318—I. ANNA⁷, b. July 18, 1782; d. Oct. 2, 1782.
319—II. ANNA⁷, b. Sept. 8, 1784.
320—III. RUTH⁷, b. Aug. 10, 1786.
321—IV. SALLY⁷, b. Oct. 18, 1788.
322—V. AARON⁷, b. Jan. 9, 1791.
323—VI. LYDIA⁷, b. July 18, 1792; d., of lung fever, Dec. 15, 1800, aged eight.
324—VII. WARNER⁷, b. July 27, 1794.
325—VIII. HARRIET⁷, b. May 22, 1796; d. May 5, 1803.
326—IX. NABBY BURRILL⁷, b. July 28, 1798.
327—X. FULLERTON⁷, b. Aug. 16, 1799; d. Aug. 29, 1814.
328—XI. ISAAC⁷, b. July 27, 1801; d., of scarlet fever, Jan. 15, 1802.
329—XII. ISAAC⁷, b. Oct. 27, 1802; d. Sept. 1, 1803.
330—XIII. ISAAC⁷, b. ———; d. Jan. 15, 1808.
331—XIV. HORACE ANSON⁷, b. Nov. 19, 1806.
332—XV. JAMES EDWIN⁷, b. Oct. 16, 1808.
333—XVI. HARRIET ALMIRA⁷, b. Sept. 22, 1810; d. Aug. 31, 1834.
334—XVII. HERMIONE⁷, b. March 18, 1812; m. George Hood.
335—XVIII. LYDIA MARIA⁷, b. Feb. 22, 1816; m. John C. Abbott Aug. 11, 1836.

186

BENJAMIN NEWHALL BREED⁶, born in Lynn June 11, 1763. He was a carman, and lived in Lynn. He married (when he was of New Haven) Ann Parrott Oct. 14, 1787; and died Feb. 16, 1847, aged eighty-three. She was his wife in 1802.

Children, born in Lynn :—

336—I. AMOS⁷, b. June 18, 1789.
337—II. ——⁷, b. Jan. 30, 1791.
338—III. SUKEY⁷, b. Sept. 9, 1792.
339—IV. LYDIA HUSEY⁷, b. Sept. 23 (25?), 1794; m. John Mansfield, 3d, Sept. 21, 1815.
340—V. NEWHALL⁷, b. July 23 (25?), 17..; d. Oct. 8, 1797.
341—VI. REBECCA⁷, b. March 4, 1798.
342—VII. IRA⁷, b. April 11, 1800; m. Elizabeth Lombard Aug. 12, 1829; and she d. Dec. 14, 1832.
343—VIII. ANNA⁷, b. May 15, 1802; d. Oct. 30, 1841, aged thirty-nine.

187

THEOPHILUS BREED⁶, born in Lynn Aug. 11, 1765. He was a cordwainer, and lived in Lynn. He married Theodate Purinton of Kensington, N. H. March 27, 1793.

Children, born in Lynn :—

344—I. LAVINA BURT⁷, b. Nov. 27, 1794; m. Jacob Huntington of Henniker, N. H., 21: 10: 1829.
345—II. ELIZA ANN⁷, b. Dec. 3, 1796.
346—III. THEOPHILUS NEWHALL⁷, b. May 2, 1805; m. Sylvina Neal May 19, 1833.

188

JAMES BREED⁶, born in Lynn July 15, 1768. He was a cordwainer, and lived in Lynn. He married Miss Phebe Nichols of Berwick 19: 9: 1798; and they were living in 1825.

Children, born in Lynn :—

347—I. STEPHEN⁷, b. Aug. 24, 1799; d. April 11, 1800.
348—II. PHEBE NICHOLS⁷, b. Sept. 11, 180..; d. Dec. 6, 1825, aged twenty-three.
349—III. MARY ELLEN⁷, b. Sept. 13, 1804; d. of brain fever, Jan. 30, 1847, aged forty-two.
350—IV. STEPHEN NICHOLS⁷, b. Oct. 12, 18..; m. Elizabeth Breed Dec. 11, 1828.
351—V. HANNAH COLLINS⁷, b. Dec. 1, 180..; d. Aug. 10, 1827.
352—VI. JAMES ALBERT⁷, b. 22: 4: 1811.

195

WILLIAM BREED⁶, born in Lynn May 13, 1768. He was a yeoman and cordwainer, and lived in Lynn. He married, first, Lydia Breed (222) in or before 1797; and she died Dec. 1, 1799. He

married, second, Lydia —— before 1806; and she was his wife in 1814. He died Dec. 31, 1846, aged seventy-eight.

Children, born in Lynn :—

353—I. EBENEZER², b. Nov. 13, 1797; d. Sept. 16, 1812.

354—II. MARY ELIZABETH², b. Feb. 23, 1806; m. Charles Merritt of Lynn March 11, 1828.

355—III. WILLIAM EBENEZER², b. March 20, 1814; m. Abigail Eastman Oct. 5, 1837.

WILL OF JOHN PICKWORTH.

The will of John Pickworth was proved in the Salem quarterly court 25 : 9 : 1663. The following is a copy of the original instrument on file in the office of the clerk of courts at Salem, volume IX, leaf 71.

The last will and testement of John Peckworth made the 27 of the 4 : month 1663

I John Peckworth being weake & seke of bodey but of Perfet memorey haue ordayned this as my laft will & Testyment

Imprymes I giuese and bequeth vnto my wellbeloued ‖ wife ‖ An Peckworth my wholle eftate as hows land and Catell and howshowlld goods and fhe to injoye the same as long as she icueth if liucing and dying in a widows estate but if fhe other wyis changh her condition and marey then fhe only to haue her thirds of wᵗ then : and after her changh eyther by deth or marege Then my Elldeft sonne John Peckworth is to haue the hows medow And 25 aekers of land wᵗʰ the pᵗ of the nek that lyeth betwene Aberham Wᵗyare and my sellfe : fᵣ the reft of my land which is 30 akers bowght of Robert morgon with the medow that belongeth to yet my 3 souns Samuell Joseph and Benciemen is to haue the same as fore mentioned by my son John as he is to haue his after my wife soe they to inJoye the sam allsoe : and my sonn Samuell is to haue the 6 aekers that lyeth vpon the nek nex to Robert Leachs lot that was giuen me by the Plantation ʃ manchester ‖ and the land that lyeth

by the saw mill : and for my Part of the samill I thus disspose of yet I leauef yet wᵗʰ my wife as the reft of my eftate only my sonn Samuell to act in her behalfe with the reft of my fortuen and he to be Payed for his labower and to haue half the Profect that yet brings in if the eftate howld out then my to elldeft dawghters Ruth marfterson and Nancw Coollens is to haue 40 fhillens a peace when the reft fore mentioned haue theyers : and to my yongeft son Beniemen and my yongeft Dawghter Abegell I giue a cow callfe the same to be thyer after my decese and the Profet that comes in by the increase furthermore yet is my will that if the hows medow & land that my son John is to haue cometh to more then a dobell Portion when the eftate is pryesed then he is to elld up out of his only he is left to his leberty for the redemeing of his land and to pay wᵗ yet comes to for to make up the sengell Portions : and for the beter Performence of this my will : I apoynt my wife An Peckworth wᵗʰ my to Sons John and Samuell to be Admineftraters and defyers and apoynts my well beloued friends Thomas Jones and William Benet to be ouer scares where unto I here set my hand

Witness
the mark ʳ[John Pickworth
John Hutson
Samuell friend

BRADFORD NOTES.

Stephen Bradford married Judith Worthen May 22, 1740.—Amesbury town records.

Robert Bradford lived in Beverly, 1670-1706; aged forty-seven in 1673; wife Hannah; yeoman and shoreman; died in Beverly Jan. 13, 1707, aged eighty; administration granted on his estate to William Bradford of Beverly Dec. 30, 1706. The inventory of his estate amounted to £203, 2s., 8d. Children, born in Beverly: 1. John, born May 29, 1672; 2. Robert, baptized March 19, 1675-6; 3. Martha, baptized Aug. 29, 1676.—Records.

SALEM IN 1700. NO. 29.

BY SIDNEY PERLEY.

The map on page 160 includes that part of South Salem, or "South fields," as it has been called since the first settlement of Salem, which is bounded on the north and west by the channel of South river, on the east by the harbor, and on the south by the present Fairfield and Lagrange streets, South fields comprises the peninsula south of South river; and was under the control of the proprietors of the South fields, especially that portion south of the great gate. The fields were used in common, although the lots were owned individually, until about 1743. The map is based on actual surveys and title deeds, and is drawn on a scale of four hundred and fifty feet to an inch. It shows the location of all houses that were standing there in 1700.

Stage point was so called in 1640, and was known by that name until within a few years. The whole of that peninsula is now generally known as The Point.

The brace marked "a", on the map, shows where Pond street begins; "b", Ropes street; "c", Porter street; "d", Cedar street; "e", Everett street; "f", Dow street; and "g", Harbor street.

When the mill was built in 1664, a new road was laid out to it from what is now High street.[*] The bridge over Forest river, at what is now the lead mills, was built by the towns of Salem and Marblehead together in the winter of 1663-4,[†] but the road from Marblehead (now the larger portion of Lafayette street) to the new mill bridge was not located until the spring of 1666. It was laid out by the committees of Marblehead and Salem; and the following is a copy of the record of their returne :—

The Returne: of thofe that weare Apoynted to laye owt the Common hie waye: betwixt salem towne and marblhed: is vydz: that the waye: shall: lye: out of the towne of marblhed: as: the Common Cart waye now lyeth: fower Rodds

*Town Records, volume II, page 64.
†Town Records, volume II, page 52.

wyde and soe to Runn: fower Rodds broade: a v.. haue m'ked trees: neere the way as It is Comanly vfed: only vppon the midle of the playne: Leaue the common waye: and goe: som.. one the Left hand of the ould waye accordu.. thee trees are marked and soe to Runn: f.. Rodd wyde: vntill wee com to: the bridg: then to goe fower Rodd wyde: vntill wee Co: the litle gate : that standeth In the south fe: ffence: and then wee haue determined that t waye shall Runn : throgh at that gate vpp.. strayght lyne vnto an ould tree that lyeth n.. that common hye waye : in the south ffeeld a.. soe to goe along the waye : as it is now vfe.. through the the south ffeeld vnto the mill dam.. and the breath of the whole waye through t.. south ffeeld to be one Rodd wyde And that t.. is owre Joynt agreement : wee haue heare v.. sett oure hands this 24 of Aprill : 1666
     William Hawthorne
     Henry Bartholmew
     Richard **T** his
     Rowland **I** mark:
     Samuell Ward:*

There was a little gate of the Sout. fields proprietors where it is marked o.. the map near the mill; but the great gate in the fence that divided the common lands of the proprietors from the lands of Ruck, Curtice and Browne was at the entrance of the lane that led to Stage point. The fence ran from the mi.. pond to the cove of the harbor.

This main street, as shown on the map, is now called by three names, From the bridge at the mill, which ran over the old dam, to the top of the hill has been called Mill street since 1812, and probably earlier. It was called a highway in 1676; highway leading to Marblehead in 1765; and South street in 1804. That part which is now Washington street was called the common road or highway in 1690; highway that leads to Marblehead in 1706; highway leading through ye Souf field, 1718 ; ye way to Marblehead, 175S; road leading from Salem to Marblehead, 1760; South street, 1795; and old road leading from mill bridge to Marblehead, 1818. That part which is now Lafayett street was called the lane commonly called Curtice's lane in 1694 ; highway, 1697; road leading from Salem to Mar..

*Town Records of Salem, volume II, page S..

blehead, 1779; South street, 1806; a
country road, 1810; the road leading
from the new South bridge to Marblehead,
1818; the public road, 1824; and Lafayette street, 1838.

The private lane leading from the mill
past the three houses was in use very
early, at least as soon as the houses were
built. In 1735, it was called ye way on
ye top of ye hill by ye mill stream; and
it is still in use, leading to Dodge street.

The ancient lane to Stage point was
laid out in 1678. At a meeting of the
selectmen of Salem, held 23 : 6 : 1678,
it was "Agred by the Selectmen, wᵗʰ
Daniell Romball & James Polland that
there shall be a highway through ther
land in the South feild of twenty foot
wide into Stage point to be allowed one
halfe by Sd Romboll out of his land &
the other halfe out of James Polands
land."* It was called ye way that leads
down to Stage point in 1706; and ye
highway that goes into Stage point in
1709. It was probably abandoned about
1764, and in that year it is described as
land formerly improved as a way to Stage
point.

Pond street was called New street in
1810.

Porter street was called a street leading
from Lafayette street to the mill pond in
1848; and Porter street in 1858. Porter
street court was called a private way in
1849.

Cedar street was, in 1839, a private way
recently laid out called Cedar street.

Everett street was called a way in
1831, and a forty-foot road lately laid
out in 1835.

Dow street was so called in 1807.

Harbor street was called the highway
leading from the highway leading from
Salem to Marblehead to Stage point, so
called, in 1779; the new road leading
down to Stage point, 1781; lane leading
from the County road to the river, 1781;
the road that leads down to the point,
1781; and Harbor street in 1800.

*Salem Town Records.

Ward street was described as land reserved for a new street forty feet wide in
1827; and was called a new street in
1837.

Peabody street was called by that name
in 1827.

Salem street was called a street from
Harbor street lately laid out in 1806; a
thirty-foot way, 1806; and a private way
in 1828.

The water to the west of the premises
was called the South river in 1671; ye
mill pond, 1675; ye mill stream, 1724;
and the river, 1741. The water to the
north of the premises was called ye
South river in 1678; the sea, 1778; and
the river, 1781. The water to the east
was called ye cove in 1678; ye harbor,
1678; Salem harbor, 1690; cove coming
out of ye harbor, 1709; the sea, 1778;
South river, 1781.

In the sketches that follow, after 1700,
titles and deeds referred to pertain to
the houses and land adjoining, and not
always to the whole lot, the design being,
after that date, to give the history of the
houses then standing principally.

Grist Mill. The town of Salem granted liberty to Mr. Will Browne, Mr. Corwine and Mr. Price, 29 : 9 : 1659, to
"build a Grift-mill vppon the South
River above mʳ Rucks houfe were it may
be Conuenient."* The mill was not
built at this time, however. The need of
another mill was again brought before the
town, at a general town meeting held 2 :
1 mo : 1662-3; but John Trask, in behalf
of his father, who conducted the mill on
North river, agreed to make as good meal
as at Lynn, and that when they could
not supply the town for want of water or
in any other respect, they would send it
to Lynn upon their own charge and have
it ground there, and the matter of building another mill again postponed.† Five
months later, however, at a town meeting,
held 22 : 6 : 1663, it was "ordered that
there is libertie granted for buildinge of a

*Town Records, volume II, page 1.
†Town Records, volume II, page 43.

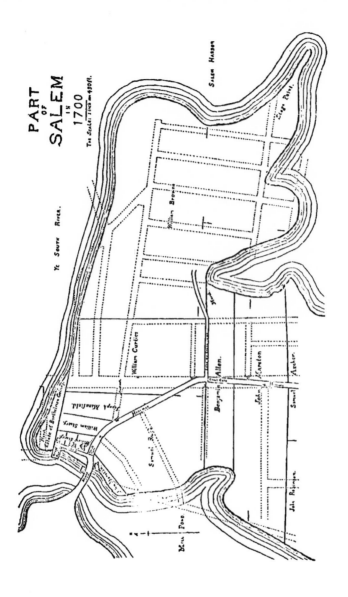

PART
OF
SALEM
IN
1700
The Scale: 1 Inch = 450 ft.

Ye South River.

Cliffs of Buckbisbury Co.

Mary Hollingsworth.

Elias Mason

William Story

Joseph Mansfield

Mill Pond

Samuel Beadle

Highway

William Curtice

Benjamin Allen

John Mason

John Marston

Samuel Archer

John Robinson

William Browne

Liger Point.

South Harbor.

mill ouer the fouth riuer neare mʳ Rucks."*
At a meeting of the selectmen, 8 : 8 :
1663, Walter Price, Henry Bartholmew,
John Gardner, George Gardner and Samuel Gardner were given " libertie to builde
a mill ouer the south riuer neare mʳ
Rucks provided it be built in two yeares
or to lofe their privilidge."† The proprietors of the mill proceeded to build a
dam and lay the foundations of the mill,
and John Pickering and Thomas Pickering, sons of John Pickering, who then
owned the "Broadfield" of Governor
Endecott, across the river, forcibly prevented the construction of the dam, and
brought an action against the said proprietors for damming up the channel of the
river below their land and hindering them
from coming by water to their land or improving it for a building place for vessels.
At the same time (11 : 9 mo : 1664), the
proprietors of the mill brought an action
against Mr. Pickering " for damage to
them by pulling up the stakes that the
millwright had set downe for placeing the
mill, and throwing part of their timber
into the River and other part of it a drift,
and throwing their wheele-barrows and
other working tools into the River by
night and indeavoring after the mill was
set down to turne it into the Channel by
night, to their great damage," etc. The
actions were tried together. It was finally
agreed between Mr. Pickering and the
proprietors of the mill that Mr. Pickering
" in regard of his damage by ftoppinge
vpp the riuer belowe his lande fhall be
alowed him twentie pounds pvided that
the ppriet︭ of the mill as aforefd fhall
haue free libertie to fett the mill where
now the dam is begun and what grounde
they fhall make vfe of to fett the mill
vpon and fullie to finish the dam he the
fd Jo : Pickeringe doth fullie grant vnto
them and will faue them harmlefs ag︭ft
Mathew Woodall or any other that fhall
molest them or Claime any damage from
the fd ppriet︭ concerninge the pmiffis."‡

*Town Records, volume II, page 47.
†Town Records, volume II, page 49.
‡Town Records, volume II, page 61.

The mill was completed that summer.

A dwelling house was also subsequently
built for the miller to live in. See section headed "John Marston House"
beyond.

The mill was originally a single grist
or corn-mill, and continued to be such
until about 1720. The miller was William Stacey from before 1682 to his death
in 1723. Because of this fact, this place
of industry was called by his name for
several years after his decease, being
known as Stacey's mills in 1735. Another
mill (that is, it is presumed, another set
of stones and machinery) was added
about 1720; and still another set about
1727. These three sets of stones or mills
continued in use until after the Revolution. They were known as the South
mills as early as 1699, and as late as 1840.
Thomas Brewer was the miller from as
early as 1729 till as late as 1739. Thomas
Osborn was the miller in 1743 and as late
as about 1760. Daniel Malloen was the
miller in 1761, and until his death in the
spring of 1783. They were known as
Malloon's mills as late as 1831. About
1769, a "scythe mill" was added, and
also a granary, the latter being in existence in 1804. The "scythe mill" existed in 1776, but was gone before 1811.
One of the grist mills was taken out before 1827. A chocolate mill was established in or before 1811, and run by
James Brown. It was leased by the owners of the mills, for ten years from July
26, 1825, to William Micklefield, a tobacconist of Salem, and changed into a
snuff mill.* There was a slaughter house
upon the premises, also, in 1813. A saw
mill had been introduced about 1812,
and that was continued as long as the
mills were run. A pulverizing mill was
established in or before 1827. There
were then upon the premises two grist,
one saw, one chocolate, and one pulverizing mill. William Frye was the miller
in 1825, and continued until 1832 or
later. In 1832, the proprietors of the

*Essex Registry of Deeds, book 239, leaf 268.

mills were called the firm of Micklefield & Co. There were dwelling apartments in the mills Jan. 20, 1836, when, for a rental of twelve hundred dollars a year, the mills were leased for ten years from Feb. 1, 1836, by Nathaniel West, merchant, William F. Gardner, merchant, William Micklefield, tobacconist, John Jewett and Elliott Smith, cabinet makers, and the guardian of Amos F. Smith, jr., all of Salem, owners, to said Micklefield, Jewett and Elliott Smith, and to Jonathan A. Kenney, all of Salem, and Thomas H. Prime of Charlestown, housewright, the lessees being the firm of Micklefield & Co.* In 1837, the mills consisted of two grist, one saw and one snuff mill. A veneering mill was added before 1846, and that was in use for a number of years, the veneer being sawn from square mahogany logs. The mills were called the City mills as early as 1846. The snuff mill was in existence as late as 1846, and another of the grist mills was discontinued between 1837 and 1846. When the proprietors sold the plant to the Eastern Railroad Company in 1854, the mills consisted of a grist, veneer and upright saw mill. The mills were run a few years after their purchase by the railroad company.

The original proprietors were interested in the mills in the following proportions: Walter Price, Henry Bartholmew and Samuel Gardner, one-quarter each, and John Gardner and George Gardner, one-eighth each. Major Price died in 167-, and his interest passed to his widow and to her children in her discretion. She conveyed one-eighth to her daughter Elizabeth, wife of John Ruck, and the other eighth to her son John Croad. George Gardner died in 1679, having devised his one-eighth interest to his son, Capt. Samuel Gardner. Mr. Bartholmew was a merchant, and, as a gift, he conveyed his interest (one-fourth) to his daughters Hannah, wife of Dr. John Swinerton, and Abigail, wife of Nehemiah

Willoughby, all of Salem, equally, Nov. 12, 1689.* Samuel Gardner died in 1689, having devised his one-fourth part to his grandchildren Abel Gardner (one-eighth), Joseph Henfield (one-sixteenth), and Mary (Henfield) Neale (one-sixteenth). John Croade, who was a merchant, conveyed his one-eighth to the miller, William Stacey, Sept. 23, 1699.† John Ruck's executors conveyed his wife's (?) interest, one-sixteenth, to Capt. Samuel Gardner of Salem, merchant,‡ and the other sixteenth to John Higginson, jr., of Salem,§ March 26, 1702. Widow Hannah Swinerton conveyed to William Browne, esq., of Salem, merchant, for fifty pounds, one-half of her interest (one-eighth) in the mill Dec. 22, 1702; and the other half, for forty pounds, Apr. 14, 1704.¶ John Gardner died in 1705, having devised his eighth interest to his grandson, John Gardner of Mendon, mariner. William Stacey, the miller, for one hundred pounds, conveyed his one-eighth interest in the mill to William Browne, esq., of Salem, merchant, at two times (one-sixteenth each time), May 5, 1708,* and April 22, 1709.†† John Gardner of Mendon conveyed his eighth interest to Capt. Samuel Gardner and the latter's son, Capt. John Gardner, equally, June 9, 1712.‡‡ William Browne, esq., conveyed one-sixteenth to his daughter Mary Lynde during his lifetime, and his other three-sixteenths he devised to her in his will, which was proved Feb. 29, 1715-6. Col. John Higginson died in 1720, having devised his sixteenth to his daughter Elizabeth, wife of John Gerrish. Capt. Samuel Gardner died in 1724, having devised his fourth part to his four grandsons, John Higginson, John Gardner, Daniel Gardner, and Samuel Gardner. Daniel Gard-

*Essex Registry of Deeds, book 8, leaf 142.
†Essex Registry of Deeds, book 13, leaf 150.
‡Essex Registry of Deeds, book 15, leaf 104.
§Essex Registry of Deeds, book 15, leaf 166.
¶Essex Registry of Deeds, book 16, leaf 20.
°Essex Registry of Deeds, book 16, leaf 112.
**Essex Registry of Deeds, book 20, leaf 127.
††Essex Registry of Deeds, book 21, leaf 60.
‡‡Essex Registry of Deeds, book 25, leaf 74.

ner and Samuel Gardner conveyed their two-sixteenths to their brother John Gardner Jan. 9, 1733.* John Gardner was a yeoman, and conveyed one-sixteenth of the mills to Jonathan Gardner of Salem, mariner, for one hundred and seventeen pounds, Dec. 10, 1735.† Mrs. Mary (Henfield) Neale, for one hundred and ten pounds, conveyed her sixteenth of "the three mills in Salem called the South Grist Mills" to Benjamin Lynde, jr., of Salem, Feb. 3, 1734-5.‡ Abel Gardner conveyed one-sixteenth of the three grist mills on South river known as the South mills, for eighty pounds, to his son Jonathan Gardner of Salem, mariner, Oct. 21, 1728;§ and died in 1739, possessed of his other sixteenth interest in the mills, which he devised to his son Abel Gardner. Abel Gardner conveyed his sixteenth to his brother Jonathan Gardner, for one hundred and twenty pounds, Dec. 28, 1739.‖ John Gardner conveyed another of his sixteenths, for one hundred and twenty pounds, to Benjamin Lynde, esq., of Salem, May 1, 1738;¶ and his other sixteenth, for a similar consideration, to William Lynde of Salem, merchant, Sept. 5, 1738.** Capt. John Gardner died possessed of his sixteenth interest; and his widow, Elizabeth Gardner, for one hundred pounds, conveyed it to Jonathan Gardner of Salem, merchant, May 13, 1742.†† Joseph Henfield died in 1743, having devised his sixteenth part to his son Edmund Henfield. John Higginson died in 1744; and his sixteenth descended to his son Francis Higginson. Francis Higginson died in 1761, having devised his interest to his wife Esther Higginson. She married Daniel Mackey of Salem, and they conveyed it to Daniel Malloon, for forty-three pounds, six shillings, and eight

peace, Feb. 22, 1762.* Mrs. Elizabeth Gerrish died in 1734; and her sixteenth interest in the mills passed to her daughter Sarah, wife of Charles King, jr., of Salem, by the division of her real estate, Dec. 1, 1756.† Mrs. King conveyed her sixteenth to James King of Salem, blockmaker, Dec. 1, 1756.‡ For forty-two pounds, James King conveyed this sixteenth interest to Daniel Malloon of Salem, miller, April 20, 1759.§ Mrs. Abigail Willoughby died, possessed of her one-eighth interest in the mills, and it descended to her son Francis Willoughby of Boston. Mr. Willoughby conveyed it to Thomas Barton of Salem June 1, 1747.‖ Colonel Barton died in 1751, and his eighth interest descended to his daughter Mary, wife of Dr. Bezaleel Toppan of Salem, merchant. She conveyed it to Daniel Malloon Feb. 4, 1764.¶ Edmund Henfield of Salem, cooper, for forty-six pounds, thirteen shillings and four pence, conveyed his sixteenth part of the South mills, being three grist mills and one scythe mill, granary, etc., to Daniel Malloon Feb. 28, 1770.** Mr. Malloon died in 1783, and his five-sixteenth interest descended to his grand-daughter Eunice (Bowles), wife of Nathaniel Andrew. William Lynde died in 1752, having devised his sixteenth to his brother Benjamin Lynde, esq. Benjamin Lynde died in 1781, and his three-sixteenths of the three grist mills and the scythe mill were divided among his three daughters, Mary, wife of Andrew Oliver, Lydia, wife of William Walter, and Hannah Lynde (unmarried, insane), equally, April 21, 1786. Jonathan Gardner died in 1783, having devised his one-fourth interest to his sons John Gardner and Jonathan Gardner, equally. Jonathan Gardner brought a suit against his brother John, who lived

*Essex Registry of Deeds, book 65, leaf 173.
†Essex Registry of Deeds, book 68, leaf 248.
‡Essex Registry of Deeds, book 71, leaf 175.
§Essex Registry of Deeds, book 46, leaf 249.
  Essex Registry of Deeds, book 80, leaf 72.
¶Essex Registry of Deeds, book 74, leaf 189.
**Essex Registry of Deeds, book 74, leaf 188.
††Essex Registry of Deeds, book 84, leaf 34.

*Essex Registry of Deeds, book 107, leaf 260.
†Essex Registry of Deeds, book 102, leaf 280.
‡Essex Registry of Deeds, book 104, leaf 107.
§Essex Registry of Deeds, book 107, leaf 91.
‖Essex Registry of Deeds, book 90, leaf 30.
¶Essex Registry of Deeds, book 113, leaf 86.
**Essex Registry of Deeds, book 127, leaf 88.

in Danvers, and recovered judgment. In satisfaction of the judgment John's one eighth interest in the saw, corn and chocolate mills and slaughter house was assigned to Jonathan Gardner July 12, 1813.* The one-sixteenth interest of Miss Hannah Lynde passed to her sister Mrs. Lydia Walter. Their mother, Madam Mary Lynde, died in the summer of 1790, and her one-fourth interest passed equally to her daughters, Mrs. Mary Oliver and Mrs. Lydia Walter. Mrs. Walter died, and her heirs conveyed one-half of her fourth interest in the mills to Jonathan Gardner of Salem, merchant, April 16, 1801;† and the other eighth, for eight hundred and seventy dollars, to John Gardner, jr., of Salem, merchant, April 16, 1801.‡ Nathaniel Andrew and his wife Eunice removed to Marblehead, and, for one hundred dollars, conveyed her five-sixteenths to Peter Hodson of Marblehead, tallow-chandler, Nov. 15, 1804.§ Mr. Hodson mortgaged the same interest to Jesse Blanchard of Marblehead, victualler, Sept. 10, 1807 ;‖ and Mr. Blanchard soon after purchased the equity of the interest or foreclosed the mortgage. Mrs. Mary Oliver died in September, 1807, having devised her estate to her three children, Dr. Benjamin Lynde Oliver, Peter Oliver and Sarah Oliver, one-sixteenth interest passing to each of them. Her three-sixteenths were then valued at sixteen hundred and fifty dollars. Sarah's interest passed to her brother, Peter Oliver, before 1810. Dr. B. L. Oliver conveyed his sixteenth interest to Jonathan Gardner of Salem, merchant, Jan. 28, 1819.¶ Jonathan Gardner had probably conveyed his first interest (one-eighth) (which he bought of the heirs of Mrs. Walter in 1801) to Nathaniel West before this time. Peter Oliver

was deranged, and his guardian, for six hundred dollars each, conveyed his two-sixteenths to Abel Lawrence, jr., and John B. Lawrence, both of Salem, by separate deeds, Feb. 26, 1821;* and Abel Lawrence, for six hundred and eighty-seven dollars and fifty cents, conveyed his one-sixteenth to Charles Lawrence of Salem, merchant, March 1, 1824.† Charles Lawrence, for nine hundred dollars, conveyed his sixteenth interest to Nathaniel West of Danvers, esquire, April 20, 1830 ;‡ and John B. Lawrence of Salem, for a similar consideration, conveyed his sixteenth to Mr. West May 27, 1831.§ John Gardner of Danvers, yeoman, for fifteen hundred dollars, conveyed his eighth interest to Mr. West Jan. 11, 1830.‖ Jesse Blanchard conveyed his five-sixteenths to William Frye of Danvers, miller, Dec. 1, 1825 ;¶ and, for forty-three hundred dollars, Mr. Frye, who had removed to Salem, miller, conveyed his five-sixteenths to William Micklefield, tobacconist, John Jewett, Elliott Smith and Amos F. Smith, cabinet makers, all of Salem, being a firm, Micklefield & Co., July 9, 1832.** Amos F. Smith died in 1833, and his interest descended to his son Amos F. Smith, jr. Jonathan Gardner died in 1821 ; and his five-sixteenths descended to his son William F. Gardner, who conveyed his five-sixteenths, equally, to Jonathan A. Kenney†† and Thomas H. Prime,‡‡ both of Salem, mahogany dealers, Jan. 27, 1846, by two deeds. Oct. 21, 1837, Elliott Smith conveyed five-sixty-fourths to William Micklefield,§§ who died in 1840, possessed of five-thirty-seconds of the mills, which interest was then appraised at three thousand, four hundred and thirty-seven dollars. The executor

*Essex Registry of Deeds, Executions, book 2, leaf 23.
†Essex Registry of Deeds, book 167, leaf 271.
‡Essex Registry of Deeds, book 175, leaf 298.
§Essex Registry of Deeds, book 174, leaf 288.
‖Essex Registry of Deeds, book 182, leaf 26.
¶Essex Registry of Deeds, book 218, leaf 214.

*Essex Registry of Deeds, book 226, leaf 9.
†Essex Registry of Deeds, book 235, leaf 46.
‡Essex Registry of Deeds, book 256, leaf 111.
§Essex Registry of Deeds, book 259, leaf 235.
‖Essex Registry of Deeds, book 255, leaf 151.
¶Essex Registry of Deeds, book 241, leaf 14.
**Essex Registry of Deeds, book 266, leaf 30.
††Essex Registry of Deeds, book 363, leaf 107.
‡‡Essex Registry of Deeds, book 363, leaf 107.
§§Essex Registry of Deeds, book 302, leaf 228.

of the will of Mr. Micklefield, for fifteen hundred and sixteen dollars, conveyed his said interest in the mills to John Jewett, Thomas H. Prime and Jonathan A. Kenney of Salem, comprising the firm of Prime, Kenney & Co., March 23, 1849.* The guardian of Amos F. Smith, for eleven hundred and twenty-five dollars, conveyed his five-sixty-fourths, at auction, to John Jewett of Salem, cabinet maker, June 2, 1846.† Nathaniel West, for sixty-five hundred and eighty dollars, conveyed his six-sixteenths to John Jewett, Thomas H. Prime, and Jonathan A. Kenney, all of Salem, equally, Oct. 12, 1849.‡ John Jewett, Thomas H. Prime and Jonathan A. Kenney, all of Salem, "owners of the City mills," for eighteen hundred and eighty-one dollars and eighty-seven cents, conveyed one-tenth of the City mills to Thomas S. Jewett of Salem, housewright, Oct. 18, 1849.§ John Jewett, cabinet maker, Thomas H. Prime, mahogany dealer, Jonathan A. Kenney, mahogany dealer, and Thomas S. Jewett, housewright, all of Salem, for fifty thousand dollars, conveyed the City mills, grist, veneer and upright saw mill, buildings and land to the Eastern Railroad Company June 17, 1854.‖

John Marston House. The executors of the will of Capt. Walter Price of Salem, merchant, conveyed this lot of land to Henry Bartholmew, Joseph Grafton, George Gardner, Samuel Gardner, sr., and said executors, "owners of the new mill," March 10, 1675.¶ They built a small house upon the lot soon after their purchase, probably the same year. Dea. John Marston of Salem, carpenter, was living in the house in 1699, and had then bought out the interests of most of the owners probably. John Croade of Salem, mariner, for ten pounds, conveyed

to him one fourth of the house and lot, "upon the entrance of the South field," Oct. 13, 1699.* Hannah Swinnerton of Salem, for five pounds, conveyed to Mr. Marston one-eighth of the house and lot, with liberty of a highway "along ye mill pond to yo mill dam," April 29, 1706.† No other conveyances of interests in this estate to Mr. Marston have been found. Mr. Marston, for love, conveyed the house and land to his grandson, Benjamin Marston of Taunton, clothier, Dec. 8, 1716.‡ Benjamin Marston, then of Barnstable, clothier, for twenty-five pounds, conveyed the house and lot to Thomas Brewer of Salem, miller, June 26, 1729 § Mr. Brewer, for forty pounds, conveyed the estate to Benjamin Lynde of Salem, esquire, Dec. 18, 1739.‖ Mr. Lynde, for fifty-three pounds, six shillings and eight pence, conveyed the land, with the house and barn thereon, to Thomas Osborn, cordwainer, and John Osborn, mariner, both of Salem, Oct. 25, 1758.* Thomas Osborn died before Oct. 9, 1765, when his administrator, for four pounds, conveyed his half of the house, barn and land, at auction, to John Warden of Salem, housewright.** Mr. Warden, for a similar consideration, conveyed the same estate to Daniel Malloon of Salem, miller (the administrator of Mr. Osborn's estate), Oct. 31, 1765.** The house was probably removed immediately.

William Stacey Houses. That part of this lot lying south of the southern dashes was a part of the lot of Capt. Walter Price of Salem, merchant, and was conveyed by him to Charles Emlett of Salem, gunsmith, "being at or near ye Southfield gate, by ye mill in Salem," Oct. 10, 1676 (?).†† Mr Emlett (Amlett) built a house upon the lot, and lived there until he died, in or before 1693. His widow,

*Essex Registry of Deeds, book 409, leaf 228.
†Essex Registry of Deeds, book 368, leaf 180.
‡Essex Registry of Deeds, book 417, leaf 282.
§Essex Registry of Deeds, book 418, leaf 93.
‖Essex Registry of Deeds, book 500, leaf 18.
¶Essex Registry of Deeds, book 4, leaf 130.

*Essex Registry of Deeds, book 14, leaf 203.
†Essex Registry of Deeds, book 26, leaf 150.
‡Essex Registry of Deeds, book 31, leaf 130.
§Essex Registry of Deeds, book 68, leaf 28.
‖Essex Registry of Deeds, book 76, leaf 219.
*Essex Registry of Deeds, book 112, leaf 82.
**Essex Registry of Deeds, book 116, leaf 255.
††Essex Registry of Deeds, book 10, leaf 10.

Mary Amlett, a Frenchwoman, then owned it until June 9, 1694, when she conveyed it to William Stacey of Salem, miller, in consideration of her life support.[*] He owned it until July 19, 1709, when, the agreement being abandoned, Mr. Stacey reconveyed the house and lot to her.[†] There was then a shop, also, upon the lot. For fifteen pounds, she conveyed the lot, with "part of an old house thereon," to George Peale of Salem, carpenter, Sept. 2, 1712.[‡] Mr. Peale probably took down the old house immediately.

That part of the lot lying between the dashes was also a part of the lot of Capt. Walter Price of Salem, merchant, and was conveyed by him to Peter Harvey of Salem, shipwright, Feb. 26, 1671.[§] Mr. Harvey built a house thereon, and, for twenty pounds, conveyed the house and lot to William Stacy of Salem, miller, May 24, 1693.[‖] The house was removed apparently soon afterward; and Mr. Stacey died possessed of the land in 1723.

That part of this lot lying north of the dashes was the property of Bartholmew Gedney of Salem; and he had a house and barn upon it. For one hundred pounds, he conveyed it, with the house and barn, to William Staccy of Salem, miller, Aug. 7, 1682.[¶] A right of way for a cart to the highway was conveyed with the estate. Mr. Stacey died in 1723, possessed of the lot and house, called in the inventory of his estate "an old house," and valued, with the land, at fifty pounds. The administrator of his estate conveyed the house and lot to Peter Windeat of Salem, currier, Dec. 31, 1724;[**] and Mr. Windeat conveyed it, for the same consideration, to Jonathan Woodwell of Salem, mariner, the administrator and son-in-law of Mr. Stacey, Jan. 4,

1724-5.[*] Mr. Woodwell lived in the house in 1735; and died in 1737, possessed of the estate, which was then appraised at eighty pounds. For seventy pounds, the administrator of his estate conveyed it to Henry Coffin of Salem, cordwainer, July 15, 1741.[†] The next day, for a similar consideration, Mr. Coffin conveyed the house and lot to Thomas Sleeman of Salem, coaster.[‡] Mr. Sleeman (or Sluman) died, and the house and lot came into the possession of John Sluman of Salem, mariner (probably son of Thomas). The house was gone before 1797, the date of Mr. Sluman's death. The deed of the administrator of John Sluman, dated Nov. 18, 1799, conveyed to John Henfield only the land, with the rocks in the old cellar.[§]

The Pound. At the time of the death of Col. Bartholmew Gedney, esq., of Salem, in 1698, he had a wharf "on ye Southfield side" called "ye pound." It has not been exactly located, but surroundings indicate that it was at the end of the lane and his lot as marked on the map. Nov. 3, 1701, in the division of his real estate, this was assigned to his daughter Deborah, wife of Francis Clark.

Estate of Bartholmew Gedney Lot. One divided half of this lot of marsh land was granted by the town of Salem 19 : 6 : 1630, in the following words: "Granted to mr Peeters the marsh lyinge over against his now dwelling containinge about an aker & halfe or therabout on the other side of the water." Charles Gott of Wenham, attorney of "Mr. Hugh Peeters, sometimes pastor of the church of Christ in Salem," for three pounds, conveyed it to George Emery of Salem, chirurgeon, July 1, 1659.[‖] Doctor Emery owned the remainder of this lot Nov. 28, 1671, when he conveyed the entire lot to Mr. John Gedney, sr., of Salem.

*Essex Registry of Deeds, book 10, leaf 11. See the bond he gave, in the probate records, July 22, 1695.
†Essex Registry of Deeds, book 25, leaf 39.
‡Essex Registry of Deeds, book 24, leaf 253.
§Essex Registry of Deeds, book 6, leaf 107.
‖Essex Registry of Deeds, book 9, leaf 107
¶Essex Registry of Deeds, book 7, leaf 4.
**Essex Registry of Deeds, book 49, leaf 269.

*Essex Registry of Deeds, book 46, leaf 156.
†Essex Registry of Deeds, book 81, leaf 251.
‡Essex Registry of Deeds, book 80, leaf 275.
§Essex Registry of Deeds, book 166, leaf 107.
‖Essex Registry of Deeds, book 1, leaf 63.

vintner.† Mr. Gedney died in 1688; and by his will his son Col. Bartholmew Gedney became possessed of the lot. He died Feb. 28, 1697-8; and the estate was not divided among his heirs until Nov. 3, 1701, when this land was assigned to his daughter Deborah, wife of Francis Clarke.

William Stacey Lot. This was a part of the lot of Walter Price of Salem, who died in 1674. It passed to his son Capt. John Price, and then to Walter's grandson, John Croade, who conveyed it to William Stacey of Salem, miller, in 1697 or 1698; and the latter owned it in 1700.

Joseph Mansfield Lot. This was a part of the lot of Walter Price, who died in 1674. It then passed by will to his son Capt. John Price and grandson John Croade of Salem, merchant. Mr. Croade became owner of the entire lot, and, for twenty-eight pounds, conveyed it to William Stacey of Salem, miller, July 19, 1697.† For thirty-two pounds, Mr. Stacey conveyed it to Joseph Mansfield of Lynn, husbandman, Dec. 29, 1698 ;‡ and Mr. Mansfield owned it until 1716.

Samuel Ruck Lot. That part of this lot lying westerly of the dashes belonged to Capt. Walter Price at an early date. He died in 1674, and the land descended to his son Capt. John Price of Salem and the deceased's grandson John Croade of Salem, merchant. Upon the death of Capt. John Price, in 1691, Mr. Croade became sole owner, and he conveyed the lot, containing five acres of upland "upon ye entrance at ye southfield," to Joseph Orne of Salem, May 18, 1697.§ The lot passed to Samuel Ruck, who owned it until 1702.

That part of the lot lying easterly of the dashes belonged to and was a part of the large lot of Daniel Rumball as early as 1653. March 18, 1681-2, he conveyed it to his daughter Alice and her husband, William Curtice, in consideration of love and his support for life ;* and Mr. Curtice, for sixteen pounds, conveyed it to Joseph Stacey of Salem, carpenter, Aug. 14, 1690.† Mr. Stacey died three months later; having orally requested that his property should descend to his mother. His father, William Stacey of Salem, miller, conveyed it, for sixteen pounds, to John Croade of Salem, merchant, July 19, 1697 ;‡ and the lot passed to Samuel Ruck, who owned it in 1702.

William Curtice Lot. This was the lot of Daniel Rumball of Salem, blacksmith, as early as 1653. For love and his support for life, he conveyed it to his daughter Alice and her husband, William Curtice, March 18, 1681-2 ;* and Mr. Curtice owned it in 1700.

William Browne Lot ("Stage Point"). This lot was known as Stage Point as early as 1640. That part of the lot lying northerly of the dashes belonged to Henry Bartholmew of Salem, merchant, in 1678; and for one hundred pounds he conveyed it to William Browne, jr., of Salem, merchant, Dec. 27, 1690.§ That part of the lot southerly of the dashes belonged to Mr. Browne as early as 1678. He died possessed of the entire lot in 1716.

That part of the lot within the dashes was conveyed by Richard Hide of Salem, ship carpenter, to John Marston, jr., of Salem, house carpenter, March 22, 1677-8 ;‖ and it became the property of William Browne soon after.

That part of the lot lying southeasterly of the dashes was the estate of Mr. William Browne, sr., in 1677-8; and was his for many years thereafter.

Benjamin Allen Lot. Widow Dorothy King of Salem owned this lot of planting ground Oct. 8, 1653, when, for seven

---

*Essex Registry of Deeds, book 4, leaf 25.
†Essex Registry of Deeds, book 12, leaf 189.
‡Essex Registry of Deeds, book 10, leaf 114.
§Essex Registry of Deeds, book 12, leaf 68.

*Essex Registry of Deeds, book 6, leaf 68a.
†Essex Registry of Deeds, book 9, leaf 26.
‡Essex Registry of Deeds, book 12, leaf 93.
§Essex Registry of Deeds, book 9, leaf 21; also, book 5, leaf 13, and book 9, leaf 22.
‖Essex Registry of Deeds, book 5, leaf 22.

pounds and ten shillings, she conveyed it to Thomas Barnes of Salem, blacksmith.* The estate came into the hands of James Powland of Salem, blacksmith, before 23 : 6 : 1678 ; and April 4, 1694, he conveyed it to Benjamin Allen of Salem, mariner, and wife Mary.† Mr. Allen owned it as late as 1702.

John Marston Lot. That part of this lot lying northerly of the dashes was conveyed by Richard Hide of Salem, ship-carpenter, to John Marston, jr., of Salem, house carpenter, March 22, 1677-8.‡

That part of the lot lying southerly of the dashes belonged apparently to George Ropes in 1662. It was the property of Mr. William Browne, sr., in 1678 ; and a few years later it came into the hands of Deacon Marston, who continued to own the entire lot as late as 1709.

WILL OF RICHARD ROOTEN.

The will of Richard Rooten of Lynn was proved in the Salem quarterly court 25 : 9 : 1663. The following is a copy of the original instrument on file in the office of the clerk of courts at Salem, volume IX, leaf 72.

This is the Last will and Testement of Richard *Rooton*

First I commit my foulle and body to God that *gave it*

First I will and bequeve all that I haue to my * * whille fhe Liues faue Sagemore hill. and * * clofe and, to steares, to cowes which I becqueue *to* my kinsman Edmond Rooton, and After my wifes Defeafe I will that all I haue to bee my kinsman, Edmond Rooton, allfoe I will that hee fhall haue a bee with al yᵗ doeth belonge to it of such as I haue of mine one Allfoe I will that Edmond Rooton haue for his Conuenefy halfe an Acor of ground vpon the hill. yᵗ was owld Tilltons to buildd him a howfe vpon : with tene Poundes towards his buildidgs I

*Essex Registry of Deeds, book 1, leaf 20.
†Essex Registry of Deeds, book 9, leaf 276.
‡Essex Registry of Deeds, book 5, leaf 22.

will; that hee haue it, where hee may *hoπe* * most Conuenient, to buildd him a howfe vpon. * Allfoe I will: that if Johnathan Hartfhorne * continew with my wife and Edmond Rooton * * tearm of yeares I doe grant vnto him fiue * Allfoe I will that our Pastor, mᵗ whiting haue forty shilling giuen vnto him Allfoe I will that Henery Rhods haue twenty fhillings to bee giuen him,

I will to giue vnto Gorge Tayler twenty fhilling.

Singhued Sealled and Deliuered in the Prefents of vs whofe names are vnder written.   the marke of h Richard this : 12ᵗʰ of June   Rooton
    1663   [SEAL.]

This his will and Testement was written when hee was in his Perfect, memory this Adicion was written beefore the figneing and fealling heare of,
    Henery Rhodes,
    Robert Diiner
    ffrancis Burrill

It is my will that * * my wife my chefe *Executrix* and Henery Rhods my ouerfers, and Gorge Tayler with him.

NOTES.

Rev. Ebenezer Bradford of Rowley, born in Canterbury, Conn., in 1746 ; graduated at Princeton college, N. J., 1773 ; preached in Danbury, Conn. ; and installed over the church in Rowley, Mass., Aug. 4, 1782 ; married Elizabeth, daughter of Rev. Jacob Green of Hanover, N. J., April 4, 1776 ; he died in Rowley Jan. 3, 1801 ; she survived him. Children : Ebenezer Green ; living in 1799 ; William, living in 1799 ; John M., at college in 1799 ; Jacob P., living in 1799 ; Elizabeth G., living in 1799 ; James, living in 1799 ; Moses, clergyman ; married Dorothy Bradstreet of Rowley Nov. 2, 1788 ; she died June 24, 1792,

aged twenty-six; he was living in 1799; Henry, living in 1799; and Mary C., living in 1799.—*Records.*

Jane Bradford married Robert Leach March 13, 1717-8, at Manchester.—*Beverly town records.*

Margaret Bradford of Bradford married Jonathan Hopkins[on] of Newbury March 28, 1738.—*Bradford town records.*

Charity Bradford married Nathaniel Collens Jan. 24, 1769, in Lynn.—*County records.*

Thomas Bradford, sojourner, married Elizabeth Denning Nov. 14, 1741.—*Gloucester town records.*

WILL OF ALEXANDER KNIGHT.

The will of Alexander Knight of Ipswich was proved in the court at Ipswich March 29, 1664. The following is a copy of the original instrument on file in the probate office at Salem.

In The Name of God Amen. The tenth day of ffebruary in the yeere of oᵣ Lord one thousand six hundred sixty & three. I Allexander Knight the vnproffitable seruant of God weake in body, but strong in mind doe willingly & with a free hart render & give againe into the hands of my Lord God & Creator my spirit, which hee of his fatherly goodnesse gaue vnto mee, when hee first fashioned mee in my mothers wombe makeing mee a liueing & a resonable creature nothing doubting but that for his infinite mercies fake set forth in the pᵗious blood of his dearely beloued sonne Jesus Chrift oᵣ onely sauiour & redeemer, hee will receiue my foule into his Glory, & place it in the Company of the heauenly Angells & blessed Saints: And for my body I Comitt it to the earth wherof it Came; nothing doubting but according to the Article of my faith at the great day of the Generall Resurrection when wee shall appeare before the Judgment seate of Chrift I shall receiue againe the same by the mighty power of God who is able to subdue all things to himselfe, not a Corruptible

weake & vile body as it is now, but an incorruptible imortall strong & pfect body in all poynts like vnto the Glorious body of my lord & Sauiour Jesus Chrift. And for the portion of these earthly things which God hath lent mee I dispose as followeth, first I giue vnto my Loueing wife my howse & howse lott & all my other goods & debts during her naturall life, (my debts being difcharged) Item I giue vnto my eldeft Daughter Hannah Knight at the age of one & twenty yeares six Acres of marsh & Six Acres of planting land, Item I giue vnto my loueing wife all the rest of my planting land & marsh during her naturall life, my will is also after my wiues deceace, that my planting land & marsh before named be equally diuided betwene my other daugters, Sarah & Mary & my sonne Nathaniell, And also that my sone Nathaniell haue my howse & house lott, besides his part in my planting land & marsh aforesaid. And further my will is that all my howsehold goods be equally diuided betwene my three daughters & my sonne Nathaniel after my wiues deceace. And I doe ordaine & appoynt my wife Hana Knight And William Inglish ‖ of Boston ‖ to be my executᵣrs of this my laft will & Teftament, And if it shall happen any of my Children before named to depart this life before there portions be due, my will is that thofe that be liueing shall share their portion or portions equally betweene them. Also my will is that if any Ambiguity doubt or queftion doe arife by reson of the impfection or defect of, or in any Claufes words or fentences in this my laft will & Teftament, or my true intent & meaning therin, I will that the further & better explanation interpᵗation & Conftruction of the faid doubt & ambiguity be by my faid execurᵗors expounded explained & interpᵗted according to their wifedome & difcretion. In witnes wherof I haue hereunto sett hand & Seale in the pᵣfents of

witnesse

John Whipple   Allexander Knight
James Chute   his ⌢ mark [SEAL]
Robert Lord Jn'r

GEORGE PEABODY.

George Peabody was born in Peabody, Mass., then a part of Danvers, Feb. 18, 1795, being a son of Thomas and Judith (Dodge) Peabody, people of ordinary means. George attended the district school of his neighborhood, and when twelve years old became a clerk in the grocery store of Capt. Sylvester Proctor, with whom he remained for three years. He then went to Thetford, Vt., where he lived for a year with his maternal grandfather, Jeremiah Dodge. A year later, he became a clerk in the store of his brother David Peabody, in Newburyport, Mass., being a clerk in that store at the time of the great fire of 1811. After the fire, he decided to enter into business on his own account, and, although but sixteen years of age, he secured the credit of two thousand dollars worth of goods from James Reed of Boston through kindly letters of recommendation from Prescott Spaulding of Newburyport, who was attracted by his manliness, vigor, and prepossessing appearance. These goods were sold at a good profit; subsequent credit was easily obtained, and he soon became a merchant of prominence.

In 1812, he engaged in business in Georgetown, D. C., with his uncle, Gen. John Peabody. The first consignment of goods made to them there was sent by Francis Todd of Newburyport. He always had the most grateful remembrances of the latter town, the home of his true and trustful friends, without whose confidence and aid he would probably have been only a clerk. In later years, he made a donation to its public library.

His uniform affability and curtesy won him many friends; and he was always unassuming in dress and deportment. In both social and business engagements he was always punctual; and his success was simply the outcome of a well balanced business mind.

He was a good conversationalist, and an attractive writer and speaker. He

never married; and his tastes were simple and personal expenses small.

In 1814, when only nineteen years old, he entered into partnership with Elisha Riggs in Georgetown, D. C., the capital being furnished by Mr. Riggs, and the business being conducted by Mr. Peabody, who frequently took long journeys on horseback to extend the sales of his house. In 1815, they removed the business to Baltimore; and, in 1822, established branch houses at New York and Philadelphia. The firm was eminently successful. Upon the retirement of Mr. Riggs, in 1830, Mr. Peabody became the senior member of the firm, and under its new name of Peabody, Riggs & Company became one of the leading concerns of the country. In the course of his business he made several trips to Europe, visiting London first in 1827.

In 1837, he withdrew from the firm, and began business with others as a merchant and broker, under the style of "George Peabody & Co., of Warnford Court, City." The firm did a banking and general brokerage business. Again he was successful in his operations; and he thus began the foundation of the large fortune which he eventually secured.

He had great faith in the country of his birth, and always sustained the credit of its bonds and other securities. He carried the state of Maryland through a critical financial period; and in London, during a time of much depression of American securities, he greatly helped in restoring confidence. He went so far in this respect that at the close of the civil war three-quarters of all his estate was invested in national and state securities.

At the time of the great exhibition of 1851, congress failed to appropriate money to enable the American division to be fitted up, and the exhibitors became disheartened. Mr. Peabody advanced the large sum required, and America was duly represented.

The list of Mr. Peabody's gifts is too long and varied to be given here. They cover the realms of science, religion, lit-

eiature, education, and general philanthro-
py, and schools, libraries, churches and
other institutions came into existence
at his word. He wished, as far as it lay
in his power, to be his own executor.

He provided the means of fitting out
the *Advance*, Doctor Kane's ship, for the
Arctic voyage in search of Sir John
Franklin.

His gifts to the town of his birth, principal for the Peabody Institute, amount
to more than two hundred thousand dollars.

He gave to the Peabody Institute at
Baltimore, Maryland, one million, five
hundred thousand dollars.

In 1859, he began to execute a long
cherished purpose of establishing homes
for the poor of London, England. The
tenements which he erected are occupied
by twenty thousand persons, who pay a
reasonable rent for pleasant, comfortable
homes. To this purpose he gave, in all,
two and one-half million dollars. That
was his largest foreign expenditure. His
largest American charity was a gift of
three million dollars known as the Southern Education Fund.

Among other donations, every Essex
county sketch of him ought to mention
his gift of one hundred and five thousand
dollars for the church and public library
in Georgetown; one hundred and forty
thousand dollars to the Peabody Academy of Science in Salem; twenty-five
thousand dollars to the Phillips Academy
at Andover; fifty thousand dollars for the
Peabody Institute in Danvers; and one
hundred and fifty thousand dollars each to
Harvard and Yale colleges.

Mr. Peabody's health began to fail
shortly before his last visit to America, in
the summer of 1869; and he returned to
London, where he passed away Nov. 4,
1869, at the age of seventy-four. The
highest honors were accorded him in
England and America, services being
held over his remains in Westminster
Abbey. The warship *Monarch*, one of
the finest ironclads in the British navy,
was ordered by Her Majesty's govern-

ment to transport the body of the dead
philanthropist to his native land. It was
conveyed by an American warship, and
also a French vessel detailed by the Em-
peror for that service. Prince Arthur ac-
companied the fleet, and attended the
funeral exercises in the South church in
Peabody, as the representative of the
queen. The burial took place, in the
midst of a great and wild snow storm, in
Harmony Grove cemetery in Salem. The
funeral oration was by Robert C. Winthrop.

Queen Victoria had offered Mr. Peabody a baronetcy, but he had refused the
title, preferring to be the simple American
that he was. His choicest mementoes,
the queen's portrait, medals, etc., are in
the Peabody Institute in Peabody, where
they can be seen.

In this number of the *Antiquarian* is
given a profile likeness of Mr. Peabody
reproduced from Ballou's Monthly Magazine for September, 1869.

NOTES.

Thomas Bragg (No. 20, page 63) married Dorothy Ingalls, not Deborah Ingalls.—*Ed.*

Edward Bray (No. 91, page 103) married Edith Doane Dec. 8, 1774; and had
children. 1. ——, married —— Loring,
and lived in Salem; 2.—— (daughter); 3.
Edward, baptized Oct. 9, 1780, married
Sally Avery (published Aug. 30, 1803;
lived in Gloucester, and had eight children; 4. Eleazar Doane, baptized July
10, 1785; 5. Nancy Russell, baptized Dec.
26, 1802; was known as Ann R. Bray,
and for many years conducted a store
on Federal street, in Salem.—*Henry C. L.
Haskell, West Gloucester.*

Moses Bray (No. 19, page 102) had a
daughter Keziah, baptized Aug. 26, 1732.
She married Samuel Denning March 14,
1754, and lived in West Gloucester.
Moses Bray died in West Gloucester of
numb palsy July 19, 1773, and his widow
died Dec. —, 1778, aged "eighty".—*Edgar Yates, Everett.*

OLD NORFOLK COUNTY RECORDS.

Continued from page 35.

Jn° Marian (his M mark) of Hampton, yeoman, to my daughter Hannah, wife of Isaac Godfrey, and their children one-half of my 12 acres of planting land above Gillese swamp (Henry Dearborne to have half); one-half of my 10 acres of fresh meadow in ye west meadows (Henry Dearborn to have half), bounded by Edw: Colcord, Robert Page, Sam⁰ Dalton and Wm. Swayne; one-half of 11 acres of salt marsh by birch island (Henry Dearborn to have half), bounded by Mr. Cris: Hussey and Tho: Levett; 10 acres of upland granted to me by Hampton, to be laid out about ye north hill; and one share of ye cow common in Hampton, Jan. 1, 1671. Wit: Hannah Dalton and Sam⁰ Dalton, jr. Ack. 2: 11 mo: 1671, before Sam⁰ Dalton, commissioner.

Will of Samuel Robins of Salisbury, planter. Gives everything " to any one or more of my owne brethren yᵗ ſhall think good to come over into new england wᵗʰ-in three years time after they ſhall heare of my deceaſe & if neither one or more of them ſhall thinke good to come over then I do giue my whole eſtate vnto my deare father John Robins of Theding worth in Liceſter ſheire in old england, if hee bee not then liueing I do giue & bequeath my whole eſtate to my deare mother Heſter Robins and if ſhe bee not liueing I doe giue my ſaid whole eſtate to my loueing brother Joſeph Robins." My friend Richard Currier of Salisbury, executor. Dated Aug. 22, 1665. Wit: Mr. Tho: Bradbury, sr., and the mark of Mary MB Bradbury. Proved by both witneſses in court at Salisbury 2: 8 mo: 1673. The executor accepted the position.

A steer taken up by William Sargent, sr., as a stray, Dec. 20, 1671.

Inventory of estate of Sam⁰ Robins attested by oath of Richard Currier in court at Salisbury April 8, 1673. Amount, all personal, £36, 7s., 6d. In hands of Sam⁰ ſſelloes, £4. Owed Robert Jones, Cpᵗ White, Mr. Dearing, Steven Swett, Capt.

Gerish, Mr. Carr, Jn° Smith, Capt. Walden, ye widow Tuck, Rich: Dole and widow Rowell.

Inventory of estate of Giles ſſuller of Hampton, taken April 8, 1673, by Tho: Marston, Abraham Pirkins and Wm. Marston. Sworn to by Richard Currier, administrator, in court at Salisbury April 8, 1673. Amount, £158, 5s., 3d. Real, £115. Personal, £43, 5s., 3d. Due to Mr. Person of Boston, Gershom Elkins, ye military company, ye jury of inquest, etc. House, barn, etc.

Inventory of estate of Thomas Lilford (also Linfurth), deceased, taken Nov. 18, 1672, by Henry Palmer and Tho: Eaton, both of Haverhill. Amount, £187, 5s. Real, £152. Personal, £35, 5s. House and land. Land sometime of James Davis, sr. Meadow at Hawks meadow, World's End meadow and Mistake meadow. Sworn to by his widow Elizabeth Linford in court at Salisbury April 8, 1673. £6 added (meadow in West meadows) April 26, 1673, in presence of Nath: Saltonstall and Wm. White.

Inventory of the estate of John Kinsbery who died 23: 11: 1670, taken by Danieli Lad, sr. (his ⌐ mark), and Robert Swan. Amount, £66, 10s. Real, £36. Personal, £30, 10s. Due to Mr. Weinwright of Ipswich, Mr. Seabell Weacker of Merimack, Jn° Johnson and Joseph Johnson. Sworn to by Elizabeth Kinsbery in court at Salisbury 11 mo: 2: 1671.

Inventory of the estate of John Dowe of Haverhill who died intestate, taken by Georg Brown and Robert Clemens. Amount, £174, 1s. Real, £107, 10s. Personal, £66, 11s. Due to Sam⁰ Plumer, Mr. Dalton, Capt. Saltonstall and Martha Heath. Due to the estate from Gilbert Eviiford and —— Belnap. Sworn to by Mary Dowe, widow of the deceased, in court at Salisbury April 8, 1673.

Inventory of the estate of widow Eaton, deceased, taken by Henry Palmer and William White Dec. 25, 1672. Amount, £11, 19s., 6d. All personal. Due from Thomas Eaton of Haverhill, Thomas Eaton of Salisbury, Thomas Whittcher,

Peter Eyer and Steven Dowe. Sworn to by Steven Dowe in court at Salisbury April 8, 1673.

John Eyers (sig. Eyer) of Haverhill, for £65 in barley and pork, conveyed to Richard Dole of Nuberie, 250 acres of land in Haverhill, bounded by Lt. Brown, Merrimack river, a highway next Spicket river and Josuah Woodman, March 27, 1673. Wit: Anthony Somerby and James Barker. Ack. in court at Ipswich 25 : 1 : 1673.

John Clough of Salisbury, house carpenter, for a 25-acre lot of upland, today conveyed to me by Isaac Colby of Haverhill, planter, conveyed to Jnº Colby of Amsbery, planter, a 2-acre division of salt marsh in Salisbury at Mr. Hall's farm, formerly of Mr. Samll Groome, and I bought it of said Isaac Colby, bounded by Richard Singletary (now in the possession of said Clough), ye great creek, Wm. Huntington (now in the possession of said Clough), Willi: Osgood and Tho: Hauxworth, Aug. 29, 1671. Wit: Tho: Bradbury and William Bradbury. Ack. in court at Salisbury April 8, 1673.

John Hoyt, jr., of Amsberie, planter, wife Mary, for £15, conveyed to Jnº Easman of Salisbury, planter, 30 acres of upand in Amsbery, bounded by grantee (formerly John Colby), Robert Jones, a highway and a brook called ye back river yt runs into ye pond, ——, 1669. Ack. in court at Salisbury April 8, 1673.

John Hoyt, jr., of Amsbery, housecarpenter, conveyed to John Colby of Amsbery a 4-acre marsh lot in Salisbury bought by Willi: Barnes of Mr. Samuell Hall then of Salisbury, and by him given to me, bounded by George Martyn, Samll ffelloes, Jnº Eaton, Jnº Ilsley and Tho: Barnard, March 25, 1672. Wit: Jeremiah Hubbard and Tho: Barnard. Ack. March 25, 1672, before Samuell Dalton, commissioner. His wife, Mary Hoyt, released dower same day.

William ffifeild of Hampton, planter, conveyed to my son Benjamin ffifeild 40 acres of upland in Hampton on ye south side of ye falls river, bounded by falls river, Lt. Swett, and highways; salt marsh on ye south side of Hampton great river, bounded by ye falls river, ye great river, widow Moulton, jr., and Wm. ffuller, sr., and one-third of my rights in common lands in Hampton except in ye great ox common, April 29, 1667. Wit: John Barsham, Jnº Redman and Abraham Cole. Ack. April 8, 1673, in court at Salisbury.

William Barnes (his 7 mark) of Salisbury, house-carpenter, for love, conveyed to his son-in-law John Hoyt, jr., of Salisbury, planter, 4 acres of marsh in Salisbury I bought of Mr. Samll Hall, bounded by Georg Martyn, Samll ffelloes, Jnº Eaton, Jnº Ilsley and Tho: Barnard, ——, 1668. Wit: Tho: Bradbury and William Scieven. Ack. March 25, 1672, before Samll Dalton, commissioner.

John Jimson (his in mark) of Emsbery conveyed to John Davis of Nubery 7 ½ acres of land in Emsbery, bounded by Robert Quenby, ye great swamp lots, Jaret Haddon and ye highway, Feb. 17, 1672. Grantor's wife Hester mentioned. Wit: Anthony Somerby and Samuell Stevens. Ack. April 8, 1673, in court at Salisbury.

Robert Swan of Haverhill, for a pair of oxen, conveyed to Joseph Williams of Haverhill two ox common rights in Haverhill, Jan. 29, 1672. Wit: Nath: Saltonstall and James Davis, jr. Ack. April 8, 1673, in court at Salisbury.

Edward Colcord, aged about fifty-six, and Willi: ffifeild deposed that when Mr. Steven Batcheller of Hampton was upon his voyage to England they heard him say to his son-in-law Mr. Christopher Hussey that as Hussey had no dowry with Batcheller's daughter when he married her, and that he had given to said Hussey all his estate. Sworn April 8, 1673, in court at Salisbury.

Richard Currier of Amsbery, planter, for £10, conveyed to Samuell ffowler of Salisbury, shipwright, four-cows common right in ye cow common in Salisbury formerly of Lewis Hulett; also, 30 acres of upland laid out to said Hulett's common right in ye great division above ye mill,

being ye 14th lot; and, also, all other commons that did belong to said Hulett's common right, except, etc., March 6, 1668-9. Wit: William Browne and Steven fflanders. Ack. March 8, 1672, before Robert Pike, commissioner.

John ffulsham (also ffoulsham) of Exiter, planter, appointed his son Peter ffulsham of Exiter his attorney, April 10, 1673. Wit: Ephraim ffulsham and Edward Smithe. Ack. April 8, 1673, in court at Salisbury.

John ffulsham, sr., of Exiter, for love, conveyed to my son Peter ffulsham of Exiter all my buildings and land (40 or 50 acres) that lately fell to me "lying in ye towne of Hinham in ye County of Norff: near Norrald comon & formerly cald by ye name of ffulfham at ye Box bufhes: being bovnded weftwd wth Norrald Comon to ye Eaftwd wth great Langhames, & little Langhams to ye northwd wth Hardingham Comon & to ye Southeaft wth ye land of John Buck formerly & ye land yt Edward ffower fformerly lived in," April 10, 1673. Wit: Ephraim ffulsham and Edward Smith. Ack. April 8, 1673, in court at Salisbury.

Francis Bates (his V/ mark) and wife Ann (her D mark) formerly Ann Oldum, acknowledged receipt of Ursula North, executrix of Richard North of Salisbury, deceased, of a legacy given to said Ann in the will of her said grandfather, Richard North, Oct. 4, 1669. Wit: Tho: Bradbury and Rich Wells. Ack. by both Oct. 5, 1669, before Robert Pike, commissioner.

Thomas Jones (his O mark) of Gloster, formerly called Cape Ann, acknowledged receipt from Ursula North of Salisbury, widow, of a legacy given to his wife Mary in the will of her father, Richard North of Salisbury, late deceased, July 24, 1669. Wit: Tho: Bradbury and William Bradbury. Proved by oath of the witnesses in court at Salisbury April 29, 1673.

Ephraim Winsly of Salisbury, cordwainer, for £5 given to Judeth Bradbury (now ye wife of Caleb Moudy of Nubery, malster) by my brother Samll Winsley,

sometimes of Salisbury, deceased, conveyed to said Caleb Moudy my interest in marsh called Rose island in ye town creek in Salisbury 24: 2: 1673. Wit Tho: Bradbury and Robert Ring. Ack. in court at Salisbury April 29, 1673.

Robert Ring of Salisbury, for £3, conveyed to Ephraim Winsly of Salisbury about an acre of marsh called Rose island, next to meadow formerly of Mr. Sam. Winsley, now in the possession of the grantee: the island was set off to grantor on execution against Salisbury on a judgment granted by the general court, May 18, 1671. Ack. 18: —: 1671, before Robert Pike, commissioner.

Tho: Marston, aged about 52, and Wm. ffifeild, aged about 55, deposed that about 1654, when Mr. Seth filetcher lived in Hampton, we were appointed to treat with Capt. Bryan Pendleton and Jno Pickerin in behalf of Portsmouth concerning ye settling of ye bounds betwixt Hampton and Portsmouth, and it was agreed "yt Hampton bounds fhould begin to meafure ten rod to ye northward of ye Cafway yt goeth over to ye beachie & from thence five miles norward neare ye fea fide." Sworn March 9, 1669, before Samll Dalton, commissioner, and in court at Salisbury April 29, 1673.

Tho: Marston and Jno Samborn, sr., depose that the next day after the line was agreed upon as above, it was meafured by Capt. Pendleton, Tho: Marston and Jno Samborn, and it "ended on yt north fide of Jocelins neck when wee fet up a ftake & layd ftones." Sworn 9: 1 mo: 1669, before Samll Dalton, commissioner, and in court at Salisbury April 29, 1673.

Jno Weed of Amsbery, husbandman, for £35 as legacies given to my children by their deceased uncle Samll Winsley, late of Salisbury, conveyed to Ephraim Winsly of Salisbury, cordwinder, 2 45 acre adjoining lots of upland in Amsbery, bounded by Burchin meadow, a highway between ye land of Wm. Osgood and Jno Colby, and land formerly of widow Rowel now Tho: Rowell's; also, my te

acre lot of upland in ye ox comon, in Amsbery, between the lots of Robert Jones and John Hoyt, jr., and next ye pond, May 3, 1671. Wit: Tho: Bradbury and Jane True. Ack. May 9, 1671, before Robert Pike, commissioner.

Isaac Cole of Hampton, carpenter, for £50, conveyed to Hezron Levitt of Hampton, shoemaker, my now dwelling house, barn, leantos and land adjoining, which land I bought of Christopher Palmer, lately in ye possession of Jn° Cass of Hampton; also, my orchard, etc., in Hampton, bounded by ye meeting house green towards ye south, a common highway and Abraham Pirkins, Jan. 15, 1666. Wit: Edward Colcord and Sarah Godfree. Ack. Jan. 17, 1666, before Sam¹¹ Dalton, commissioner.

John Payne of Boston, merchant, for boards paid by Lt. Peter Coffyn of Dover, conveyed to Peter ffulsham of Exiter, my fourth of a saw mill at Exiter, the other three fourths being at present in ye possession of Jn° Gillman, Jonathan Thing and John ffulsham, jr., Nov. 12, 1670. Wit: Allexander Waldern and George Resare. Ack. Nov. 14, 1670, before Richard Waldern, commissioner.

Jn° Stevens of Salisbury, husbandman, and wife Katherine, for two house lots (one ye house lot of Tho: Hauxworth and the other Jn° Cleford's, containing two acres), conveyed to Onezephorus Page and wife Mary 7 acres of upland and swamp in Salisbury, bounded by common land and grantor, 3 : 9 mo : 16—. Wit: John Pike and John Presse. Ack. by both May 15, 1673, before Robert Pike, commissioner.

Execution: Daniell Ela v. Wm. Neff; dated 30 : 2 : 1673. Addressed to Abraham Drake, marshall, who assigned it for service to his deputy, Jn° Griffyn, May —, 1673. Jn° Griffin demanded payment at the house of William Neff of Haverhill, who was not at home, but his wife directed the deputy to his land, and desired her brother John Corlis to show him the land, on which the execution was levied, May 6, 1673. The land was appraised

by Robert fford, who was chosen by the wife, and by Jn° Haseltine, chosen by Daniell Ela, 11¼ acres of it being measured and set off to Daniell Ela, bounded by Hauk's meadow way in Haverhill, Thomas Davis, etc.

Mr. George Peirson (Pearson—signature), now dwelling in Boston, appoints Edward Colcord of Hampton his attorney to receive claim from Sam¹¹ Levitt, "now dwelling in ye towne of Exon, in new england," March 19, 1672. Ack. at Great Island March 19, 1672, before Elias Stileman, commissioner.

John Warrin (his | W mark) of Exiter, card maker, for £22, conveyed to Sam¹¹ Levitt and Jonathan Robinson of Exiter 40 acres of land in Exiter, bounded by Will: Tayler, way from Exeter to Hampton and Hampton line, Sept. 29, 1668. Wit: John Redman and mark X of Edward Clarke. Ack. March 2, 1668-9, before Sam¹¹ Dalton, commissioner.

James Chase of Hampton released to Jn° Ilsly (also Ilsley) of Salisbury a bond dated Jan. 28, 1672, to be delivered to James Chase or Tho Philbrook, and conveyed to said Jn° Ilsly my two divisions of upland I bought of him in Salisbury in Hall's farm, bounded by Edward ffrench, Mr. Stanian,—one being 16¾ acres sold by Jn° Easman to said Jn° Ilsly, and the other 9 acres 13 rods sold by Abraham fitts to said Jn° Ilsly, being lots 7 and 8 in Salisbury town records, June 5, 1673. Wit: Tho: Philbrick and Joseph Dow. Ack. June 5, 1673, before Sam¹¹ Dalton, commissioner.

Moses Worcester of Salisbury, planter, for £58, conveyed to John Allin of Salisbury, mariner, a dwelling house and a 16-acre planting lot adjoining in Salisbury, bounded by Mr. Sam¹¹ Dudley (now in ye possession of Georg Goldwyer), Mr. Batts (now in ye possession of Maj. Robert Pike), Mr. Dudley and highway leading to Hampton, June 23, 1673. Wit: Mary Bradbury (her MB mark) and Caleb Moody. Ack. June 23, 1673, before Samuel Symonds, deputy-governor.

Capt. Matthew ffuller of Barnstable, Mass., and Wm. Chandler of Newbury, cooper, deposed that upon consideration of a contract of marriage being accomplished between Caleb Moody and Sarah Peirce, both of Newbury, her father Daniell Peirce, sr., of Newbury, farmer, made to her a deed of gift of land in Salisbury he bought of Phillip Wallidge of Salisbury, lately the land of Mr. Munday. Sworn before Willia Stoughton, assistant, and Robert Pike, commissioner, June 23, 1673.

John Eyres (Eyer—*signature*) of Haverhill, yeoman, with consent of wife Mary, for £250, conveyed to my son Zakerie Eyres of Haverhill my now dwelling house and farm adjoining in Haverhill, containing 250 acres, bounded by Lt. Brown, Josuah Woodman, Spickett river and Merimack river, June 30, 1673. Wit: Anthony Somerby and Rebecah Somerby. Ack. July 1, 1673, before Robert Pike, commissioner.

Nicolas Norris (his N mark) of Exiter, tailor, conveyed to John ffuller of Hampton a 2½-acre houselot in Hampton on ye north plain, formerly ye land of Abraham Pirkins who conveyed it to Thomas Webster, and by him to me, bounded by Abraham Pirkins, a way and ye commons, April 29, 1671. Wit: Willi: ffuller, sr., W: ffuller, jr., and Abraham Pirkins, sr. Ack. April 29, 1671, before Samll Dalton, commissioner. Grantor's wife, Sarah Norris, released dower 5: 11 mo: 1671, before Samll Dalton, commissioner.

Robert Jones (his | mark) of Amsbery, planter, for love, conveyed to my son William Jones my house and three acres of land, and my part of ye saw mill; the land lies below ye country way, bounded by Richard Currier and Pawwaus river, also, ten acres above ye country highway, bounded by ye power river, Thomas Barnard and the country highway; and, also, 20 acres near Whitcher's hill; all lying in Amesbury, July 4, 1673. Grantee is to pay money to his brother Joseph Jones, to his three sisters and his mother Jones. Wit: William Osgood

(his WO mark) and John Osgood. A. July 4, 1673, before Robert Pike, commissioner.

John Hoyt, jr., of Salisbury newtown and wife Mary, for £13, conveyed John Davis, jr., of Newbury 40 acre land in Amsbery or Salisbury newt above ye pond, bounded by highway Wm. Barnes and John Hoyt, sr., June 1669. Wit: Anthony Somerbie and Anthony Mors, jr. Ack. Jan. —, 1669, fore Robert Pike, commissioner.

Mr. Thomas Bradbury and John Stevens sr. (his | mark), divide land the bought of Mr. Anthony Stanian in 500 acres granted by Salisbury to the habitants, bounded by ye highway lead to the mill, Merimack main river, He: Brown, Jno Bayly, and a white oak stan ing near ye millway by ye now dwell house of Jno Stevens, jr., July 7, 167 Wit: Richd Crisp and John Buss. Ack July 10, 1673, before Robt Pike, commissioner.

John Williams, sr., of Haverhill, wi Jane (her | mark), conveyed to my s. Joseph Williams my now dwelling house house lot, orchard, hop yards, eight common rights in Haverhill, and a parcel the ox common which was laid out to beyond ye fishing river towards the s mill; also, my duck meadow, March 1673. Wit: John Jonson and Na Smithe. Ack. July 14, 1673, before Na Saltonstall, commissioner.

Henry Green of Hampton, house ca penter, for 7 acres of upland made today to Isaac Green by Joseph ffren of Salisbury, tailor, conveyed to s Joseph ffrench my 12-acre lot cf upla in Salisbury in Mr. Hall's farm, forme ye lot of George Goldwyer, bounded Mr. Willi: Hooke, Edward Goue, a co of meadow and a highway running thre said farm, 10: 10: 1671. Wit: Willia Bradbury and John Stanyan. Ack. court at Salisbury April 8, 1673.

George Goldwyer (his O mark) Salisbury, yeoman, for £18, conveyed Jededia Andros of Salisbury, house penter, my division of ye first higled

pigledee lots of salt marsh in Salisbury, granted to Joseph Moys, containing five acres, bounded by Wm. Sargent, sr., Abraham Morrill and Richard Wells of Salisbury, deceased, March 21, 1672-3. Wit: Tho: Bradbury and Jabez Bradbury. Ack., and wife Martha Goldwyer released dower, March 21, 1672-3, before Rob't Pike, commissioner.

Moses Worcester of Salisbury, planter, for £20, conveyed to Cornelius Conner of Salisbury, husbandman, my 6-acre lot of cow-common marsh in Salisbury, bounded by Jn° Severans, Tho: Carter, ye little river or creek w'ch comes from Hampton river and common marsh, June 24, 1673. Wit: Phillip Greelee and Jabez Bradbury. Ack. June 30, 1673, before Robert Pike, commissioner.

Peter Green (his ꝑ mark) of Haverhill, wife Elizabeth, for £26, conveyed to Michell Emerson of Haverhill my dwelling house and one acre of land in Haverhill belonging thereto with the apple trees upon said land, bounded " by y° highway y't goeth to y° west bridg," and ye little river "comonly called y° Saw mill River," June 14, 1673. Wit: Robert fford and Joseph Jonson (his | mark). Ack. before Daniell Denison.

Benjamin Shaw receipts for one-half of the carpenter's tools, pewter platters, sword, colt, housing, land, etc., given to him in the will of his father, 20: 11: 1661. Wit: Samuell ffogge, Joseph Shawe and Daniell Tilton. Ack. in court at Hampton 14: 8: 1673.

Joseph ffoulsham, sr., of Exiter, yeoman, conveyed to William Samborn of Hampton 30 acres of land (being one-half of 60 acres laid out to Jn° ffoulsham, jr., and to grantor in Hampton, upon an agreement with Mr. Jn° Gillman and Henry Robie, in ye behalf of ye town of Hampton, bounded by Exiter bounds, "towards y't playne comonly called y° Indian graues," the Hampton comons and ye old way y't leadeth towards Salisbury; the other half of said 60 acres is in the hands of the grantee, March 31, 1673. Wit: Sam'll Dalton and Benj:

Moulton (his E mark). Ack. in court at Sarisbury April 8, 1673. Mr. Sam'll Dudley of Exiter warrants the title of above lot of land, Sept. —, 1673. Wit: John Gillman and Moses Gillman. Ack. 16: 8: 1673, before Sam'll Dalton, commissioner.

John ffolsham, jr., of Exiter conveyed to William Samborn of Hampton 30 acres of land in Hampton (being one-half of 60 acres allowed to John ffolshon, sr., and Jn° ffolsham, jr., by an agreement made by Mr. John Gillman of Exiter and Henry Robie in behalf of Hampton), bounded by Exiter line, grantee, Hampton comons, etc., 15: 3: 1673. Wit: Edw: Smith and Linsley Hall. Ack. by Jn° ffoulsham, jr., 16: 8: 1873, before Sam'll Dalton, commissioner.

John Garland (his ꙩ mark) of Hampton, planter, for £26, conveyed to John Philbrick of Hampton 100 acres of upland and fresh meadow (thirty acres) in Hampton, being one-half of the farm I lately bought of Mr. Seaborne Cotton in Hogpen plain, bounded by Wm. ffuller (now in ye hands of John ffuller), land granted to Mr. Seahorn Cotton, and land laid out to Jn° ffilbrick, Aug. 5, 1671. Wit: James Pirkins (his J P mark) and John ffuller. Ack. Aug. 5, 1671.

John Philbrick (his J mark) of Hampton, planter, for £17, conveyed to Isaac Chase of Hampton 50 acres of upland and meadow (being one-half of that I bought of John Garland of Hampton) in Hampton, in Hog pen plain, and being one-fourth of ye farm granted by Hampton to Mr. Seaborn Cotton, and by him sold to Jn° Garland, 1: 11 mo: 1672. Wit: Joseph Dow, Jonathan Philbrick and Jacob Pirkins. Ack. 23: 8: 1673, before Sam'll Dalton, commissioner.

To be continued.

NOTE.

Elizabeth Bradford, alias Dennen, of Gloucester, widow of Thomas Bradford, late of Gloucester, deceased, 1756.— *Registry of deeds.*

BRICKETT GENEALOGY.

NATHANIEL BRICKETT[1], born about 1648, lived in Newbury, being a cooper. He was living in Newbury in 1711.

Children, born in Newbury :—

2—I. NATHANIEL[2], b. Dec. 20, 1673 ; drowned Oct. 17, 1687, in Newbury.
3—II. JOHN[2], b. May 3, 1676.
4—III. SARAH[2], b. Feb. 13, 1677-8 ; m. Henry Lunt, 3d, Jan. 1, 1700-1.
5—IV. JAMES[2] (twin), b. Dec. 11, 1679. See below (5).
6—V. MARY[2] (twin), b. Dec. 11, 1679.
7—VI. HANNAH[2], b. Sept. 23, 1683; "Hannah Brickett, a singlewoman, had a son born in Newbury Jan. 31, 1708."

5

JAMES BRICKETT[2], born in Newbury Dec. 11, 1679. He was a yeoman, and lived in Newbury. He married Mary Haynes before 1705; and died about 1763; his will, dated April 9, 1753, being proved March 12, 1764. She survived him, and died, his widow, before Nov. 27, 1770, when administration was granted upon his estate.

Children, born in Newbury :—

8—I. MARY[3], b. Aug. 13, 1705; m. Solomon Holman May 23, 1722.
9—II. SARAH[3], b. April 2, 1707; m. Abel Chase of Newbury May 14, 1728.
10—III. JAMES[3], b. June 27, 1711. See below (10).
11—IV. JOHN[3], b. July 19, 1716; d. Aug. 28, 1736, aged twenty.
12—V. BARNARD[3], b. April 3, 1719. See below (12).

10

JAMES BRICKETT[3], born in Newbury June 27, 1711. He was a house carpenter, and lived in Newbury. He married Susanna Pilsbury of Newbury Aug. 7, 1729. He died July 21, 1770, aged fifty-nine. His estate was appraised at £549. She survived him, and died, his widow, Dec. 22, 1788, aged seventy-nine.

Children, born in Newbury :—

13—I. NATHANIEL[4], b. May 21, 1731. See below (13).
14—II. JAMES[4], b. Dec. 7, 1733; d. young.
15—III. ABIGAIL[4], b. Oct. 12, 1735; lived in Newbury; d., unmarried; her will, dated Nov. 26, 1782, was proved Feb. 4, 1783.

16—IV. JAMES[4], b. Feb. 16, 1738. See (16).
17—V. JOHN[4], b. March 13, 1740. See (17).
18—VI. MOSES[4], b. May 4, 1742. See (18).
19—VII. SUSANNA[4], b. Jan. 8, 1745; m. Chase Haddock of Haverhill Oct. 22, 1772 and d. Feb. 4, 1781, aged thirty.
20—VIII. MARY[4], b. Aug. 20, 1749; m. Abel Adams, 4th, Nov. 18, 1768; and was living in 1782.
21—IX. BARNARD[4], b. July 25, 1751. See (21).

12

BARNARD BRICKETT[3], born in Newbury April 3, 1719. He was a husbandman and lived in Newbury. He married Sarah Hale of Newbury Dec. 21, 1737 and died April 9, 1748, aged twenty-nine. His estate was valued at £373 8s. She survived him, and married, secondly, Moses Morss Oct. 25, 1759.

Children, born in Newbury :—

22—I. MARY[4], b. Feb. 20, 1738; m. Step Merrill Nov. 25, 1756; and was living in 1764.
23—II. SARAH[4], m. Enos (Enoch?) Bartlett, jr., of Newbury, cordwainer, May 1, 1768.
24—III. BARNARD[4], b. Oct. 7, 1742; lived in Newbury, where he was a cordwainer, and removed, in 1765, to Chester, N. H., where he was a yeoman; m. Mary Hall March 5, 1772.
25—IV. THOMAS[4], b. Oct. 1, 1744. See (25).
26—V. ——[4], d. Dec. 19, 1747, aged 14 hours.

13

LT. NATHANIEL BRICKETT[4], born Newbury May 21, 1731. He was a yeoman, and lived in Newbury. He married Anna Wooden Nov. 13, 1750; and she was his wife in 1801. He died in 1805; his will, dated March 12, 1801, being proved Sept. 26, 1805.

Children, born in Newbury :—

27—I. ANNA[5], b. Feb. 26, 1756; m. Benja. Hills, jr., of Newbury Sept. 1774; and was living in 1801.
28—II. SUSANNA[5], b. April 20, 1759; m. Stephen Coffin of Newbury May 23, 1777 and was living in 1801.
29—III. NATHANIEL[5], b. May 1, 1761. See low (29).
30—IV. JAMES[5], b. Jan. 15, 1765. See (30).

::—v. JUDITH⁵, b. April 8, 1767; m. Caleb
        Titcomb of Newbury (pub. Dec. 25,
        1784); living in 1801.
.:—vi. AMOS⁵, b. April 11, 1769. *See below*
        (32).
:3—vii. MARY⁵, b. May 12, 1771; m. Enoch
        Little, jr., of Newbury Sept. 15,
        1796; and was living in 1801.
::—viii. ELIZABETH⁵, b. May 17, 1773; m. Steph-
        en Moody Little of Newbury Oct. 9,
        1794; and was living in 1801.

16

DR. JAMES BRICKETT⁴, born in Newbury Feb. 16, 1738. He was a physician, and settled in Haverhill in 1762.
He was surgeon's mate in Colonel Frye's
regiment at Fort Frederick from March
30, 1759, to July 30, 1760; and was a
patriot of the Revolution. He became
lieutenant-colonel in Colonel Frye's regiment, and commanded the regiment at
the battle of Bunker hill, being wounded.
He became colonel, and finally brigadier-
general of the forces to be sent to Canada in 1776, commanding the Massachusetts levies for the Northern Army. The
next year he was a brigadier under General Gates. Doctor Brickett's services
were too numerous to be recorded here.
He married, first, Edna Merrill Oct. 8,
1760; and she died Sept. 21, 1802. He
married, second, Abigail Moody Jan. 24,
1803; and died Dec. 10, 1818, at the
age of four-score years.
Children :—
35—i. DANIEL⁵, b. Aug. 20, 1761, in New-
        bury. *See below* (35).
36—ii. JAMES⁵, b. Jan. 28, 1763, in Haverhill;
        d. Sept. 19, 1775, aged twelve.
37—iii. MARY⁵, b. March 6, 1765, in Haver-
        hill; probably m. James Ayer, jr.,
        Dec. 8, 1782; and d. April 28, 1838.
38—iv. MOSES⁵, b. Nov. 19, 1766, in Haverhill.
39—v. SARAH⁵, b. Dec. 21, 1768, in Haver-
        hill; d. Nov. 15, 1775, aged six.
40—vi. THEODORE⁵, b. Jan. 7, 1772, in Haver-
        hill; m. Sally Swett of Haverhill
        Sept. 27, 1795; and probably settled
        in Andover, Me.
41—vii. JOHN⁵, b. June 2, 1774, in Haverhill.
        See below (41).

17

JOHN BRICKETT⁴, born in Newbury
March 13, 1740. He was a blacksmith;
and lived in Newbury until 1780, when
he settled in Haverhill. He married,
first, Prudence Adams April 17, 1760;
and she died April 25, 1783, aged forty-
four. He married, second, Mary, widow
of Leonard Sawyer of Haverhill June 29,
1783; and she died Feb. 18, 1817. He
died Feb. 28, 1825, aged eighty-four.
Children, born in Newbury :—
42—i. JOHN⁵, b. Dec. 13 (14?), 1762. *See
        below (42).*
43—ii. HANNAH⁵, b. March 1, 1765; probably
        m. Joseph Snow June 8, 1783; and
        d. (?) before 1799.
44—iii. ABRAHAM⁵, b. Feb. 10, 1767; shop
        joiner; lived in Newbury, in Coos,
        Vt., in 1796.
45—iv. EDMUND⁵, b. Dec. 25, 1772; black-
        smith; lived in New Salem, N. H.
46—v. JOSEPH⁵, b. about 1779; lived in New-
        bury in 1799.

18

COL. MOSES BRICKETT⁴, born in Newbury May 4, 1742. He was a housewright and yeoman; and lived in the
West parish of Newbury. He married
Miss Sarah Chase of Newbury Oct. 5,
1768; and died in 1813, his will, dated
Sept. 16, 1805, being proved Jan. 4,
1814. She survived him; and died in
West Newbury early in the year 1827.
Children, born in Newbury :—
47—i. SARAH⁵, b. May 29, 1770; m. Abial
        Swett of Newbury Oct. 13, 1792; and
        was living in 1816.
48—ii. MOSES⁵, b. Jan. 19, 1772; lived in
        Newbury, chaise-maker, in 1814; and
        in West Newbury, a wheelwright, in
        1827.
49—iii. DAVID⁵ (twin), b. Feb. 20, 1774; living
        in 1816.
50—iv. JAMES⁵ (twin), b. Feb. 20, 1774; living
        in 1816.

21

BARNARD BRICKETT⁴, born in Newbury
July 25, 1751. He was a husbandman,
and lived in Newburyport until 1777
when he settled in Haverhill. He married Deborah Towne of Topsfield Dec.
3, 1772; and she was living in 1824. He
died Feb. 7, 1829, aged seventy-seven.
Children :—
51—i. JOSEPH⁵, b. June 26, 1775, in New-
        bury; living in 1824.

52—II. BARNARD⁵, b. July 17, 1778, in Haverhill; m. Miriam Stewart May 2,
1799; lived in Haverhill; esquire; d.
April 15, 1836, aged fifty-seven, leaving nine children.

25

THOMAS BRICKETT⁴, born in Newbury
Oct. 1, 1744. He was a blacksmith, and
lived in Newbury until after 1777, being
of Pembroke, N. H., in 1790. He married Mary Noyes Aug. 27, 1766; and she
was his wife in 1777.
Children, born in Newbury:—
53—I.   SARAH⁵, b. July 13, 1767.
54—II.   RHODA⁵, b. July 24, 1769.
55—III. ——HARD⁵ (son), b. Nov. 24, 1771.
56—IV.   ——⁵ (dau.), b. Jan. 25, 1775.
57—V.   ——ATHAN⁵ (son), b. March 11, 1776.

29

NATHANIEL BRICKETT⁵, born in Newbury
May 1, 1761. He was a yeoman, and
lived in Newbury until about 1789, when
he became a resident of Newburyport.
He married Judith Allen of Newbury
June 11, 1783; and she was his wife in
1795. He was living in Newburyport in
1805.
Children :—
58—I.   ANNA⁶, b. April 19, 1784, in Newbury.
59—II.   NATHAN ALLEN⁶, b. Jan. 10, 1786, in
Newbury.
60—III. JOSEPH⁶, b. Jan. 12, 1791, in Newburyport.
61—IV.   JUDITH⁶, b. Sept. 15, 1792, in Newburyport.
62—V.   NATHANIEL⁶, b. April 12, 1795, in Newburyport.

30

JAMES BRICKETT⁵, born in Newbury
Jan. 15, 1765. He married Anna
Wheeler of Salem, N. H., Feb. 14, 1786;
and lived in Newbury. She was living in
1793, and he in 1801.
Children, born in Newbury :—
63—I.   HANNAH⁶, b. Dec. 14, 1786.
64—II.   JONATHAN⁶, b. May 31, 1789.
65—III. NATHANIEL⁶, b. March 17, 1793.

32

AMOS BRICKETT⁵, born in Newbury
April 11, 1769. He was a yeoman, and
lived in Newbury. He married Abigail

Thurla of Newbury April 18, 1793; and
he was living in Newbury in 1805.
Child, born in Newbury :—
66—I.   MOODY⁶, b. July 31, 1791; lived
West Newbury; m. Elizabeth T.
she d. Sept. 27, 1879, aged ei
seven years and nine months; an
d. May 26, 1888, aged ninety-three.

35

DR. DANIEL BRICKETT⁵, born in Haverhill Aug. 20, 1761. He was a soldier of
the Revolution, and a pensioner. He
married Polly West Sept. 23, 1784; and
lived in Haverhill, where he was a phy-
cian. She died March 20, 1815 ; and he
died Jan. 16, 1835, aged seventy-three.
Children, born in Haverhill :—
67—I.   SARAH⁶, b. Dec. 24, 1784; d. Oct. 21,
1810, aged twenty-five.
68—II.   JAMES⁶, b. in 1786; d. Nov. 12, 1786,
aged nine months.
69—III. MARY⁶, b. Jan. 1, 1787; d. before 18—
70—IV.   ANNA⁶, b. Feb. 5, 1789; d. before 18—
71—V.   FANNY (FRANCES)⁶, b. Sept. 23, 1791;
m. Phineas Carleton of Haverhill;
and she was the only child living in
Massachusetts in 1835.
72—VI.   HARRIET⁶, b. Sept. 1, 1796; m. Eb-
zer A. Porter; and lived in New York
City.
73—VII. ABIGAIL⁶, b. Oct. 15, 1798; m. Charles
Robbins; and lived in Ithaca, N. Y.,
in 1842.
74—VIII. EDWIN⁶, living in 1842.

41

DR. JOHN BRICKETT⁵, born in Haver-
June 2, 1774. He married Eliza(?)
Ayer of Haverhill Sept. 29, 1795 ; and
they were living in Newburyport in 179
and 1798; in Newbury in 1800 an
1805; and in Newburyport in 1807 an
1808.
Children, born in Newburyport :—
75—I.   LAVINIA⁶, b. Aug. 17, 1796.
76—II.   MARTHA KIMBALL⁶, b. March 23,
1798; d. Aug. 18, 1807.
77—III. SARAH A.⁶, d. Aug. 25, 1825.
78—IV.   JOHN JAMES⁶, b. Feb. 1, 1802; d. Sept.
30, 1824.
79—V.   ELIZA⁶, b. May 30, 1804; d. Jan. —
1873.
80—VI.   ELIZABETH WHITE⁶, b. June (July?)
1806 (5?); d. April 19, 1807.

42

JOHN BRICKETT[5], born in Newbury Dec. 13 (14?), 1762. He married Abigail Haseltine of Haverhill about 1785; and lived in Haverhill. He died Dec. 27, 1845, aged eighty-three; and she died March 17, 1848, aged eighty-five.

Children, born in Haverhill :—

81—I.   SUSANNA[6], b. March 13, 1786; d., unmarried, Aug. 7, 1826, aged forty.
82—II. ABIGAIL[6], b. April 18, 1788.
83—III. POLLY[6], b. in 1791; d. May 22, 1791, aged fifteen weeks.
84—IV. JOHN[6], b. July 11, 1792.
85—V.   JAMES[6], b. Dec. 14, 1794; d. Dec. 10, 1807, aged thirteen.
86—VI. POLLY[6], b. in 1796; d. Nov. 28, 1797, aged fourteen months.
87—VII. DANIEL, b. in 1800; d. June 9, 1803, aged two years and eight months.
88—VIII. MOSES[6], b. in 1802; d. Sept. 23, 1803, aged fifteen months.
89—IX. SALLY[6], b. Oct. 14, 1808.

JOHN AUSTIN.

The following deposition is copied from the record in the Essex county registry of deeds, Executions, book 3, leaf 170.

I Joseph Bradeen of Marblehead in the County of Essex yeoman, on oath depose testify and say that I was born in the Town of york in the County of york that in the year of our Lord seventeen hundred and seventy I left that place and came to Marblehead where I have lived ever since, and I further Testify that I well knew Matthew Austin of said york who was a Respectable Farmer in said Town, he lived within about one mile of the place where I was born, I was about twenty seven years old when I left york. some years after my residence at Marblehead a Stranger came to my house and enquired if I knew him. I told him I did not, he then asked me whether I did not once belong to the Town of york, and whether I was not acquainted with Matthew Austin of that place. I told him I was born in york and well knew Matthew Austin of that place. He then said that he was the son of said Matthew and that he knew me very well and had often seen me at york and he well knew all my friends there, and told me their names, and told me whom my Sisters were married to. I was frequently at york to see my friends, but John Austin who was the person who called on me, must have been quite young and I do not recollect I ever saw him there. He lived a number of years in Marblehead and always went by the name of old york. He afterwards left Marblehead and went with his family to live in Boston, and further your Deponent says not.   Joseph Bradeen.

Sworn to at Marblehead Dec. 16, 1819, before Nathan Bowen and Ralph H. French, justices of the peace, at the request of the town of Marblehead.

NOTES.

Perez Bradford of Marblehead, shoreman, and wife Mary, 1756.—*Registry of deeds.*

Robert Bracket published to Miss Sarah Goodhue, both of Newburyport, Sept. 21, 1765.

Miss Sarah Bradish married William Tarbox, both of Newburyport, Oct. 29, 1782.

Capt. John Bradish married Miss Sarah Greenough, both of Newburyport, July 1, 1784.

Miss Anne Bradish married Capt. Benaiah Titcomb, jr., both of Newburyport, March 13, 1786.

Miss Mary Bradish married Capt. Jonathan Titcomb, jr., both of Newburyport, Sept. 16, 1792.

— *Newburyport town records.*

Rebecca Bradeen (Bradner?) published to Richard Priar Nov. 7, 1712.—*Ipswich town records.*

Thomas Brackett's children : Joseph, died May 15, 16—; Lidea, died Jan. 1, 1667 ; Thomas, died Jan. 15, 1667.

Mary Bradaway married John Allen May 30, 1698.

James Brace married Polly Doyle, both of Salem, Dec. 11, 1791.

Sally Bradish married Joseph Felt Dec. 29, 1793.

—*Salem town records.*

Josiah Bradley married Polly Duston
July 8, 1787; she died March 5, 1803.
Children: Joshua, born June 19, 1788;
Hazen, born March 14, 1790; Betsey,
born Oct. 19, 1792; Hezekiah; Maria;
Isaiah; Loisa.—*Haverhill town records.*

SUFFOLK COUNTY DEEDS.

VOLUME IV.

The following are abstracts of all records in volume IV of the Suffolk county
registry of deeds relating to Essex
county persons and property, where parties are given as residing, or property is
mentioned as being located in Essex
county. The records in this volume
cover the period from 1661 to 1665.

Execution: Edward Lane of Boston,
merchant, v. Samuell Archard of Salem,
for £10, 13s., 4d., judgment by the court
of assistants at Boston Feb. 12, 1660:
addressed to Edw. Michelson, marshall-
general; signed by Edw. Rawson, secretary. Returned satisfied April 10, 1661,
by Rich. Wayte, deputy.—*Page IX.*

Execution: Jn° Williams of Marblehead, mariner, v. William Russell of Boston, mariner, for £30; dated at Boston
Feb. 3, 1661; addressed to the marshall
of Suffolk county; signed by Edw. Rawson, recorder. Return by Richard Wayte,
marshall; that he committed the defendant to prison Feb. 3, 1661.—*Page XI.*

Execution: Edward Lane of Boston,
merchant, v. Samuell Archar of Salem,
for £10, 13s., 4d., judgment by the court
of assistants at Boston Sept. 7, 1658;
addressed to Edward Michelson, marshall-
general; dated Feb. 12, 1660. Returned
satisfied April 10, 1661, by Rich: Wayte,
deputy-marshall.—*Page XII.*

Execution: Robert Hazeltine v. George
Hadley, for £5, 1s., 6d., and possession
of land sued for at Salem court, judgment
by the court of assistants at Boston Sept.
1, 1663; addressed to Edward Michelson, marshall-general; signed by Edw.
Rawson, secretary. Return by John Pickard, deputy-marshall, of possession of land

given and costs satisfied.—*Page XII.*

Antipas Newman of Wenham and wife
Elizabeth conveyed to Mr. Amos Richison
of Boston the neck of land which was
given to me by my father Winthrop, who
bought it of Hugh Calkin in the Pequitt
country at or near the place called Qua-
docke adjoining Quandocke farm belonging to said Richison, bounded by said
farm east, Caulkin's brook west, the sea
south, and Capt. Denison's north, Oct.
29, 1661. Wit: Elizabeth Richards and
Lucy Winthrop. Ack. 16: 11: 1661,
before Samuel Symonds.—*Page 9.*

John Alcock of Roxbury, physician, for
£13, conveyed to Nathaniell Winslow of
Salisbury, planter, one-thirty-second part
of Block island, being twelve and one-
half acres, the grantor having bought of
Gov. John Endecott, esq., Maj.-gen. Daniell Denison and Maj. Wm. Hathorne
their respective interests in said island,
namely, three-fourths, to them given by
the colony, May 3, 1661. Wit: Edward
Rawson and Rachell Rawson. Ack. 3: 5
mo: 1661, before Jo: Endecott, gov.—
Page 30.

Joshua Lasker, "Cittizen and Girdler
of London appointed his friend Thomas
Lucke of Pensurst in Kent, merchant, at
present bound on a voyage for New England, to recover money due from Samuell
Sherman now or late of New England,
merchant, and Walter Price of Salem,
merchant, May 12, 1662. Wit: Henry
Minchard, scr., John Peirce, Edward Williams servant to Rob' Minchard, notary
public, and Samuell Warkman. Proved
by oaths of Mr. John Peirce and Samuell
Warkman 25: 5: 1662, before Dep.-gov.
Ri: Bellingham. Thomas Luck receipts
for £46, 8s., received of Mr. Walter
Price of Salem July 25, 1662. Wit:
Richard Page, Samuell Warkman and
John Peirce. Ack. before Ri. Bellingham,
dep.-gov.—*Page 34.*

Bond of Walter Price of Salem, merchant, for £86, 8s., sterling, to Joshua
Lasker "Cittizen and Girdler of London,"
whose attorney is Thomas Lucke of Pent-
hurst, county of Kent, merchant, to pay

balance of debt, in sugar sent from Barbadoes, etc., July 26, 1662. Wit: Jo: Endecott, gov., and Jo: Endecott, jr.—*Page* 35.

Ezekiel Woodward of Ipswich, carpenter, and wife Anne, conveyed to Thaddeus Riddan of Lynn, merchant, house, wharf and lot in Boston, Aug. 14, 1662. Wit: Wm. Halsey. Ack. Aug. 15, 1662, before Jo. Endecott, gov.—*Page* 42.

Peter Nash, "now Inhabiting within the bounds" of Rowley, bind to Theodor Atkinson of Boston, merchant, my house and lot in Charlestown on northeast side of Charlestown river, and northwest side of the highway, to pay £30 in pipe staves, July 8, 1661. Wit: William Howard, Theodor Atkinson, jr., and Rob' Howard, notary public. Ack. July 9, 1661, before Ri Bellingham, dep.-gov.— *Page* 72.

John Johnson of Haverhill and wife Elizabeth conveyed to Peter Nash of Charlestown my dwelling house, shop and orchard in Charlestown, Aug. 20, 1660. Wit: Richard Littlehale and Robert Clements. Ack. Dec. 13, 1662, before Jo: Endecott, gov. Possession given in presence of Nathaniell Atkinson, Peter Nash, Joseph Stower and Josias Wood.—*Page* 73.

Samuel Rogers of Ipswich, for £100, conveyed to William Hubbard of Ipswich my interest in one-fourth of houses and land in the possession of Joshua Hewes, and given to me by my grandfather, Mr. Robert Crane, Sept. 23, 1662. Wit: John Appleton and John Paine. Ack. before Daniel Denison.—*Page* 107.

John Payne of Boston, merchant, for £1,500 in legacies under the will of my father William Payne of Boston, deceased, mortgaged to the three children of Samuel Apleton of Ipswich, gent", my interest in the Prudence island, houses, land, etc., Jan. 20, 1663. Wit: Thomas Danforth, Joell Jacooms, John Evens and Caleb Cheesahteannutk. Ack. Jan. 21, 1663, before Daniel Gookin.—*Page* 176.

Joseph Humphry, one of the sons of the late John Humphrey of Lynn, esquire,

petitioned the general court May 27, 1663, to grant him "three hundred acres of land in the wilderness where it may be found free from former grants and not hindering a Plantation," which was done, said Joseph Humfry, for £20, conveyed to Antipas Boyce of Boston said three hundred acres of upland June 25, 1664. Wit: James Oliver and John Evered.— *Page* 200.

Richard Cooke of Boston, one of the assignees of Thomas Broughton of Boston (the other assignee being Walter Price of Salem, merchant), conveyed to Sir Thomas Temple, now resident in Boston, knight and baronet, the interest of said Broughton in Noddle's island, near or in Boston, which said assignees received on execution, dated March 31, 1663, Aug. 4, 1664.—*Page* 210.

Thomas Shearer of Boston, tailor, for £64, 16s., 4d., mortgaged to Simon Lynde of Boston, merchant, house and lot of land in Boston, bounded by house late of Thomas Roberts, now in the hands of Unis, relict of said Roberts, and now wife of Moses Mavericke of Marblehead, and at present in the occupation of Zechariah Phillips, etc., Sept. 23, 1665. Discharged on margin July 8, 1668.—*Page* 220.

Harlakenden Simons of Gloucester, gent., and wife Elizabeth, for £122, conveyed to James Bill of Pulling point, in Boston, husbandman, our farm house and 70 acres of land at said Pulling point, Jan. 16, 1664. Wit: Increase Mather and Jo: Endicott, jr., Rob' Howard, notary public, John Tuttle and Thomas Bill. Ack. Jan. 19, 1664, before Samuel Simonds.—*Page* 261.

John Burnell of Salem, planter, for £30, conveyed to John White of Boston, joiner, a house and small lot of land between the street leading by the water towards the north Battery and the highway leading towards the meeting house at the north end of Boston, unto the well and wharf, Oct. 17, 1665. Wit: Joshua Rice and William Pearse, scr. Ack. 17: 8: 1665, before Eliazer Lusher. Posses-

sion given same day in the presence of William Pearse, scr.—*Page* 324.

Deposition of Jn° Gifford, aged forty years, that having received a letter from England from a kinswoman of his, Mrs. Hargrave, living in Horsley downe neer London about the year 1663-4, which desired information about the estate of Samuell Bennet, sr., of Lyn or Boston, and to inquire of said Bennett how far forth he would be assenting to the match of his son Samuell Bennet, jr., with the daughter of said Mrs. Hargrave, and as to what estate he would possess his said son, I went to Mr. Bennet to inform him of Mrs. Hargrave's desire, and he said that he would give his son the estate that he is dwelling in in the roadway between Boston and Lynne, which was worth, he said, £800, and also £80 stock of cattle, the son to allow his father £20 a year for the latter's life, in case he needed it, on condition that the son should not sell the property. Sworn to Dec. 5, 1665, before Tho Clarke, commissioner.

Samuell Maverick, aged 63 years, deposed that some time last year he had some speech with Samuell Bennet, sr., of Lynne as to a match intended between his son Samuell Bennet, jr., and a daughter of Capt. William Hargrave of Horsey downe, mariner. Mr. Bennet promised that if the marriage took place he would convey to his son the house he now lives in, with barns, stables, orchards, gardens, and all upland and meadow fenced in and belonging to said farm, with several acres of woodland adjacent and £80 worth of stock with the provision that the son should pay the father £20 a year during the latter's life, if he needed it or demanded it, and to the best of my remembrance he so wrote to Capt. Hargrave. He also tied his son not to alienate the premises during his life. Sworn at Boston Dec. 8, 1665, before Thomas Clarke, commissioner.

Recorded at request of Samuell Bennet, jr.

—Page 328.

IMPORTANCE OF LOCAL HISTORY.

BY DANIEL S. DURRIE.

There are few branches of knowledge whose importance has been so generally and justly extolled, as that of history. From the days of Cicero, who proclaimed it to be "the light of truth, the life of memory and the preceptress of life," the world has been accustomed to hear its praises and listen to the recital of its powers. History has been justly termed "philosophy teaching by example," and in a broad sense "the whole past course of humanity from the first moment of its existence to the present hour."

The love of history seems inseparable from human nature. It is natural for man to preserve as far as is in his power the memory of those of his own time and of those that preceded it. Rude heaps of stone and earth have been raised and ruder hymns or rythmes have been composed by nations who had not yet the use of arts and letters. An application of the study of history that does not tend to make us better men and better citizens is at least but an ingenious sort of idleness; and the knowledge thus acquired is at best a creditable kind of ignorance. The study of history, however, of all others is the most proper to train us up to private and public virtue.

Important, however, and instructive as is the narrative of past events and the influence they have exerted on the world in civilization and refinement, history is seldom so interesting as when descending from the loftier and more splendid regions of general narration, it dwells for a while in an humbler place, and delights in the details of events of every-day life, and of the history of the people.

"The struggles of empires and the convulsions of nations," says a writer, "while they have much of sublimity have also much of uncertainty and indistinctness. They are too large for the grasp of ordinary minds, or too indefinite to act on common sensibilities: while the interests awakened by the details of local history are such as from the facility of compre-

hension and the identity of the objects presented, must necessarily come home at once to the feelings of every reader. They place us by the firesides, or walk with us among the graves of our fathers, attaching a living story to the thousand inanimate objects with which they are surrounded."

Under all forms of government, in this country, whether colonial, provincial or republican, many important measures have been submitted to the primary assemblies of the people to be examined and acted on by them. Thus we find in the revolutionary war, in particular, towns and parishes not only expressed their opinion on many subjects connected with that event, but they actually exercised much of the jurisdiction of a national government in prosecuting that war. How these small corporations organized solely for municipal or parochial purposes, transacted that business in that war, as well as the more subsequent ones, in procuring soldiers, stores and the means for carrying them forward is well known.

"The great object of local history," says Mr. Shattuck, "is to furnish the first elements of general history, to record facts rather than deductions from facts. In these small settlements dotted over this country (as well as others) are to be found many of the first moving causes which operate upon and revolutionize public opinion. Many facts, minute in themselves, and regarded by many as trivial and unimportant, are really of great service. The details, which it is the appropriate province of the local historian to spread before the public, are not so much history itself as materials for history. It is the work of the general historian, who has before him all the particulars of the great natural and political landscape, to exhibit the connection of the several parts and to show how they depend one upon another in bringing about the great changes which have been taking place and affecting the condition of society."

No people in the world can have so great an interest in the history of their country as that of the United States; for there are none who enjoy an equally great share in their country's historical acts.

John Quincy Adams once made a remark which contains a world of truth: "That posterity delights in details." And it is highly creditable to the intelligence of the American people, that so much of the early history of the towns and villages of the country has been written, and nothing comes closer to the sensibilities of the people than the details of events that occured when their fathers or ancestors were on the field of action and took their part in building up their several locations. This attachment to our homes is a wise provision of Divine economy. It is eminently proper that every person should entertain a particular attachment to the place where he was born, and where he has made his home. Change of location does not always wean the affection away from the old fireside. By the aid of memory we are privileged to call back the early bygone scenes, and appreciate the lessons we received that had so important a bearing on our subsequent life.

To trace the history of our ancestors, and transmit a record of their deeds to posterity, is a duty we owe to the past and to the future. Such a record must be preserved as invaluable by the immediate descendants and kindred of those who once lived and acted where they now do, and whose ashes repose in their soil, and it cannot be without interest to those who have gone out from their kindred to dwell in other parts of the country, nor to those who have come to dwell in the habitations made vacant by the removal or death of the original occupants. What the present place of our residence once was, who originally occupied it and by what means and by whom it has become what it now is—are questions which can be answered only by minute topographical history.

This work, however, must be done from unselfish motives. It is useless to disguise the fact that the labor of collecting the materials and preparing the same

for publication, brief and imperfect as they may be, is one of magnitude. No one until he has tried the experiment can fully appreciate the labor and patience which are requisite in connecting isolated facts, and the perplexity which is caused in reconciling apparent contradictions and removing doubts. Such kind of labor is never remunerative, but the consciousness of having redeemed from undeserved neglect the history of our homes and of our forefathers, and rescuing from oblivion many facts which would otherwise have been lost, will be a source of gratification if no other reward is received.

We wish we could suitably impress the importance of this subject on the attention of the people.

NOTES.

RAN away on Sabbath day Night the 29th of August last past, from his Master Elisha Odlin of Salem, Innholder, an English Man-servant, named Anthony Pearl, about Sixteen years of Age, well set, short bushy black Hair, his Right hand has been burnt, and the finger drawn up, He has on a Kersey Coat with brass Buttons, a linnen Jacket and Breeches, French fall shoes. Whosoever shall apprehend the said Runaway, and him safely Convey to his said Master, living at the Sign of the Globe in Salem, or to Mr. Ezekill Cleasby near Salutation Tavern in Boston, shall have Forty Shillings reward, and all necessary charges paid.—*Boston News Letter, Aug.* 30—*Sept.* 6, 1714.

Anna Bradstreet married David Ingersoll April 12, 1756, in Newbury.—*Court records.*

James Brady married Jane Stevens Dec. 7, 1730 ; lived in Gloucester ; their daughter Jane born July 12, 1732 ; he died Nov. 14, 1732 ; and she married, secondly, John Curtis Nov. 6, 1733.

Lydia Broadstreet married Josiah Thurston (record Nov. 26, 1796).

Polly Bradey (Brodey?) married James Lane Dec. 16, 1792.
—*Gloucester town records.*

Joseph Bragdon married Miss Martha Noyes, both of Newburyport, Nov. 22, 1792. Children : Sarah Wyer, born May 2, 1793 ; Joseph, born Aug. 7, 1795 ; Martha, born Feb. 6, 1798. —*Newburyport town records.*

Samuel, son of Samuel and Mary Bragden, baptized April 26, 1691.

James Brady married Mary Parsons Feb. 11, 1830-1.
—*Church records, Marblehead.*

Samuel Bragg published to Mary Brown both of Salem, April 9, 1748.

Henry Bragg married Elizabeth Mackmallen 17 : 10 : 1677 ; children : Elizabeth, born 7 : 7 : 1678 ; Mary, born March 24, 1680 ; Henry, born April 12, 1682 ; William, born Oct. 17, 1684 ; Sarah, born March 26, 1687 ; Alexander, born March 6, 1689.

John Brady, late of Gloucester, now resident in Salem, published to Mary Hubbard of Salem April 15, 1775.

Jonathan Bragg married Phebe Pease, both of Salem, Dec. 7, 1779.
—*Salem town records.*

Mary Brage married Joshua Moulton Dec. 20, 1774.—*Danvers town records.*

Mercy Bragg married Ebenezer Larrabe of Danvers May 27, 1773.

Rebeccah Bragg of Lynn married Ephraim Larribee, jr., of Danvers May 13, 1773.

Jacob, son of Josiah Bragg, died, of bloody flux, Aug. 21, 1775, aged eight.

An infant of Josiah Bragg died July -, 1766.
Lynn town records.

Sally Bragg published to Elisha Towle of Hampton April 8, 1797.—*Salisbury town records.*

Widow Anstice Bragg of Andover was appointed administratrix of the estate of John Bragg of Andover, cordwainer, June 26, 1796. He left a widow.—*Probate records.*

James, son of widow Sarah Bragg, baptized July 31, 1785.—*Beverly First church records.*

Bridget, daughter of John and Sarah Bragg, born Aug 26, 1772.

John Bragg married widow Alta Frost Nov. 22, 1792.
—*Andover town records.*
James Bragg married Abigail Gallichan April 21, 1774.
Abigail Bragg married Joseph Smith (recorded May 22, 1784).
—*Gloucester town records.*
Joseph, son of Allen Braid, jr., born 12 : 12 : 1657, in Lynn.
Edward Brammidge of Haverhill(?), 1665.
Alexander Bravendear of Wenham, 1665.
Sarah Bran married Timothy Bread Feb. -, 1693-4.
William, son of John Braman, born in Marblehead Dec. 20, 1676.
Thadeus Bran's children born in Lynn: Mary, born 12 : 12 : 1670; Elizabeth, born 16 : 6 : 1673.
—*County records.*
Sarah, wife of Thadeus Bran, died Dec. 13, 1675.—*Lynn town records.*
Rev. Isaac Braman,* born in Norton, Mass., July 5, 1770; H. C., 1794; ordained over the congregational church in the West parish of Rowley, now the town of Georgetown, June 7, 1797; married, first, Hannah Palmer of Norton (published June 27, 1797). Children born in Rowley: Harriet, born July 17, 1798; Milton Palmer, born Aug. 6, 1799; D. D.; clergyman at Danvers; James Chandler, born Sept. 29, 1801; Adeline, born July 10, 1805; Isaac Gordon, born March 12, 1813; became an eminent physician. Mrs. Braman died in 1835; and Mr. Braman married, secondly, Miss Sarah Balch of Newburyport; and died.Dec. 26, 1858, at the age of eighty-eight. His wife Sarah survived him, and died in Georgetown Feb. 8, 1893, aged one hundred and two.
Capt. Edward Brattle of Marblehead, merchant, esquire and gentleman, 1693-1719; came from Boston, where he was l ving when he married Mary Legg March 23, 1692-3; she survived him and married, secondly, Nathaniel Norden, esq.,

*See volume III, page 87.

7 : 20 : 1722. Captain and Mrs. Brattle had a daughter Mary, baptized in Marblehead Feb. 24, 1694-5; and married James Smith of Boston March 20, 1711-2. Captain Brattle made his will Feb. 5, 1718-9, and it was proved Nov. 22, 1719. In it he mentions his sisters Elizabeth Oliver, Katherine Winthrop and Mary Mico; his nephew William Brattle; his son-in-law Mr. James Smith of Boston; his wife Mary Brattle; his kinsman Jacob Wendell of Boston, merchant, and his children by "my cozen" Sarah Wendell his wife; and his kinswoman Eliz⁴ Keeling. Amount of inventory, £1,233, 16s., 11d.
Thomas Bray of Salem, 1725-1732; fishermen and mariner; married Elizabeth Glandfield of Salem April 1, 1723; he died before July 19, 1732, when administration was granted upon his estate, which was appraised t £131, 13s., 10d.; she survived him and was his widow in 1733. He left a young child.
—*Records.*

THE OLD HOME.

BY EBEN E. REXFORD.

It stands in a desolate, weed-grown garden,
  Where once the rose and the lilac grew,
And the lily lifted a waxen chalice
  To catch the wine of the summer's dew.
The grass creeps in o'er the mossy threshold,
  The dust lies deep on the rotting floor,
And the wind at will is coming, going
  Through broken window and open door.

O poor old house, do you grieve as men do
  For the vanished things that were yours of yore,
Like a heart in whom love was one time tenant,
  But has gone away to come back no more?
Do you dream of the dead as the days pass over?
  Of the pang of parting and joy of birth
In hearts turned dust? Ah, that dust is scattered
  By winds of lifetimes to the ends of earth!

See! Here by the path is one little blossom!
  It lifts to the sunshine a fragile face.
It springs from a root that some dead hand planted
  A century back in the dear home place.
Little thought they whom the old house sheltered
  That life would fade as the leaves that fall.
They had their day and are quite forgotten—
  The little flower has outlived them all!

NOTES.

Abigail and Mary, daughters of Elizabeth Bray, baptized Dec. 11, 1737.—*Salem church records.*

Ichabod Nichols of Salem was appointed guardian of Hannah Bray, aged thirteen years, daughter of Ann Wyatt, late of Salem, singlewoman, deceased, Nov. 7, 1799. She released her guardian Sept. 24, 1812.

John Bray, jr., of Harpswell, Me., coaster, was appointed administrator of the estate of Noah Bray of Marblehead, fisherman, Jan. 4, 1779.
—*Probate records.*

Elizabeth Bray married William Nicolls, Oct. 16, 1702.—*Topsfield town records.*

John Bray married Mrs. Rebecca Dennis (published July 4, 1778); children: John, baptized March 17, 1782; Alce, bapt. Nov. 16, 1783; Jane, baptized Aug. 6, 1786; Jane, baptized May 11, 1788; and Sarah, baptized March 21, 1790.—*Marblehead records.*

"BOSTON, *July* 31.

"*Laft Monday arrived here the Brig Hannah, Capt. Jarvis, in 7 Weeks from London; and Yefterday arrived Capt. Jacobfon from the fame Place, but laft from Portfmouth in 8 Weeks, in whom came Paffenger* JOHN FISHER, *Efq.; Collector of the Cuftoms for the Port of* SALEM, JOHN SOBER, *Efq; with his Lady and Family, and feveral other Perfons.*"

John Cushing, esq., was appointed as a justice of the peace for Essex county July 27; and the council consented thereto.

"*S A L E M, Auguft* 1.

"Saturday, July 23, SAMUEL-GILES PARSONS, the Son of Capt. Jonathan Parsons, of Newbury-Port, was unfortunately drowned from one of the Wharfs in that Place. He was a Lad near 12 Years old, and his virtuous Life, promifing Genius, and clofe Application to Books, render'd his Life very amiable to his Friends, and his Death greatly lamented by them.

"The Inftallment of the Reverend NATHANIEL WHITAKER, D.D. into the paftoral Office over the Church and Congregation, of which the late Reverend Mr. HUNTINGTON was Paftor, was performed on Friday laft."
—*Essex Gazette, July 25-Aug. 1, 1769.*

"S A L E M, Auguft 8.

"We hear that the Lightning, Yefterday fe'nnight, ftruck a Tree in Danvers, and killed an Ox and a Cow, which were ftanding near it. About the fame Time, a Child, in the fame Town, was ftruck down, but not much hurt.

"John Fifher, Efq; Collector of his Majifty's Cuftoms for this Port, arrive! at Portfmouth laft Wednefday.

"Laft Saturday failed for Liverpool, the Brig Britannia, Capt. John Rojes, belonging to this Place; with whom went Paffenger, Mr. Van Cofter, a Native of the Eaft-Indies.
—*Essex Gazette, Aug. 1-8, 1769.*

Mary Bond married Thomas Little Jan. 12, 1737-8.—*Haverhill town records.*

John Bradish of Marblehead, baker, 1772 and 1775, was a brother of Billings Bradish, who was also a baker. Billings Bradish married Sarah Austin of Charlestown Feb. 1, 1765; lived in Salem, 1765-1773; and removed to Danvers in 1774, where he was a yeoman. He died about 1791. His wife Sarah survived him, living in Salem, his widow, in 1797. His son George Bradish lived in Danvers, 1784, and January, 1793, moving to Salem that month. He was an innholder in Salem in 1789, and a mariner in 1797.
—*Records.*

James Brading married Hannah York Oct. 11, 1657.—*Newbury town records.*

Mary, daughter of John Bradley, baptized "at Haverhill, West Parish," Oct. 14, 1764.—*Topsfield church records.*

John Bradley of Haverhill, 1724-1749; husbandman, 1730-1749; "jr.," 1730, 1739; married Susannah Staples Sept. 16, 1724, in Haverhill; she probably married, secondly, William Whittaker, jr., Dec. 21, 1752. Children, born in Haverhill: Obediah, born Nov. 15, 1724; David, born Nov. 30, 1726; died Dec. 30, 1728; Mary, born Feb. 6, 1728; Susanna, born June 15, 1731; David,

born June 16, 1733; Elizabeth, born April 17, 1736; John and Susanna (twins), born Aug. 17, 1738.—*Records*.

—— Bradley married Moses Bricket before 1793; first child was born in Wiscasset; and she died in Haverhill Oct. —, 1798.

Sally Bradley of Andover married Moses McFarland, jr., of Haverhill Aug. 6, 1797.

Joseph Bradley of Haverhill married Miriam Currier of Amesbury Sept. 22, 1796. Children: James, born Oct. 12, 1797; Nathan, born Jan. 2, 1799; Joseph, born May 14, 1800; died July 23, 1821; Benjamin, born Jan. 26, 1802; Sarah, born Nov. 21, 1804; Israel, born Aug. 5, 1806; died March 7, 1830; Maria, born April 9, 1808; Sophia, born April 22, 1810; Eliza, born March 22, 1812; died July —, 1813; Lois, born Aug. 9, 1813; Abigail, born March 18, 1815; Ira, born July 12, 1816; Emily, born Jan. 14, 1819.

Henry Bradley of Newbury married widow Hannah Hendrick of Haverhill April 17, 1729.

Mehitable Bradley married William Wingate March 7, 1767; and she died July 22, 1796.

Mehitable Bradley of Amesbury married Barnabas Tyler of Haverhill Feb. 28, 1799.

Ruth Bradley married Josiah Chase Feb. 17, 1780.

Sarah Bradley of Haverhill married Warren Wheeler of Salem, N. H., April 1, 1784.

Polly Bradley of Haverhill married Robert Eastman of Concord Nov. 13, 1785.

Elizabeth Bradley of Haverhill married David Dexter of Hampstead Nov. 12, 1786.

John Bradley, jr., married Sarah Eaton Jan. 9, 1734-5; and they had son William born Aug. 1, 1735.

Elizabeth Bradley married Josiah Foulsom before 1747, perhaps in Exeter, N. H. She died, and he married, secondly, Abigail Farnom.

Susanna Bradley married Philbrook Colby July 13, 1758.

John Bradley married Mary Heath March 21, 1760; and had children: David, born Dec. 15, 1760; Mary, born Sept. 15, 1764.

Susanna Bradley married Eliezer Emerson Feb. 26, 1760.

Elizabeth Bradley of Haverhill married Henry Hall, jr., of Chester May 14, 1761.

—Haverhill town records.

Hannah Bradley, resident in Andover, married John Gutheson July 28, 1735.—*Andover town records.*

Sarah Bradley published to Lt. Daniel Quimby March 4, 1780.

Susanna Bradley married Humphrey Hoyt Jan. 27, 1791.

Joshua Bradley published to Sally Osgood April 19, 1794.

Hannah Bradley married Moses Kimball of Haverhill Jan. 31, 1796.

Sarah Bradley married John Johnson of Haverhill Aug. 30, 1795.

—Amesbury town records.

Thomas Bradley married Mehitable Carleton June 2, 1796.—*Bradford town records.*

Timothy Bradley, jr., married Sarah Foster, in Andover, Dec. 23, 1773.—*County records.*

Dolly, daughter of Briant and Dorothy Bradley, baptized July 4, 1784.

Bryant Bradley married Dorothy Williams Oct. 14, 1780.

Caroline, daughter of Briant and Sarah Bradley of Penobscot, baptized Aug. 9, 1801.

—Marblehead church records.

Henry Bradley married widow Judith Davis Jan. 7, 1695-6. She died, his wife, Nov. 15, 1728.—*Newbury town records.*

Joshua Bradley married Judith Lumbe, in Rowley, May 26, 1663.

Martha, daughter of Joshua Bradley, born 12 : 20 : 1663.

Mary Bradley married Thomas Leaver Sept. 1, 1643.

—Rowley town records.

Samuel, daughter of Thomas and Sarah Bradley, born in Salisbury Oct. 14, 1733.

Joshua Bradley of Amesbury married Sally Osgood (published April 18, 1794). Children: Oliver Osgood, born Feb. 16, 1796; Hannah Challis, born Sept. 25, 1797.

—Salisbury town records.

Samuel Bradley of Haverhill, hatter, 1791; trader, 1798; wife Abigail, 1798.

Sarah Bradley of Amesbury, singlewoman, 1792, 1794.

—Registry of deeds.

Stephen Bradshaw married Mary ——, and had son Stephen, born Sept. 15, 1764.—*Amesbury town records.*

Joseph Bradshaw died of small pox in 1777.

Stephen Bradshaw died July 29, 1778, aged thirty-nine.

—Beverly town records.

Mrs. Sarah Bradshaw married Joseph Severy Feb. 22, 1798.

Thomas Bradshaw married Sarah Green Aug. 4, 1789; and their daughter Sarah was baptized Oct. 18, 1789.

—Marblehead records.

Joseph Bradshaw[1] married Sarah Fortin Dec. 11, 1755, and lived in Marblehead. Children, born in Marblehead: 1. *Joseph*[2], baptized Sept. 12, 1756. 2. *John Paine*[2], baptized Jan. 1, 1758. 3. *John*[2], baptized Oct. 19, 1760; married Tabitha (Dane), widow of Joseph Lovett, Oct. 6, 1782, in Beverly; he died Feb. 13, 1827, aged sixty-six; children, born in Beverly: 1. Ruth[3], born Feb. 26, 1784; married James Gano; 2. John[3], born June 8, 1786; married Hannah Stickney and Elizabeth Hobson of Ipswich in 1812; 3. Joseph[3], born Aug. 13, 1788; married Clarissa Foster; 4. Henry[3], born Aug. 10, 1790; died about 1810; 5. Lucy[3], born July 19, 1792; married Aaron Foster June 7, 1810; 6. Nathaniel[3], born Aug. 13, 1794; married Betsey Bowen of Philadelphia; and died at Philadelphia June 20, 1851.—*Records.*

Hannah (Anna) Bradshaw of Newbury married David Ingersoll (Engerson) of Gloucester April 12, 1756.

Sarah Bradstreet married Henry Brewins Dec. 14, 1766.

John Bradstreet of Ipswich married Judith Hale of Newbury Feb. 14, 17.

—Newbury town record

Polly Bradshaw married William Lee Sept. 12, 1790.

Widow Mary Bradshaw married Robert Peele, both of Salem, Feb. 28, 1781.

William Bradshaw published to Elizabeth Hubbard, both of Salem, April 1 1779.

—Salem town records.

Children of John and Mary Bradstreet: Christopher, Elizabeth and Samuel, baptized May 19, 1734.—*Marblehead church records.*

Ann Bradstreet married Nathaniel Clarke March 10, 1768.

Mary Bradstreet married Thomas Robie July 26, 1759.

Nancy Bradstreet married Capt. Samuel Dugard Feb. 22, 1778.

Rebecca Bradstreet married Rev. Isaac Story Dec. 19, 1771.

Samuel, illegitimate son of Ann Bradstreet, baptized June 10, 1770.

—Marblehead records.

Lois Bradstreet married Stephen Nichols June 17, 1778.—*Middleton town records.*

Mary Bradstreet married Joel Harriman Dec. 11, 1755.—*Haverhill town records.*

Rebecca Bradstreet of Marblehead, spinster, 1771.

Moses Bradstreet of Ipswich, yeoman, 1754, 1755; gentleman, 1763-1771.

Samuel Bradstreet of Topsfield, husbandman, 1740, 1763, 1764; jr., 1755, 1762.

Ruth Bradstreet of Topsfield, singlewoman, 1791.

—Registry of deeds.

Moses Bradstreet, jr., of Rowley, 1774-1795; gentleman, 1790; married (when he was of Ipswich) Sarah Mighill, jr., of Rowley Jan. 26, 1775: and they had the following named children, born in Rowley: Dolly, born Jan. 5, 1776; Sarah, born March 27, 1777; Moses, born Dec.

1, 1779; of Rowley, yeoman, 1799; Lois, born Nov. 21, 1780; Nathaniel, born Dec. 18, 1782; Hannah, born May 6, 1786; Thomas, born March 10, 1791; died young; Irene, born Feb. 15, 1793; and Thomas, born Feb. 19, 1795; died June 27, 1800, aged five years and two months.—*Records.*

QUERIES.

Queries are inserted for one cent a word.
Answers are solicited.

484. Miss Fuller married William Jessep. Her pa came over in the Mayflower. What was her mother's name?
Miami, Fla. A.

485. Wanted, genealogy and names of children of Richard Gardner, who came over in the Mayflower. M.

486. Francis Harrington and his two brothers came over in the Mayflower, second time, and settled in Rhode Island. Where did they come from and where settle? C.

ANSWERS.

476. Oliver Knight, who married Sarah Coffin in 1742, was probably son of Tristram[4] (Joseph[3], John[2], John[1]) Knight and Sarah Greenleaf his wife. Oliver was born in Newbury May 20, 1722.—*Annie Hale Knight, Newburyport.*

480. Joseph Pilsbury, who married Eunice Coffin Jan. 26, 1766, was son of Joshua and Mary (Somerby) Pilsbury of Newbury, where he was born June 24, 1745. Joshua Pilsbury was son of Daniel[3] (Job[2], William[1]) Pilsbury, and Mary Somerby was daughter of Abiel Somerby. See Pilsbury Genealogy for further information.—*Ed.*

EDITORIAL.

This number completes volume eleven of *The Essex Antiquarian.* There have been published during the year the wills proved in Essex county from 1662 to 1664; the gravestone inscriptions in the town of Hamilton before 1800; the genealogies of Essex county families from Bradley to Brickett inclusive; the record of the Essex county Revolutionary soldiers and sailors from Bond to Bradbury; abstracts of the old Norfolk county records, 1672 and 1673; Ipswich quarterly court records and files, 1655 to 1657 inclusive; and miscellaneous genealogical notes from the records from Boovy to Bradstreet.

NEW PUBLICATIONS.

WATERMAN, ILLINOIS, YEAR BOOK, 1905. *Compiled by George Edward Congdon.* Hiawatha, Kansas, 1907. This little year book, though somewhat delayed in its appearance, is larger and more interesting even than the preceding editions. As before, it contains the local events of the year, notices of deceased persons, directories of societies, etc., births and deaths, and much other information of local interest. It has seventy-eight pages, bound in paper, and is embellished with fifteen half-tone engravings. The price is fifty cents, and it is for sale by the compiler at Hiawatha.

A CONDENSED GENEALOGY OF ONE BRANCH OF THE EDWARDS FAMILY OF CONCORD AND ACTON, MASSACHUSETTS, AND OF THE ALLIED FAMILIES. *By John Harrington Edwards, D. D.* Brooklyn, N. Y., 1907. This is a pamphlet of twenty-eight octavo pages, containing brief notes of the Chetlain, Clemens, Conant, Crandall, Edwards, Fletcher, Harrington, Haskell, Haven, Heald, Knickerbocker, Locke, Pierson, Starr, Tower and Van Veghten families, etc., especially referring to the first of these names in America. Dr. Edwards' address is 122 Willow street, Brooklyn, N. Y.

VITAL RECORDS OF BRADFORD, MASSACHUSETTS, to the End of the Year 1849. Topsfield, Mass., 1907. The Topsfield Historical Society has collected, arranged and published in a volume of 373 octavo

pages, bound in cloth, the births, marriages and deaths, which have occurred in the town of Bradford before 1850. It also includes the baptisms of children when the date of birth is not known, and also the intention of marriage if the record of the marriage is not found in the records. It includes not only the information derived from the town records, but also from court records, church records, gravestone inscriptions and family bibles. This volume is uniform with those published at the expense of the state; and will be sent postpaid for $3.90 by The Topsfield Historical Society, Topsfield, Mass.

A HISTORY OF THE UNITED STATES AND ITS PEOPLE. *By Elroy McKendree Avery.* Volume III. Cleveland, O., 1907. This is the third volume of Doctor Avery's work on the history of the nation, which he has been preparing for a quarter of a century. This volume contains 446 pages, and is even better in every way, if possible, than the preceding ones. There are more illustrations, covering a greater variety of subjects, but the beautiful artistic effect of the mechanical execution of the first volumes it is difficult to surpass. The illustrations delight the antiquarian and historian as well as the general reader, and almost every page has portraits, maps, or other engravings. The frontispiece is a bust portrait of William Penn. Comprehensively, the engravings also include portraits of Edward Hyde, John Locke, Sir George Carteret, Anthony Ashley Cooper, George Monk, Henry Morgan, Lord Culpepper, Lord Howard, Charles Calvert, Augustine Herman, James II., Sir Edmund Andros, Josiah Winslow, Simon Bradstreet, Charles II., Thomas Thacher, Isaac Jogues, Bishop Laval, Jacques Marquette, Queen Mary II., King William, King Louis XIV., Queen Anne, Robert Walpole, Thomas Pelham Holles, King George I., William Rhett, James Logan, Earl of Bellomont, Peter Schuyler, Isaac Addington, Increase Mather, William Stoughton, Samuel Sewall, Joseph Dudley, Cotton Mather, Fitz-

John Winthrop, and many other portraits, maps, seals, autographs, title pages, documents, coats of arms, coins, badges, flags, etc. The printing of the in colors enables many points to be br out with perfect clearness, which be impossible in black and white. typography is in correspondence with former volumes, being exceptionally ple ing; and we would again express our admiration of this beautiful work, so sump tuous as well as substantial in all its part

The scheme of the work is what known as the horizontal method of presenting history. Doctor Avery carries along the history of each section of country at once. This is done by writing it in chronological periods. This is the only way, in our opinion, that history this kind should be written, as contemporaneousness is a most important factor the understanding of the occurrences a situations of a complex history.

This volume covers a period which more familiar and therefore more interesting to the general reader than thos previously issued. The years included are from 1660 to 1745, the period between active colonization and the final struggle for the conquest of New France It is the neglected period of American history, and lacks many of the dramatic characteristics of the times preceding and succeeding it. Much new matter is introduced, and a new interest in this period of our history will arise from the presentation.

Doctor Avery is entirely unprejudiced in his statements, insisting upon the truth in each instance, in many cases making original investigations to learn the actual facts in controverted cases, and always consulting the best authorities. His simple, lucid and graphic style makes his chapters interesting aside from the intrinsic attractiveness of the subject matter.

The work is to be issued in fifteen volumes, and the price for the edition cloth binding is $6.25 net. The publishers are The Burrows Brothers Company, Cleveland, Ohio.

Volume XII.   JANUARY, 1908.   Number 1.

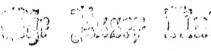

An Illustrated Quarterly Magazine

Devoted to the

Biography, Genealogy, History and Antiquities

of

Essex County, Massachusetts.

SIDNEY PERLEY, *Editor.*
GEORGE FRANCIS DOW, *Business Manager.*

CONTENTS.

Notes and Queries.

PER ANNUM, $1.50.   SINGLE COPIES, 50 CENTS.
FOREIGN SUBSCRIPTIONS, EXCEPT FROM CANADA AND MEXICO, $1.75.

SALEM, MASS.
The Essex Antiquarian.
1908.

2879 X